Boarding Juliet

To LOVE, or not to LOVE

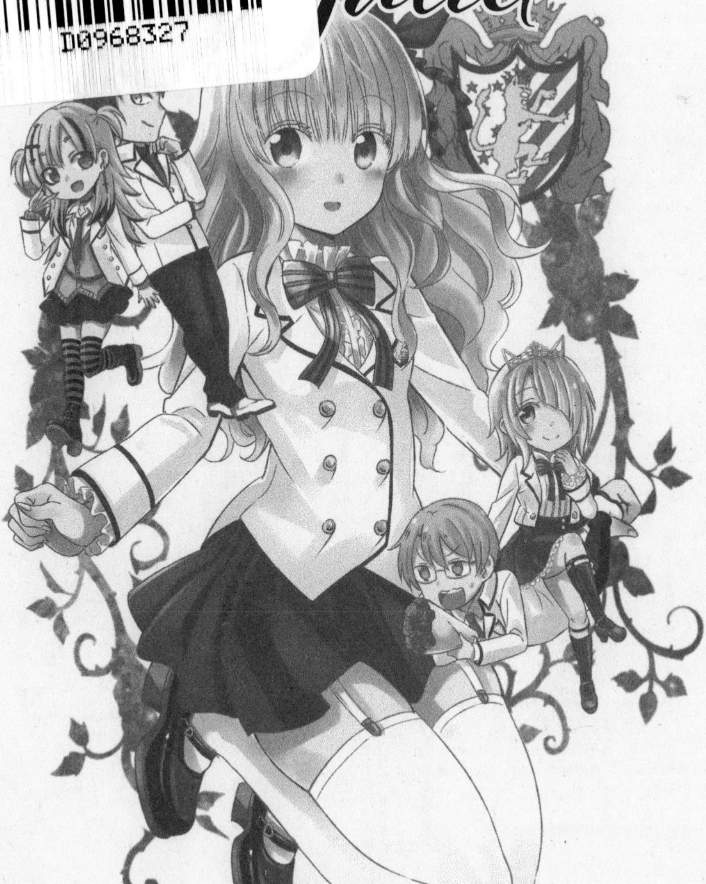

vol. 3

YOUSUKE KANEDA

THE PLAYERS

character

HASUKI

Inuzuka's best bud since they were little. It broke her heart when she found out about him and Persia.

BLACK DOGGY HOUSE
(NATION OF TOUWA DORM)

BEST BUDS

ROMIO INUZUKA

Leader of the Black Doggy first-years. All brawn and no brains. Has had one-sided feelings for Persia since forever.

SECRETLY DATING

KOHITSUJI

Idiot.

TOSA

Idiot.

WANTS TO KILL

WANTS TO KILL

MARU

A Black Doggy outlaw. Has seen Inuzuka as an enemy ever since Inuzuka foiled his plan to defeat Persia.

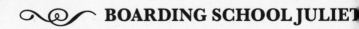

BOARDING SCHOOL JULIET

To LOVE, or not to LOVE

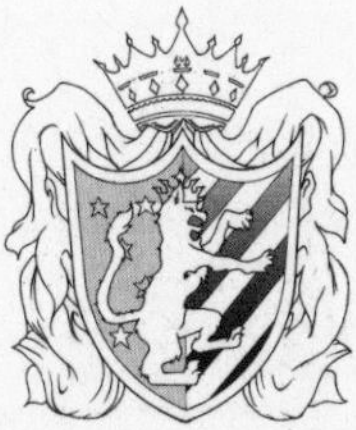

WHITE CAT HOUSE
(PRINCIPALITY OF WEST DORM)

SCOTT

Walks a fine line between worshipping and stalking Persia.

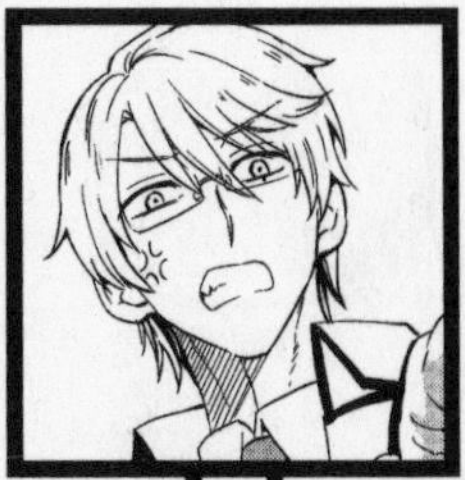

WORSHIPS

WANTS TO KIL

JULIET PERSIA

Leader of the White Cat first-years. A noble. Her dream is to change the world so that she can carry on the family estate.

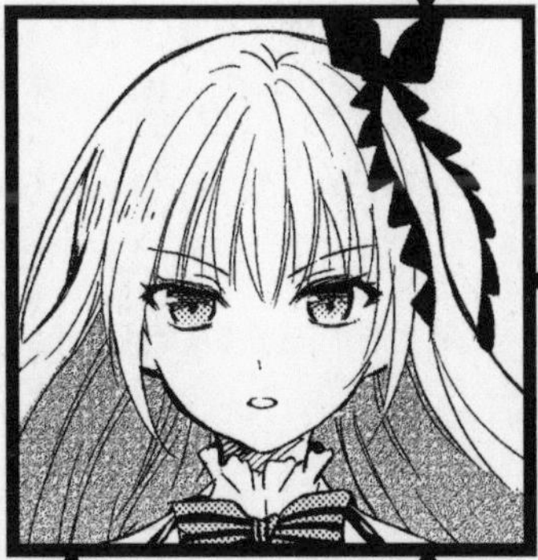

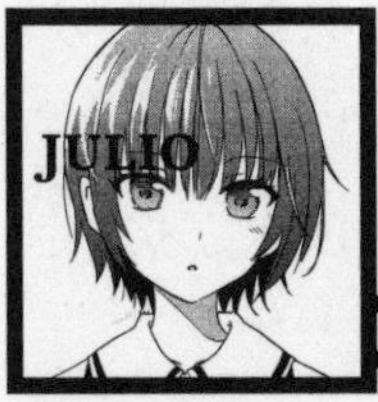

JULIO

Persia's Black Doggy middle school boy disguise.

SAME PERSON

INTERESTED?

BEST FRIENDS

CHARTREUX WESTIA

Princess of the Principality of West
Secretly in love with
Persia. Knows abou
Inuzuka and Persia'
relationship.

ABY FACTION

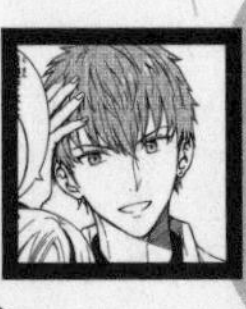

ABY SINIA

Ladies' man. Wants to take over as the White Cats' leader.

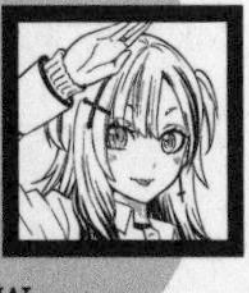

SOMALI

Infatuated with Aby. Stupidly strong and just plain stupid.

contents

story

At Dahlia Academy, a boarding school attended by students from two feuding countries, one first-year longs student for a forbidden love. His name: Romio Inuzuka, leader of the Black Doggy House first-years. The apple of his eye: Juliet Persia, leader of the White Cat House first-years. It all begins when Inuzuka confesses his feelings to her. This is Inuzuka and Persia's star-crossed, secret love story...

It's Dahlia Academy's traditional sports festival, and the two dorms are competing fiercely. When Persia gets injured due to Aby's scheming, Inuzuka heads back to the games with wrath in his heart!

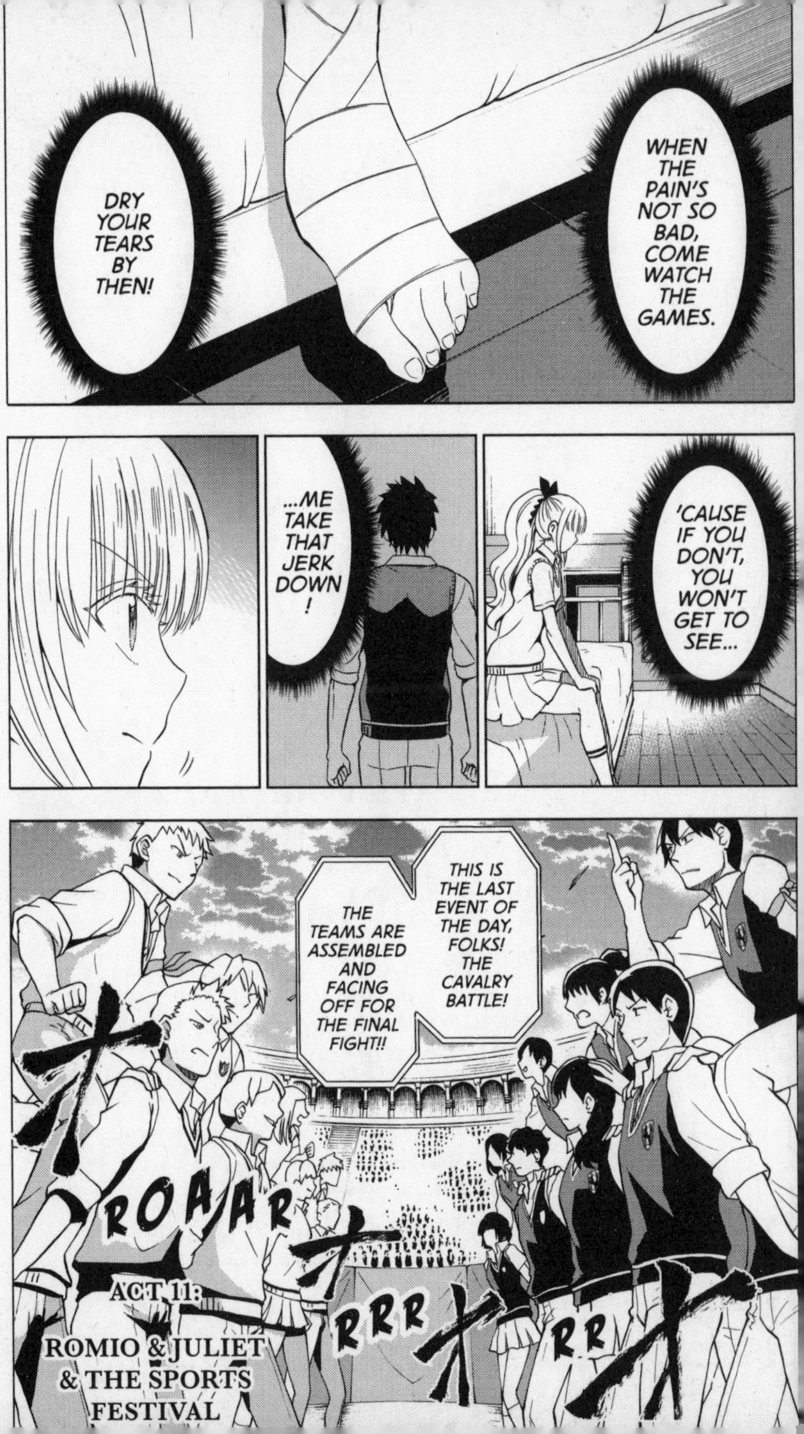
WHEN THE PAIN'S NOT SO BAD, COME WATCH THE GAMES.
DRY YOUR TEARS BY THEN!
'CAUSE IF YOU DON'T, YOU WON'T GET TO SEE...
...ME TAKE THAT JERK DOWN!
THIS IS THE LAST EVENT OF THE DAY, FOLKS! THE CAVALRY BATTLE!
THE TEAMS ARE ASSEMBLED AND FACING OFF FOR THE FINAL FIGHT!!
ROAAR
RRR
RR
ACT 11: ROMIO & JULIET & THE SPORTS FESTIVAL

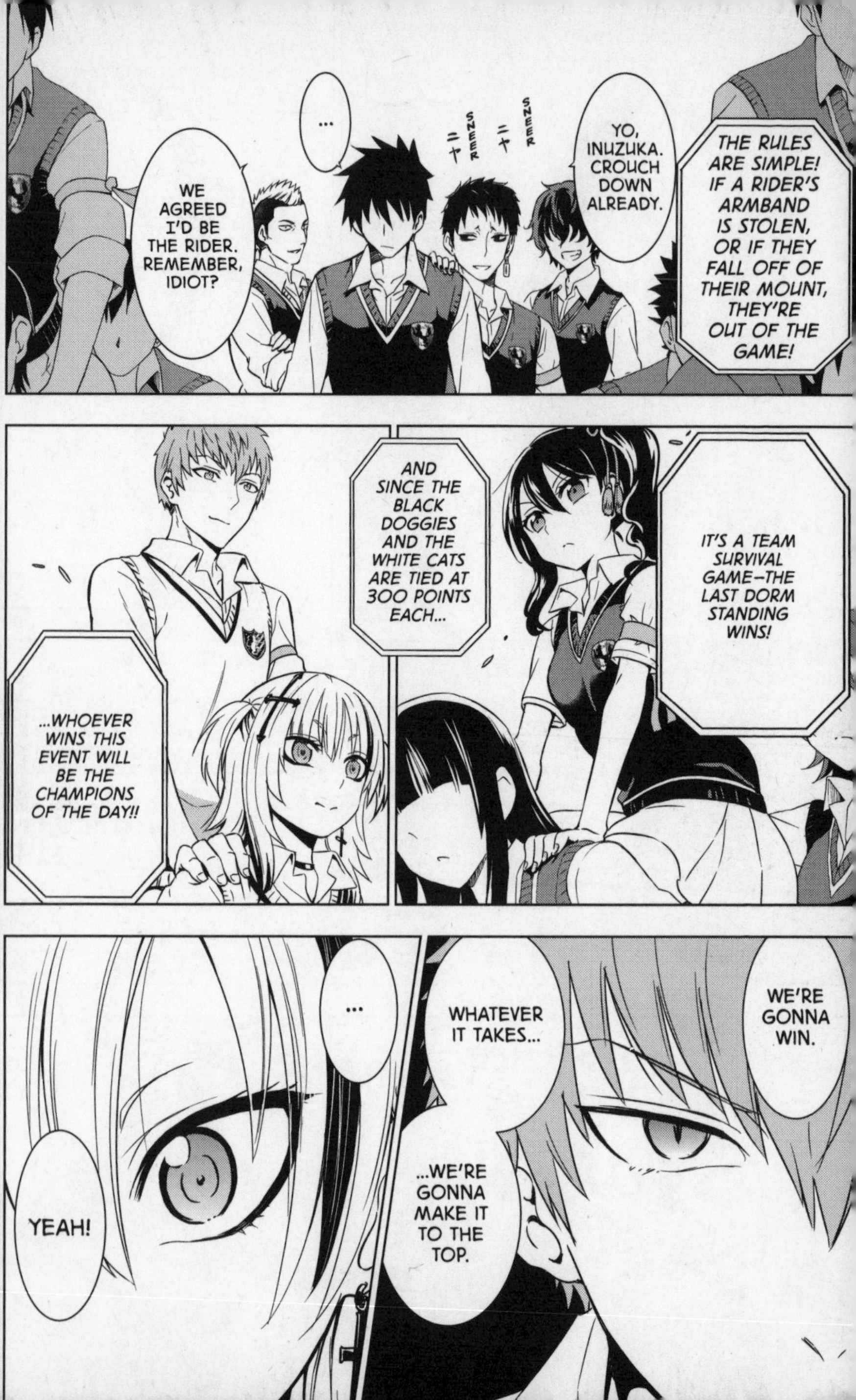
THE RULES ARE SIMPLE! IF A RIDER'S ARMBAND IS STOLEN, OR IF THEY FALL OFF OF THEIR MOUNT, THEY'RE OUT OF THE GAME!
YO, INUZUKA. CROUCH DOWN ALREADY.
ニヤ SNEER
ニヤ SNEER
...
WE AGREED I'D BE THE RIDER. REMEMBER, IDIOT?
IT'S A TEAM SURVIVAL GAME—THE LAST DORM STANDING WINS!
AND SINCE THE BLACK DOGGIES AND THE WHITE CATS ARE TIED AT 300 POINTS EACH...
...WHOEVER WINS THIS EVENT WILL BE THE CHAMPIONS OF THE DAY!!
WE'RE GONNA WIN.
WHATEVER IT TAKES...
...WE'RE GONNA MAKE IT TO THE TOP.
...
YEAH!

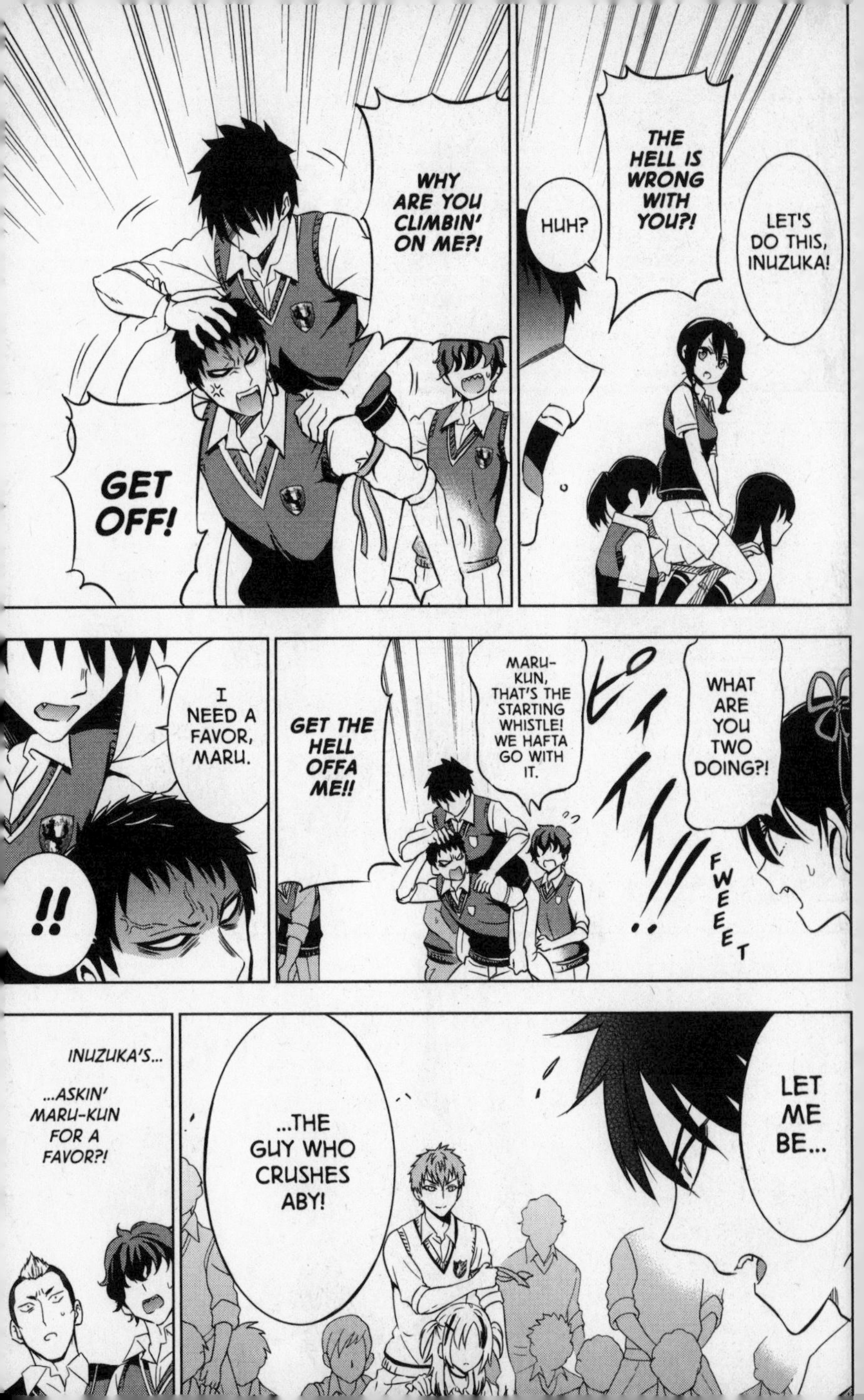
LET'S DO THIS, INUZUKA!
THE HELL IS WRONG WITH YOU?!
HUH?
WHY ARE YOU CLIMBIN' ON ME?!
GET OFF!
WHAT ARE YOU TWO DOING?!
FWEEET
MARU-KUN, THAT'S THE STARTING WHISTLE! WE HAFTA GO WITH IT.
GET THE HELL OFFA ME!!
I NEED A FAVOR, MARU.
!!
LET ME BE...
...THE GUY WHO CRUSHES ABY!
INUZUKA'S...
...ASKIN' MARU-KUN FOR A FAVOR?!

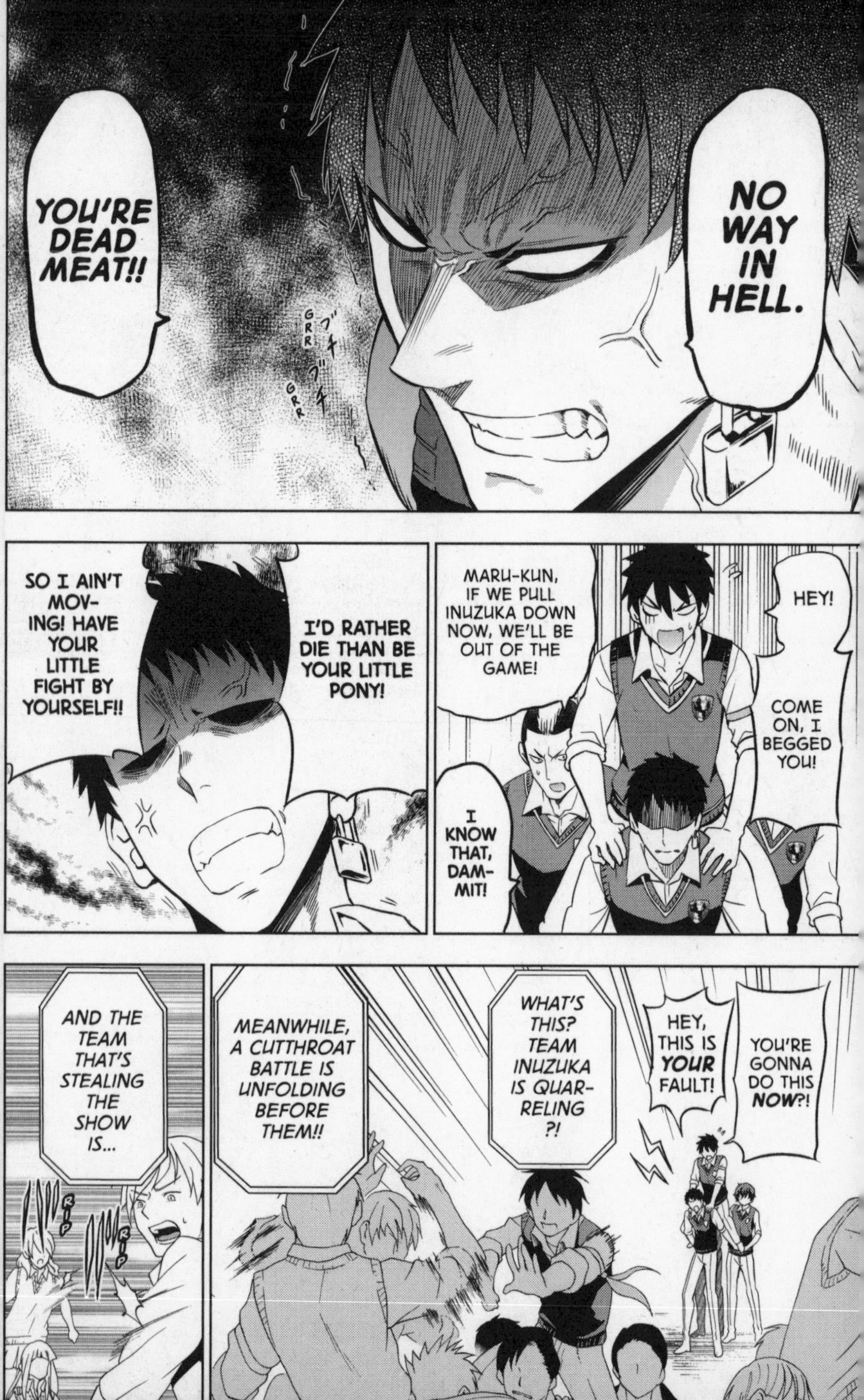
NO WAY IN HELL.
YOU'RE DEAD MEAT!!
GRR GRR
HEY!
COME ON, I BEGGED YOU!
MARU-KUN, IF WE PULL INUZUKA DOWN NOW, WE'LL BE OUT OF THE GAME!
I KNOW THAT, DAMMIT!
I'D RATHER DIE THAN BE YOUR LITTLE PONY!
SO I AIN'T MOVING! HAVE YOUR LITTLE FIGHT BY YOURSELF!!
YOU'RE GONNA DO THIS *NOW*?!
HEY, THIS IS *YOUR* FAULT!
WHAT'S THIS? TEAM INUZUKA IS QUARRELING?!
MEANWHILE, A CUTTHROAT BATTLE IS UNFOLDING BEFORE THEM!!
AND THE TEAM THAT'S STEALING THE SHOW IS...
RIP RIP

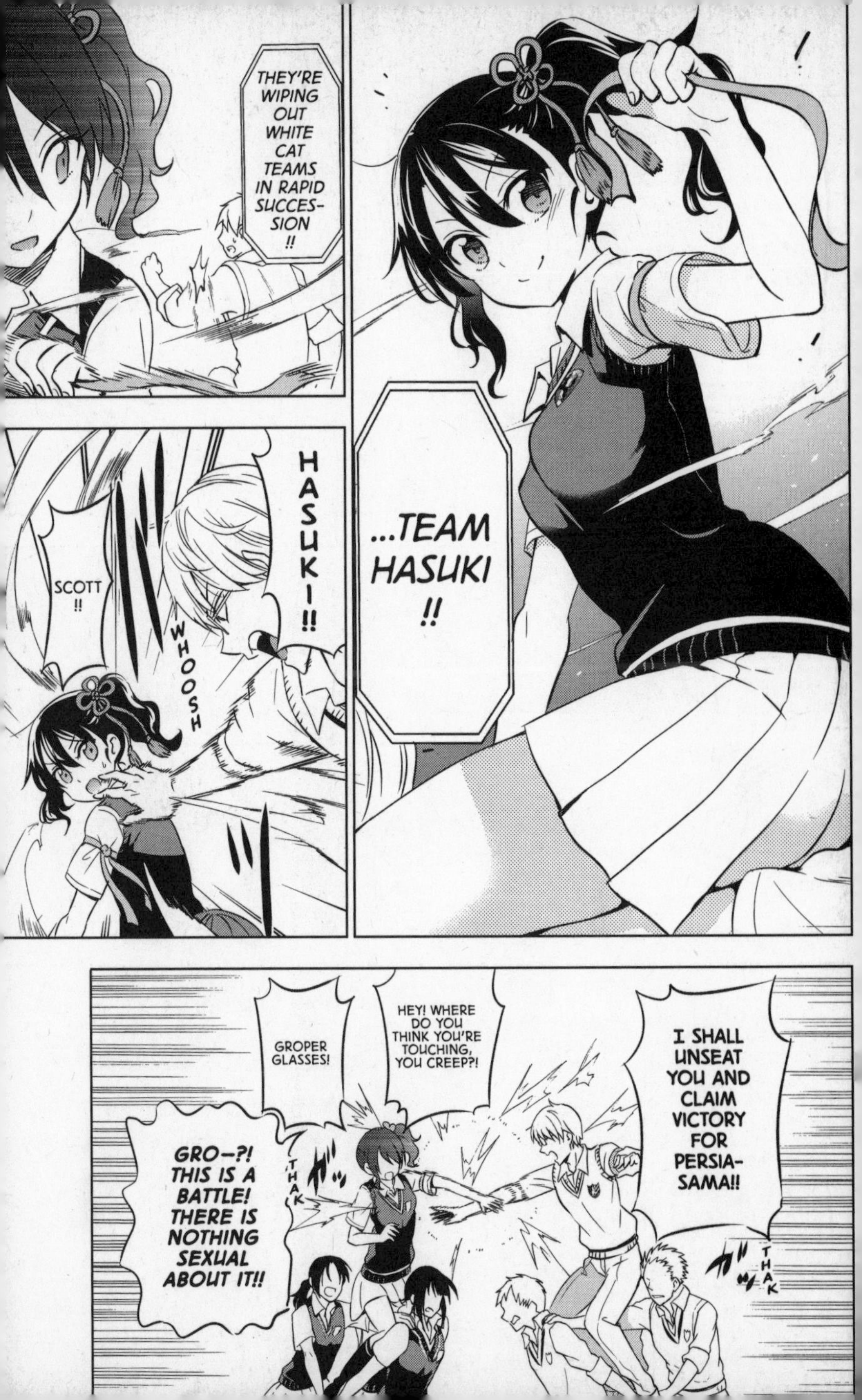
...TEAM HASUKI!!
THEY'RE WIPING OUT WHITE CAT TEAMS IN RAPID SUCCESSION!!
HASUKI!!
SCOTT!!
WHOOSH
I SHALL UNSEAT YOU AND CLAIM VICTORY FOR PERSIA-SAMA!!
HEY! WHERE DO YOU THINK YOU'RE TOUCHING, YOU CREEP?!
GROPER GLASSES!
GRO—?! THIS IS A BATTLE! THERE IS NOTHING SEXUAL ABOUT IT!!
THAK
THAK

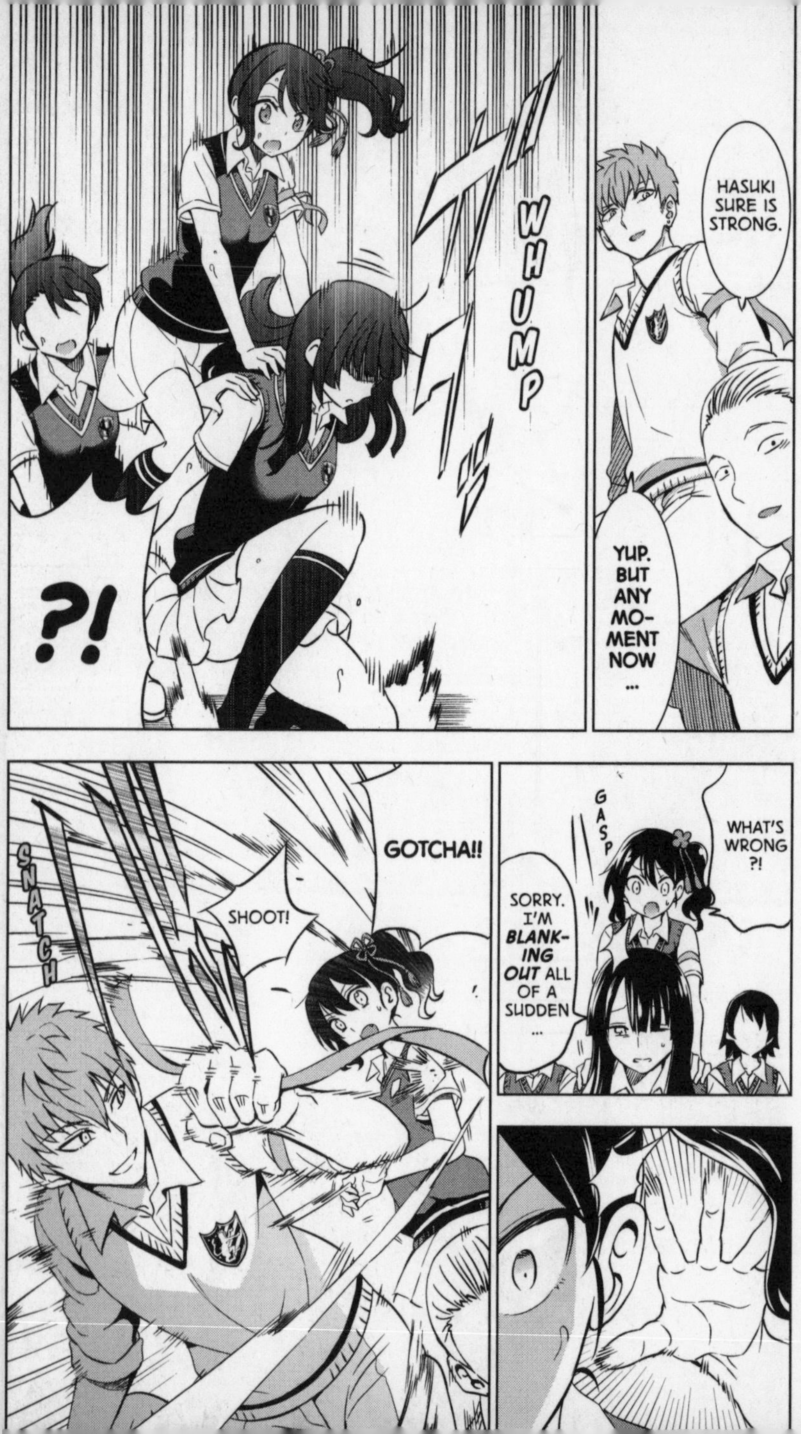
HASUKI SURE IS STRONG.
YUP. BUT ANY MO-MENT NOW ...
WHUMP
?!
WHAT'S WRONG ?!
GASP
SORRY. I'M *BLANK-ING OUT* ALL OF A SUDDEN ...
GOTCHA!!
SHOOT!
SNATCH

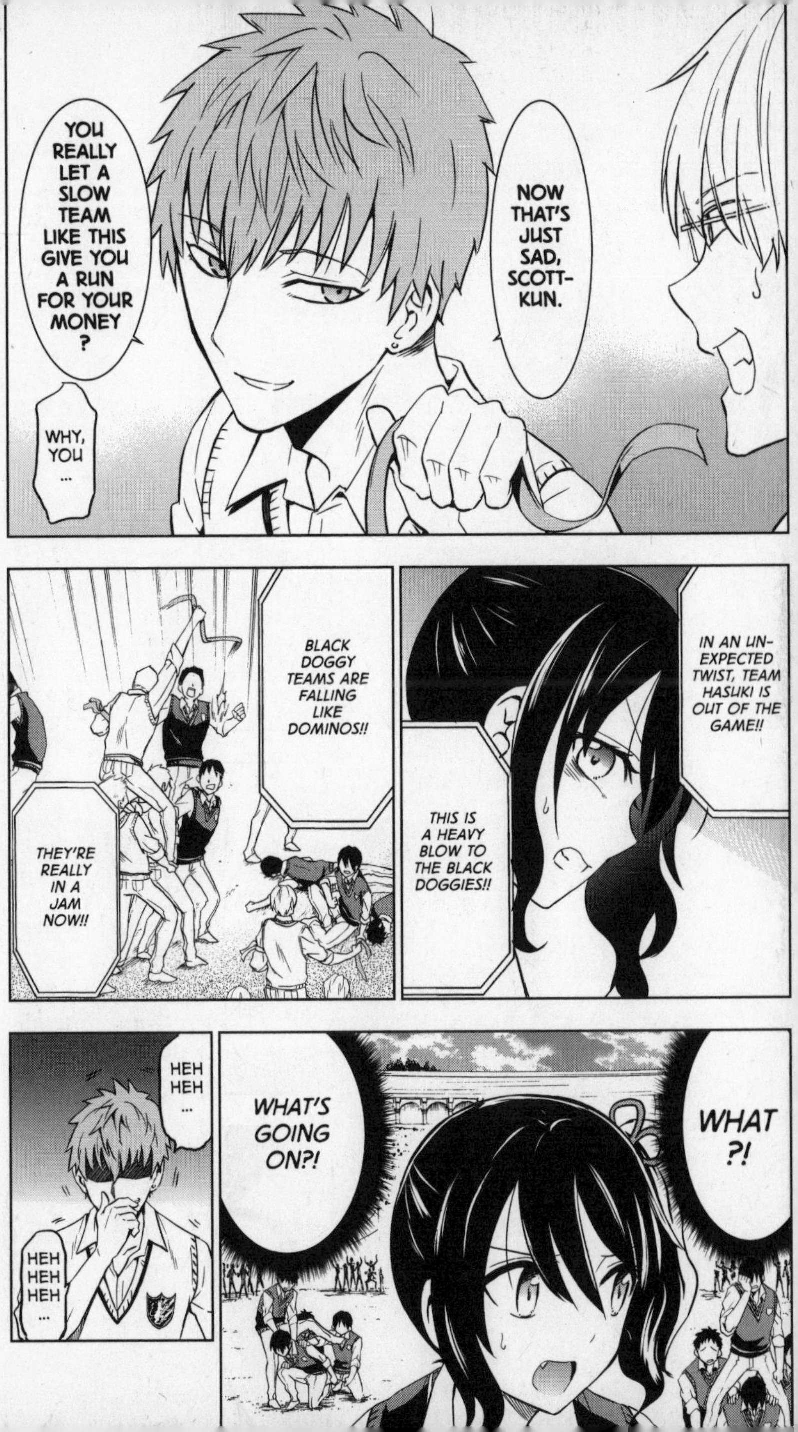
NOW THAT'S JUST SAD, SCOTT-KUN.
YOU REALLY LET A SLOW TEAM LIKE THIS GIVE YOU A RUN FOR YOUR MONEY ?
WHY, YOU ...
IN AN UN-EXPECTED TWIST, TEAM HASUKI IS OUT OF THE GAME!!
THIS IS A HEAVY BLOW TO THE BLACK DOGGIES!!
BLACK DOGGY TEAMS ARE FALLING LIKE DOMINOS!!
THEY'RE REALLY IN A JAM NOW!!
WHAT ?!
WHAT'S GOING ON?!
HEH HEH ...
HEH HEH HEH ...

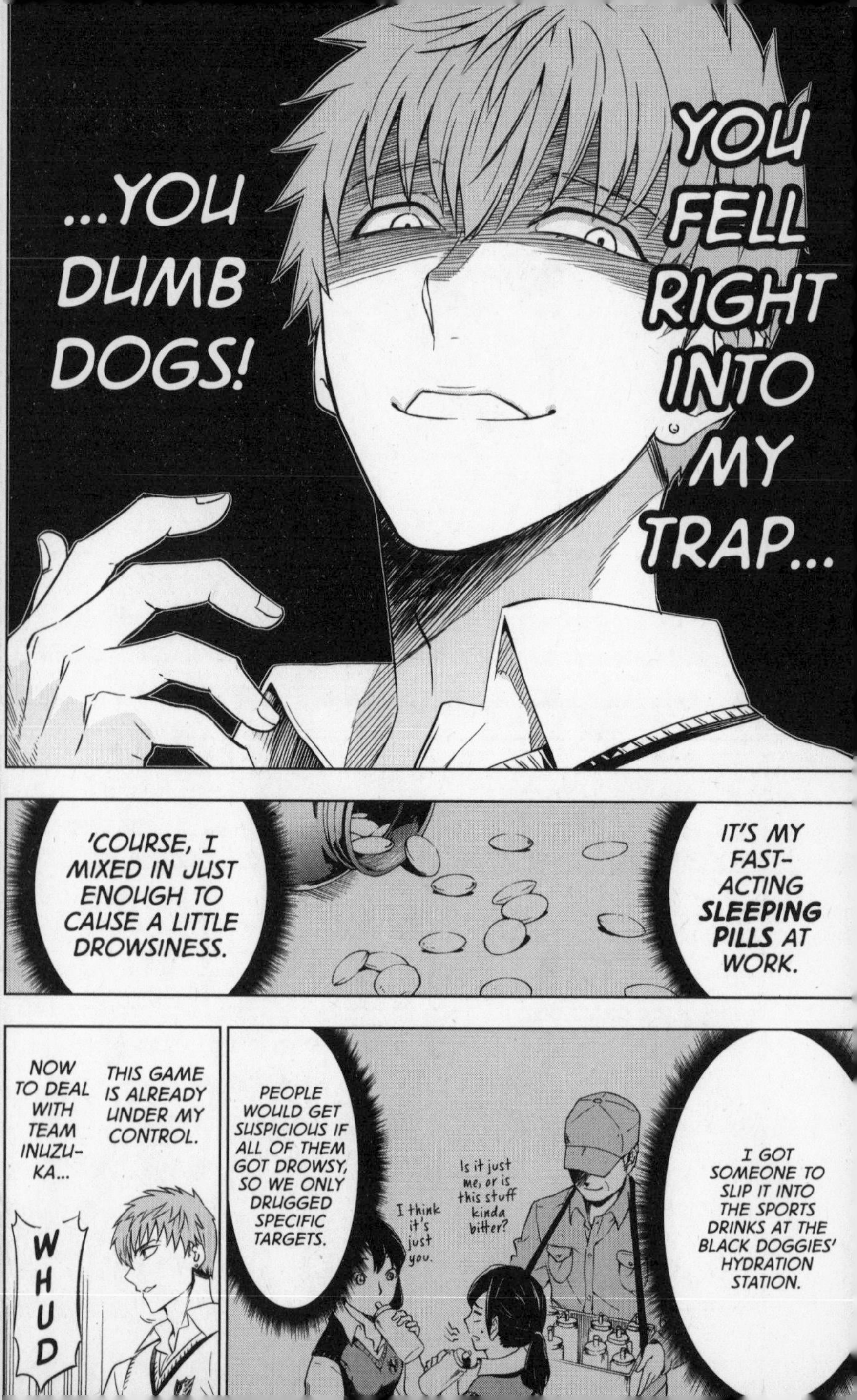
YOU FELL RIGHT INTO MY TRAP...
...YOU DUMB DOGS!
IT'S MY FAST-ACTING **SLEEPING PILLS** AT WORK.
'COURSE, I MIXED IN JUST ENOUGH TO CAUSE A LITTLE DROWSINESS.
I GOT SOMEONE TO SLIP IT INTO THE SPORTS DRINKS AT THE BLACK DOGGIES' HYDRATION STATION.
Is it just me, or is this stuff kinda bitter?
I think it's just you.
PEOPLE WOULD GET SUSPICIOUS IF ALL OF THEM GOT DROWSY, SO WE ONLY DRUGGED SPECIFIC TARGETS.
THIS GAME IS ALREADY UNDER MY CONTROL.
NOW TO DEAL WITH TEAM INUZUKA...
WHUD

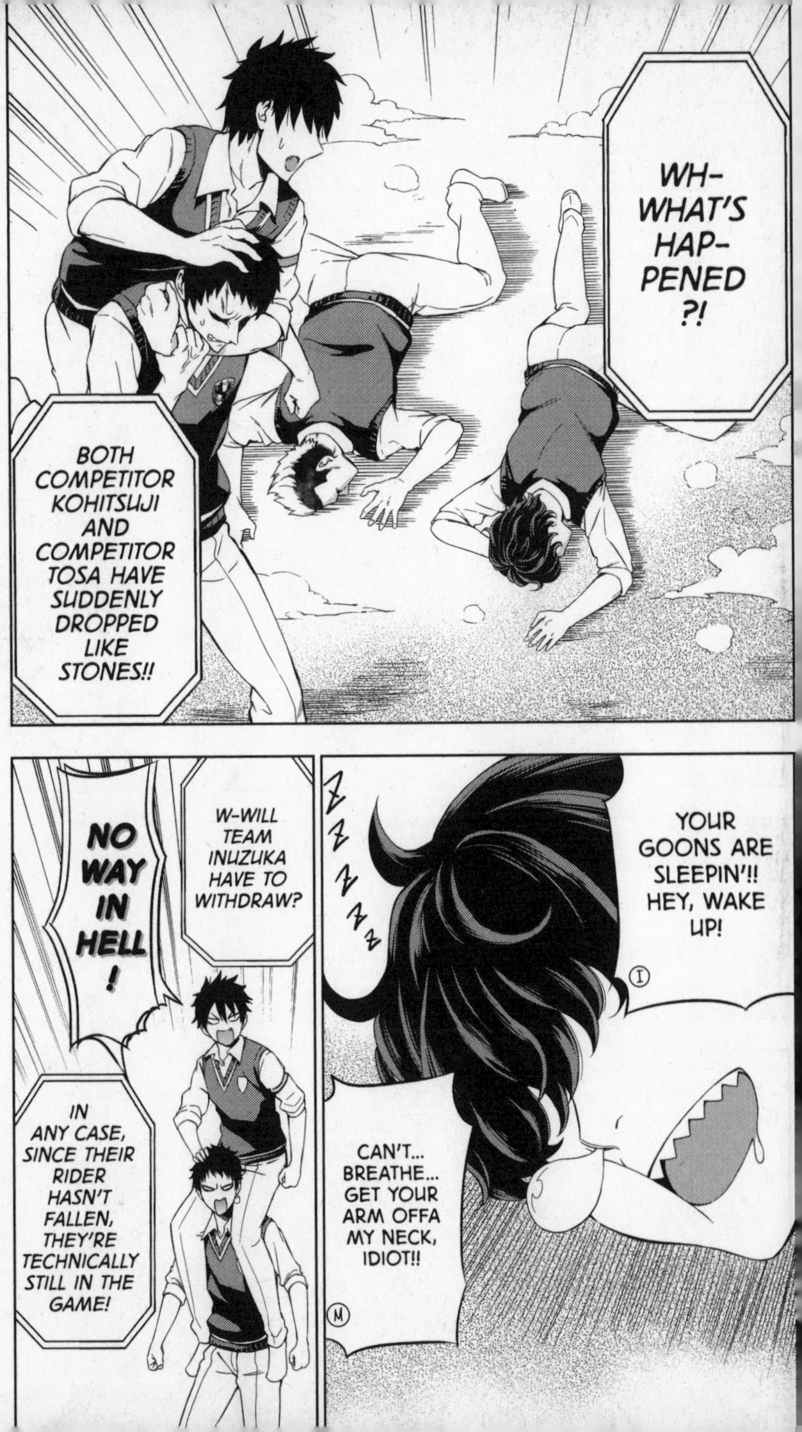
WH- WHAT'S HAP-PENED?!
BOTH COMPETITOR KOHITSUJI AND COMPETITOR TOSA HAVE SUDDENLY DROPPED LIKE STONES!!
YOUR GOONS ARE SLEEPIN'!! HEY, WAKE UP!
ZZZZZ
CAN'T... BREATHE... GET YOUR ARM OFFA MY NECK, IDIOT!!
W-WILL TEAM INUZUKA HAVE TO WITHDRAW?
NO WAY IN HELL!
IN ANY CASE, SINCE THEIR RIDER HASN'T FALLEN, THEY'RE TECHNICALLY STILL IN THE GAME!

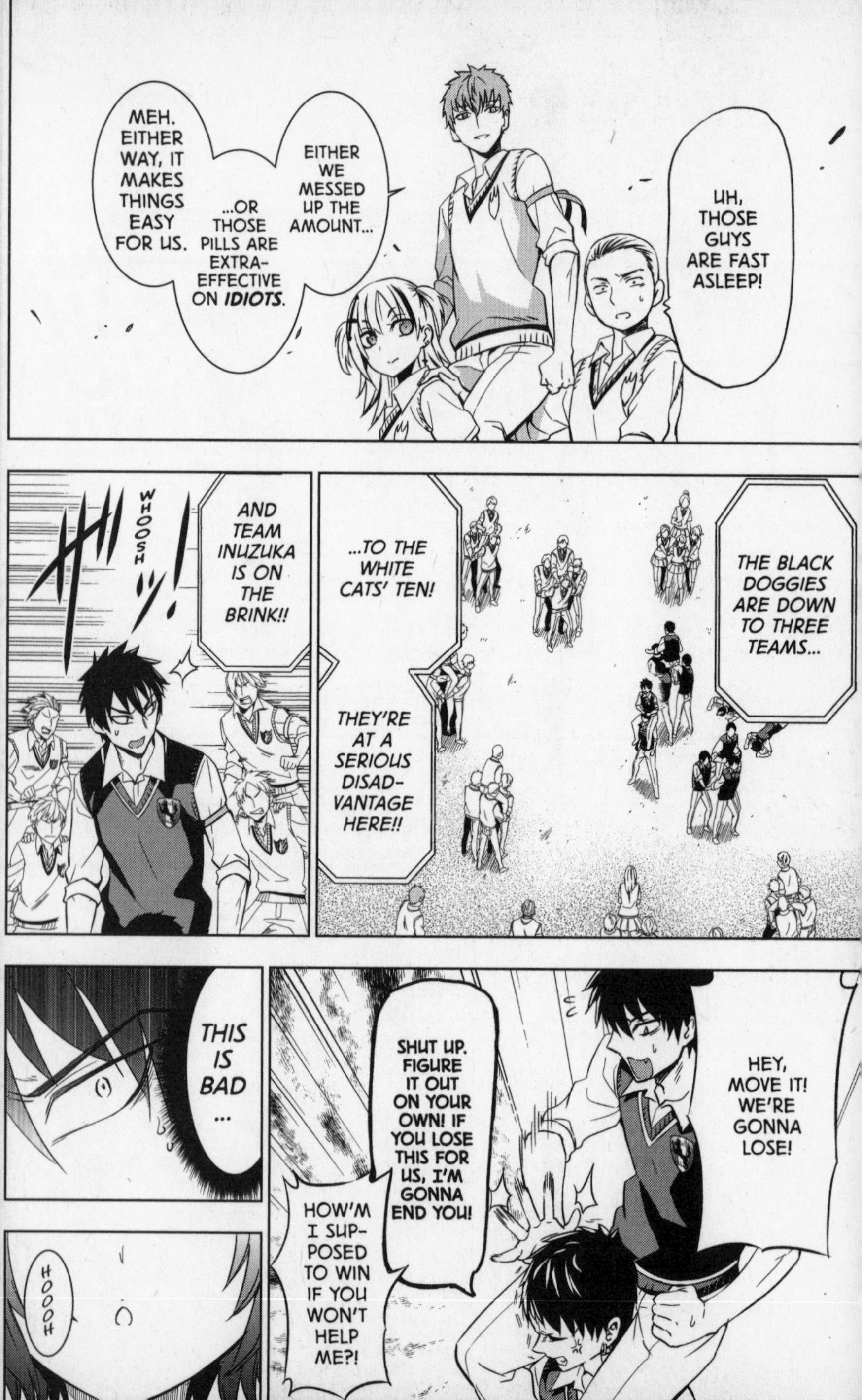
UH, THOSE GUYS ARE FAST ASLEEP!
EITHER WE MESSED UP THE AMOUNT...
...OR THOSE PILLS ARE EXTRA-EFFECTIVE ON IDIOTS.
MEH. EITHER WAY, IT MAKES THINGS EASY FOR US.
THE BLACK DOGGIES ARE DOWN TO THREE TEAMS...
...TO THE WHITE CATS' TEN!
THEY'RE AT A SERIOUS DISAD-VANTAGE HERE!!
AND TEAM INUZUKA IS ON THE BRINK!!
WHOOSH
HEY, MOVE IT! WE'RE GONNA LOSE!
SHUT UP. FIGURE IT OUT ON YOUR OWN! IF YOU LOSE THIS FOR US, I'M GONNA END YOU!
HOW'M I SUP-POSED TO WIN IF YOU WON'T HELP ME?!
THIS IS BAD ...
HOOOH

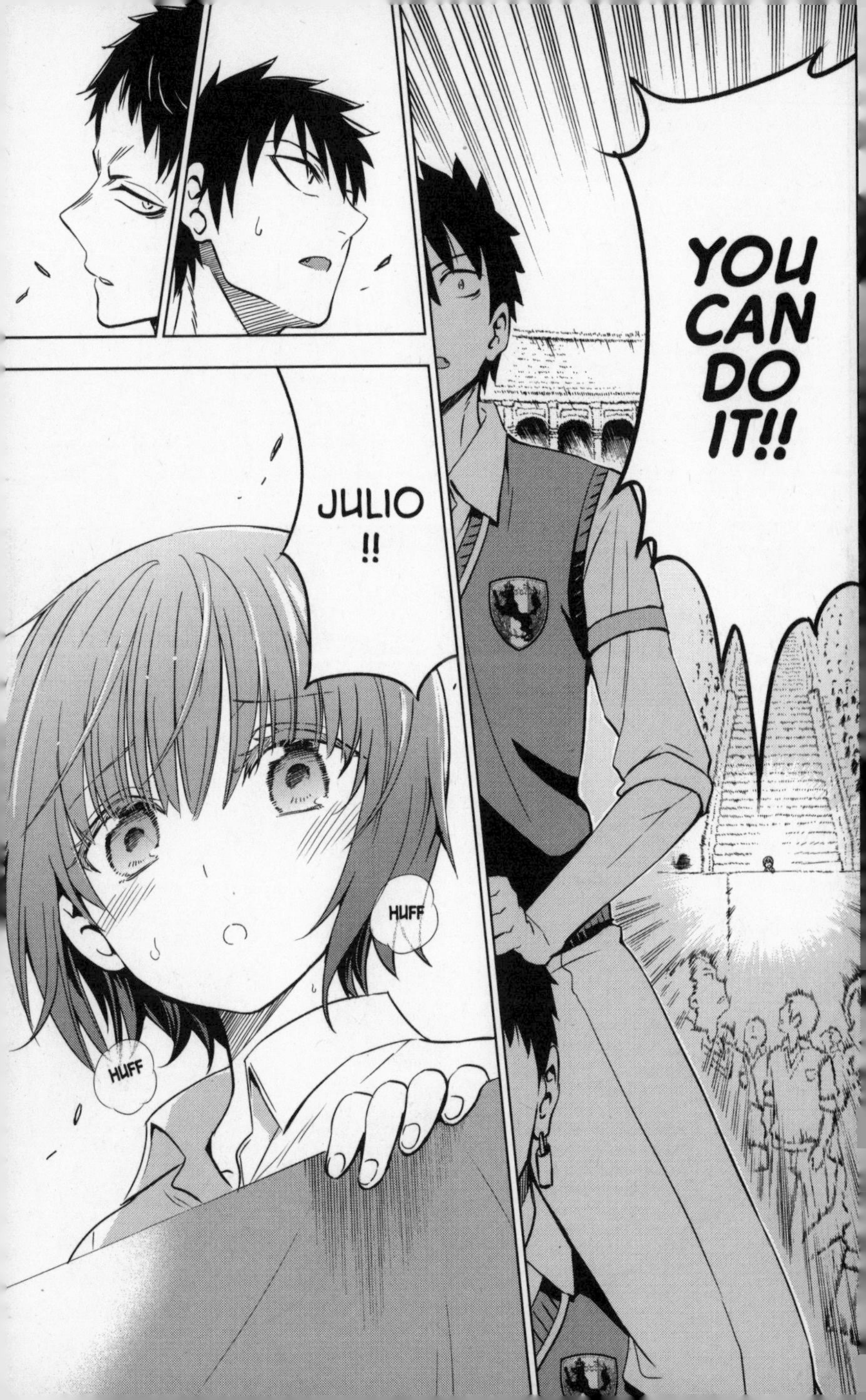
YOU CAN DO IT!!
JULIO!!
HUFF
HUFF

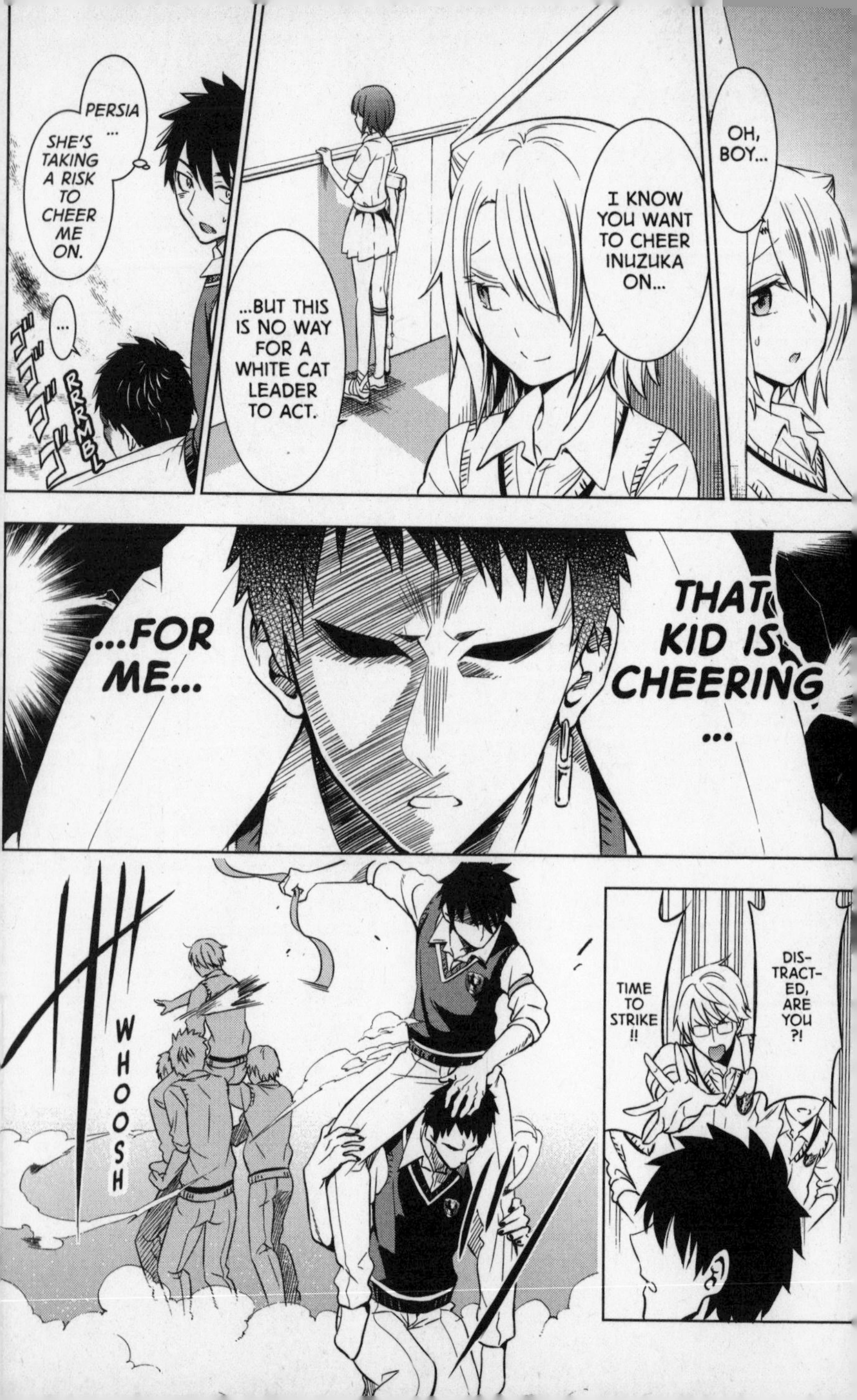
OH, BOY...
I KNOW YOU WANT TO CHEER INUZUKA ON...
...BUT THIS IS NO WAY FOR A WHITE CAT LEADER TO ACT.
PERSIA ... SHE'S TAKING A RISK TO CHEER ME ON.
...
RRRMBL
THAT KID IS CHEERING ...
...FOR ME...
DIS-TRACT-ED, ARE YOU ?!
TIME TO STRIKE !!
!
WHOOSH

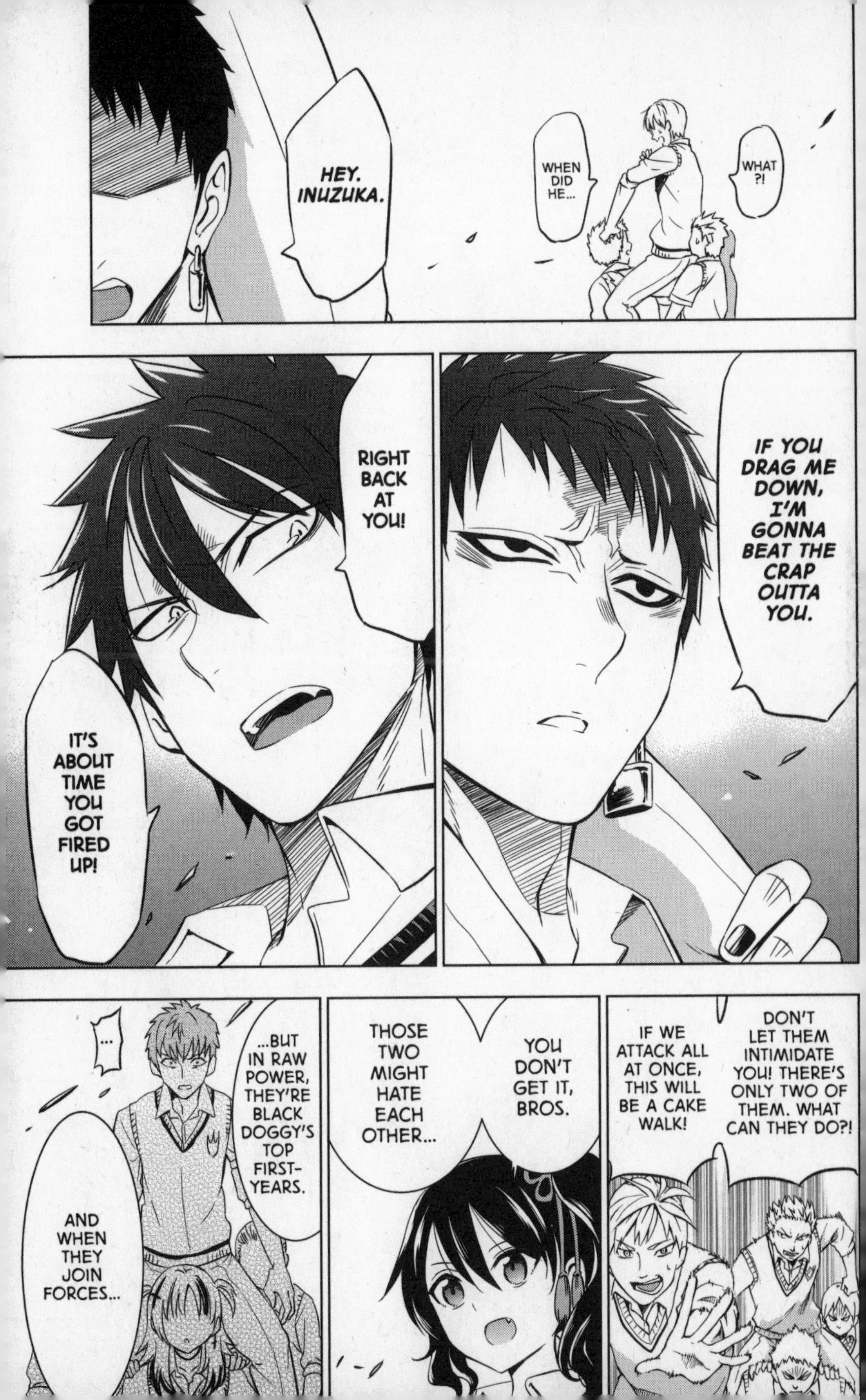
WHAT?!
WHEN DID HE...
HEY. INUZUKA.
IF YOU DRAG ME DOWN, I'M GONNA BEAT THE CRAP OUTTA YOU.
RIGHT BACK AT YOU!
IT'S ABOUT TIME YOU GOT FIRED UP!
DON'T LET THEM INTIMIDATE YOU! THERE'S ONLY TWO OF THEM. WHAT CAN THEY DO?!
IF WE ATTACK ALL AT ONCE, THIS WILL BE A CAKE WALK!
YOU DON'T GET IT, BROS.
THOSE TWO MIGHT HATE EACH OTHER...
...BUT IN RAW POWER, THEY'RE BLACK DOGGY'S TOP FIRST-YEARS.
...
AND WHEN THEY JOIN FORCES...

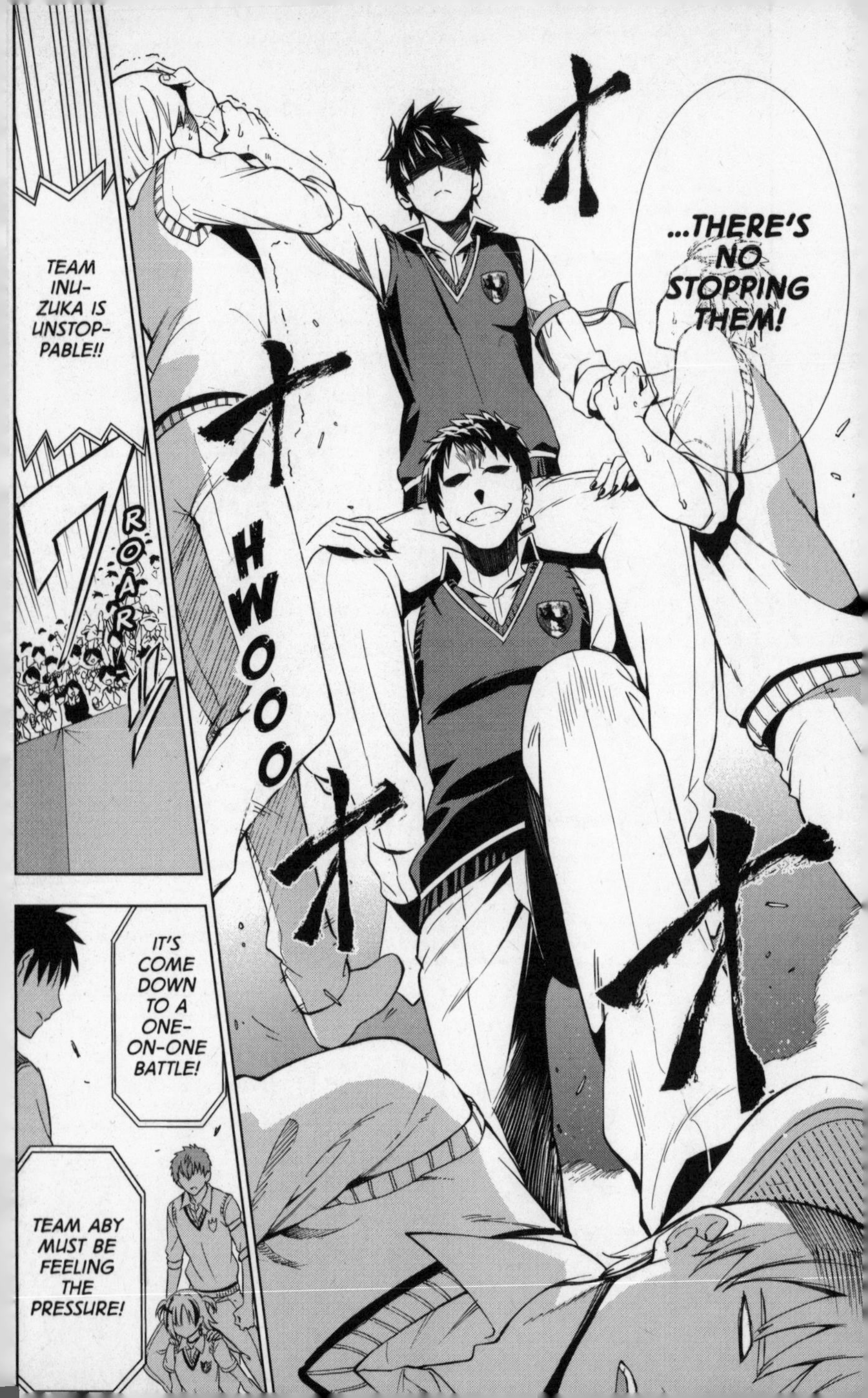
...THERE'S NO STOPPING THEM!
オ
オ
HWOOOO
オ
オ
TEAM INUZUKA IS UNSTOPPABLE!!
ROAR
IT'S COME DOWN TO A ONE-ON-ONE BATTLE!
TEAM ABY MUST BE FEELING THE PRESSURE!

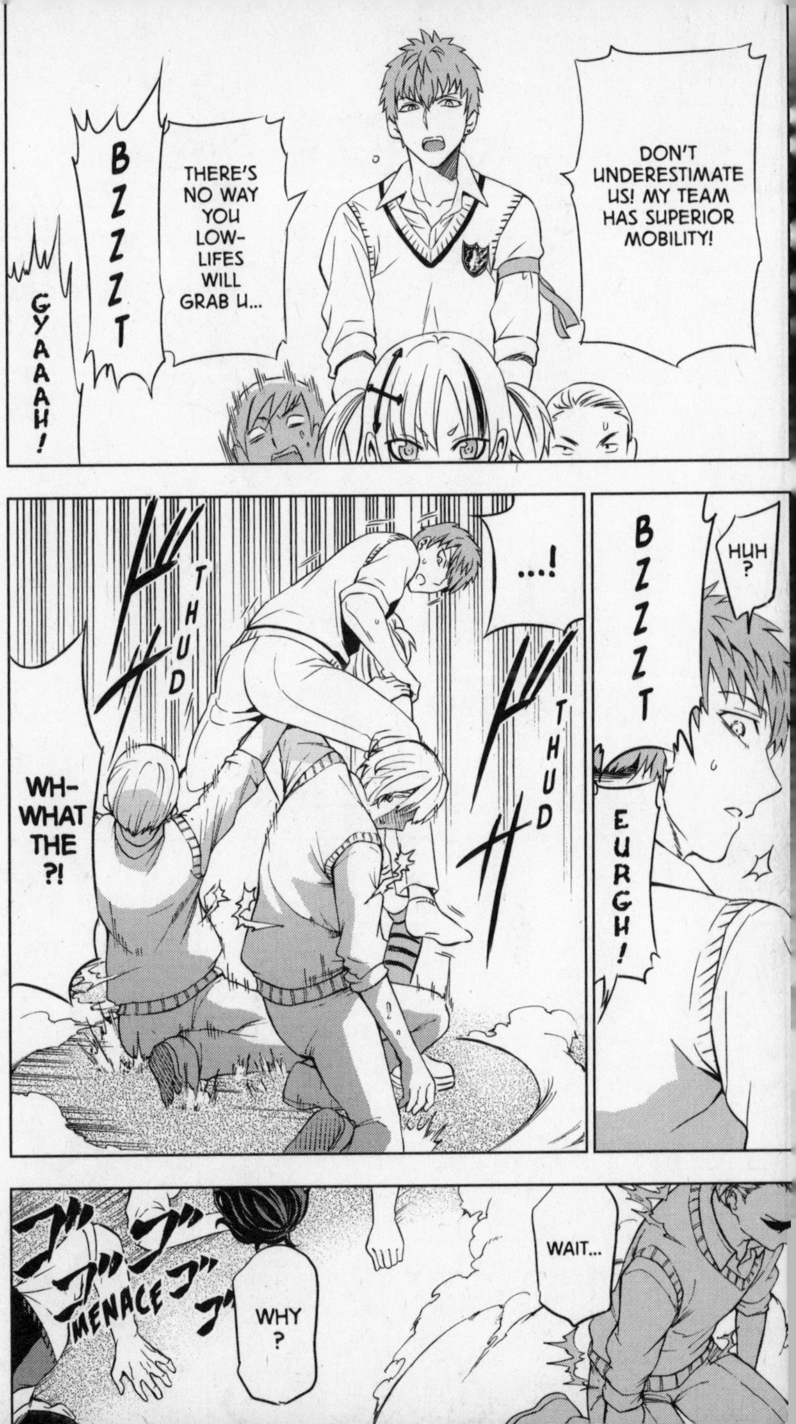
DON'T UNDERESTIMATE US! MY TEAM HAS SUPERIOR MOBILITY!
THERE'S NO WAY YOU LOW-LIFES WILL GRAB U...
BZZZT
GYAAAH!
HUH?
BZZZT
EURGH!
...!
THUD
THUD
WH-WHAT THE ?!
WAIT...
WHY?
MENACE

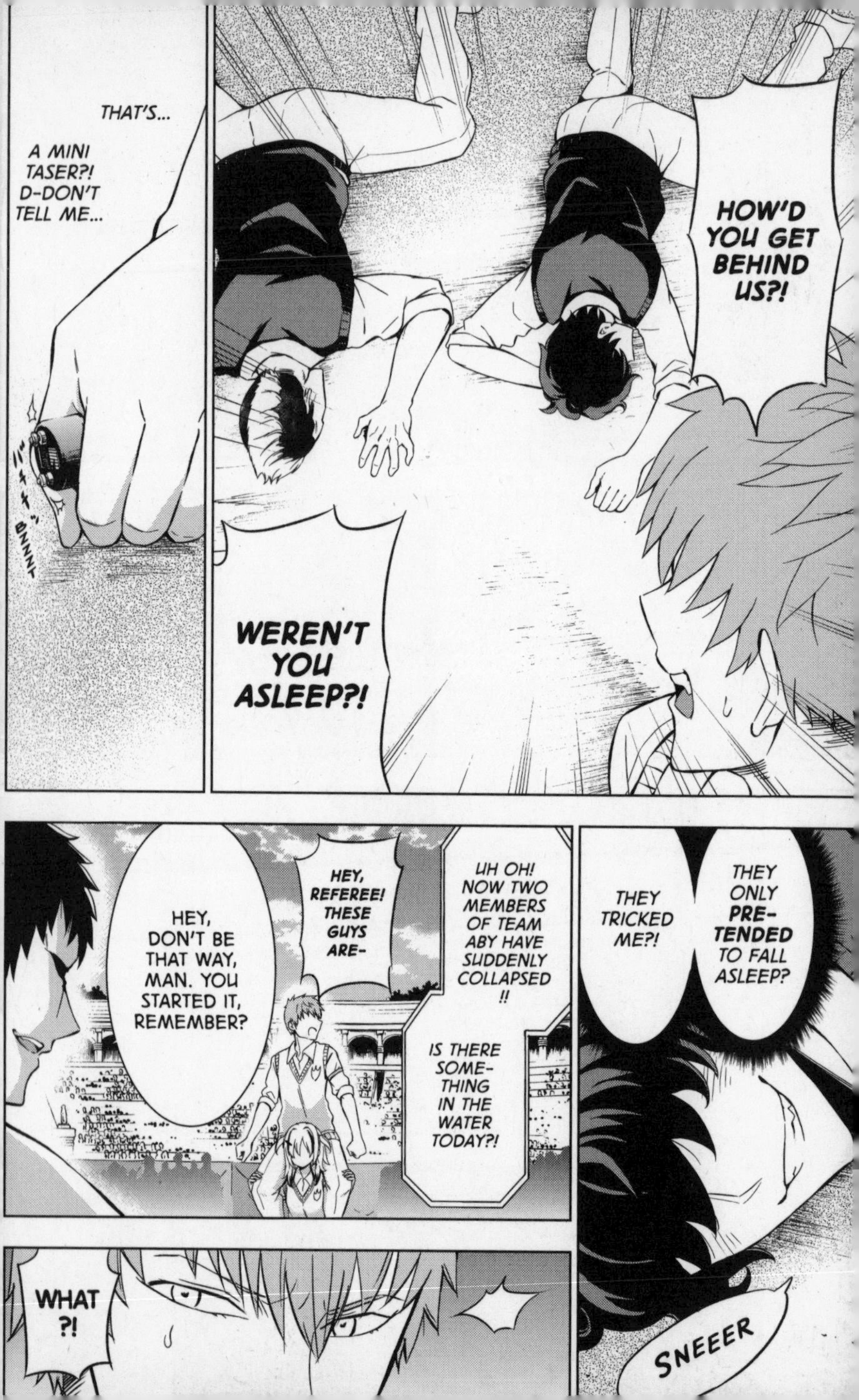
HOW'D YOU GET BEHIND US?!
WEREN'T YOU ASLEEP?!
THAT'S...
A MINI TASER?! D-DON'T TELL ME...
BZZZT
THEY ONLY PRE-TENDED TO FALL ASLEEP?
THEY TRICKED ME?!
SNEEER
UH OH! NOW TWO MEMBERS OF TEAM ABY HAVE SUDDENLY COLLAPSED !!
IS THERE SOME-THING IN THE WATER TODAY?!
HEY, REFEREE! THESE GUYS ARE-
HEY, DON'T BE THAT WAY, MAN. YOU STARTED IT, REMEMBER?
WHAT ?!

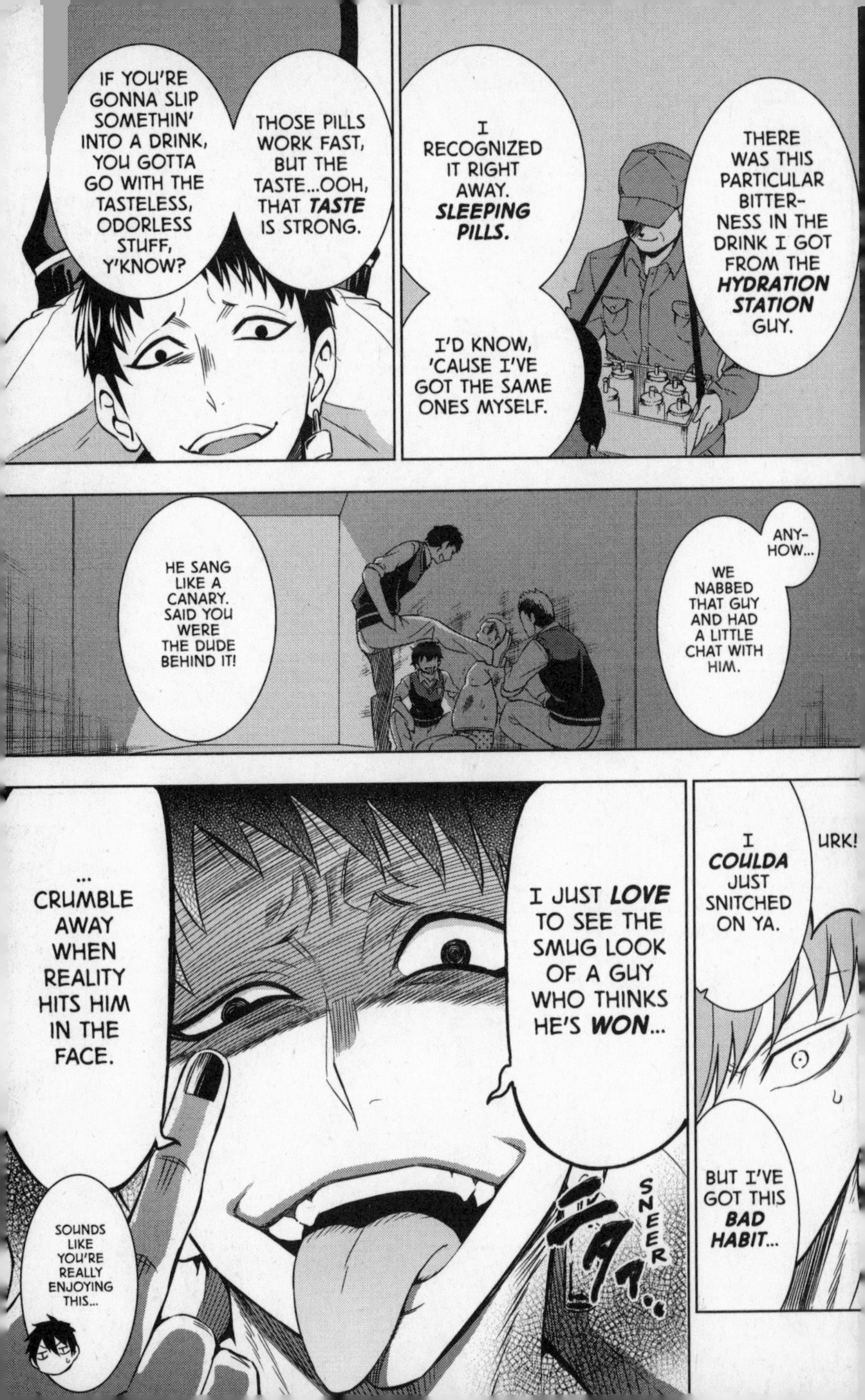
THERE WAS THIS PARTICULAR BITTERNESS IN THE DRINK I GOT FROM THE HYDRATION STATION GUY.
I RECOGNIZED IT RIGHT AWAY. SLEEPING PILLS.
I'D KNOW, 'CAUSE I'VE GOT THE SAME ONES MYSELF.
THOSE PILLS WORK FAST, BUT THE TASTE...OOH, THAT TASTE IS STRONG.
IF YOU'RE GONNA SLIP SOMETHIN' INTO A DRINK, YOU GOTTA GO WITH THE TASTELESS, ODORLESS STUFF, Y'KNOW?
ANYHOW...
WE NABBED THAT GUY AND HAD A LITTLE CHAT WITH HIM.
HE SANG LIKE A CANARY. SAID YOU WERE THE DUDE BEHIND IT!
URK!
I COULDA JUST SNITCHED ON YA.
BUT I'VE GOT THIS BAD HABIT...
I JUST LOVE TO SEE THE SMUG LOOK OF A GUY WHO THINKS HE'S WON...
...CRUMBLE AWAY WHEN REALITY HITS HIM IN THE FACE.
SNEER
SOUNDS LIKE YOU'RE REALLY ENJOYING THIS...

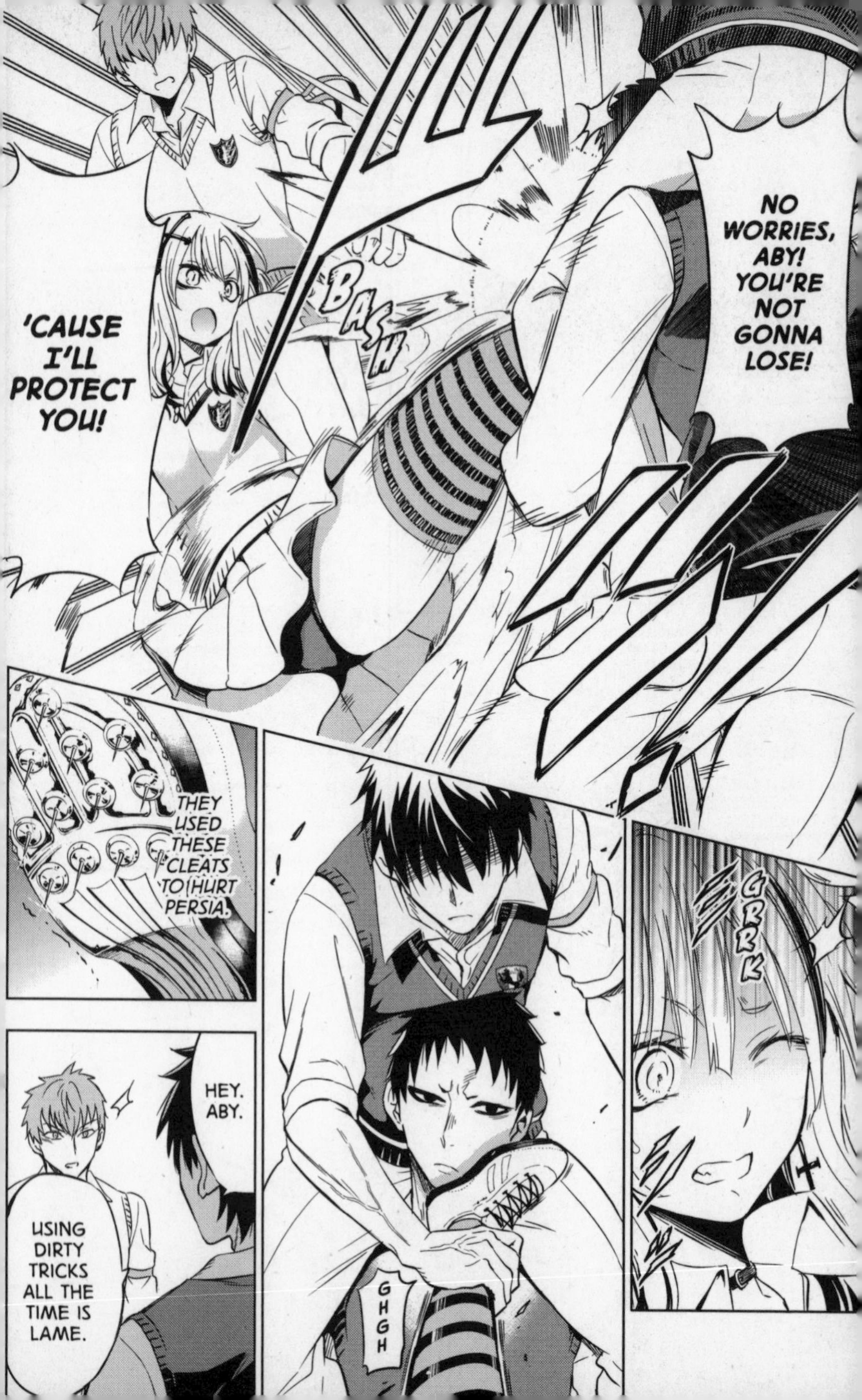
NO WORRIES, ABY! YOU'RE NOT GONNA LOSE!
BASH
'CAUSE I'LL PROTECT YOU!
GRRK
GHGH
THEY USED THESE CLEATS TO HURT PERSIA.
HEY. ABY.
USING DIRTY TRICKS ALL THE TIME IS LAME.

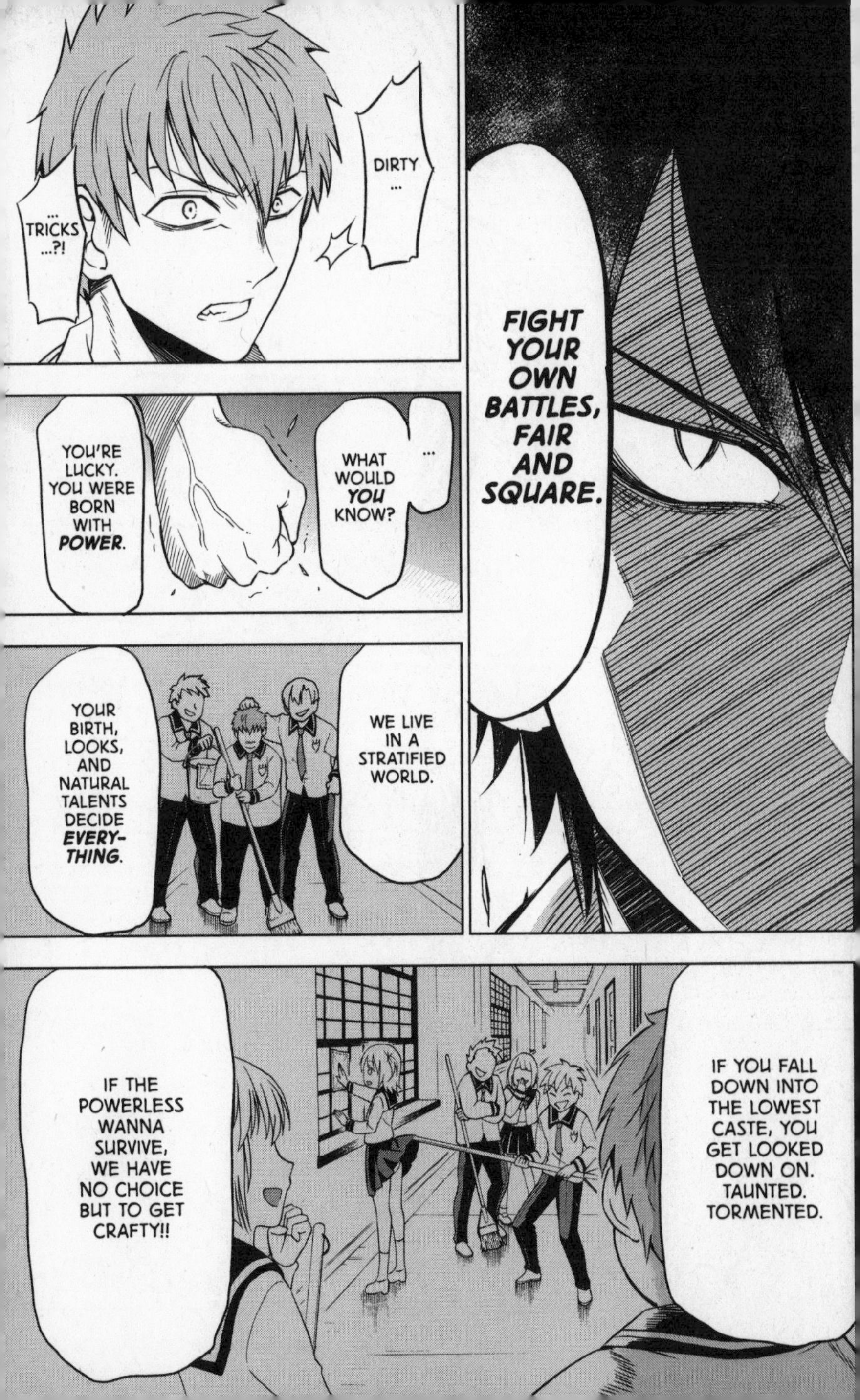

FIGHT YOUR OWN BATTLES, FAIR AND SQUARE.
DIRTY ...
... TRICKS ...?!
... WHAT WOULD YOU KNOW?
YOU'RE LUCKY. YOU WERE BORN WITH POWER.
WE LIVE IN A STRATIFIED WORLD.
YOUR BIRTH, LOOKS, AND NATURAL TALENTS DECIDE EVERY-THING.
IF YOU FALL DOWN INTO THE LOWEST CASTE, YOU GET LOOKED DOWN ON. TAUNTED. TORMENTED.
IF THE POWERLESS WANNA SURVIVE, WE HAVE NO CHOICE BUT TO GET CRAFTY!!

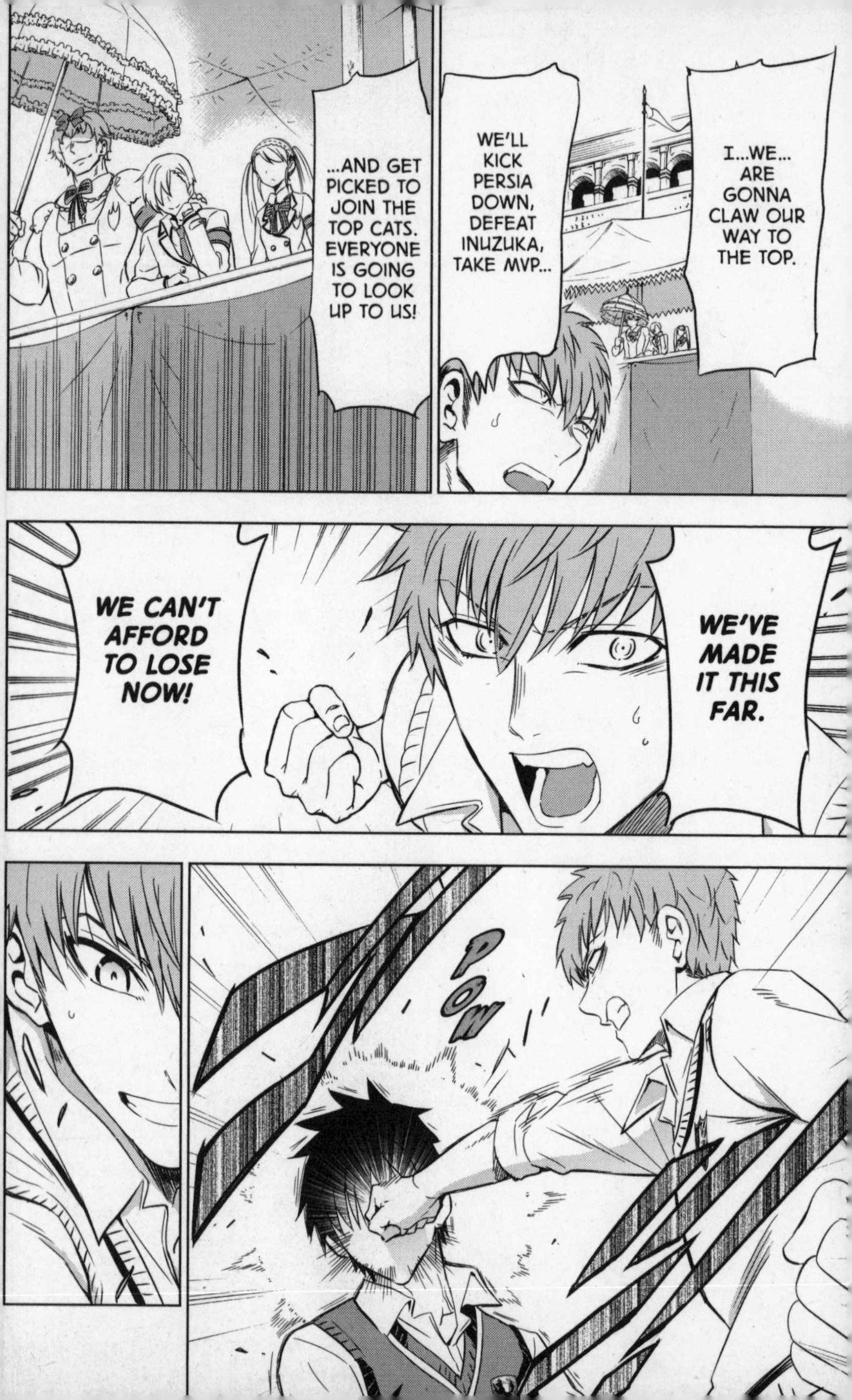
I...WE... ARE GONNA CLAW OUR WAY TO THE TOP.
WE'LL KICK PERSIA DOWN, DEFEAT INUZUKA, TAKE MVP...
...AND GET PICKED TO JOIN THE TOP CATS. EVERYONE IS GOING TO LOOK UP TO US!
WE'VE MADE IT THIS FAR.
WE CAN'T AFFORD TO LOSE NOW!
POW

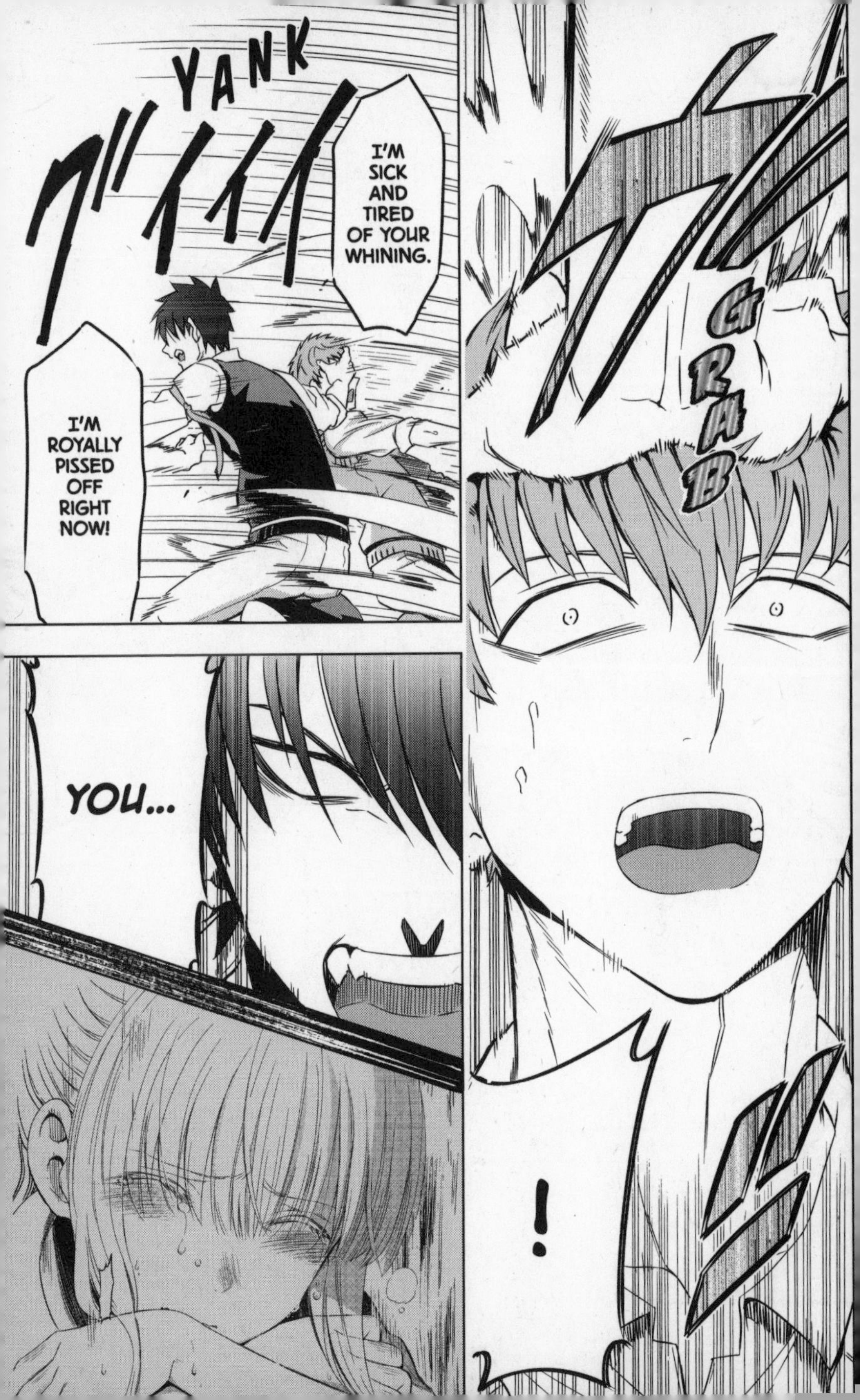
GRAB
!
I'M SICK AND TIRED OF YOUR WHINING.
YANK
グイイイ
I'M ROYALLY PISSED OFF RIGHT NOW!
YOU...

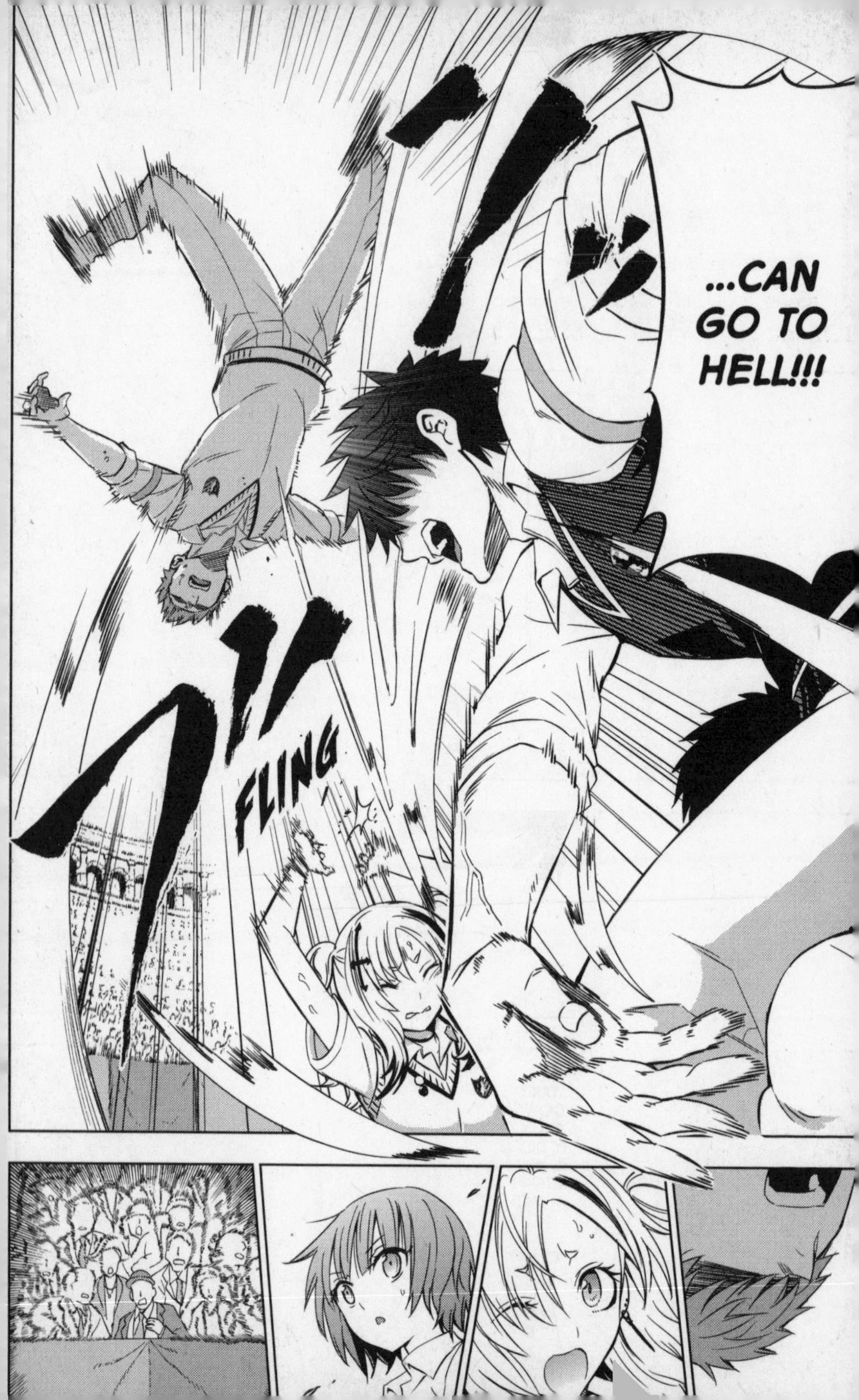
...CAN
GO TO
HELL!!!
FLING

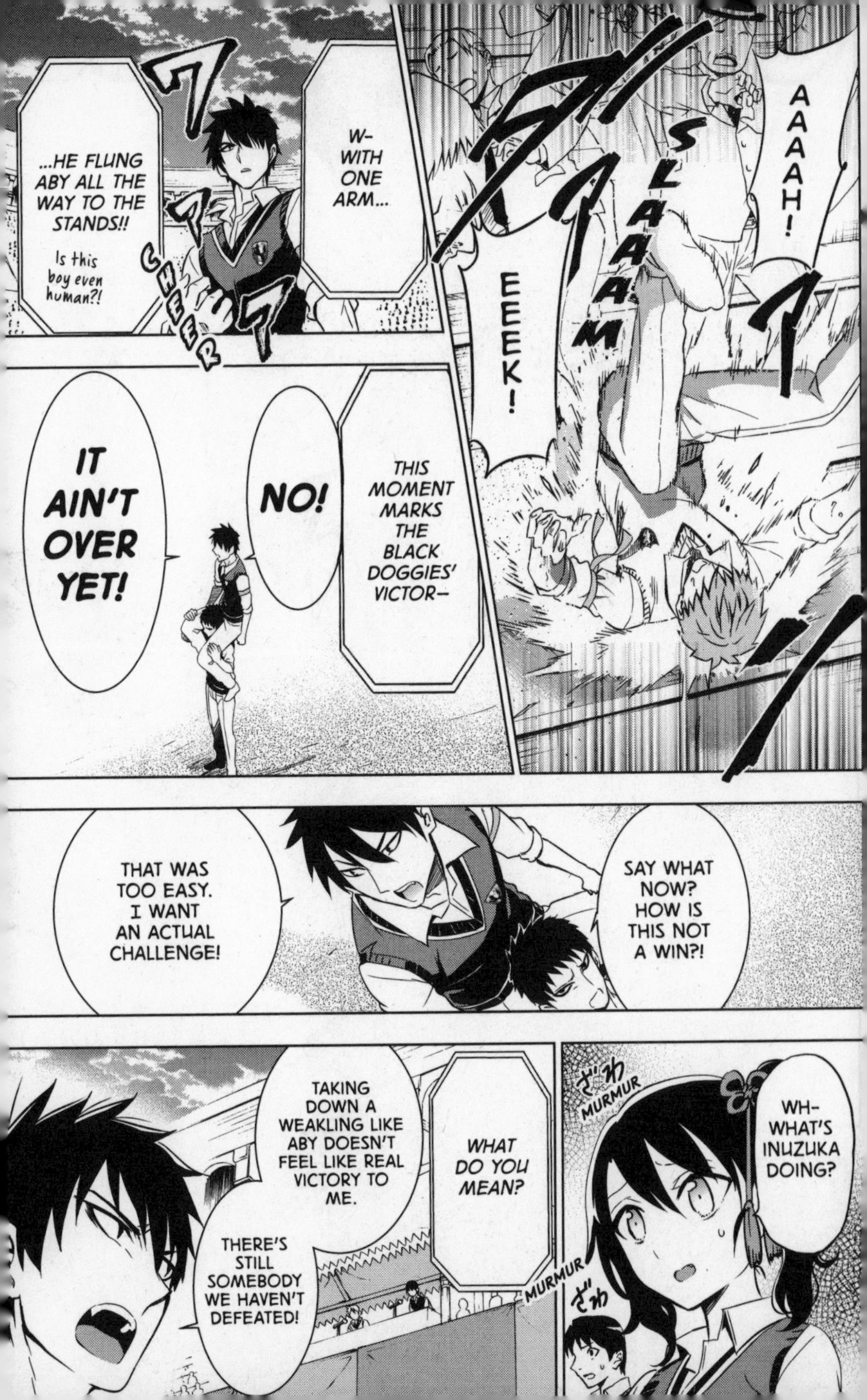
AAAAAH!
SLAAAAM
EEEK!
W- WITH ONE ARM...
...HE FLUNG ABY ALL THE WAY TO THE STANDS!!
Is this boy even human?!
CHEER
THIS MOMENT MARKS THE BLACK DOGGIES' VICTOR–
NO!
IT AIN'T OVER YET!
SAY WHAT NOW? HOW IS THIS NOT A WIN?!
THAT WAS TOO EASY. I WANT AN ACTUAL CHALLENGE!
WH- WHAT'S INUZUKA DOING?
MURMUR
MURMUR
WHAT DO YOU MEAN?
TAKING DOWN A WEAKLING LIKE ABY DOESN'T FEEL LIKE REAL VICTORY TO ME.
THERE'S STILL SOMEBODY WE HAVEN'T DEFEATED!

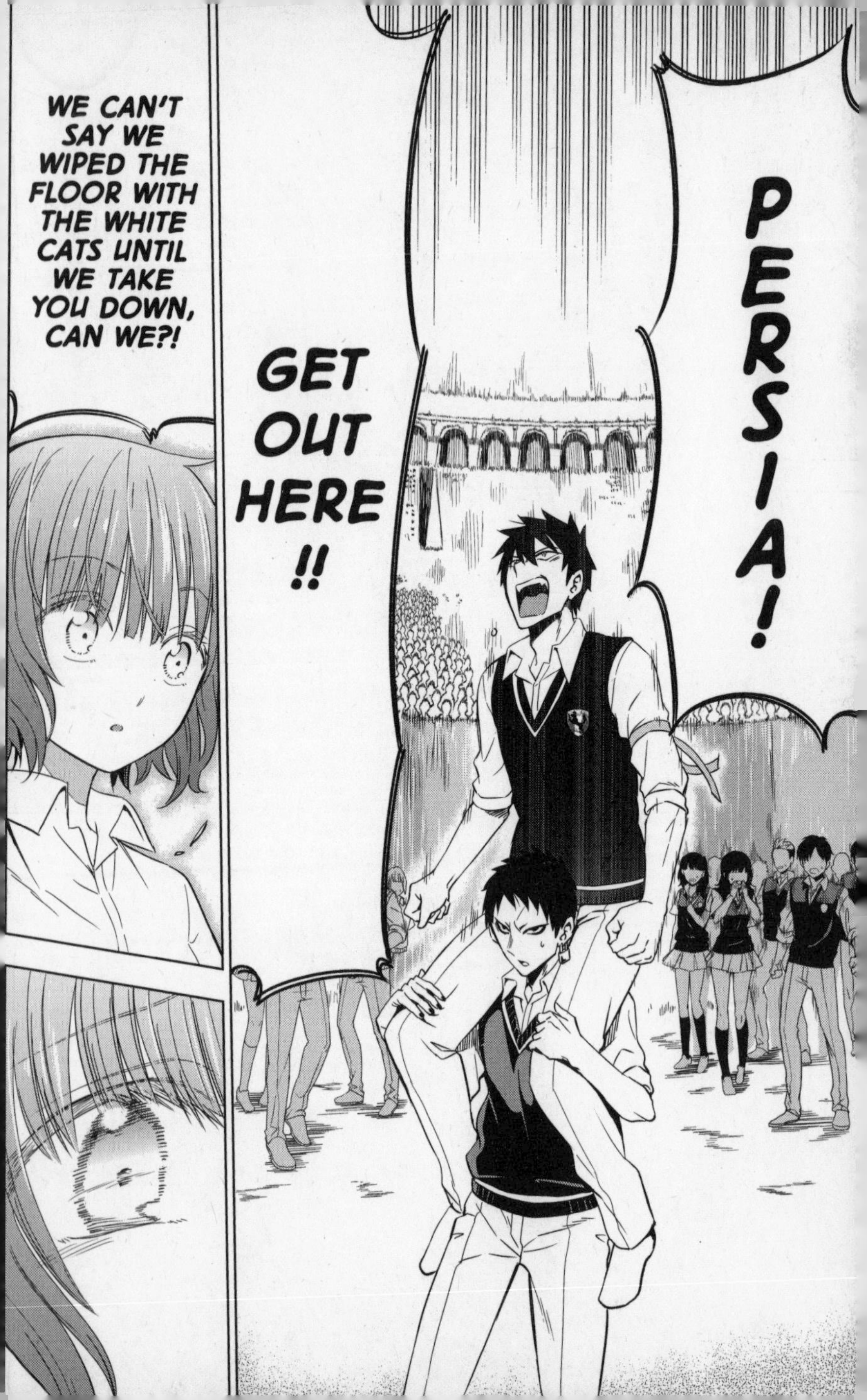
PERSIA!
GET OUT HERE!!
WE CAN'T SAY WE WIPED THE FLOOR WITH THE WHITE CATS UNTIL WE TAKE YOU DOWN, CAN WE?!

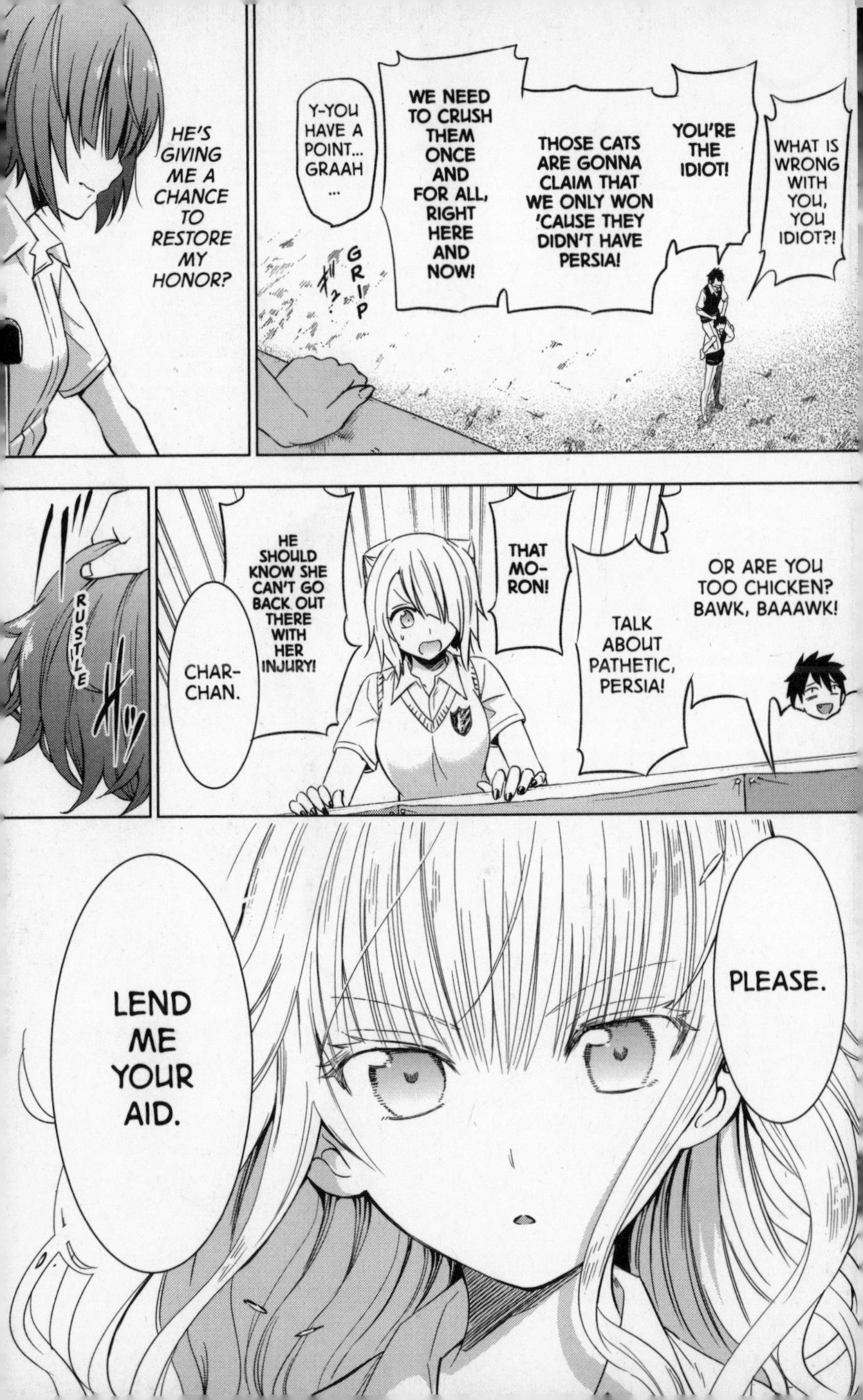
WHAT IS WRONG WITH YOU, YOU IDIOT?!
YOU'RE THE IDIOT!
THOSE CATS ARE GONNA CLAIM THAT WE ONLY WON 'CAUSE THEY DIDN'T HAVE PERSIA!
WE NEED TO CRUSH THEM ONCE AND FOR ALL, RIGHT HERE AND NOW!
Y-YOU HAVE A POINT... GRAAH ...
GRIP
HE'S GIVING ME A CHANCE TO RESTORE MY HONOR?
OR ARE YOU TOO CHICKEN? BAWK, BAAAWK!
TALK ABOUT PATHETIC, PERSIA!
THAT MO-RON!
HE SHOULD KNOW SHE CAN'T GO BACK OUT THERE WITH HER INJURY!
CHAR-CHAN.
RUSTLE
PLEASE.
LEND ME YOUR AID.

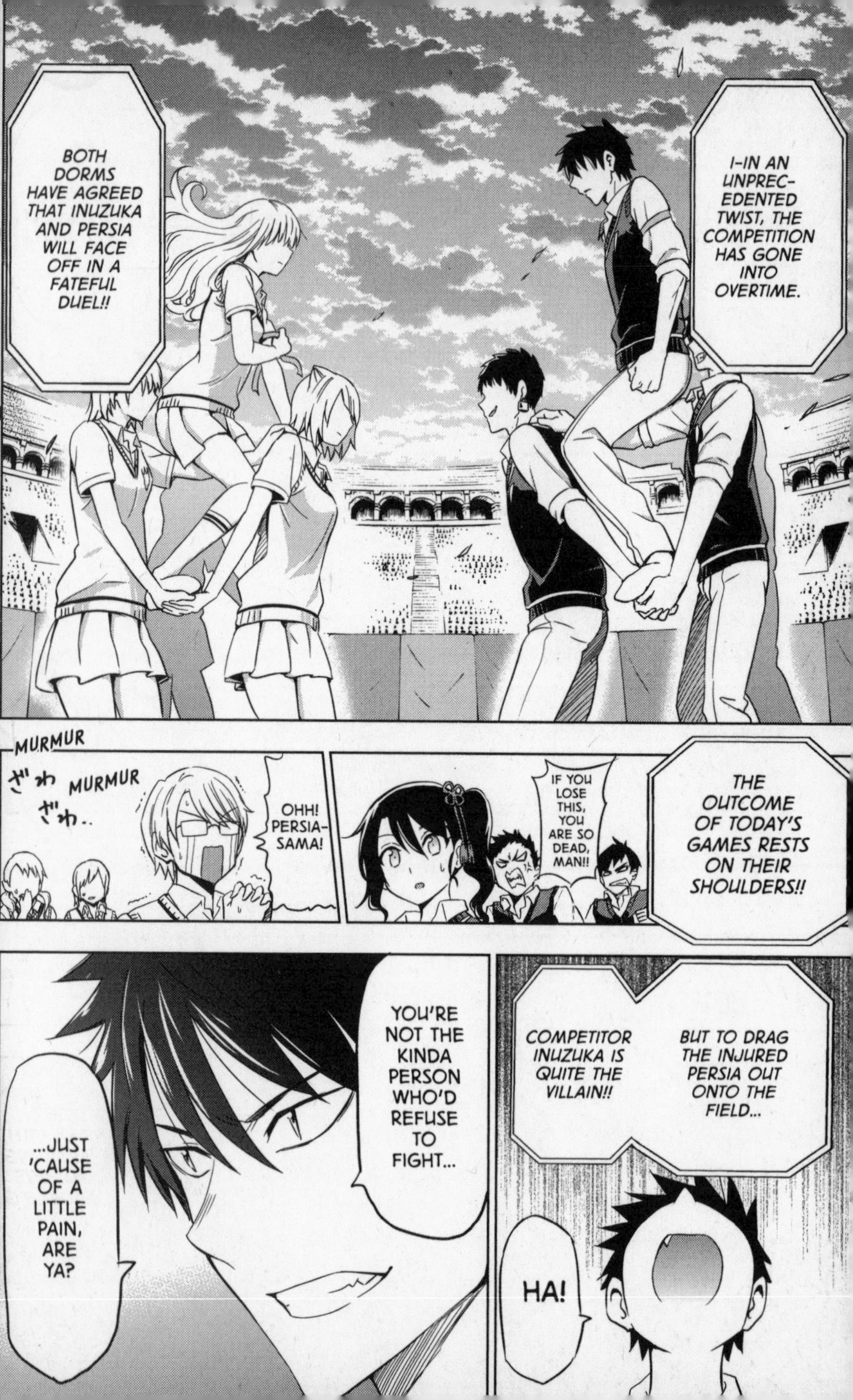
I-IN AN UNPRECEDENTED TWIST, THE COMPETITION HAS GONE INTO OVERTIME.
BOTH DORMS HAVE AGREED THAT INUZUKA AND PERSIA WILL FACE OFF IN A FATEFUL DUEL!!
MURMUR
THE OUTCOME OF TODAY'S GAMES RESTS ON THEIR SHOULDERS!!
IF YOU LOSE THIS, YOU ARE SO DEAD, MAN!!
OHH! PERSIA-SAMA!
MURMUR
ざわ ざわ..
BUT TO DRAG THE INJURED PERSIA OUT ONTO THE FIELD...
COMPETITOR INUZUKA IS QUITE THE VILLAIN!!
HA!
YOU'RE NOT THE KINDA PERSON WHO'D REFUSE TO FIGHT...
...JUST 'CAUSE OF A LITTLE PAIN, ARE YA?

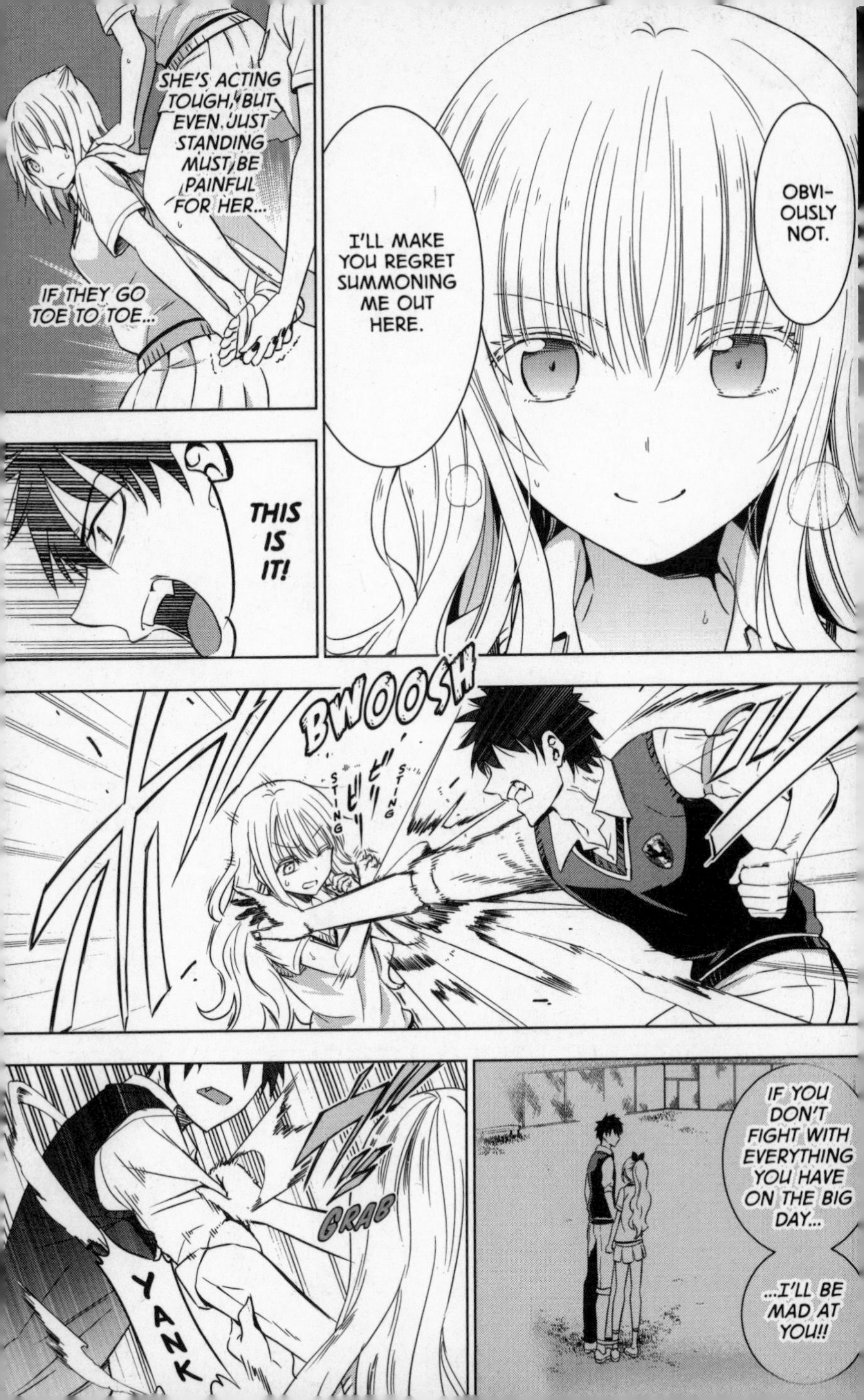
OBVI-OUSLY NOT.
I'LL MAKE YOU REGRET SUMMONING ME OUT HERE.
SHE'S ACTING TOUGH, BUT EVEN JUST STANDING MUST BE PAINFUL FOR HER...
IF THEY GO TOE TO TOE...
THIS IS IT!
BWOOSH
STING
STING
IF YOU DON'T FIGHT WITH EVERYTHING YOU HAVE ON THE BIG DAY...
...I'LL BE MAD AT YOU!!
GRAB
YANK

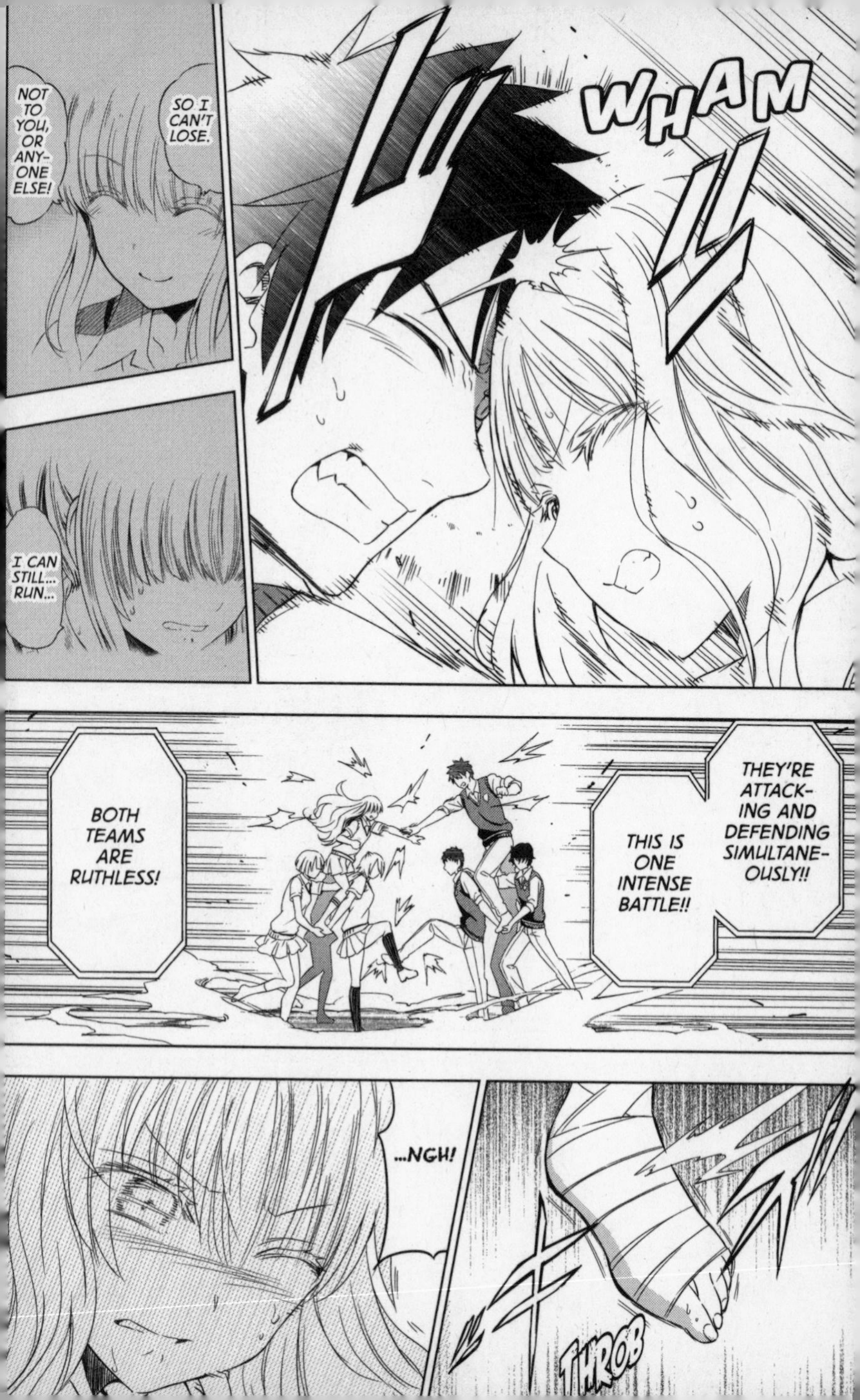
WHAM
SO I CAN'T LOSE.
NOT TO YOU, OR ANYONE ELSE!
I CAN STILL... RUN...
THEY'RE ATTACKING AND DEFENDING SIMULTANEOUSLY!!
THIS IS ONE INTENSE BATTLE!!
BOTH TEAMS ARE RUTHLESS!
THROB
...NGH!

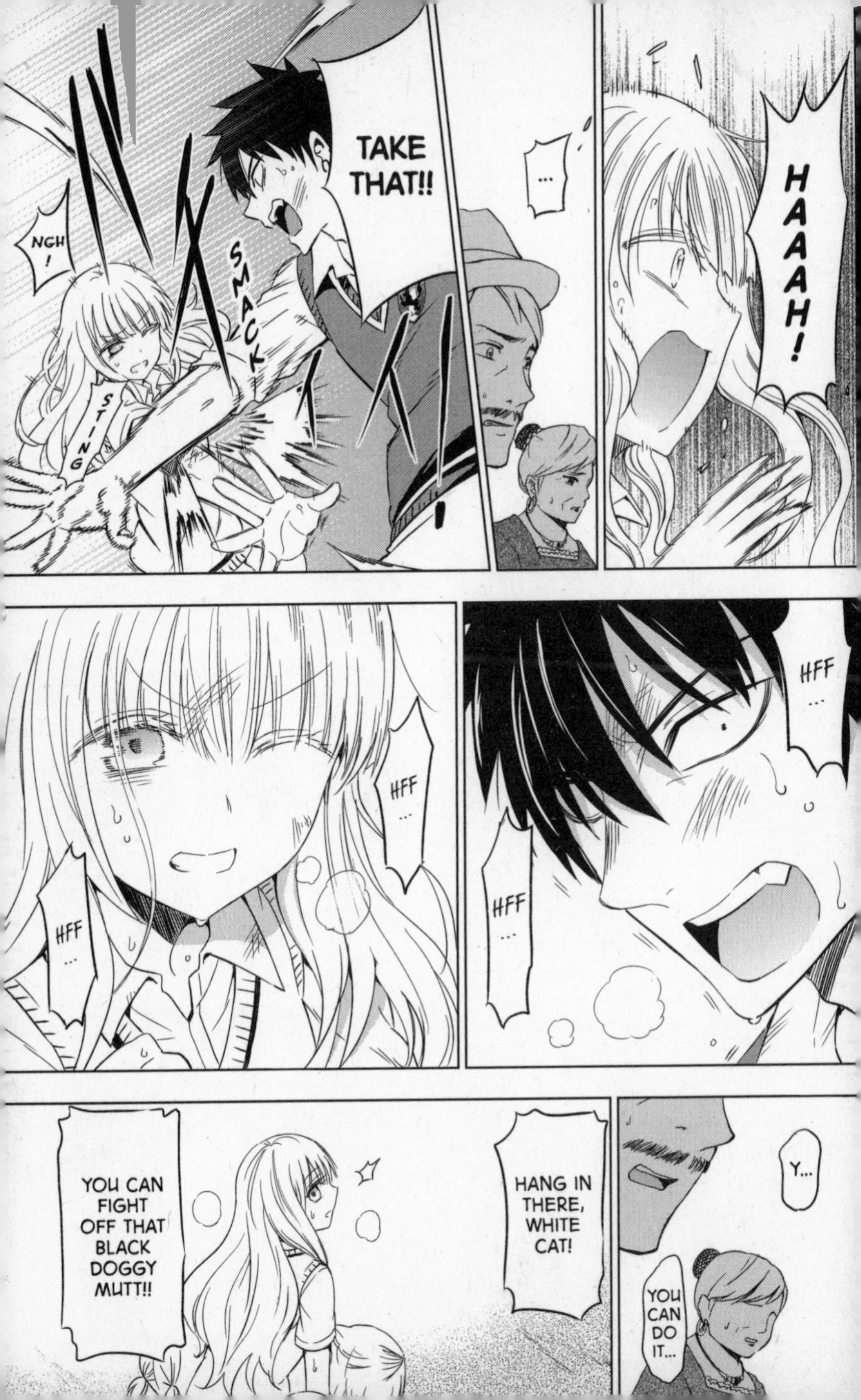
HAAAAH!
...
TAKE THAT!!
SMACK
NGH!
STING
HFF...
HFF...
HFF...
HFF...
Y...
YOU CAN DO IT...
HANG IN THERE, WHITE CAT!
YOU CAN FIGHT OFF THAT BLACK DOGGY MUTT!!

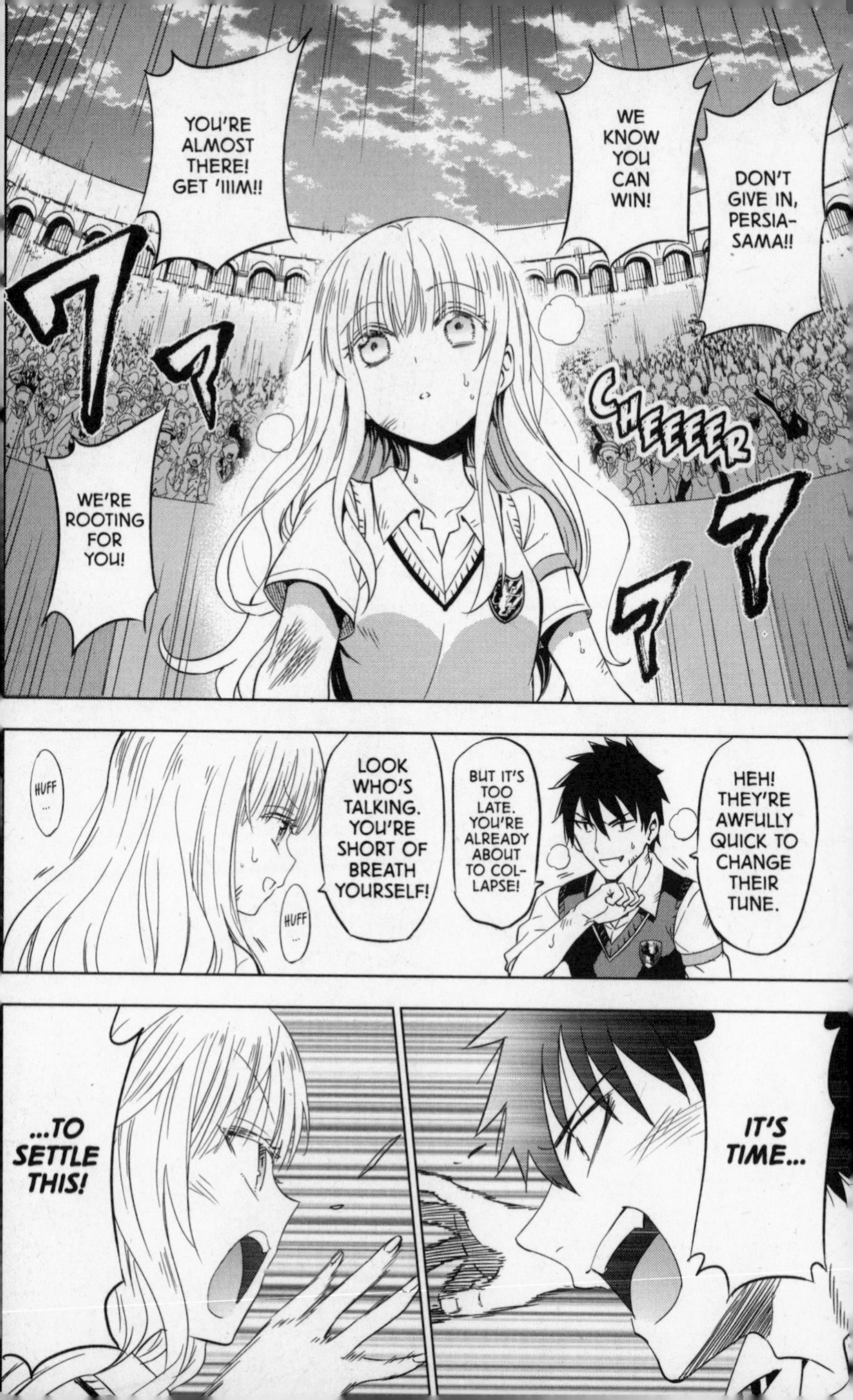
DON'T GIVE IN, PERSIA-SAMA!!
WE KNOW YOU CAN WIN!
CHEEEER
YOU'RE ALMOST THERE! GET 'IIIM!!
WE'RE ROOTING FOR YOU!
HEH! THEY'RE AWFULLY QUICK TO CHANGE THEIR TUNE.
BUT IT'S TOO LATE. YOU'RE ALREADY ABOUT TO COL-LAPSE!
LOOK WHO'S TALKING. YOU'RE SHORT OF BREATH YOURSELF!
HUFF...
HUFF...
IT'S TIME...
...TO SETTLE THIS!

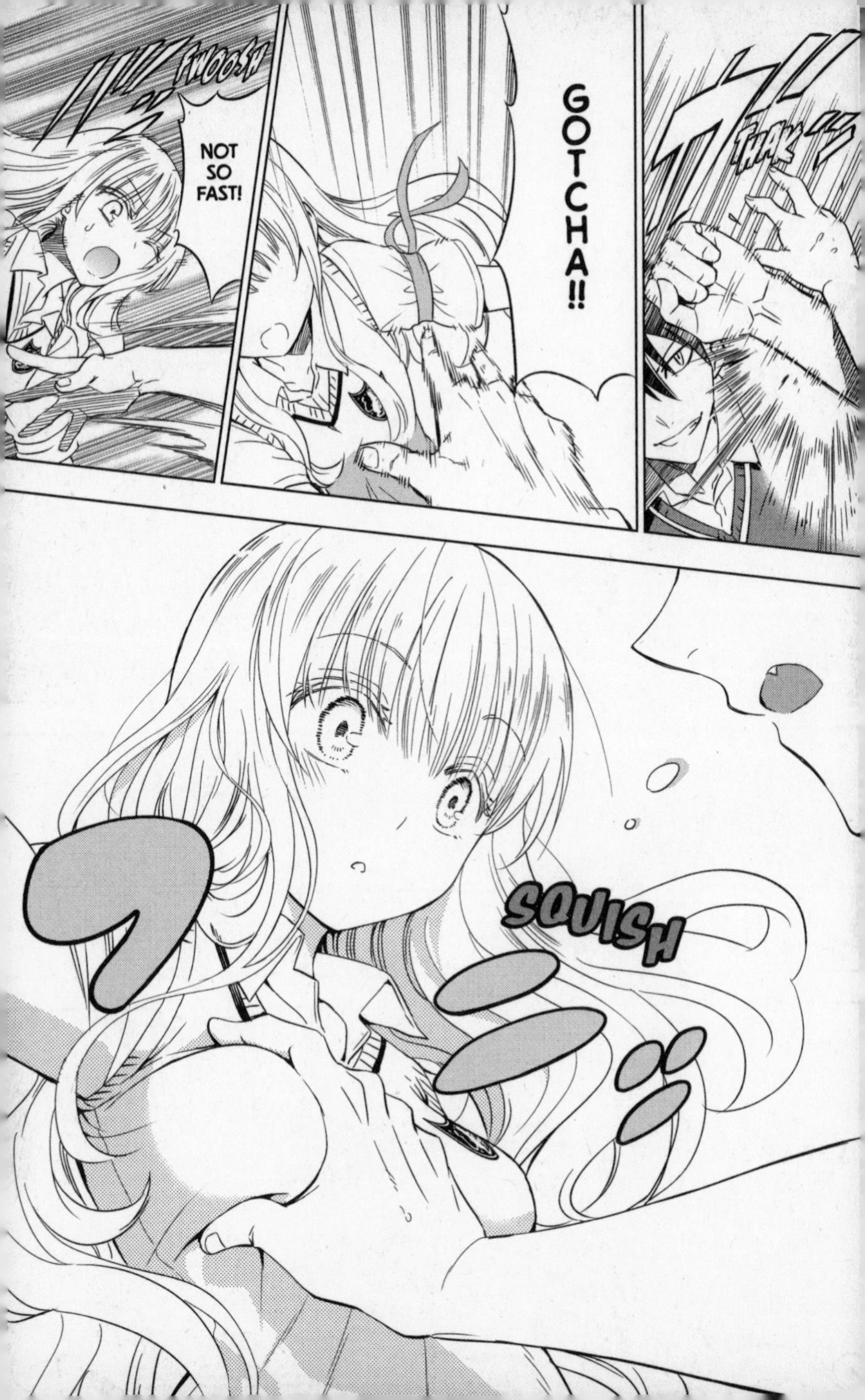
THAK
GOTCHA!!
FWOOSH
NOT SO FAST!
SQUISH

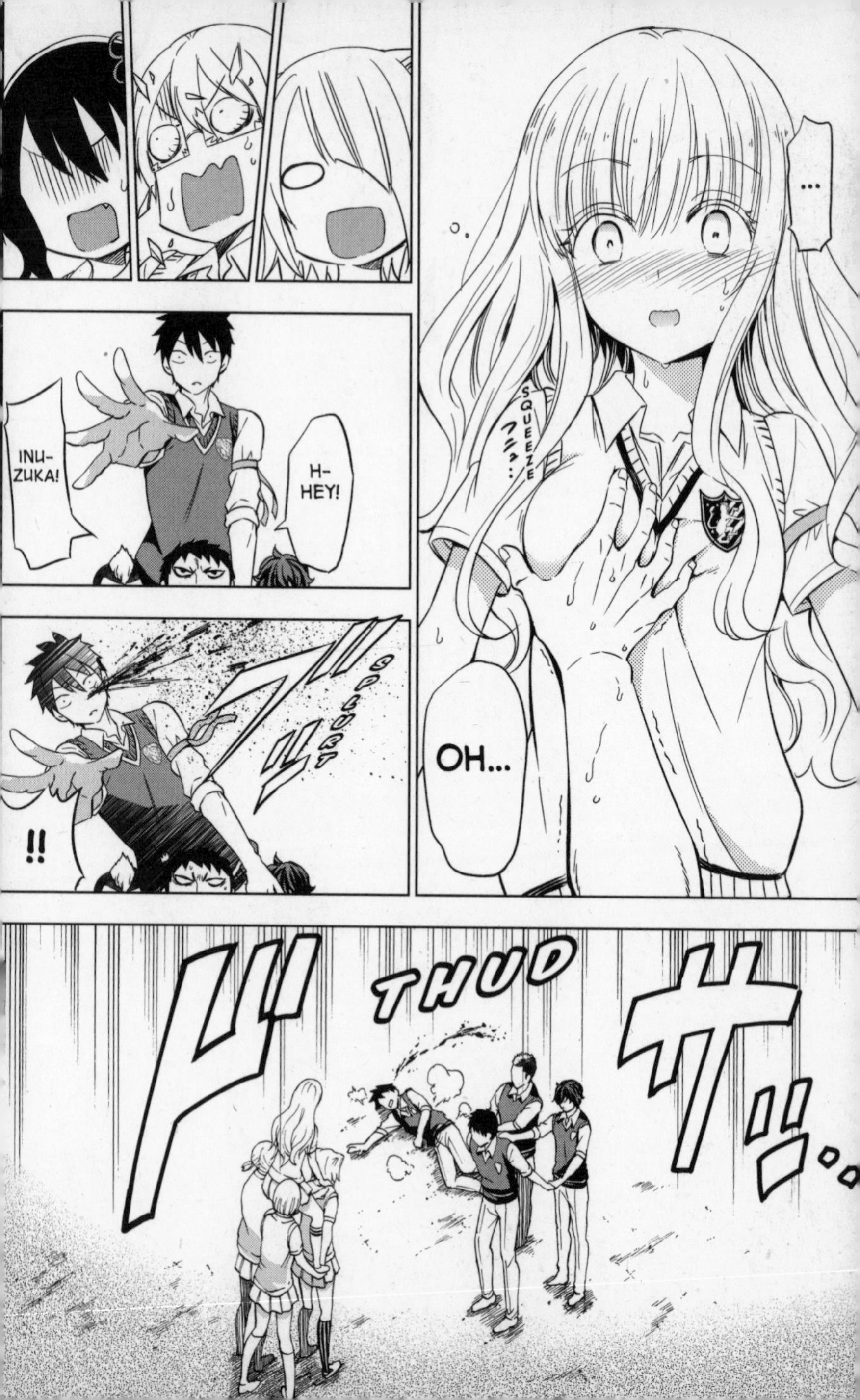
...
SQUEEZE
OH...
H-
HEY!
INU-
ZUKA!
SPLURT
!!
THUD

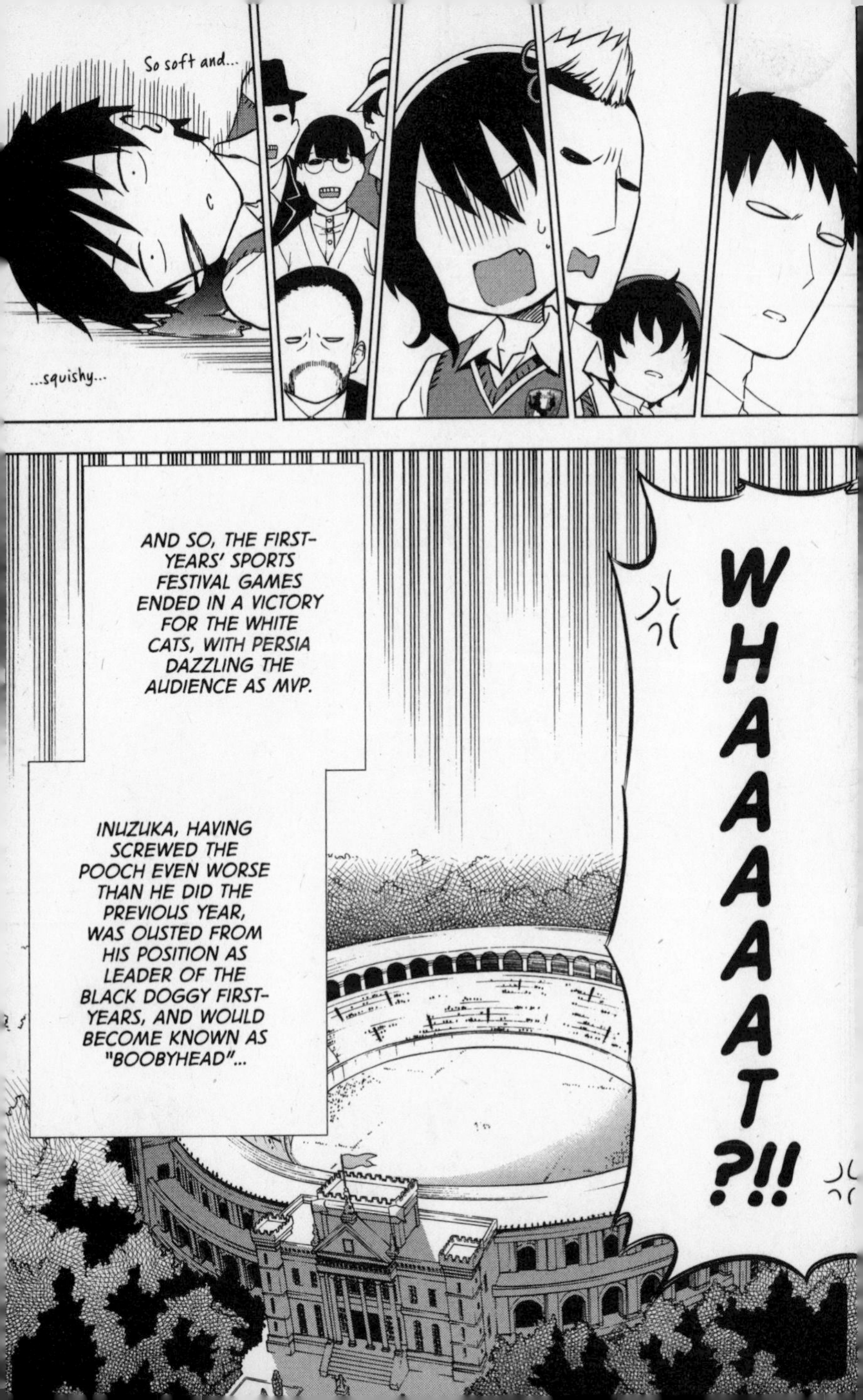
So soft and...
...squishy...
WHAAAAAT?!!
AND SO, THE FIRST-YEARS' SPORTS FESTIVAL GAMES ENDED IN A VICTORY FOR THE WHITE CATS, WITH PERSIA DAZZLING THE AUDIENCE AS MVP.
INUZUKA, HAVING SCREWED THE POOCH EVEN WORSE THAN HE DID THE PREVIOUS YEAR, WAS OUSTED FROM HIS POSITION AS LEADER OF THE BLACK DOGGY FIRST-YEARS, AND WOULD BECOME KNOWN AS "BOOBYHEAD"...

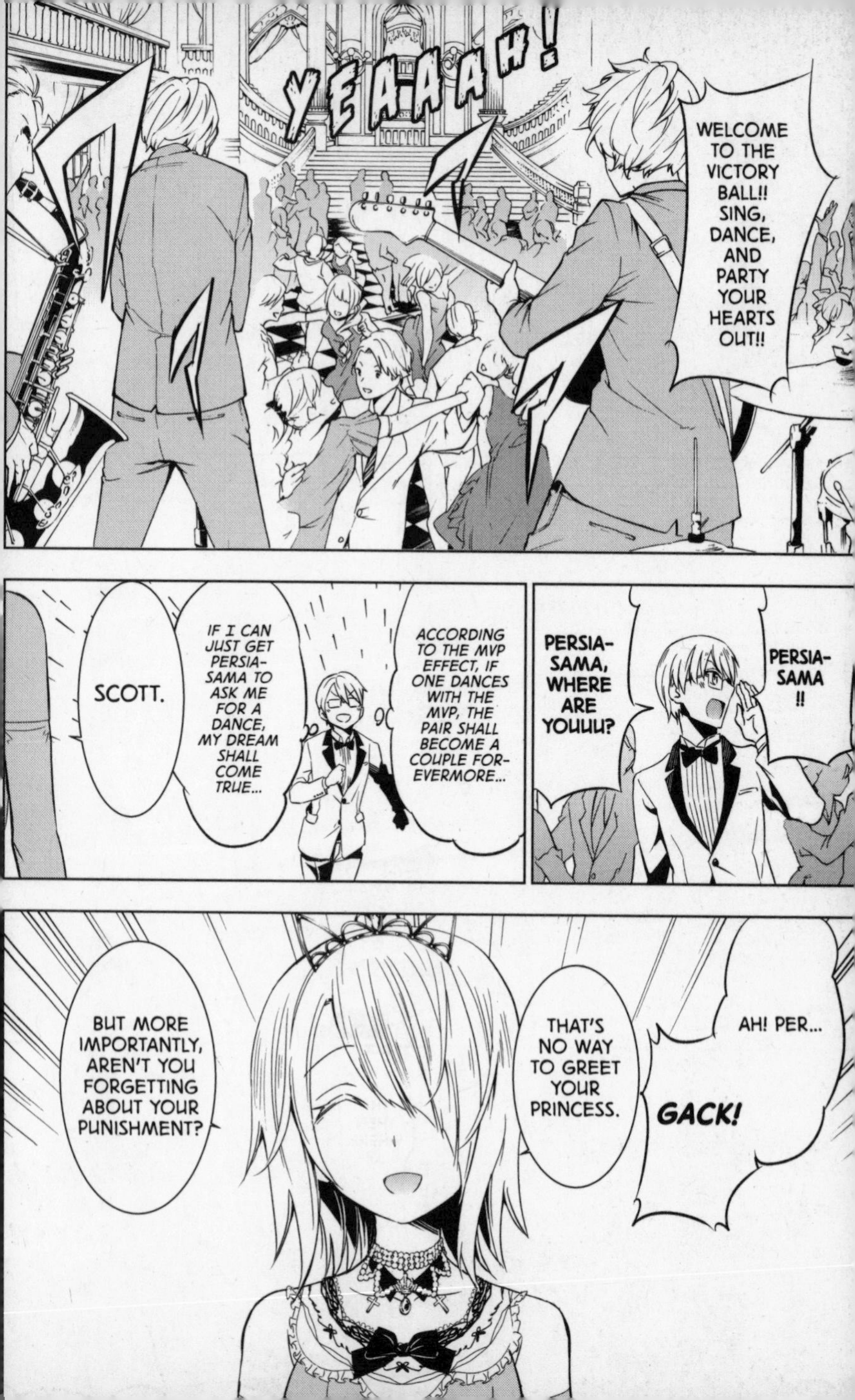
WELCOME TO THE VICTORY BALL!! SING, DANCE, AND PARTY YOUR HEARTS OUT!!
YEAAAAH!
PERSIA-SAMA!!
PERSIA-SAMA, WHERE ARE YOUUU?
ACCORDING TO THE MVP EFFECT, IF ONE DANCES WITH THE MVP, THE PAIR SHALL BECOME A COUPLE FOR-EVERMORE...
IF I CAN JUST GET PERSIA-SAMA TO ASK ME FOR A DANCE, MY DREAM SHALL COME TRUE...
SCOTT.
AH! PER...
GACK!
THAT'S NO WAY TO GREET YOUR PRINCESS.
BUT MORE IMPORTANTLY, AREN'T YOU FORGETTING ABOUT YOUR PUNISHMENT?

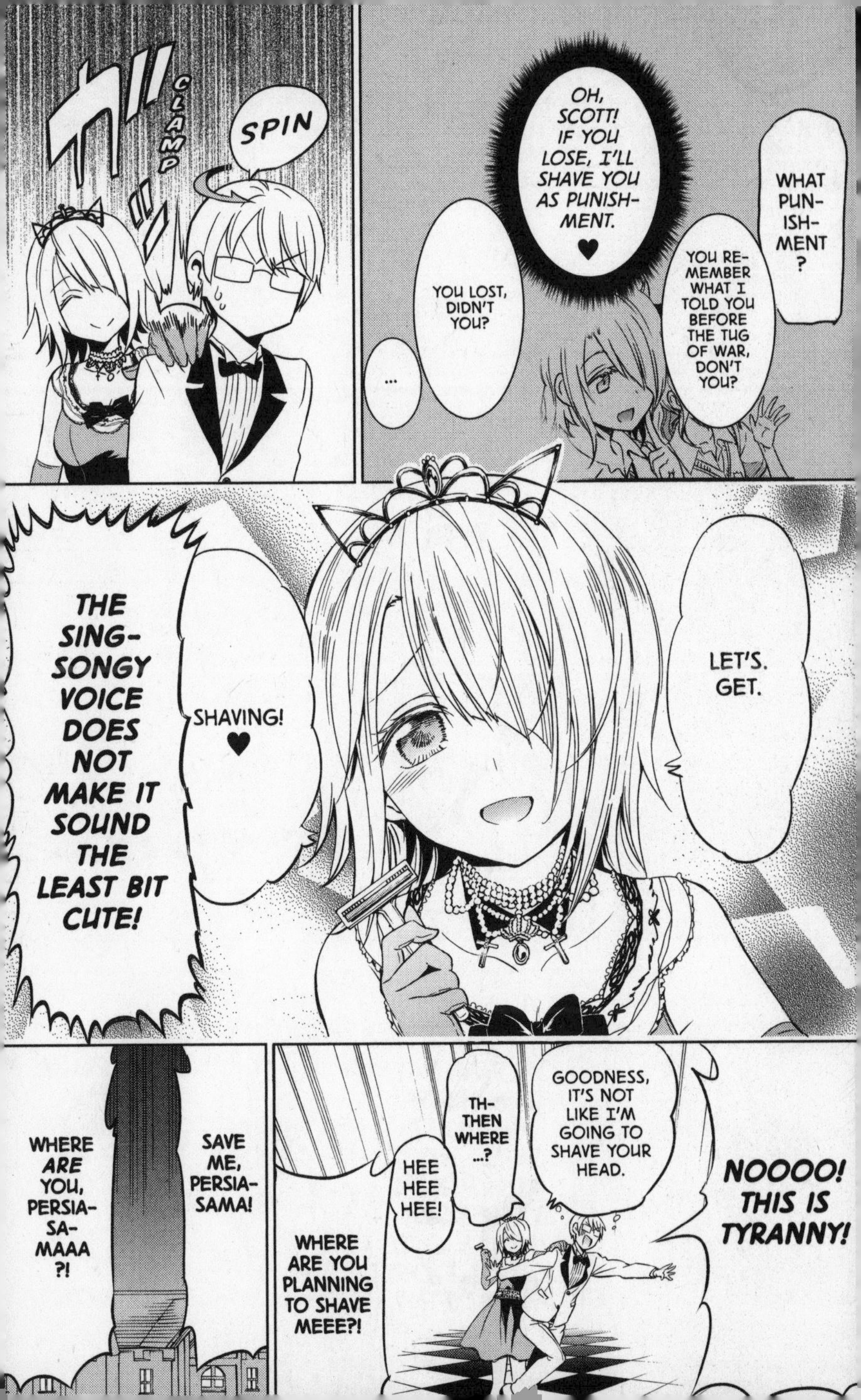
WHAT PUNISHMENT?
YOU REMEMBER WHAT I TOLD YOU BEFORE THE TUG OF WAR, DON'T YOU?
OH, SCOTT! IF YOU LOSE, I'LL SHAVE YOU AS PUNISHMENT. ♥
YOU LOST, DIDN'T YOU?
...
SPIN
CLAMP
LET'S. GET.
SHAVING! ♥
THE SING-SONGY VOICE DOES NOT MAKE IT SOUND THE LEAST BIT CUTE!
NOOOO! THIS IS TYRANNY!
GOODNESS, IT'S NOT LIKE I'M GOING TO SHAVE YOUR HEAD.
TH-THEN WHERE...?
HEE HEE HEE!
WHERE ARE YOU PLANNING TO SHAVE MEEE?!
SAVE ME, PERSIA-SAMA!
WHERE ARE YOU, PERSIA-SAMAAA?!

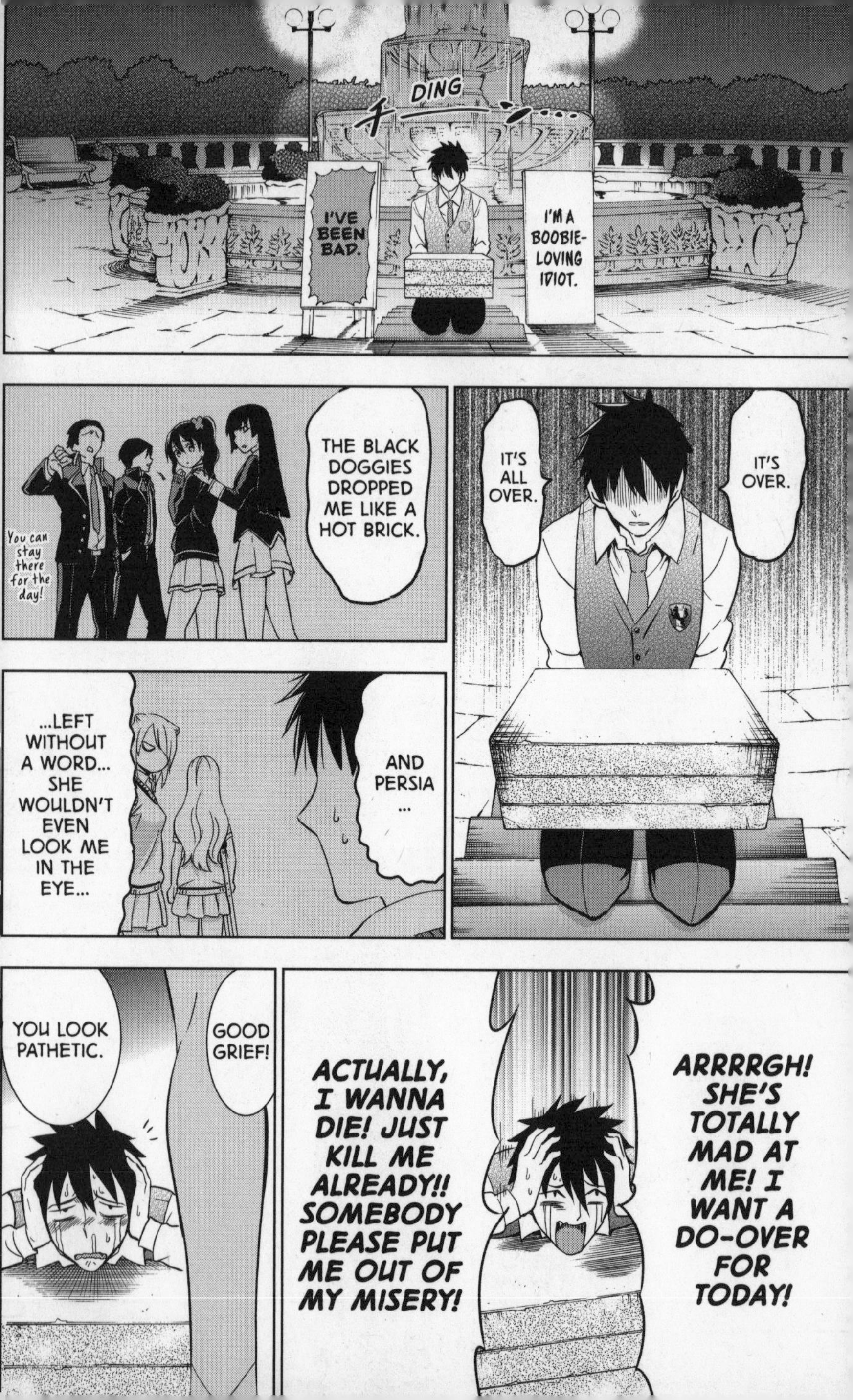
DING
I'M A BOOBIE-LOVING IDIOT.
I'VE BEEN BAD.
IT'S OVER.
IT'S ALL OVER.
THE BLACK DOGGIES DROPPED ME LIKE A HOT BRICK.
You can stay there for the day!
AND PERSIA ...
...LEFT WITHOUT A WORD... SHE WOULDN'T EVEN LOOK ME IN THE EYE...
ARRRRGH! SHE'S TOTALLY MAD AT ME! I WANT A DO-OVER FOR TODAY!
ACTUALLY, I WANNA DIE! JUST KILL ME ALREADY!! SOMEBODY PLEASE PUT ME OUT OF MY MISERY!
GOOD GRIEF!
YOU LOOK PATHETIC.

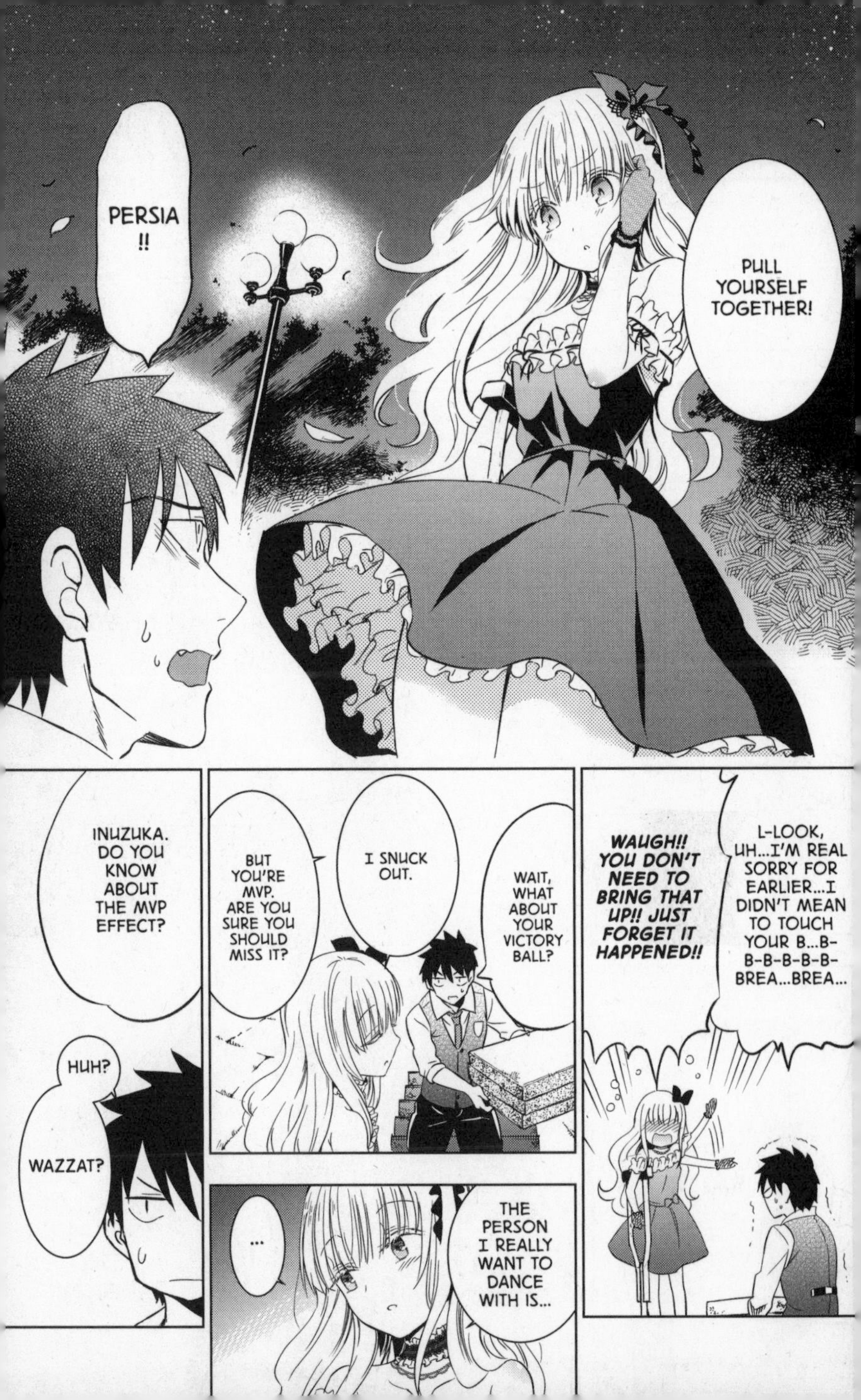

PULL YOURSELF TOGETHER!
PERSIA !!
L-LOOK, UH...I'M REAL SORRY FOR EARLIER...I DIDN'T MEAN TO TOUCH YOUR B...B-B-B-B-B-B-BREA...BREA...
WAUGH!! YOU DON'T NEED TO BRING THAT UP!! JUST FORGET IT HAPPENED!!
WAIT, WHAT ABOUT YOUR VICTORY BALL?
I SNUCK OUT.
BUT YOU'RE MVP. ARE YOU SURE YOU SHOULD MISS IT?
THE PERSON I REALLY WANT TO DANCE WITH IS...
...
INUZUKA. DO YOU KNOW ABOUT THE MVP EFFECT?
HUH?
WAZZAT?

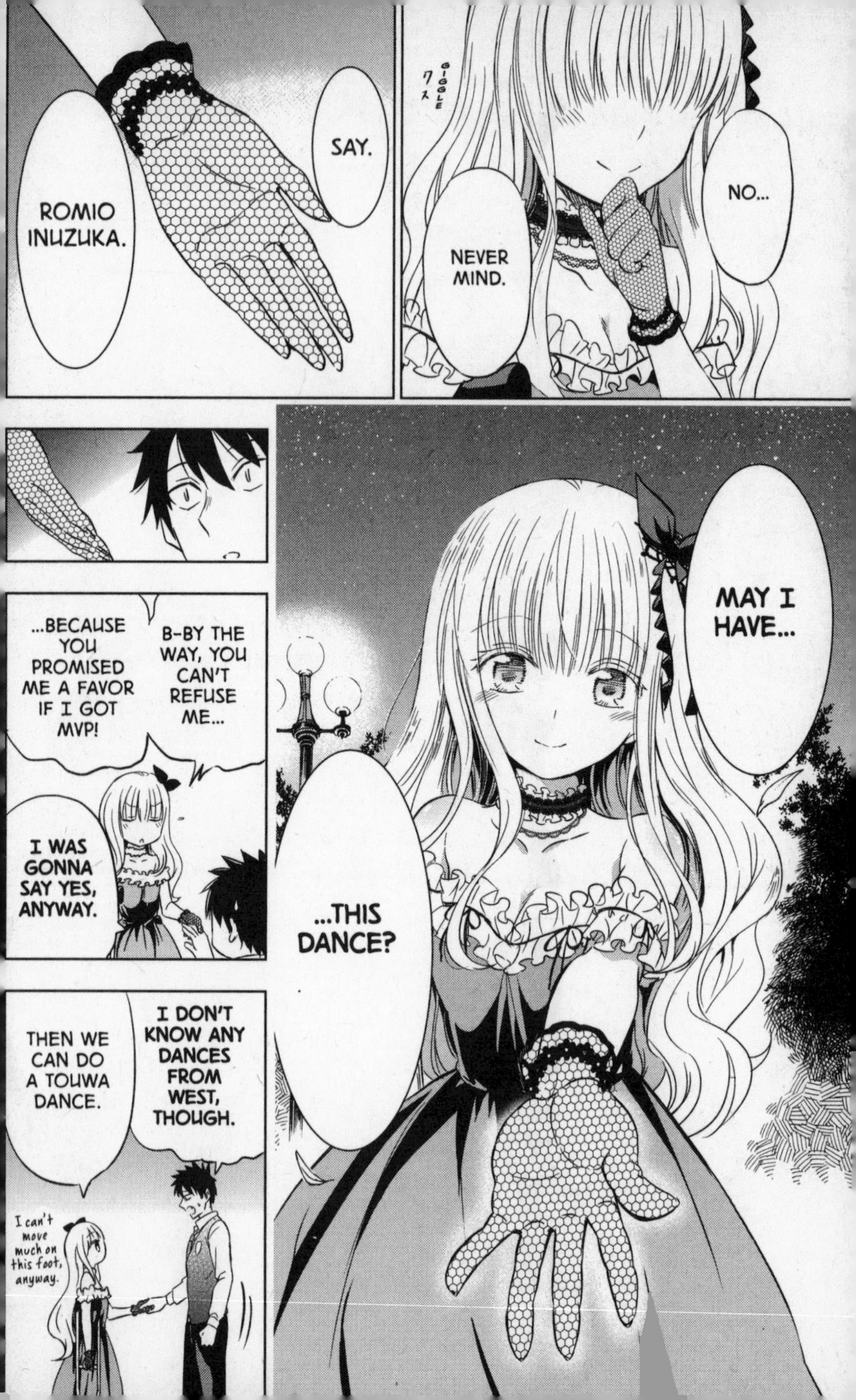
NO...
クス GIGGLE
NEVER MIND.
SAY.
ROMIO INUZUKA.
MAY I HAVE...
...THIS DANCE?
B-BY THE WAY, YOU CAN'T REFUSE ME...
...BECAUSE YOU PROMISED ME A FAVOR IF I GOT MVP!
I WAS GONNA SAY YES, ANYWAY.
I DON'T KNOW ANY DANCES FROM WEST, THOUGH.
THEN WE CAN DO A TOUWA DANCE.
I can't move much on this foot, anyway.

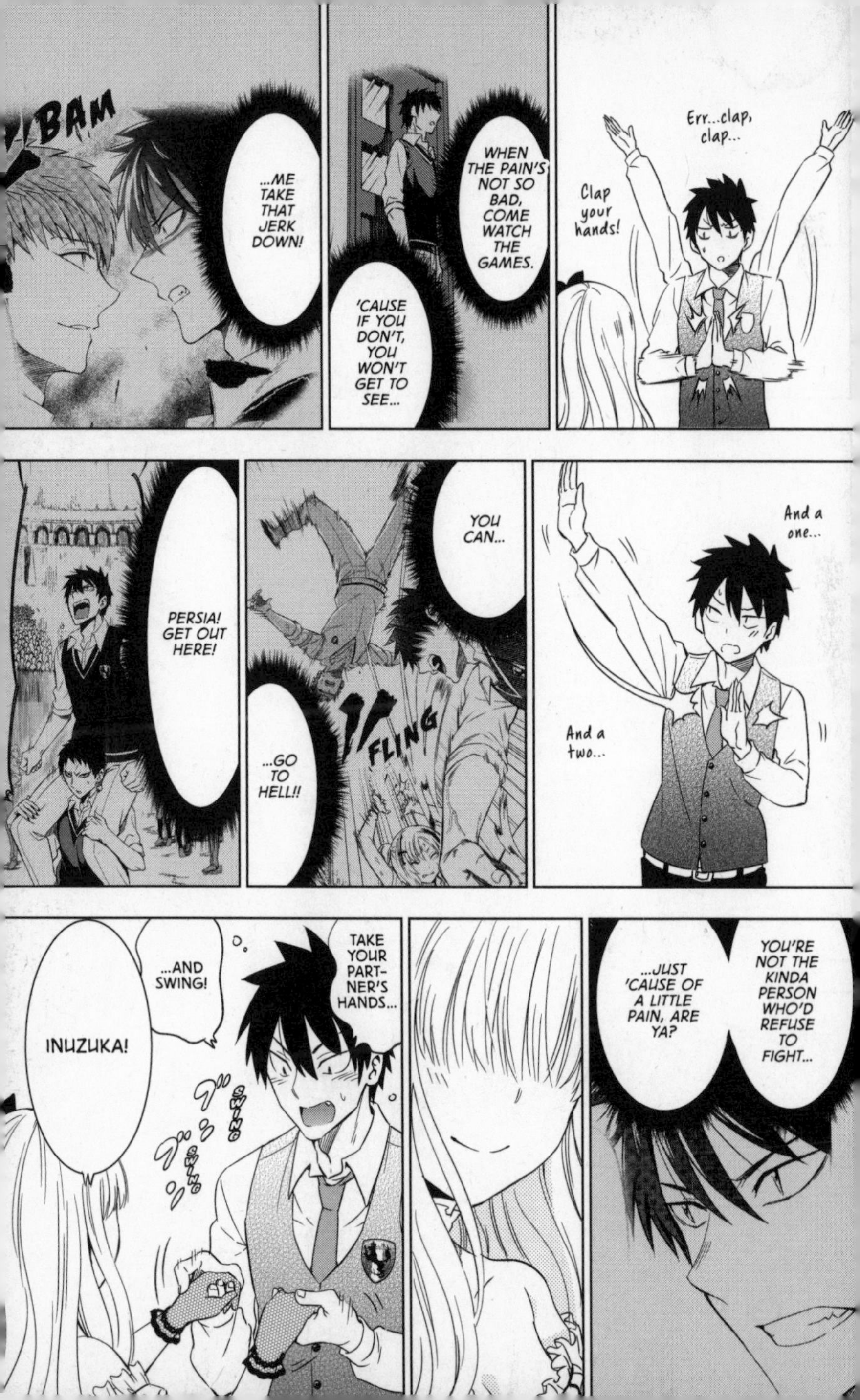
Err...clap, clap...
Clap your hands!
WHEN THE PAIN'S NOT SO BAD, COME WATCH THE GAMES.
'CAUSE IF YOU DON'T, YOU WON'T GET TO SEE...
...ME TAKE THAT JERK DOWN!
BAM
And a one...
And a two...
YOU CAN...
...GO TO HELL!!
FLING
PERSIA! GET OUT HERE!
YOU'RE NOT THE KINDA PERSON WHO'D REFUSE TO FIGHT...
...JUST 'CAUSE OF A LITTLE PAIN, ARE YA?
TAKE YOUR PARTNER'S HANDS...
...AND SWING!
SWING
SWING
INUZUKA!

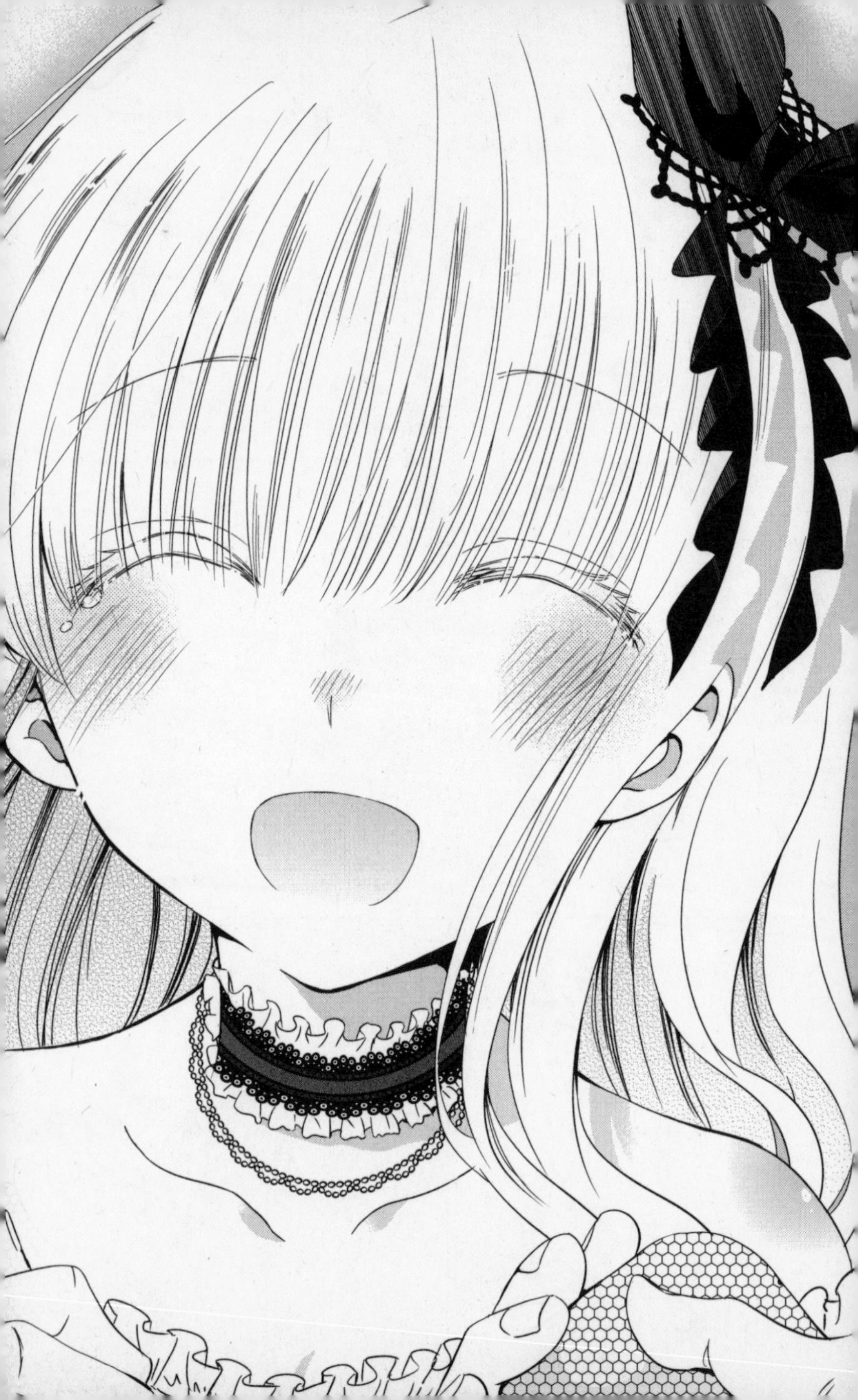

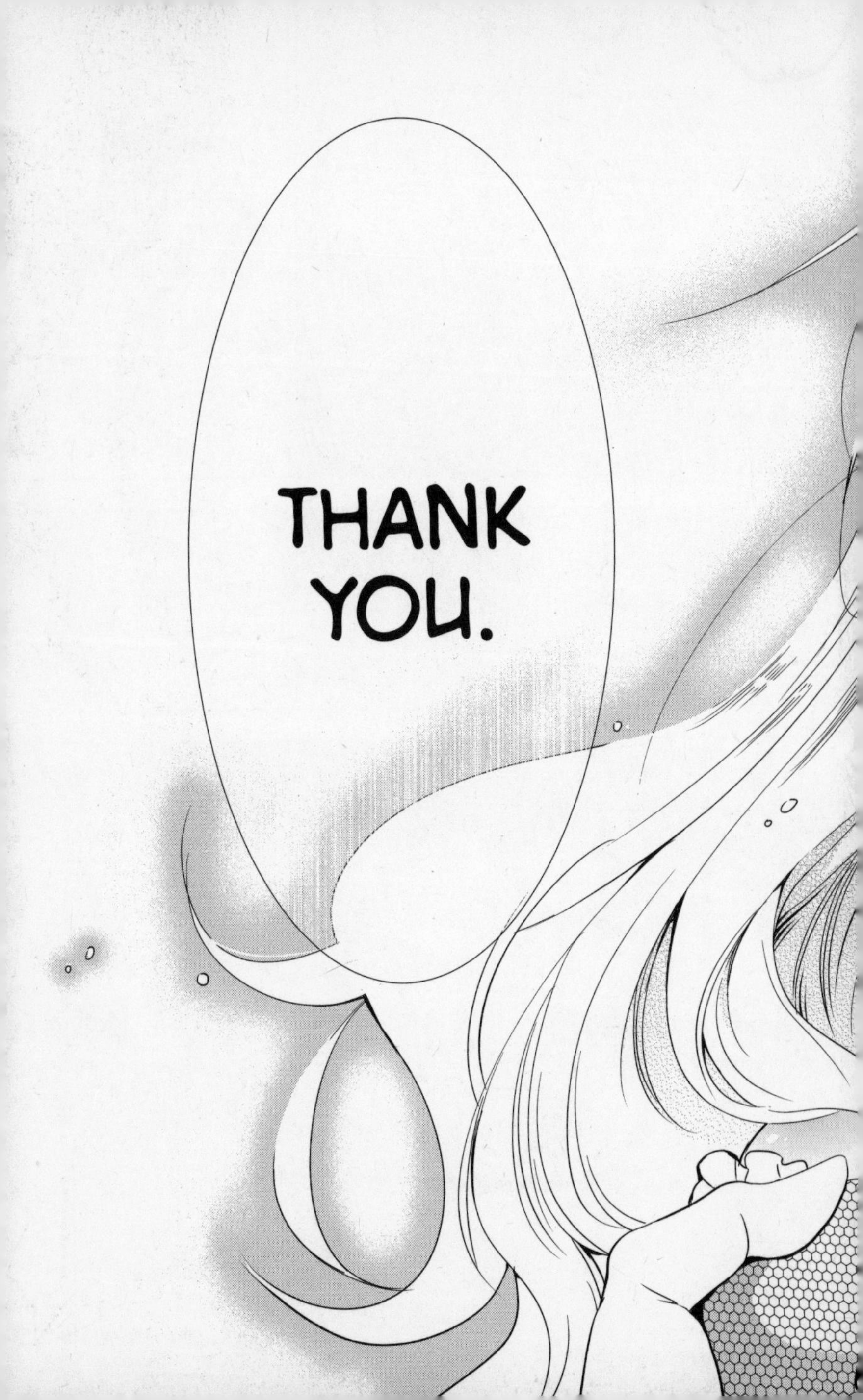
THANK YOU.

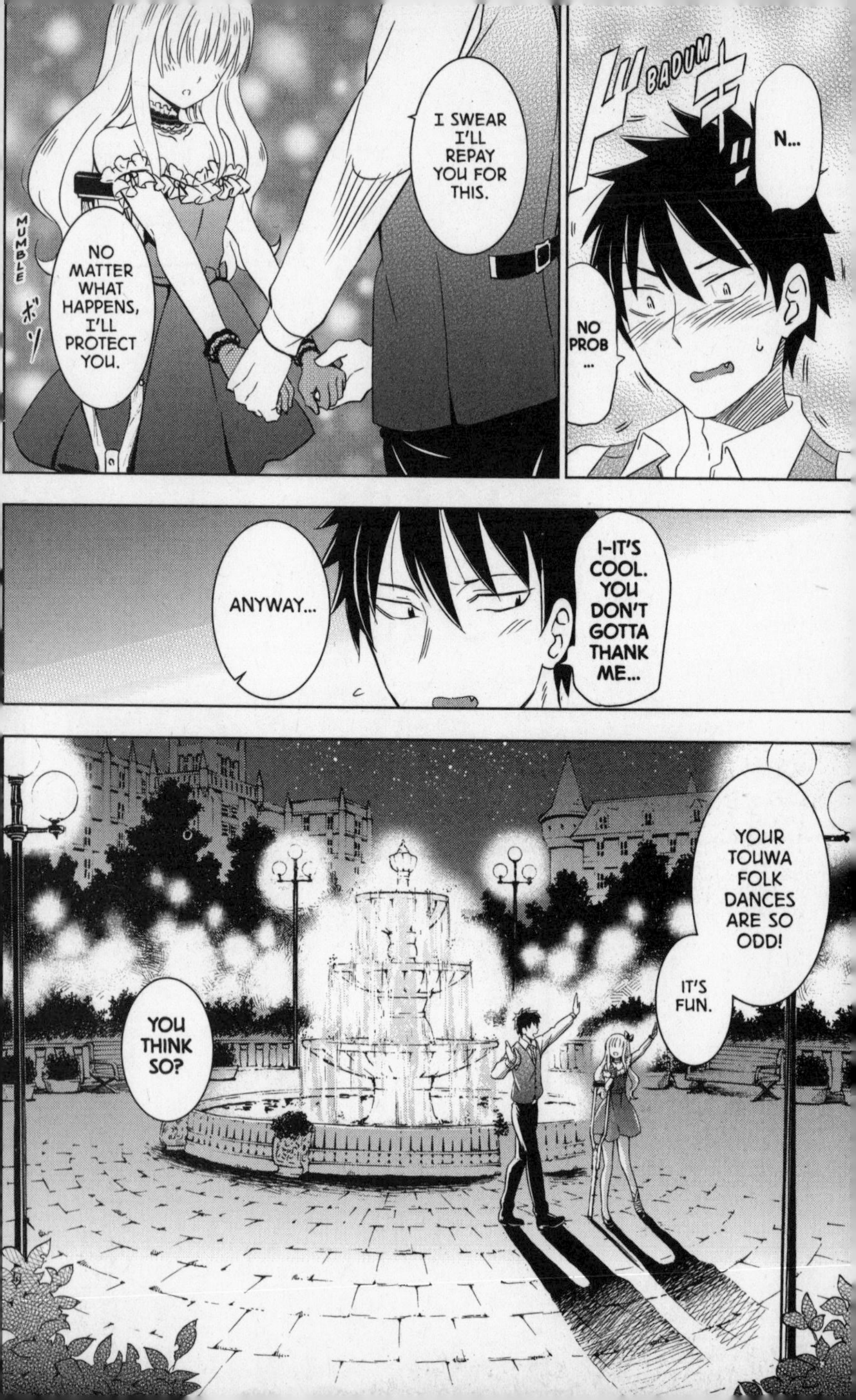
BADUM
N...
NO PROB...
I SWEAR I'LL REPAY YOU FOR THIS.
NO MATTER WHAT HAPPENS, I'LL PROTECT YOU.
MUMBLE
I-IT'S COOL. YOU DON'T GOTTA THANK ME...
ANYWAY...
YOUR TOUWA FOLK DANCES ARE SO ODD!
IT'S FUN.
YOU THINK SO?

ACT 12:

NURSING & JULIET

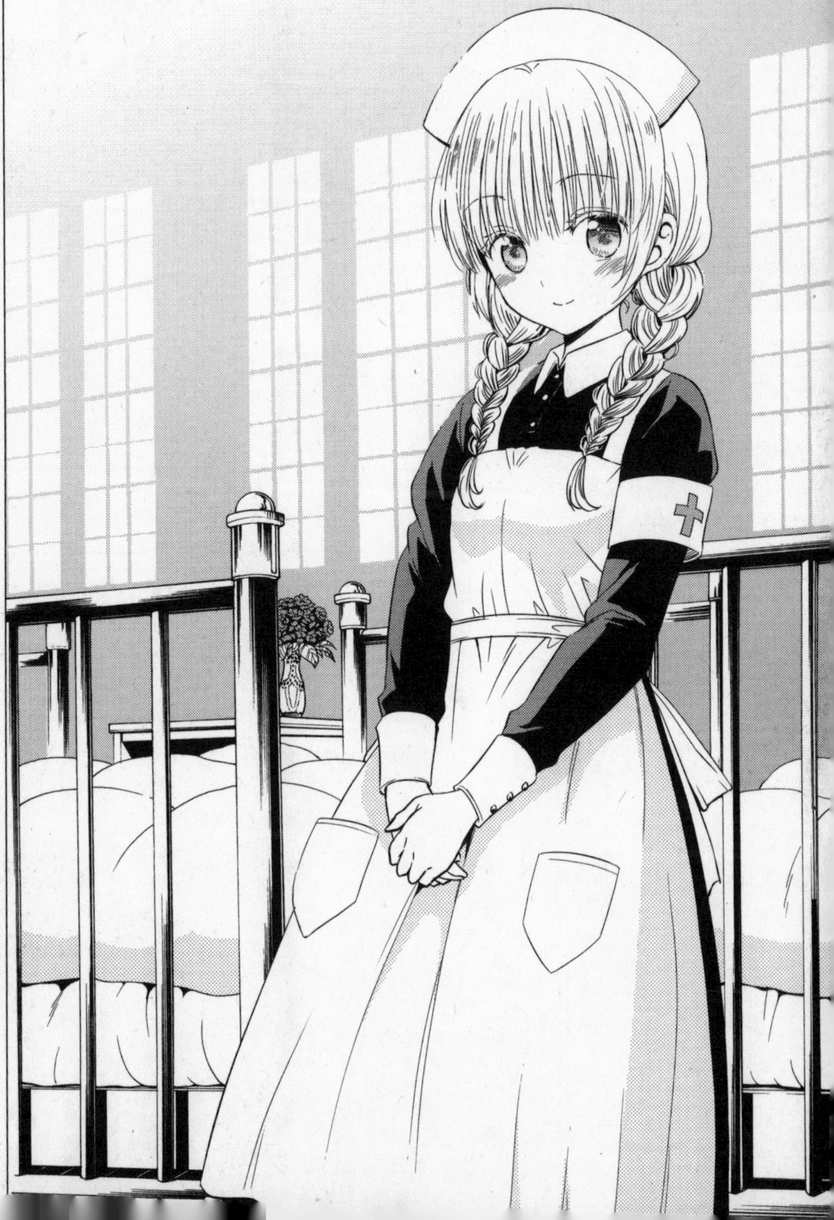

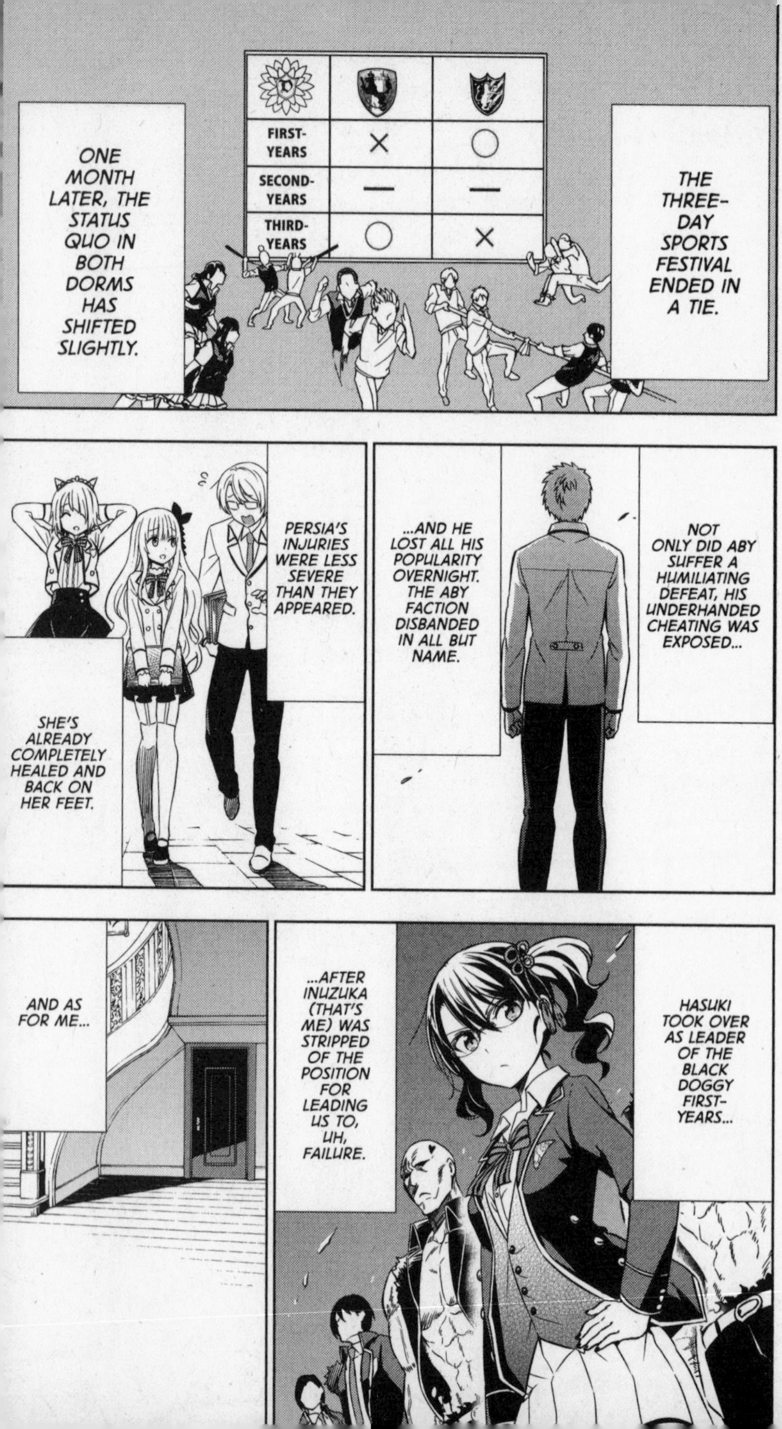
THE THREE-DAY SPORTS FESTIVAL ENDED IN A TIE.
FIRST-YEARS
SECOND-YEARS
THIRD-YEARS
ONE MONTH LATER, THE STATUS QUO IN BOTH DORMS HAS SHIFTED SLIGHTLY.
NOT ONLY DID ABY SUFFER A HUMILIATING DEFEAT, HIS UNDERHANDED CHEATING WAS EXPOSED...
...AND HE LOST ALL HIS POPULARITY OVERNIGHT. THE ABY FACTION DISBANDED IN ALL BUT NAME.
PERSIA'S INJURIES WERE LESS SEVERE THAN THEY APPEARED.
SHE'S ALREADY COMPLETELY HEALED AND BACK ON HER FEET.
HASUKI TOOK OVER AS LEADER OF THE BLACK DOGGY FIRST-YEARS...
...AFTER INUZUKA (THAT'S ME) WAS STRIPPED OF THE POSITION FOR LEADING US TO, UH, FAILURE.
AND AS FOR ME...

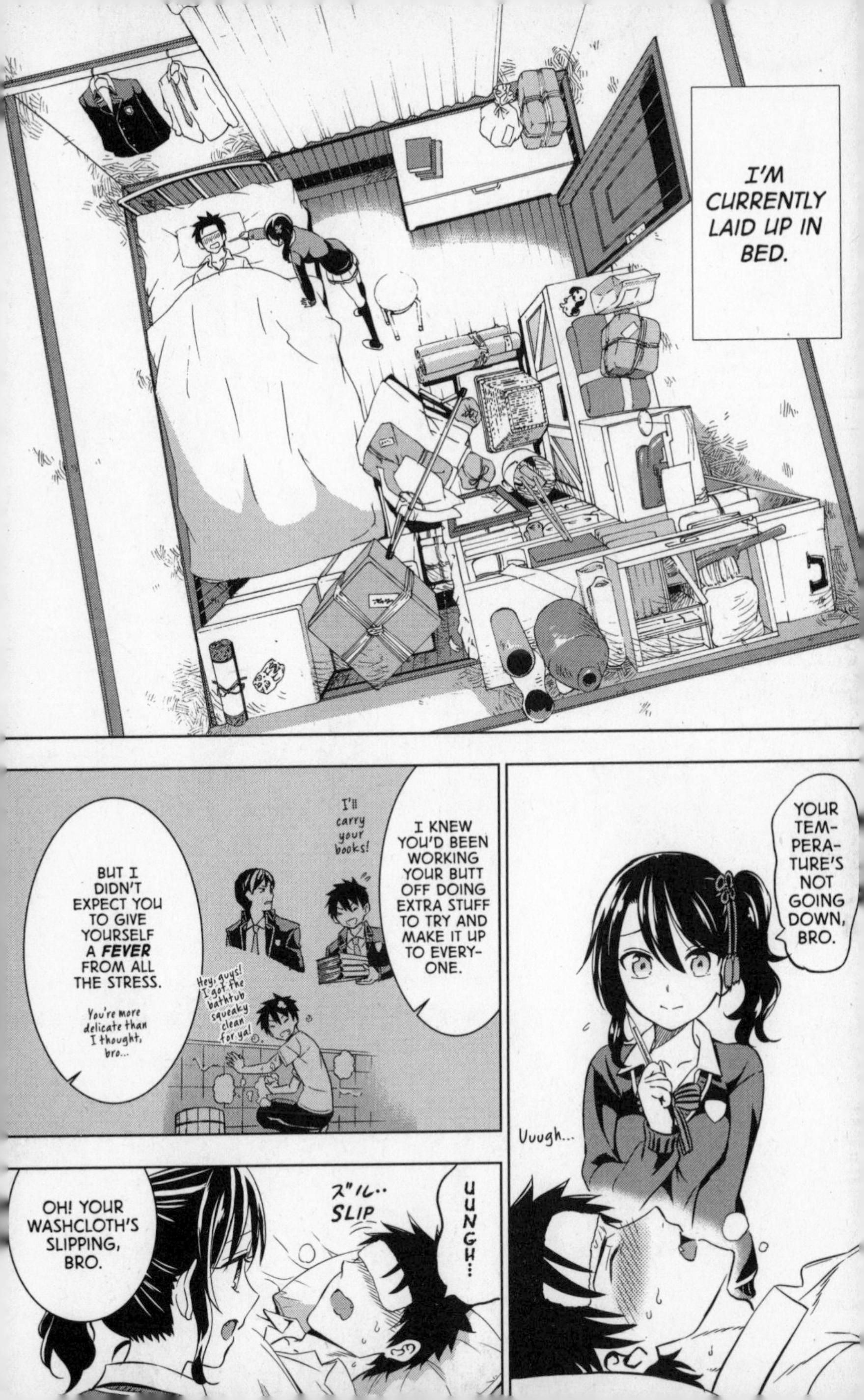
I'M CURRENTLY LAID UP IN BED.
YOUR TEMPERATURE'S NOT GOING DOWN, BRO.
Uuugh...
I KNEW YOU'D BEEN WORKING YOUR BUTT OFF DOING EXTRA STUFF TO TRY AND MAKE IT UP TO EVERYONE.
I'll carry your books!
Hey, guys! I got the bathtub squeaky clean for ya!
BUT I DIDN'T EXPECT YOU TO GIVE YOURSELF A ***FEVER*** FROM ALL THE STRESS.
You're more delicate than I thought, bro...
UUNGH...
ズル.. SLIP
OH! YOUR WASHCLOTH'S SLIPPING, BRO.

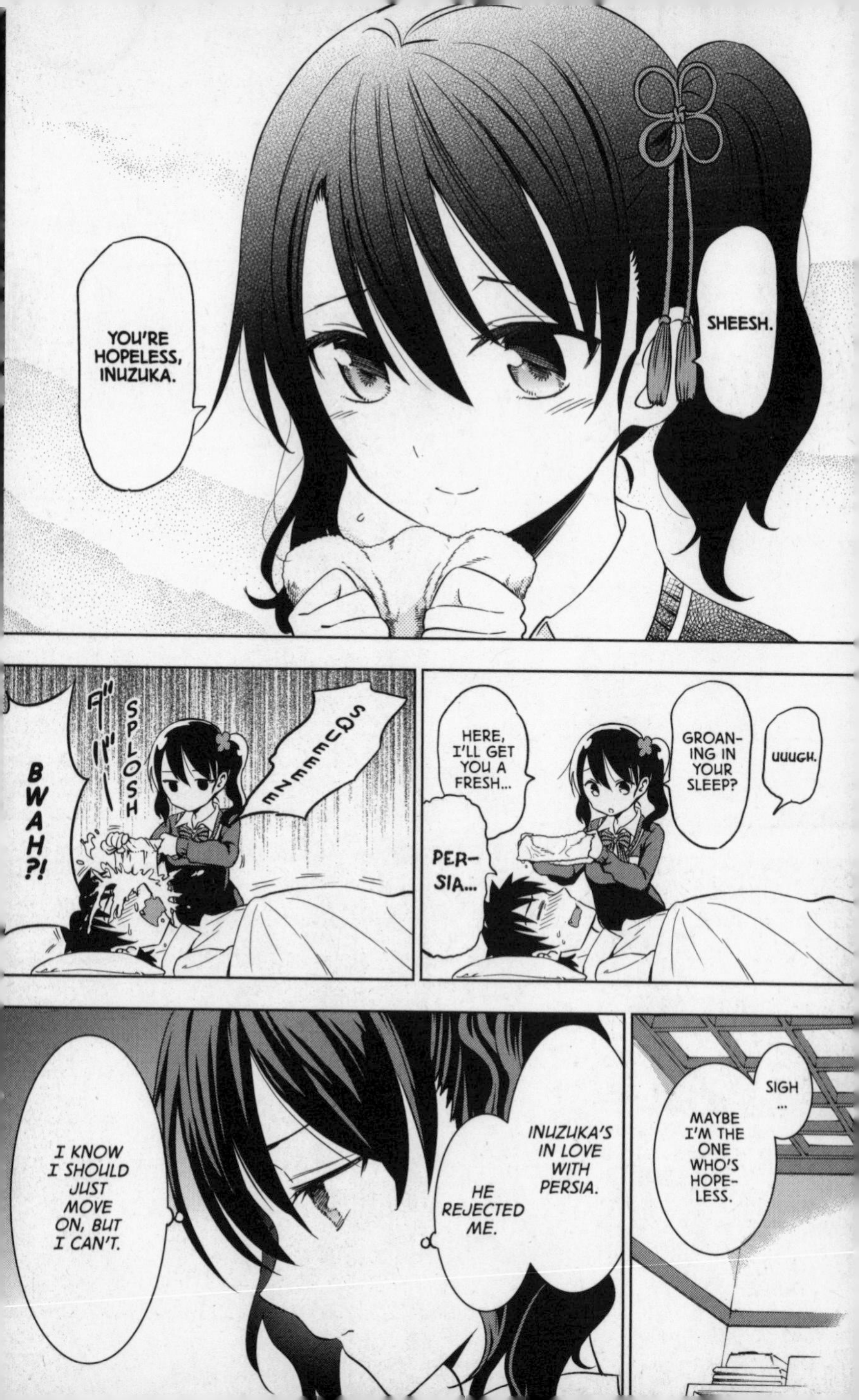
SHEESH.
YOU'RE HOPELESS, INUZUKA.
UUUGH.
GROAN-ING IN YOUR SLEEP?
HERE, I'LL GET YOU A FRESH...
PER-SIA...
SQUEEEEEZE
SPLOSH
BWAH?!
SIGH...
MAYBE I'M THE ONE WHO'S HOPE-LESS.
INUZUKA'S IN LOVE WITH PERSIA.
HE REJECTED ME.
I KNOW I SHOULD JUST MOVE ON, BUT I CAN'T.

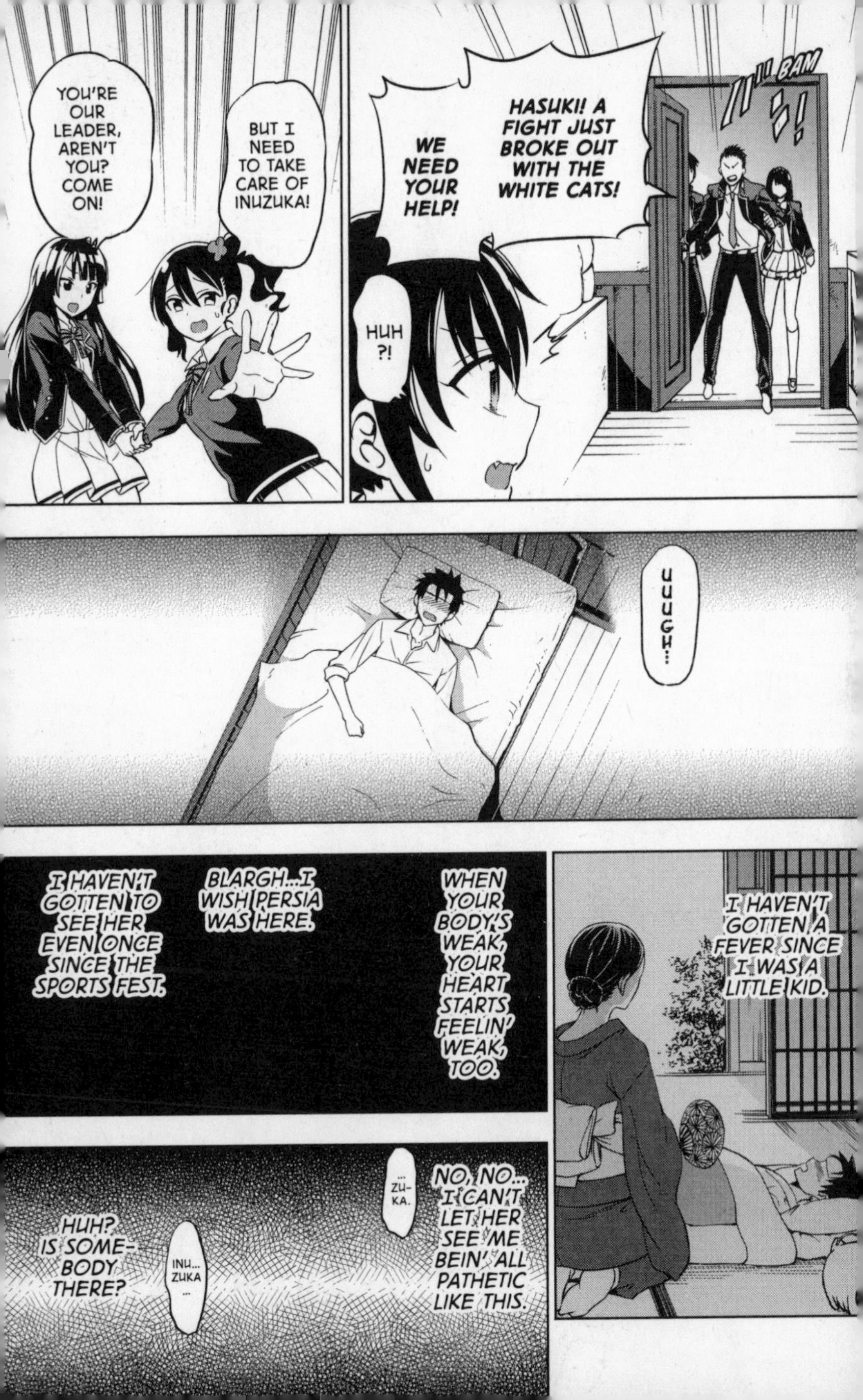
BAM
HASUKI! A FIGHT JUST BROKE OUT WITH THE WHITE CATS!
WE NEED YOUR HELP!
HUH?!
BUT I NEED TO TAKE CARE OF INUZUKA!
YOU'RE OUR LEADER, AREN'T YOU? COME ON!
UUUGH...
I HAVEN'T GOTTEN A FEVER SINCE I WAS A LITTLE KID.
WHEN YOUR BODY'S WEAK, YOUR HEART STARTS FEELIN' WEAK, TOO.
BLARGH...I WISH PERSIA WAS HERE.
I HAVEN'T GOTTEN TO SEE HER EVEN ONCE SINCE THE SPORTS FEST.
NO, NO... I CAN'T LET HER SEE ME BEIN' ALL PATHETIC LIKE THIS.
...ZU-KA.
INU... ZUKA...
HUH? IS SOMEBODY THERE?

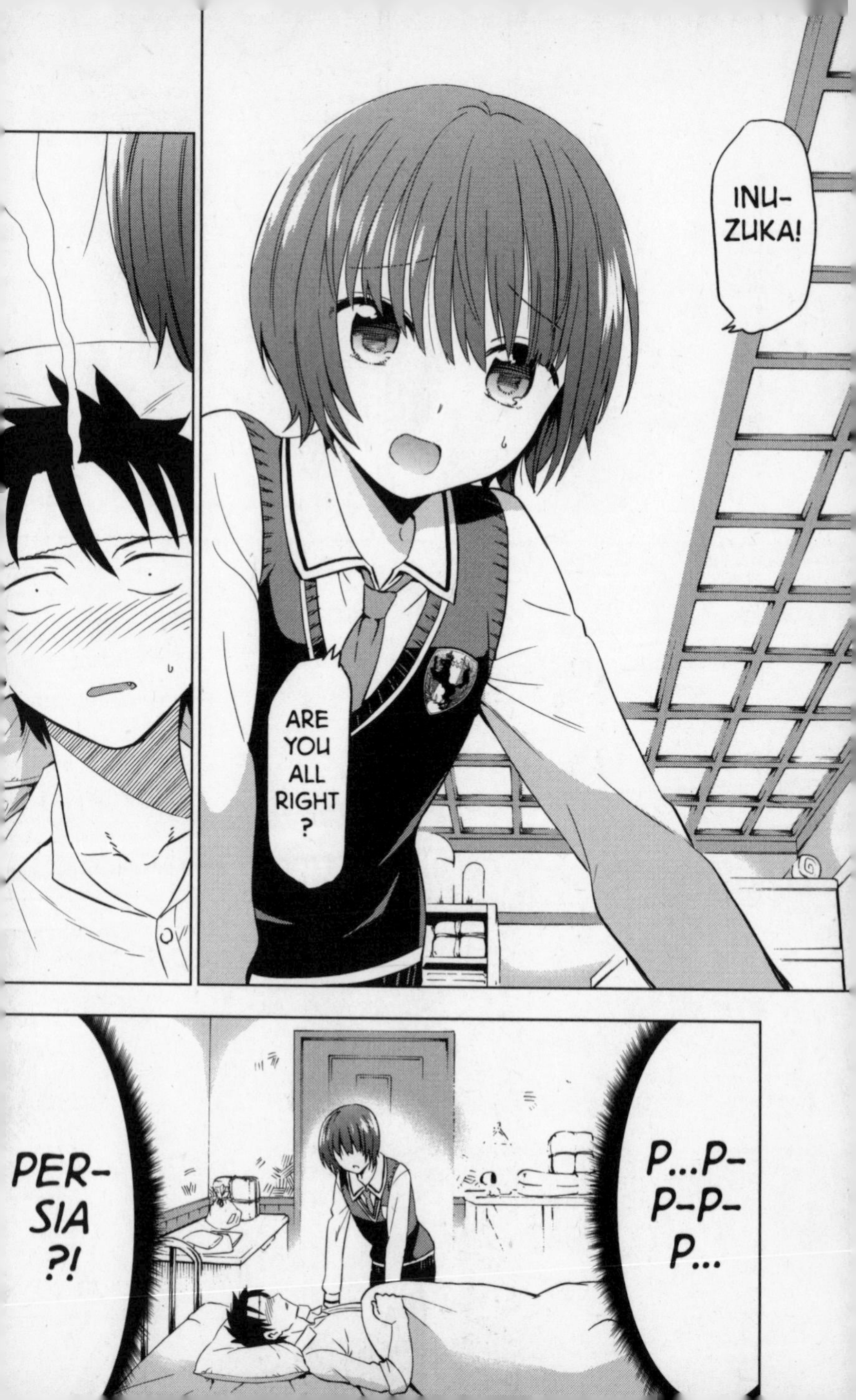
INU-ZUKA!
ARE YOU ALL RIGHT?
P...P-P-P-P...
PER-SIA?!

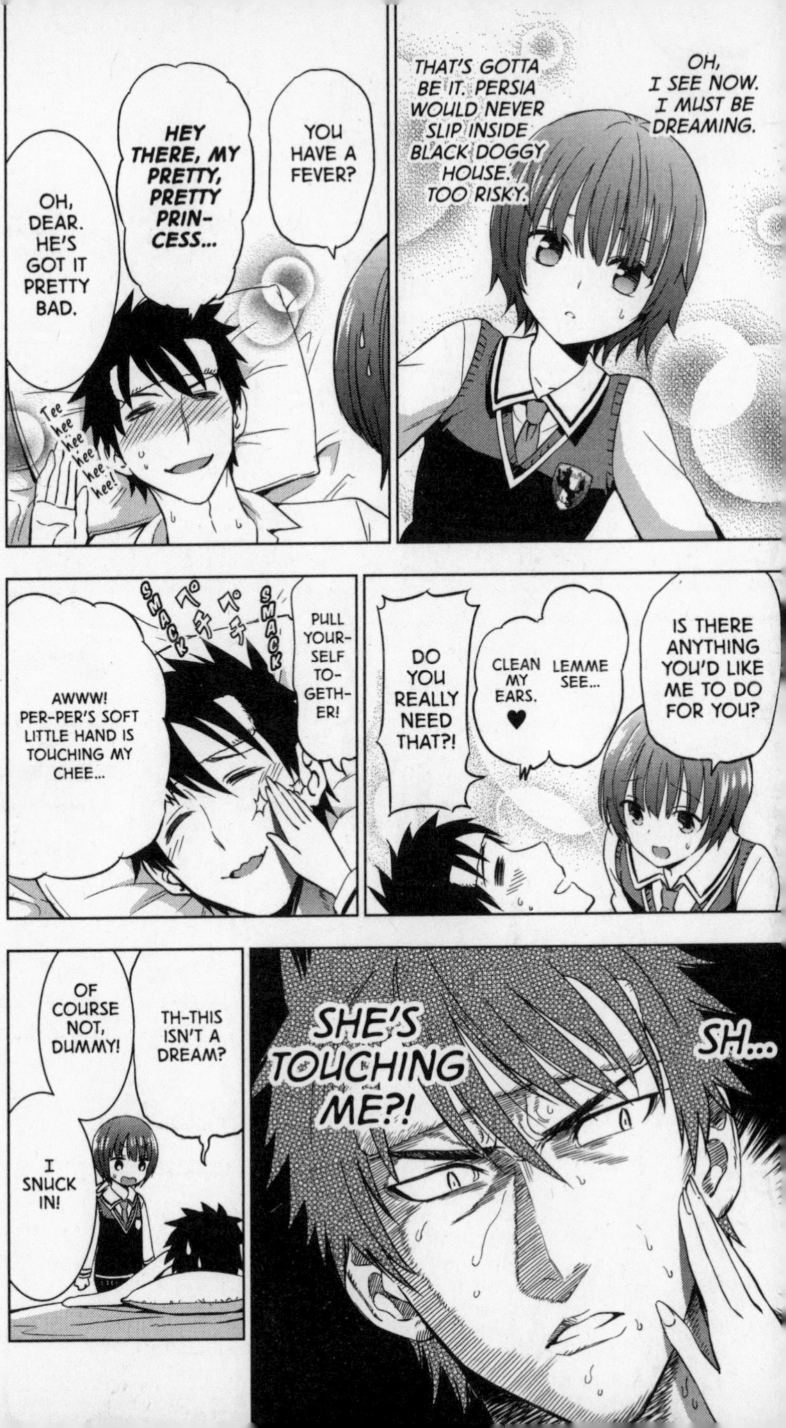
OH, I SEE NOW. I MUST BE DREAMING.
THAT'S GOTTA BE IT. PERSIA WOULD NEVER SLIP INSIDE BLACK DOGGY HOUSE. TOO RISKY.
YOU HAVE A FEVER?
HEY THERE, MY PRETTY, PRETTY PRINCESS...
OH, DEAR. HE'S GOT IT PRETTY BAD.
Tee hee hee hee hee hee!
IS THERE ANYTHING YOU'D LIKE ME TO DO FOR YOU?
LEMME SEE...
CLEAN MY EARS. ♥
DO YOU REALLY NEED THAT?!
PULL YOURSELF TOGETHER!
SMACK
ペチ
ペチ
SMACK
AWWW! PER-PER'S SOFT LITTLE HAND IS TOUCHING MY CHEE...
SH...
SHE'S TOUCHING ME?!
TH-THIS ISN'T A DREAM?
OF COURSE NOT, DUMMY!
I SNUCK IN!

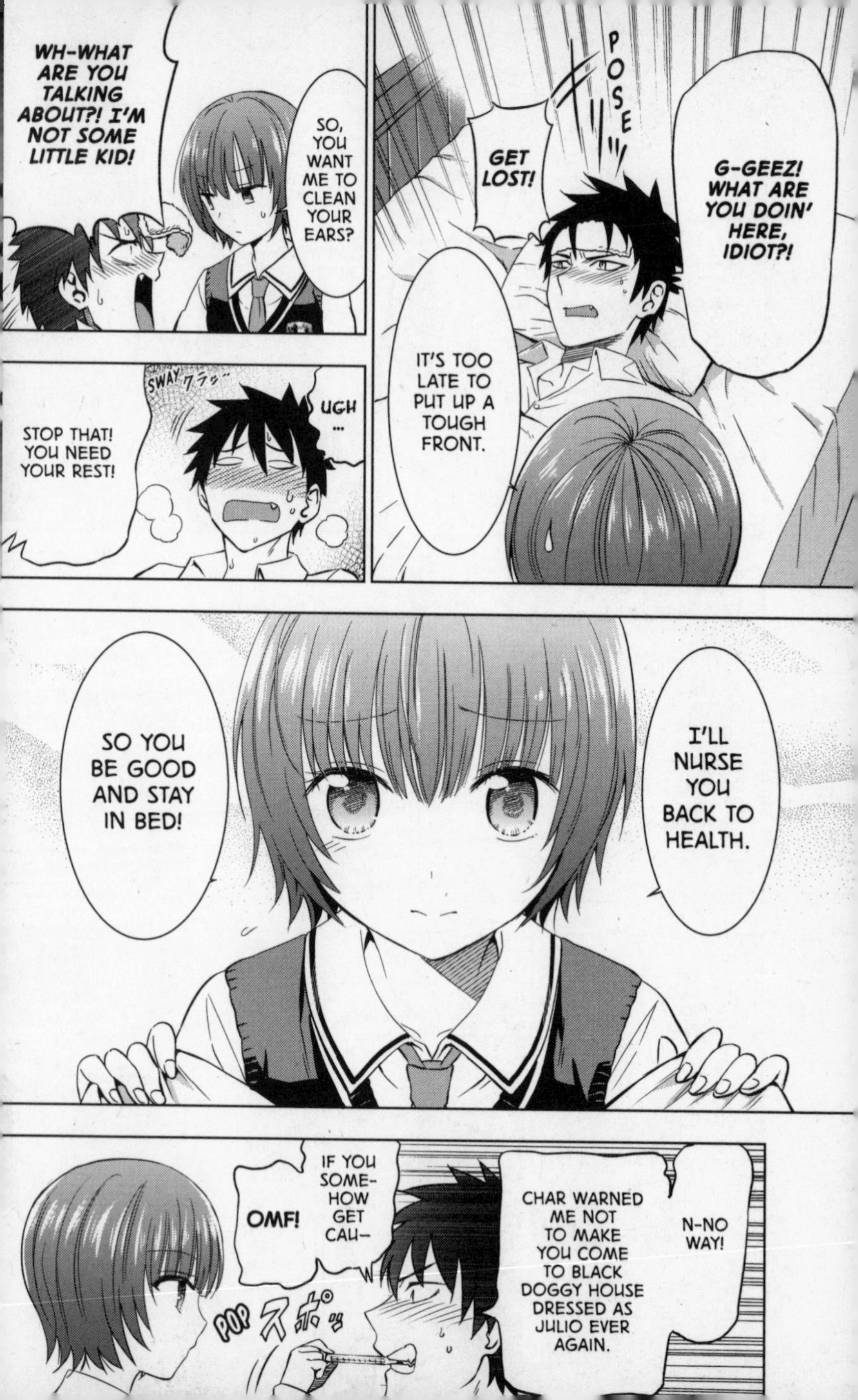

G-GEEZ! WHAT ARE YOU DOIN' HERE, IDIOT?!
POSE
GET LOST!
IT'S TOO LATE TO PUT UP A TOUGH FRONT.
SO, YOU WANT ME TO CLEAN YOUR EARS?
WH-WHAT ARE YOU TALKING ABOUT?! I'M NOT SOME LITTLE KID!
SWAY クラッ
UGH ...
STOP THAT! YOU NEED YOUR REST!
I'LL NURSE YOU BACK TO HEALTH.
SO YOU BE GOOD AND STAY IN BED!
N-NO WAY!
CHAR WARNED ME NOT TO MAKE YOU COME TO BLACK DOGGY HOUSE DRESSED AS JULIO EVER AGAIN.
IF YOU SOMEHOW GET CAU-
OMF!
POP スポッ

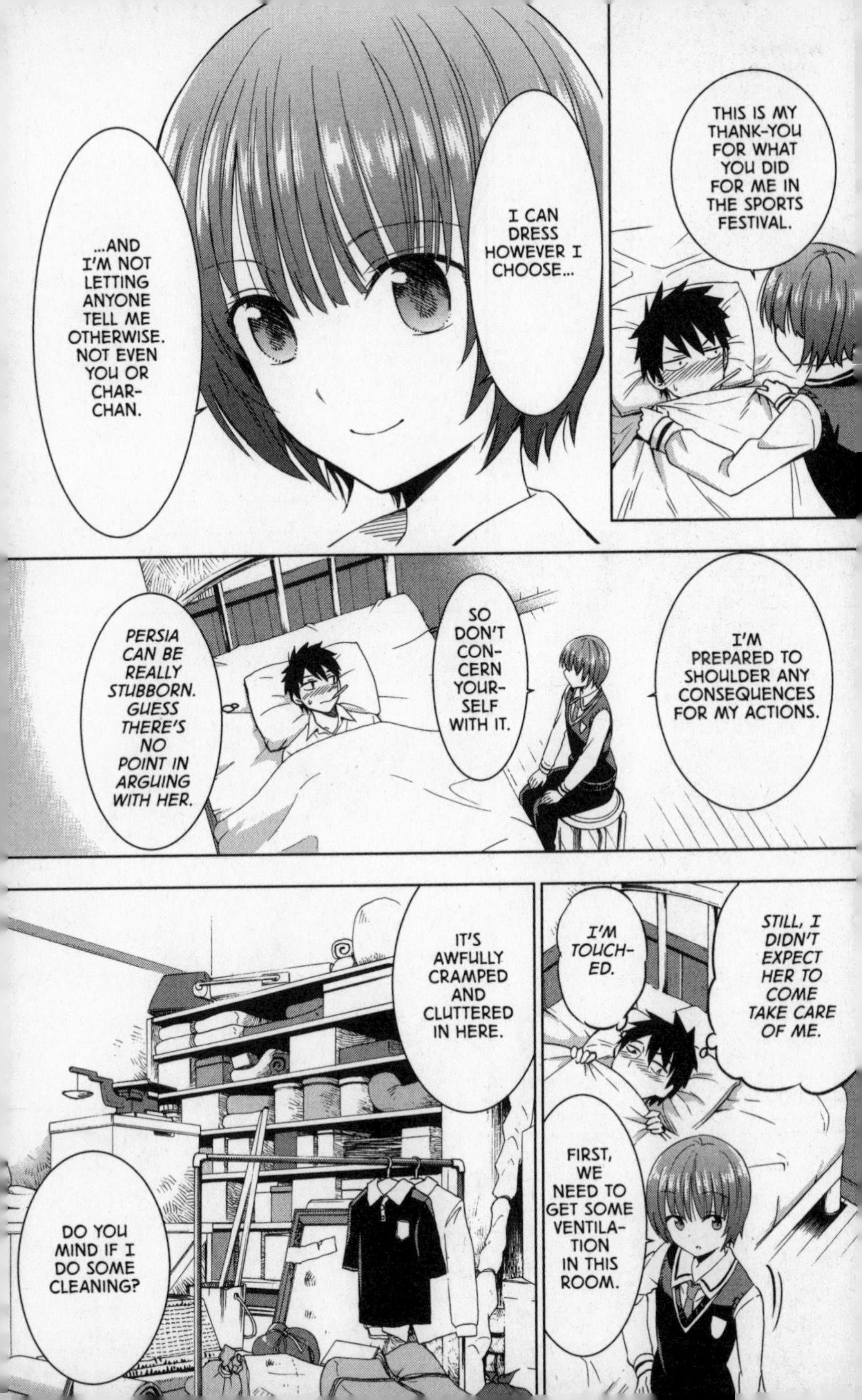
THIS IS MY THANK-YOU FOR WHAT YOU DID FOR ME IN THE SPORTS FESTIVAL.
I CAN DRESS HOWEVER I CHOOSE...
...AND I'M NOT LETTING ANYONE TELL ME OTHERWISE. NOT EVEN YOU OR CHAR-CHAN.
I'M PREPARED TO SHOULDER ANY CONSEQUENCES FOR MY ACTIONS.
SO DON'T CONCERN YOURSELF WITH IT.
PERSIA CAN BE REALLY STUBBORN. GUESS THERE'S NO POINT IN ARGUING WITH HER.
STILL, I DIDN'T EXPECT HER TO COME TAKE CARE OF ME.
I'M TOUCHED.
FIRST, WE NEED TO GET SOME VENTILATION IN THIS ROOM.
IT'S AWFULLY CRAMPED AND CLUTTERED IN HERE.
DO YOU MIND IF I DO SOME CLEANING?

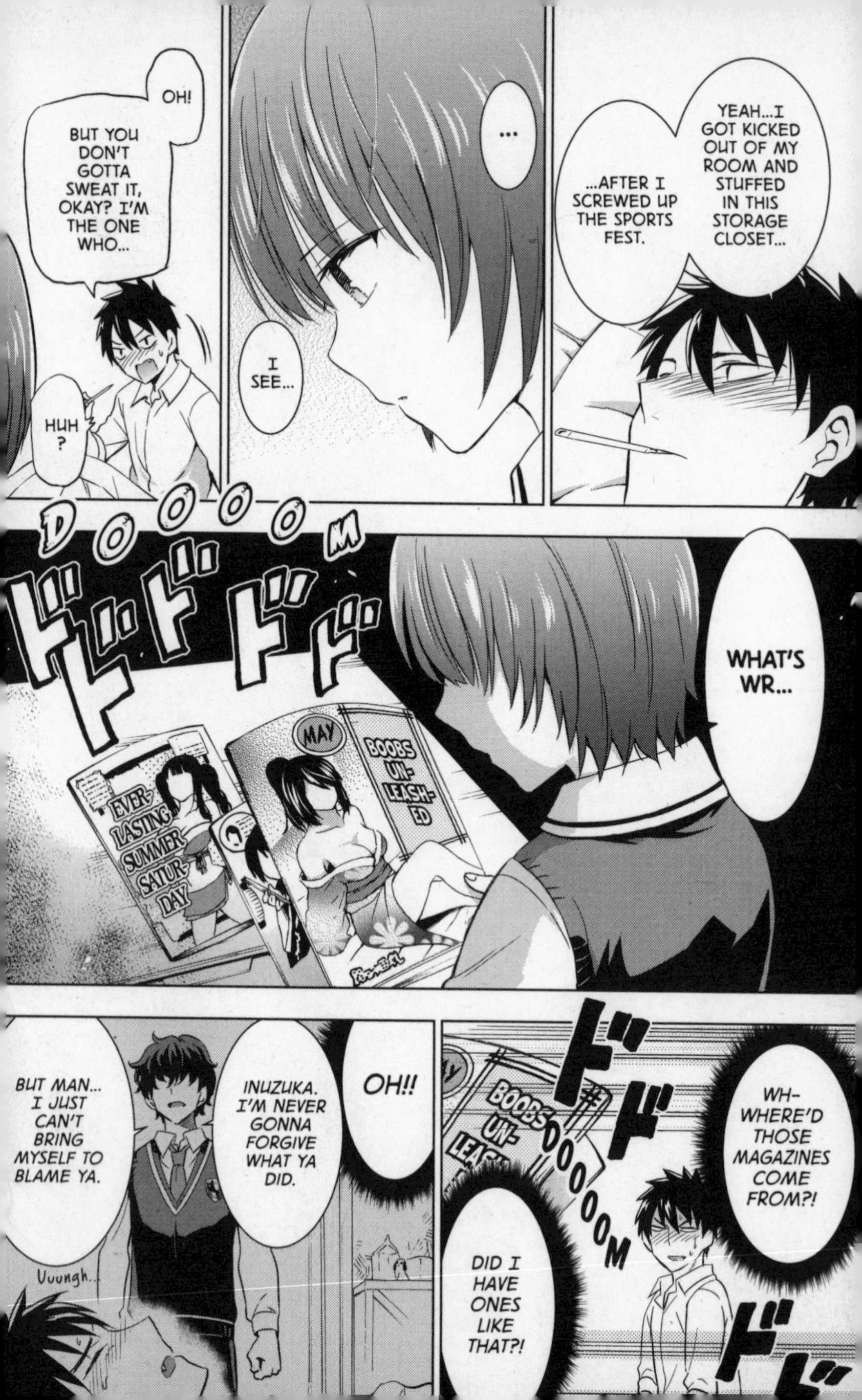
YEAH...I GOT KICKED OUT OF MY ROOM AND STUFFED IN THIS STORAGE CLOSET...
...AFTER I SCREWED UP THE SPORTS FEST.
...
I SEE...
OH!
BUT YOU DON'T GOTTA SWEAT IT, OKAY? I'M THE ONE WHO...
HUH ?
DOOOOOM
ドドドドド
WHAT'S WR...
MAY
BOOBS UN-LEASH-ED
EVER-LASTING SUMMER SATUR-DAY
WH-WHERE'D THOSE MAGAZINES COME FROM?!
ドドド
DOOOOOM
DID I HAVE ONES LIKE THAT?!
OH!!
INUZUKA. I'M NEVER GONNA FORGIVE WHAT YA DID.
BUT MAN... I JUST CAN'T BRING MYSELF TO BLAME YA.
Uuungh...

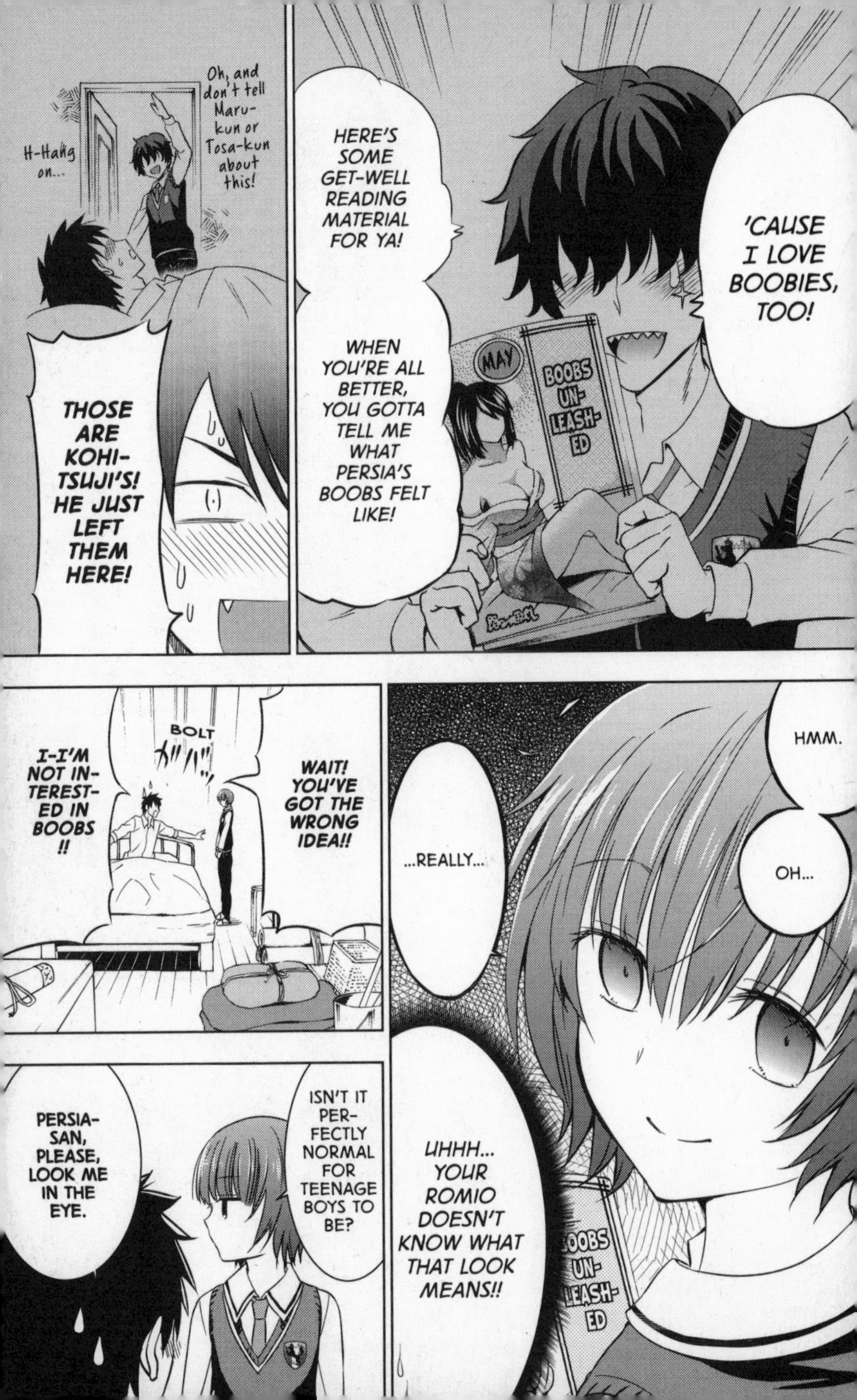

HERE'S SOME GET-WELL READING MATERIAL FOR YA!
WHEN YOU'RE ALL BETTER, YOU GOTTA TELL ME WHAT PERSIA'S BOOBS FELT LIKE!
'CAUSE I LOVE BOOBIES, TOO!
MAY
BOOBS UN-LEASH-ED
Oh, and don't tell Maru-kun or Tosa-kun about this!
H-Hang on...
THOSE ARE KOHI-TSUJI'S! HE JUST LEFT THEM HERE!
HMM.
OH...
...REALLY...
UHHH... YOUR ROMIO DOESN'T KNOW WHAT THAT LOOK MEANS!!
BOOBS UN-LEASH-ED
WAIT! YOU'VE GOT THE WRONG IDEA!!
BOLT
I-I'M NOT INTER-EST-ED IN BOOBS!!
ISN'T IT PER-FECTLY NORMAL FOR TEENAGE BOYS TO BE?
PERSIA-SAN, PLEASE, LOOK ME IN THE EYE.

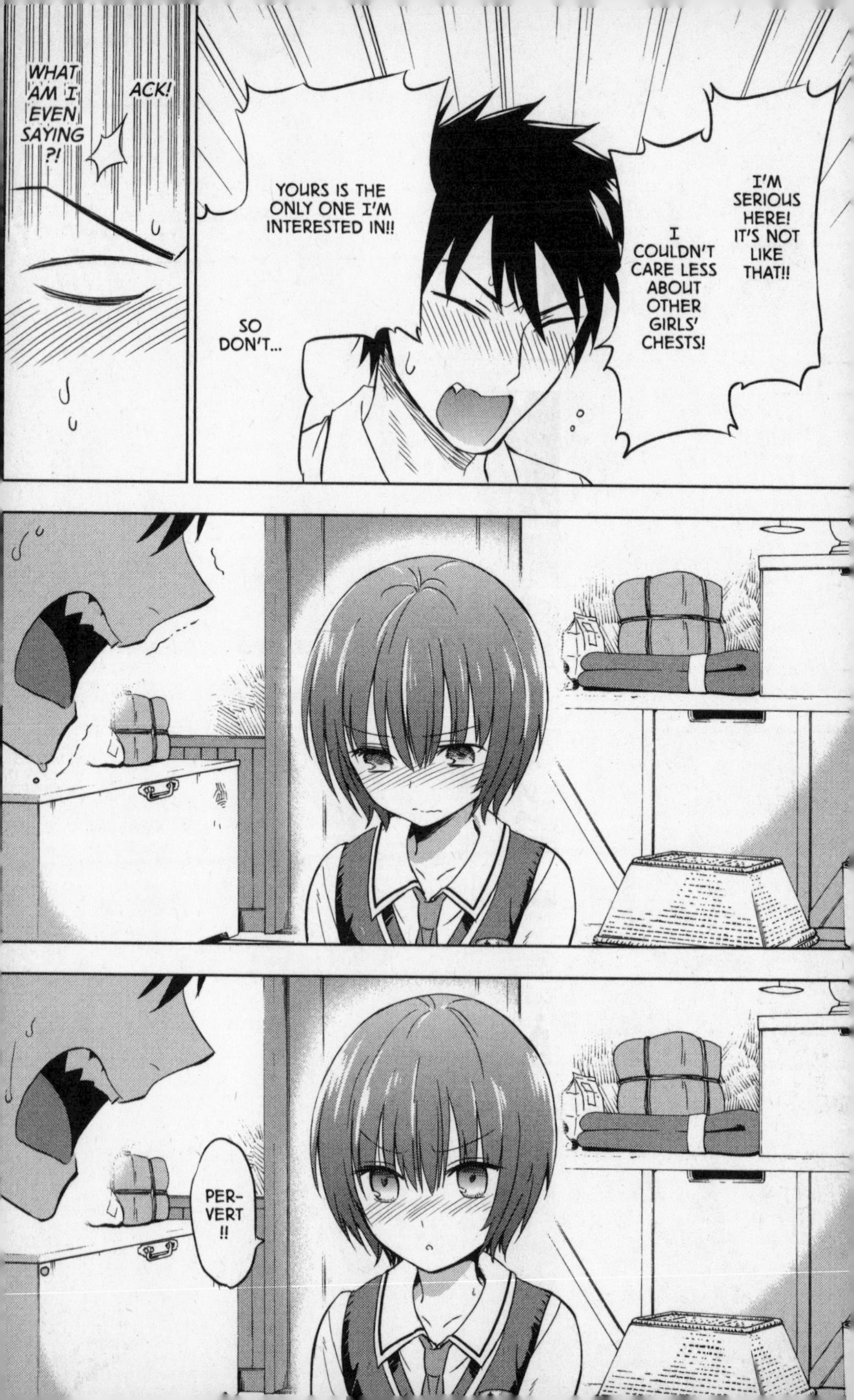
I'M SERIOUS HERE! IT'S NOT LIKE THAT!!
I COULDN'T CARE LESS ABOUT OTHER GIRLS' CHESTS!
YOURS IS THE ONLY ONE I'M INTERESTED IN!!
SO DON'T...
ACK!
WHAT AM I EVEN SAYING?!
PER-VERT!!

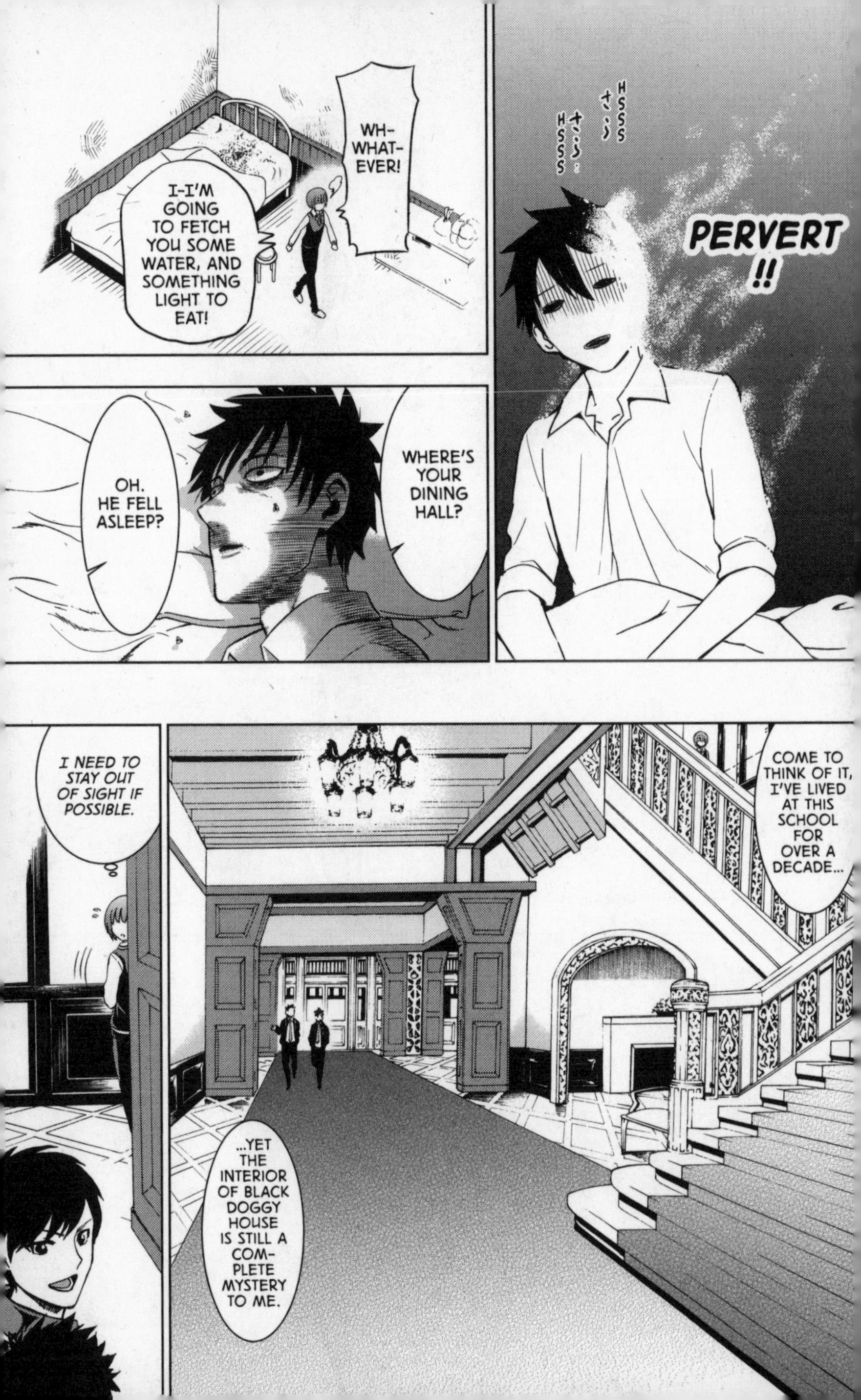
HSSS
HSSS
PERVERT!!
WH-WHAT-EVER!
I-I'M GOING TO FETCH YOU SOME WATER, AND SOMETHING LIGHT TO EAT!
WHERE'S YOUR DINING HALL?
OH. HE FELL ASLEEP?
COME TO THINK OF IT, I'VE LIVED AT THIS SCHOOL FOR OVER A DECADE...
I NEED TO STAY OUT OF SIGHT IF POSSIBLE.
...YET THE INTERIOR OF BLACK DOGGY HOUSE IS STILL A COM-PLETE MYSTERY TO ME.

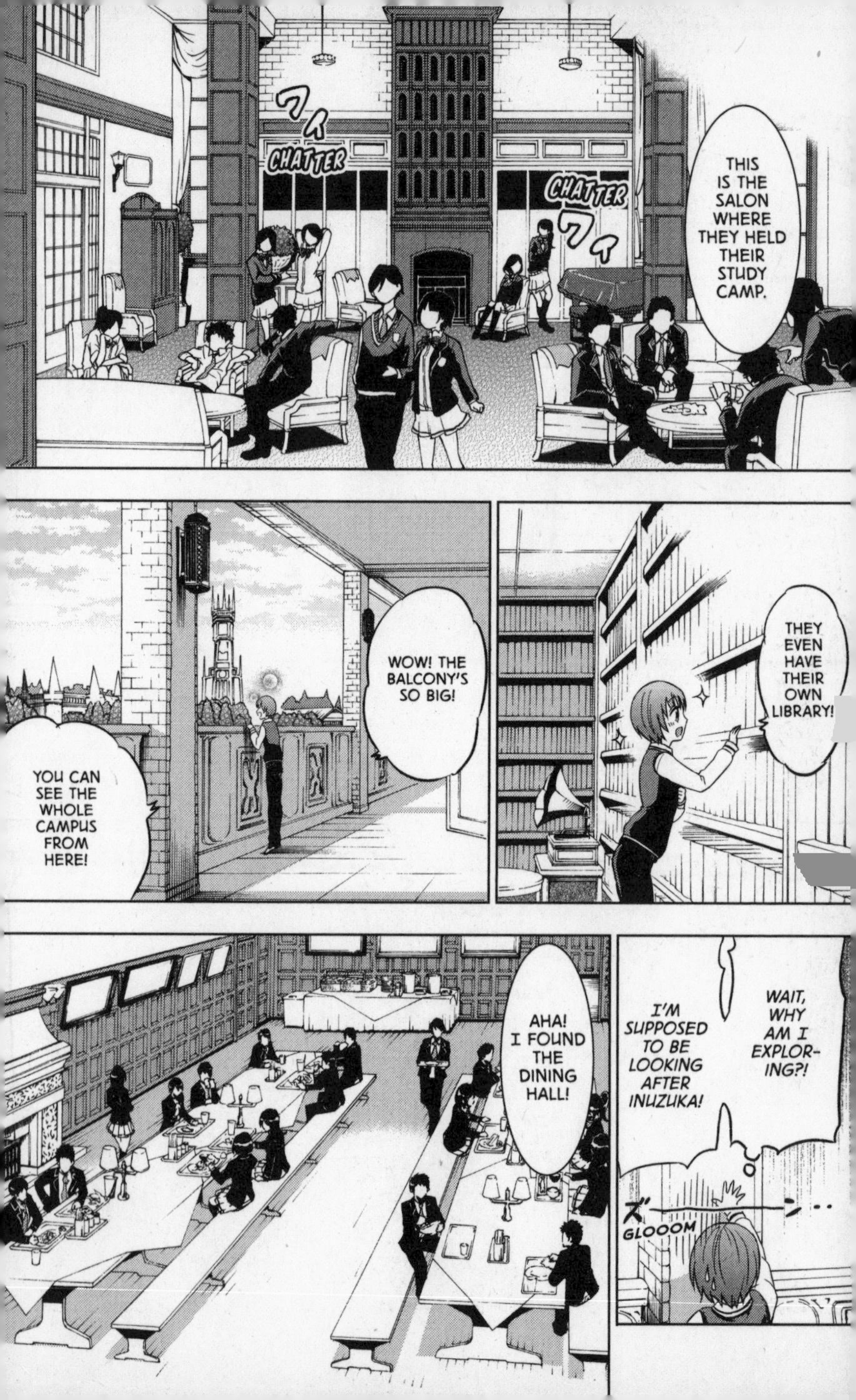
THIS IS THE SALON WHERE THEY HELD THEIR STUDY CAMP.
CHATTER
ワイ
ワイ
CHATTER
THEY EVEN HAVE THEIR OWN LIBRARY!
WOW! THE BALCONY'S SO BIG!
YOU CAN SEE THE WHOLE CAMPUS FROM HERE!
WAIT, WHY AM I EXPLORING?!
I'M SUPPOSED TO BE LOOKING AFTER INUZUKA!
ズーン…
GLOOOM
AHA! I FOUND THE DINING HALL!

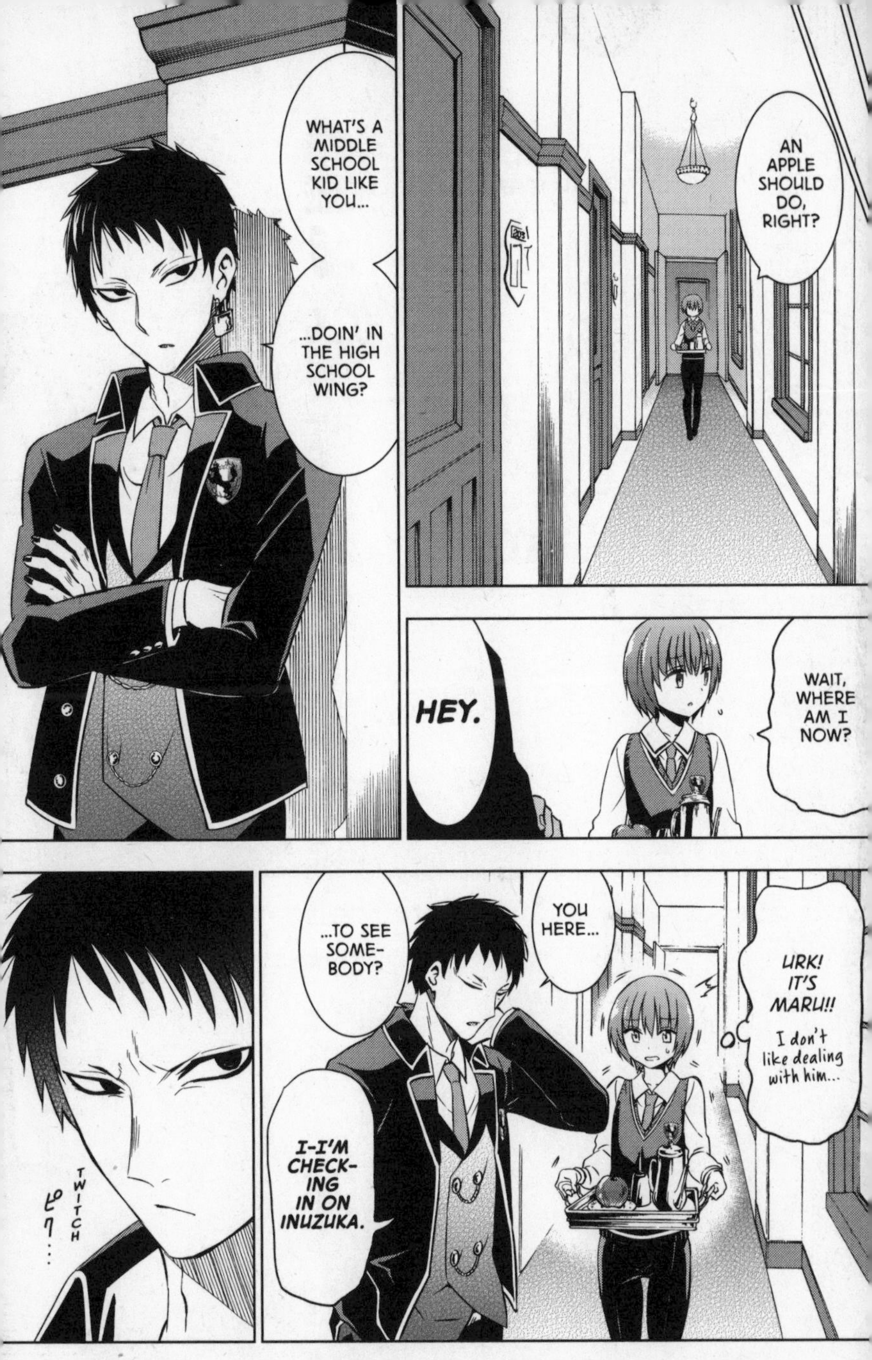
AN APPLE SHOULD DO, RIGHT?
WAIT, WHERE AM I NOW?
HEY.
WHAT'S A MIDDLE SCHOOL KID LIKE YOU...
...DOIN' IN THE HIGH SCHOOL WING?
URK! IT'S MARU!!
I don't like dealing with him...
YOU HERE...
...TO SEE SOME-BODY?
I-I'M CHECK-ING IN ON INUZUKA.
ピク...
TWITCH

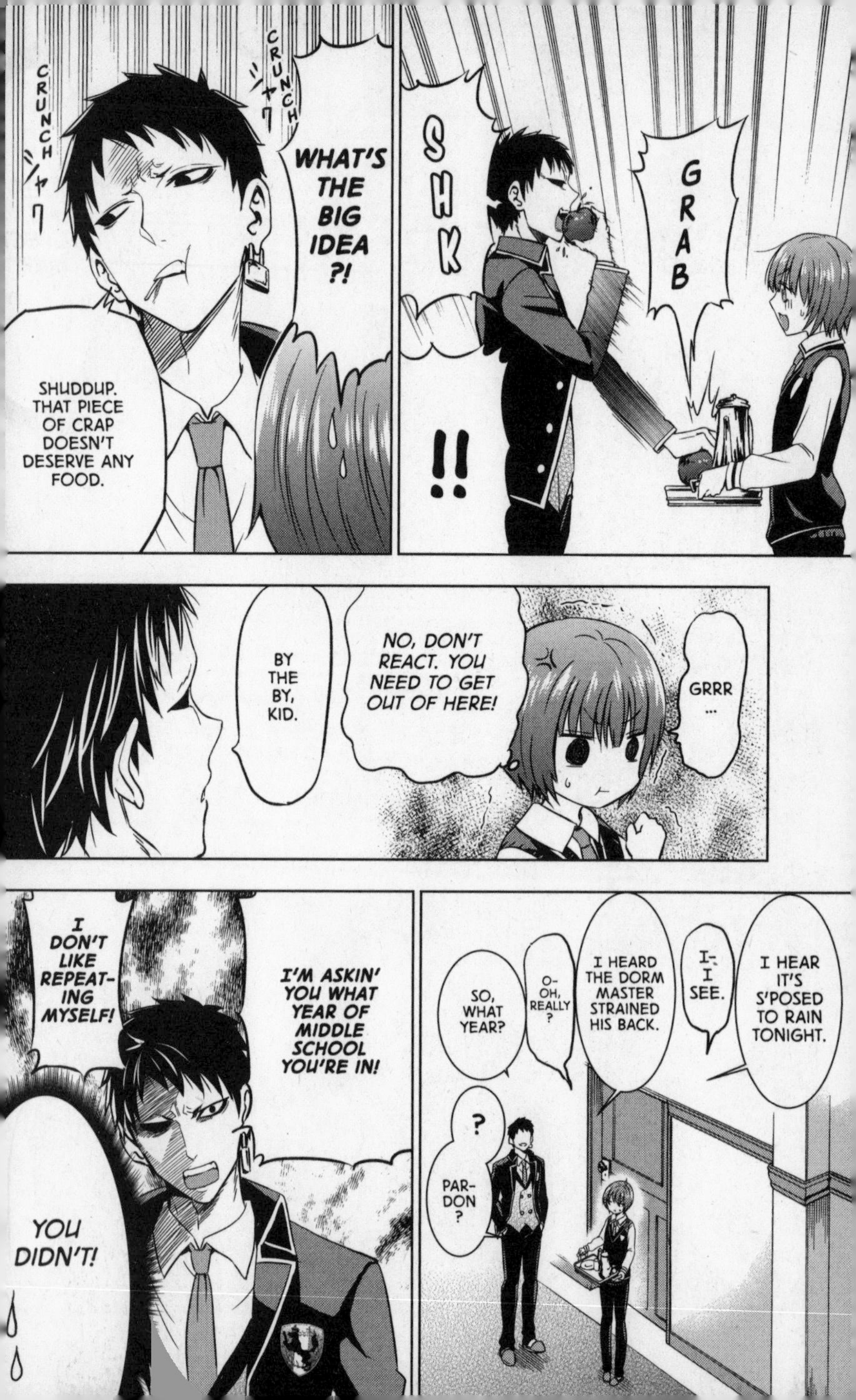
GRAB
SHK
!!
CRUNCH
WHAT'S THE BIG IDEA?!
CRUNCH
SHUDDUP. THAT PIECE OF CRAP DOESN'T DESERVE ANY FOOD.
GRRR...
NO, DON'T REACT. YOU NEED TO GET OUT OF HERE!
BY THE BY, KID.
I HEAR IT'S S'POSED TO RAIN TONIGHT.
I-. I SEE.
I HEARD THE DORM MASTER STRAINED HIS BACK.
O-OH, REALLY?
SO, WHAT YEAR?
?
PAR-DON?
I'M ASKIN' YOU WHAT YEAR OF MIDDLE SCHOOL YOU'RE IN!
I DON'T LIKE REPEAT-ING MYSELF!
YOU DIDN'T!

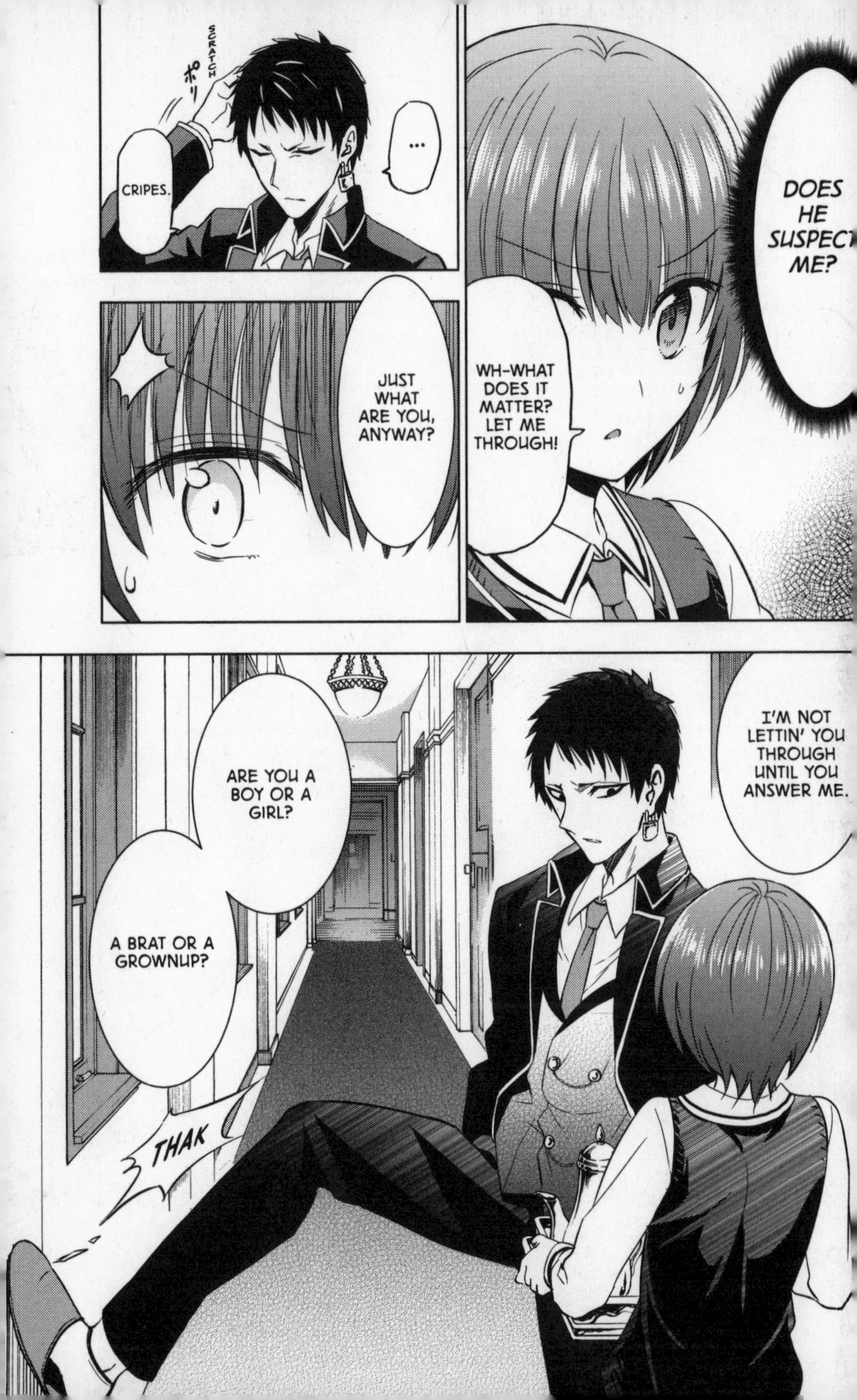
DOES HE SUSPECT ME?
WH-WHAT DOES IT MATTER? LET ME THROUGH!
...
SCRATCH
CRIPES.
JUST WHAT ARE YOU, ANYWAY?
I'M NOT LETTIN' YOU THROUGH UNTIL YOU ANSWER ME.
ARE YOU A BOY OR A GIRL?
A BRAT OR A GROWNUP?
THAK

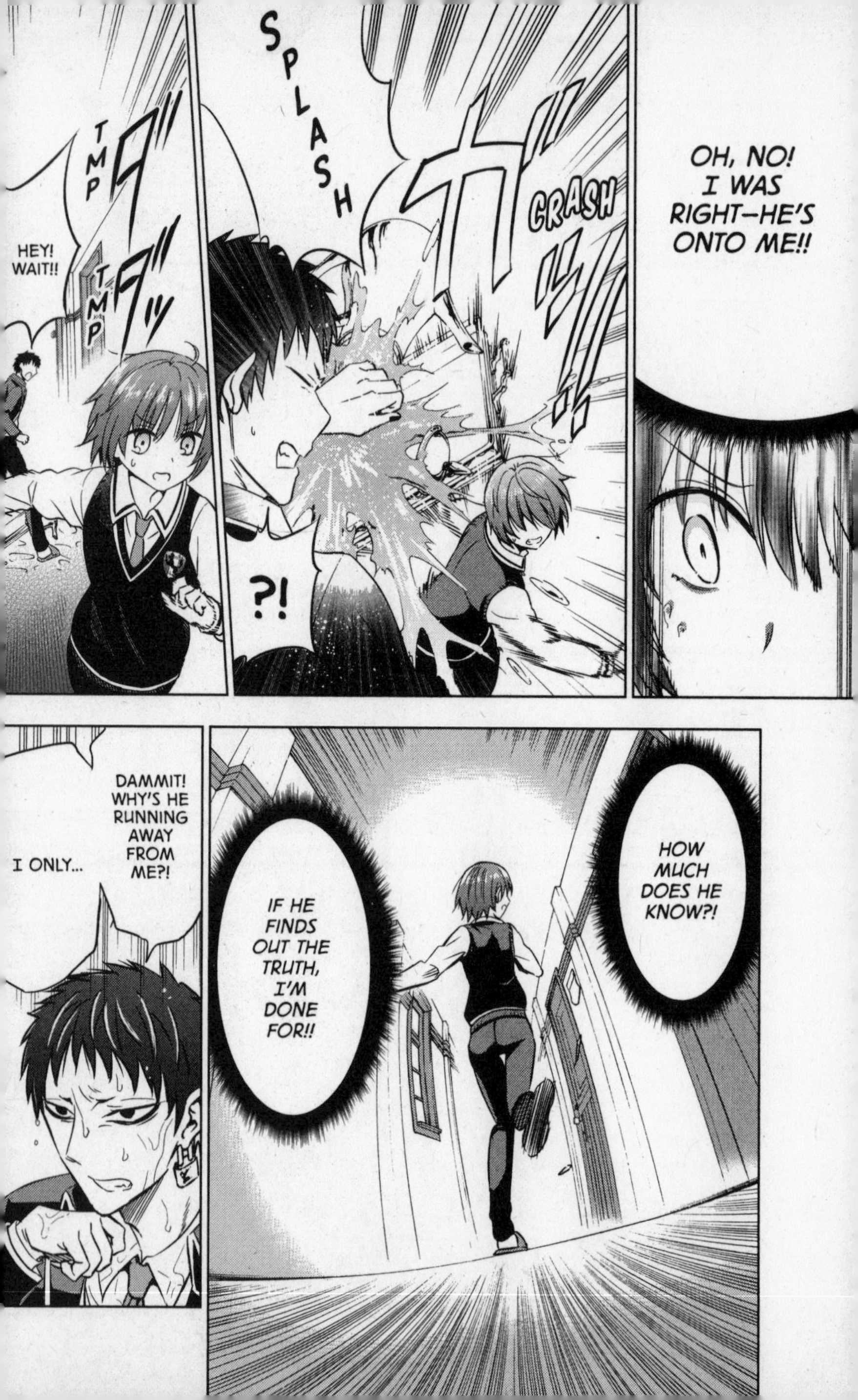
OH, NO! I WAS RIGHT—HE'S ONTO ME!!
SPLASH
CRASH
?!
TMP
TMP
HEY! WAIT!!
HOW MUCH DOES HE KNOW?!
IF HE FINDS OUT THE TRUTH, I'M DONE FOR!!
DAMMIT! WHY'S HE RUNNING AWAY FROM ME?!
I ONLY...

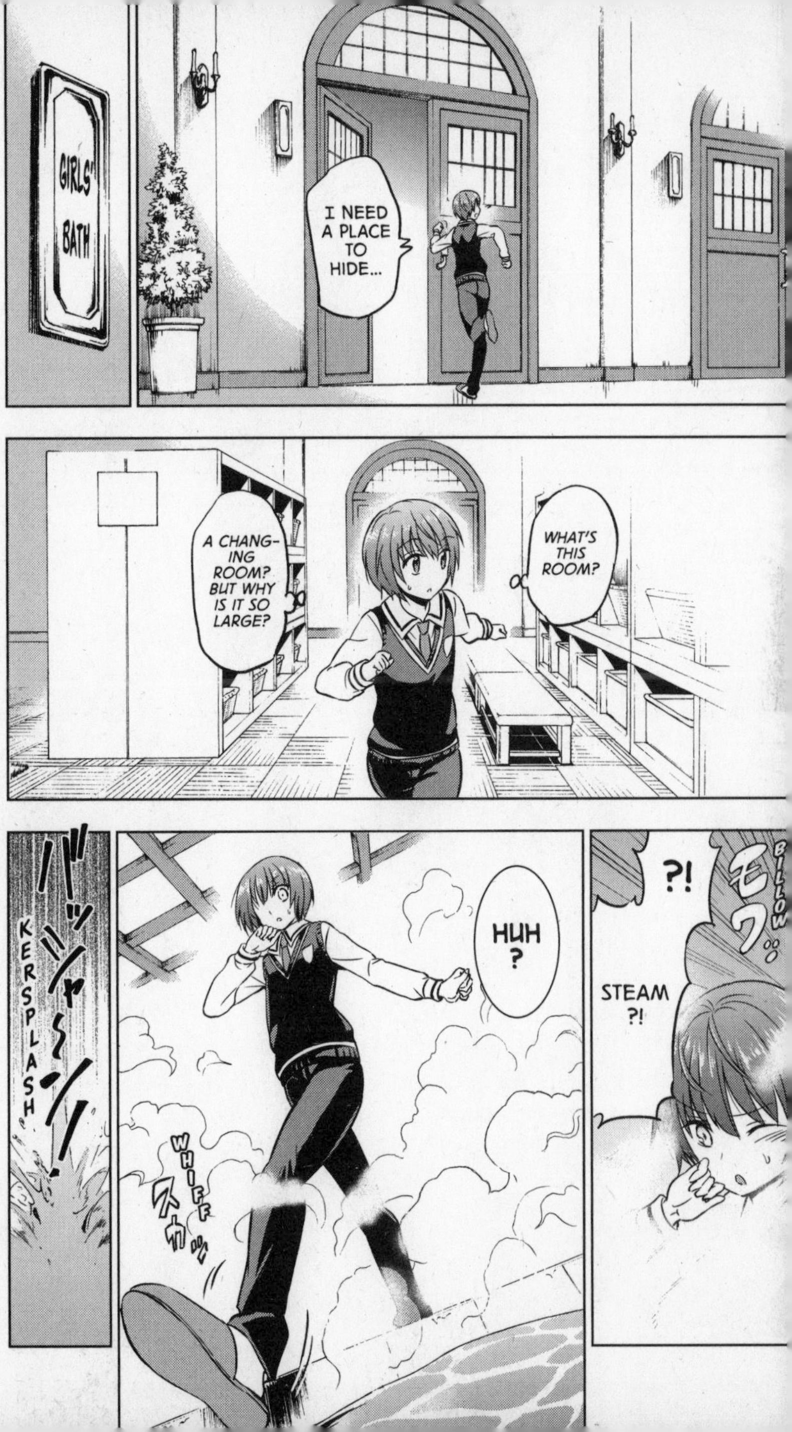
I NEED A PLACE TO HIDE...
GIRLS' BATH
WHAT'S THIS ROOM?
A CHANGING ROOM? BUT WHY IS IT SO LARGE?
?!
BILLOW
STEAM ?!
HUH ?
WHIFF
KERSPLASH

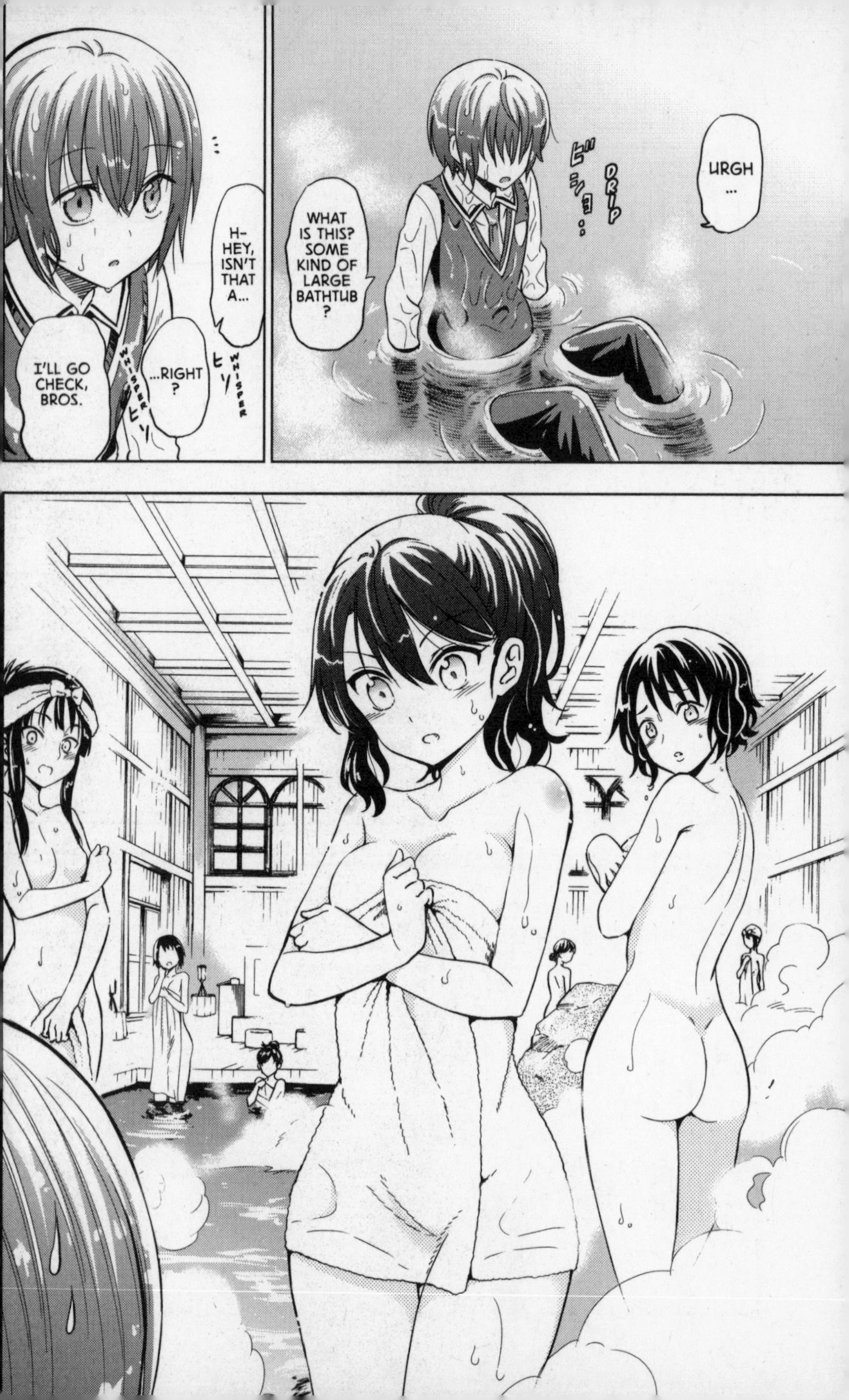
URGH ...
DRIP
WHAT IS THIS? SOME KIND OF LARGE BATHTUB?
H-HEY, ISN'T THAT A...
WHISPER
...RIGHT?
WHISPER
I'LL GO CHECK, BROS.

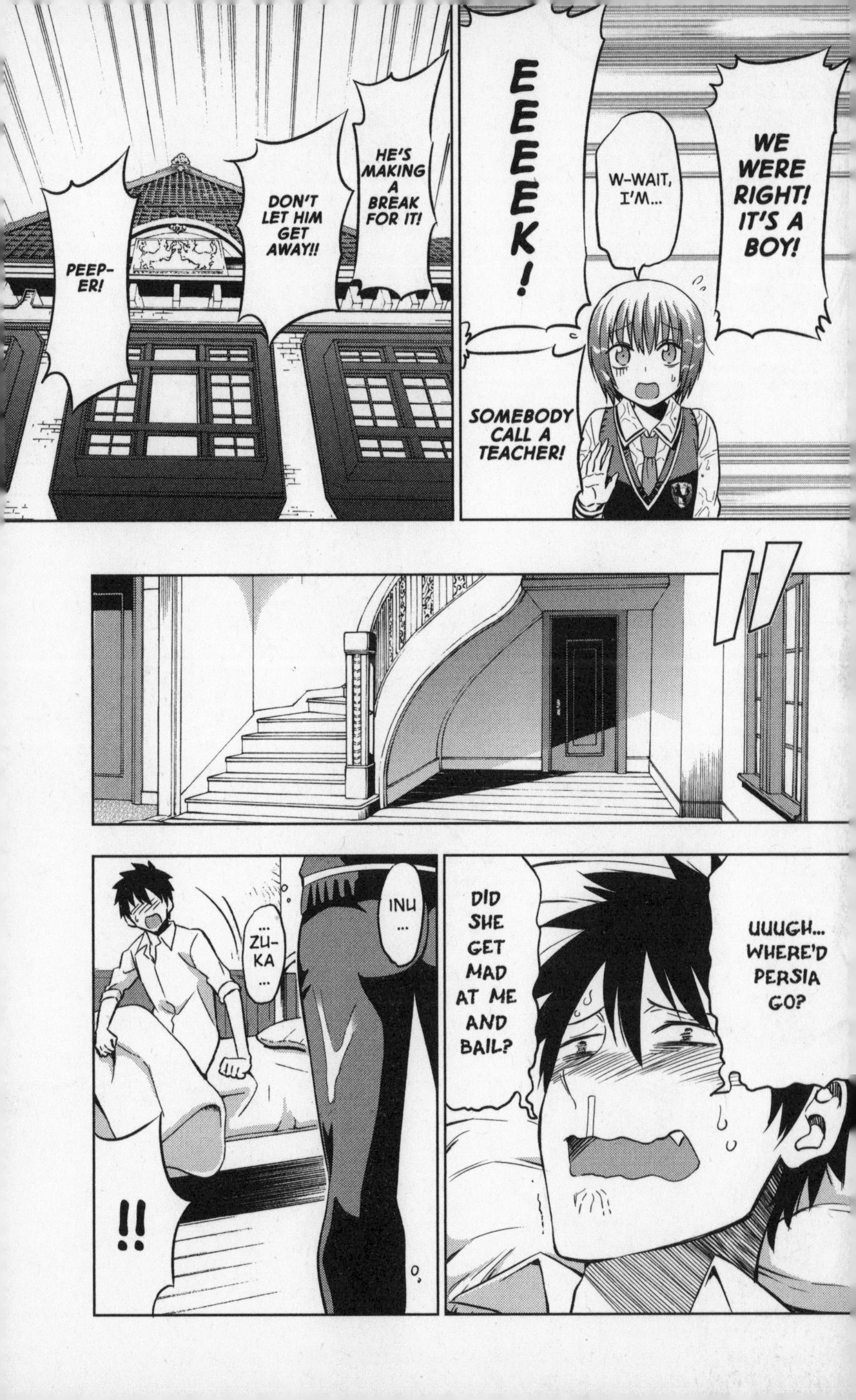
WE WERE RIGHT! IT'S A BOY!
W-WAIT, I'M...
EEEEK!
SOMEBODY CALL A TEACHER!
HE'S MAKING A BREAK FOR IT!
DON'T LET HIM GET AWAY!!
PEEPER!
UUUGH... WHERE'D PERSIA GO?
DID SHE GET MAD AT ME AND BAIL?
INU...
...ZU-KA...
!!

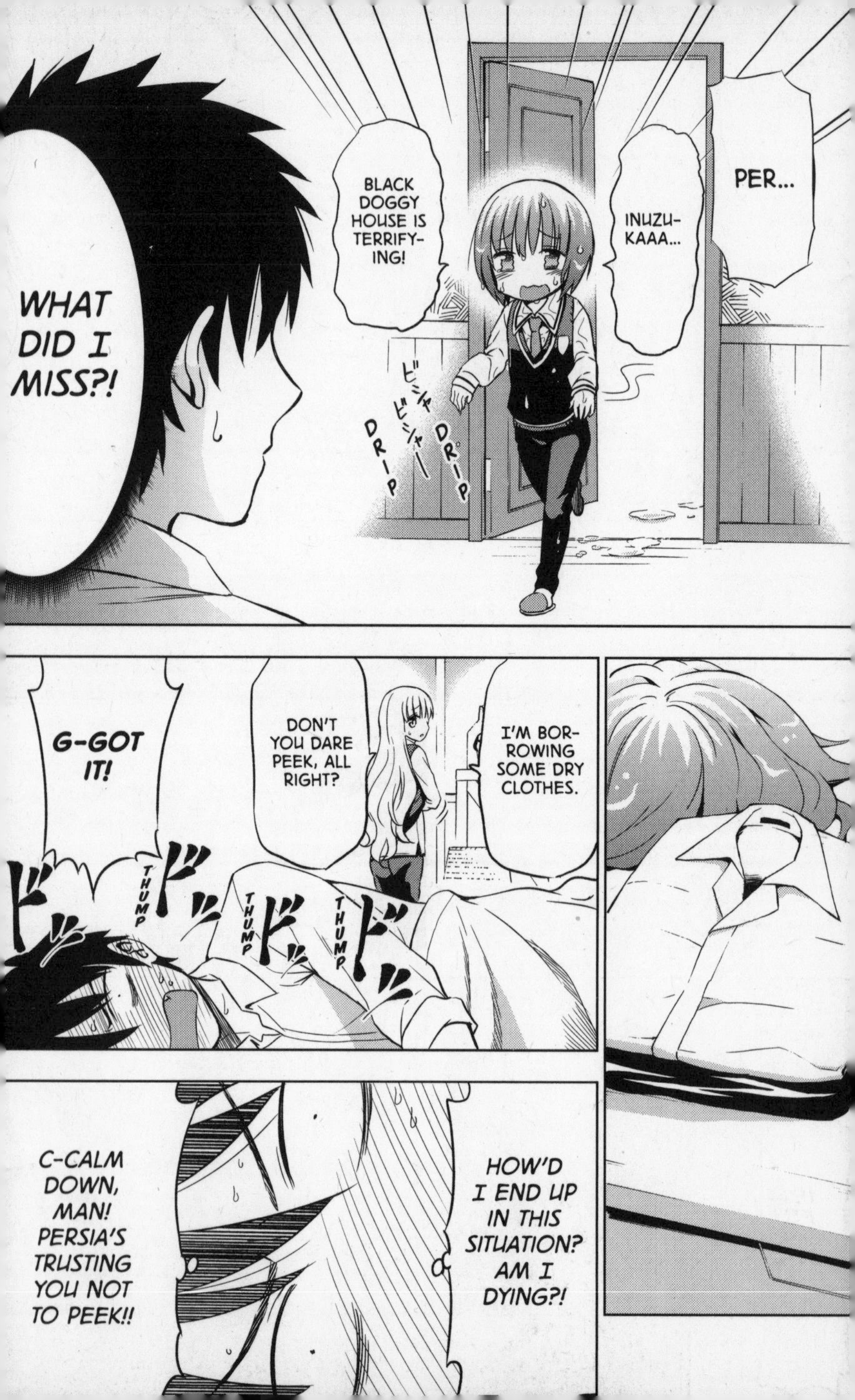
PER...
INUZU-KAAA...
BLACK DOGGY HOUSE IS TERRIFY-ING!
ビシャ ビシャー
DRIP DRIP
WHAT DID I MISS?!
I'M BOR-ROWING SOME DRY CLOTHES.
DON'T YOU DARE PEEK, ALL RIGHT?
G-GOT IT!
ドッ ドッ ドッ
THUMP THUMP THUMP
HOW'D I END UP IN THIS SITUATION? AM I DYING?!
C-CALM DOWN, MAN! PERSIA'S TRUSTING YOU NOT TO PEEK!!

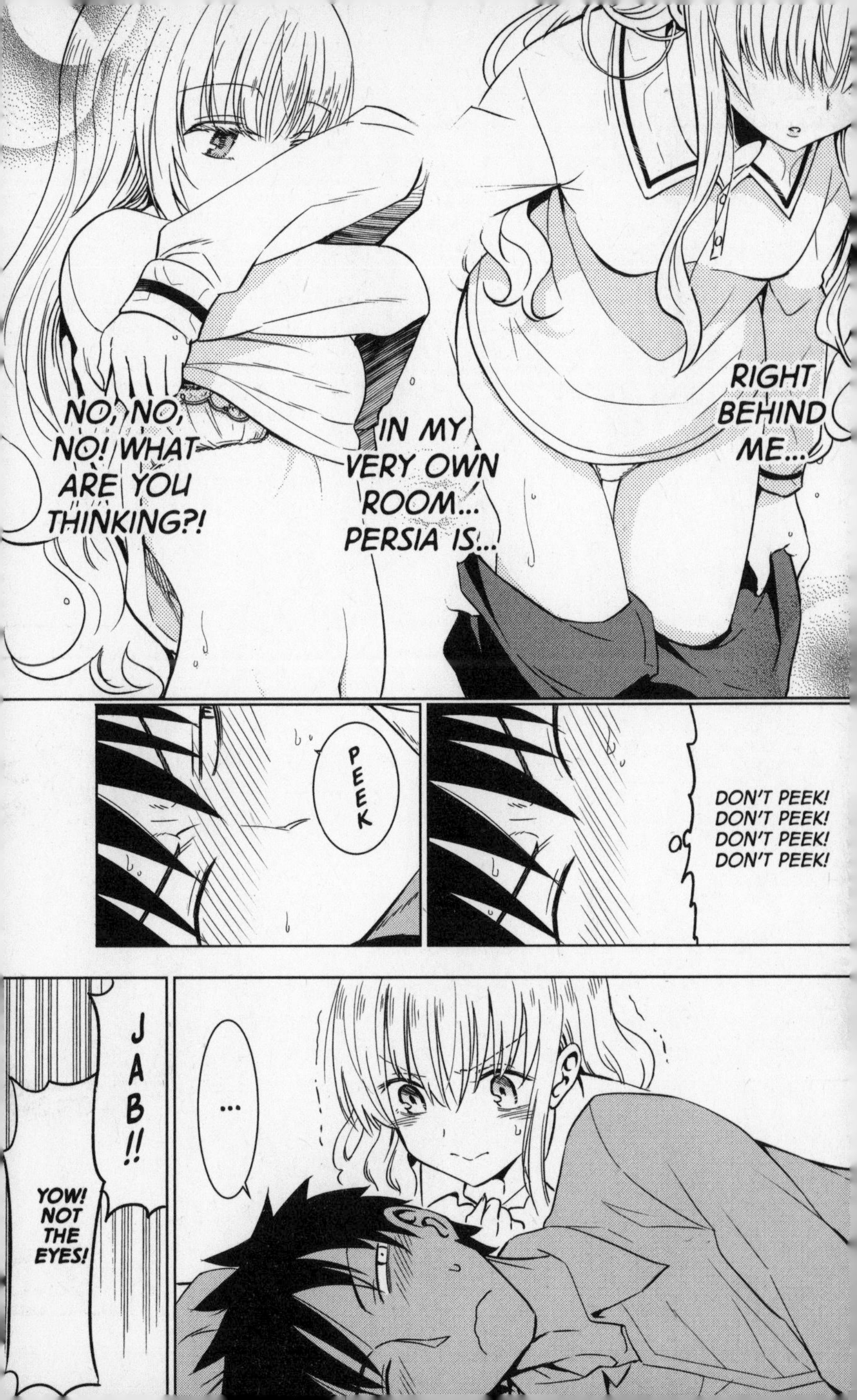
RIGHT BEHIND ME...
IN MY VERY OWN ROOM... PERSIA IS...
NO, NO, NO! WHAT ARE YOU THINKING?!
DON'T PEEK! DON'T PEEK! DON'T PEEK! DON'T PEEK!
PEEK
...
JAB!!
YOW! NOT THE EYES!

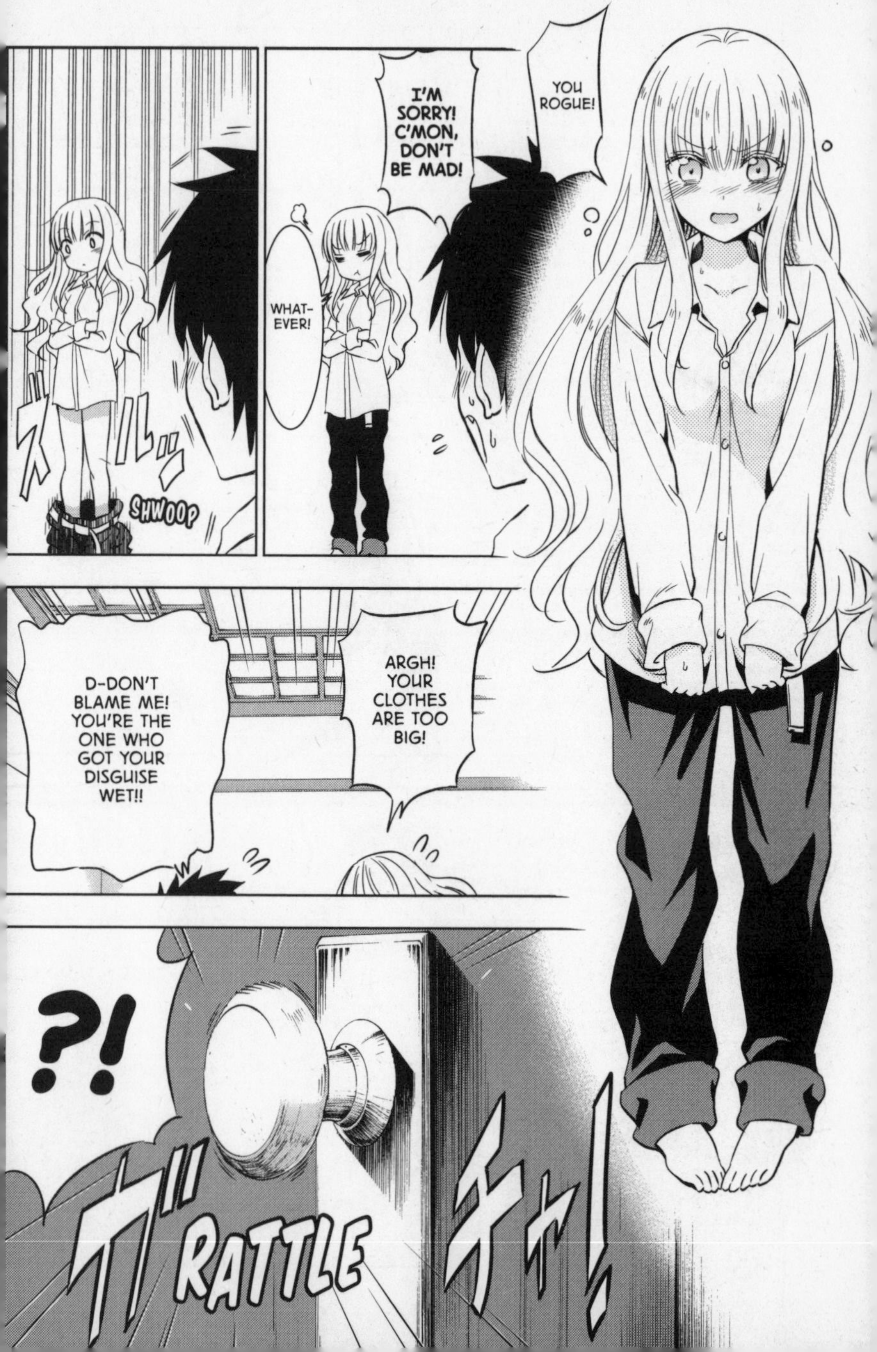
YOU ROGUE!
I'M SORRY! C'MON, DON'T BE MAD!
WHAT-EVER!
ズルッ
SHWOOP
ARGH! YOUR CLOTHES ARE TOO BIG!
D-DON'T BLAME ME! YOU'RE THE ONE WHO GOT YOUR DISGUISE WET!!
?!
ガチャ!
RATTLE

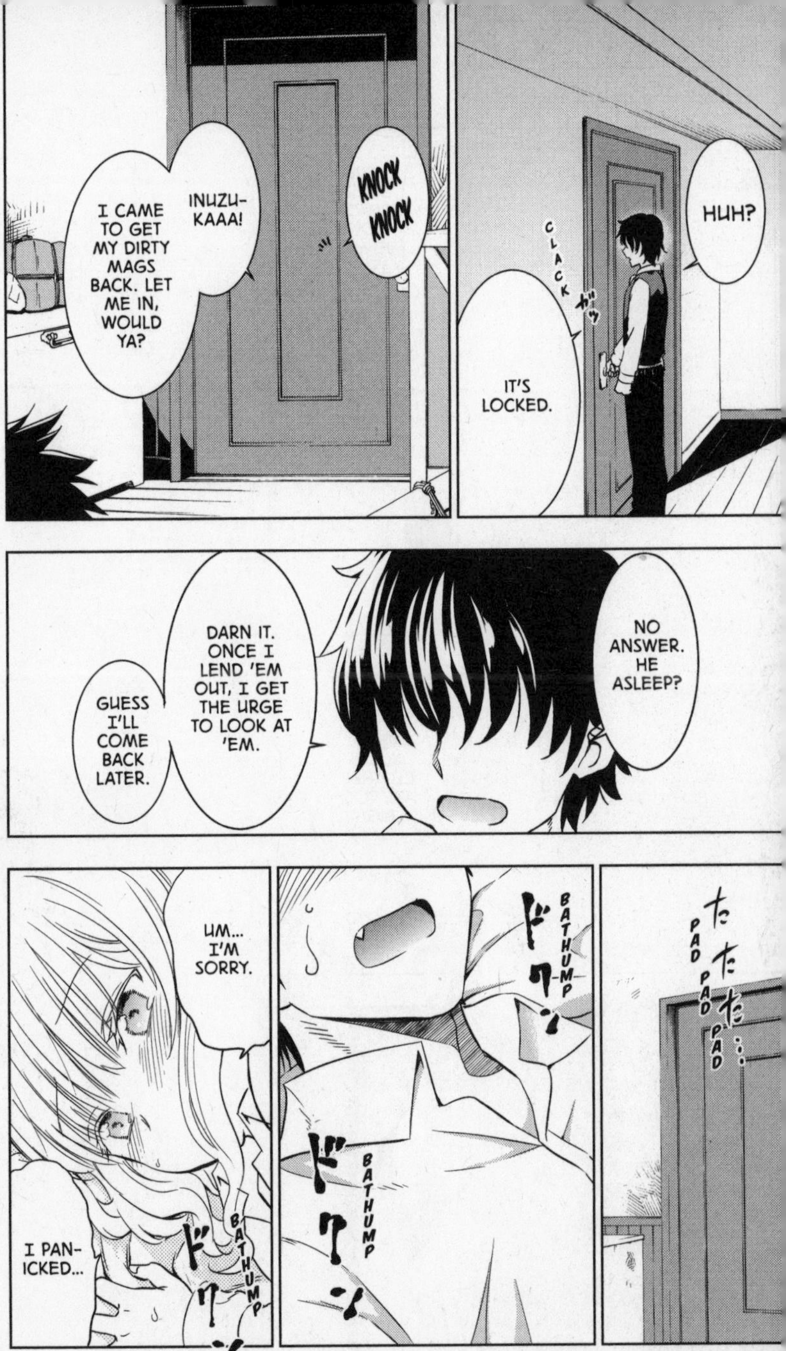
HUH?
CLACK
IT'S LOCKED.
KNOCK KNOCK
INUZU-KAAA!
I CAME TO GET MY DIRTY MAGS BACK. LET ME IN, WOULD YA?
NO ANSWER. HE ASLEEP?
DARN IT. ONCE I LEND 'EM OUT, I GET THE URGE TO LOOK AT 'EM.
GUESS I'LL COME BACK LATER.
PAD PAD PAD
BATHUMP
BATHUMP
UM... I'M SORRY.
BATHUMP
I PANICKED...

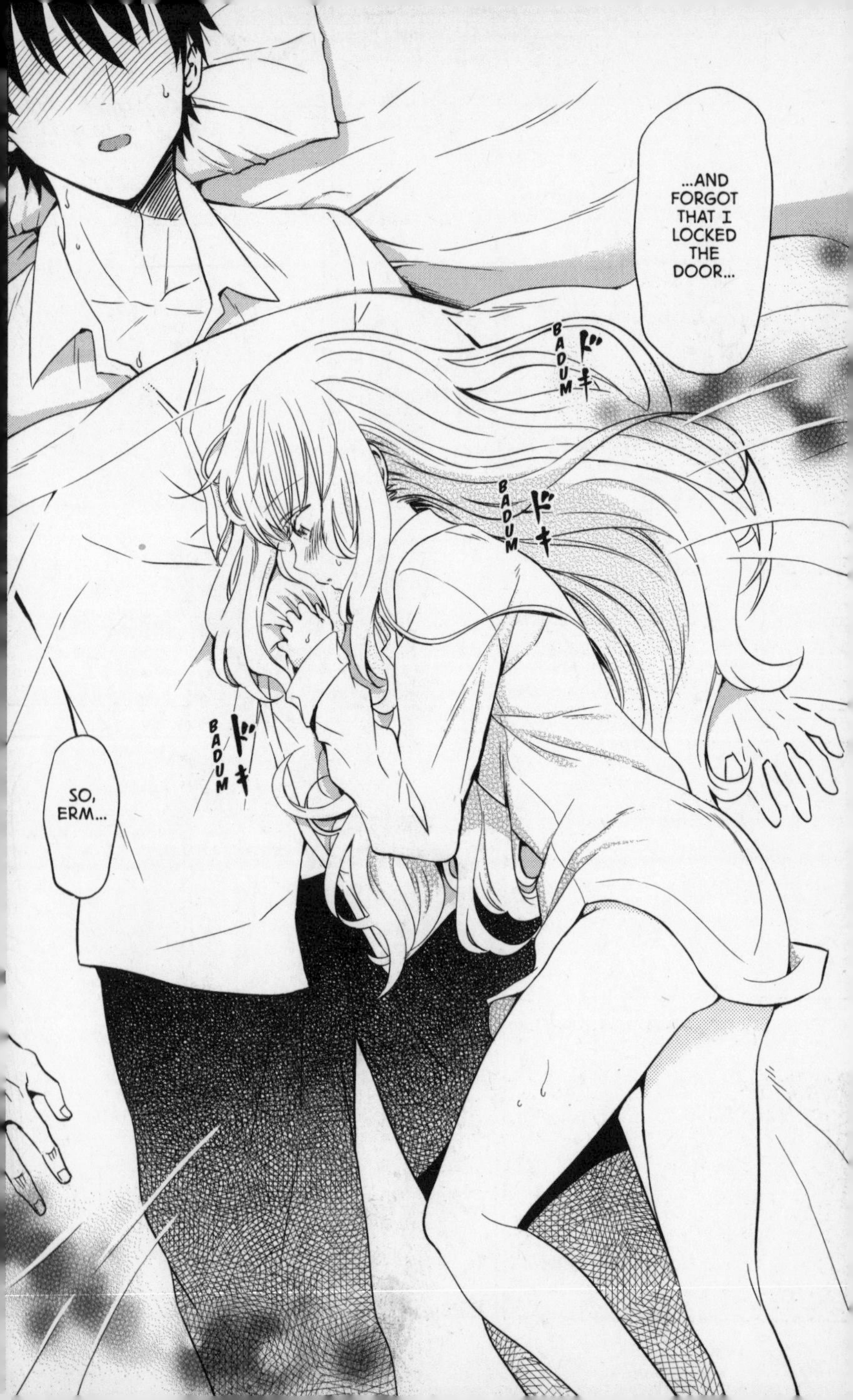
...AND FORGOT THAT I LOCKED THE DOOR...
BADUM ドキ
BADUM ドキ
BADUM ドキ
SO, ERM...

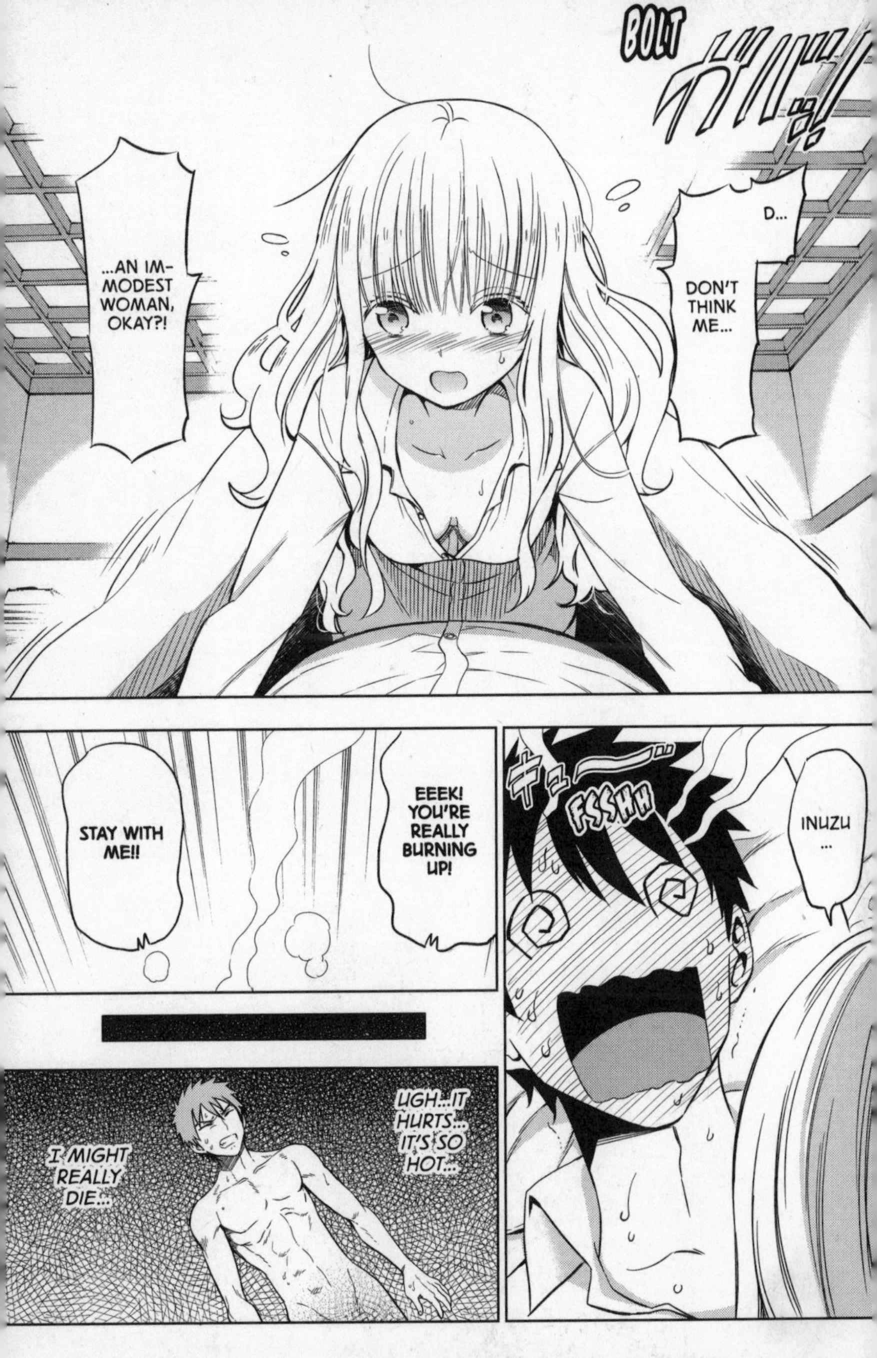
BOLT
D...
DON'T THINK ME...
...AN IM-MODEST WOMAN, OKAY?!
INUZU ...
FSSHH
EEEK! YOU'RE REALLY BURNING UP!
STAY WITH ME!!
UGH...IT HURTS... IT'S SO HOT...
I MIGHT REALLY DIE...

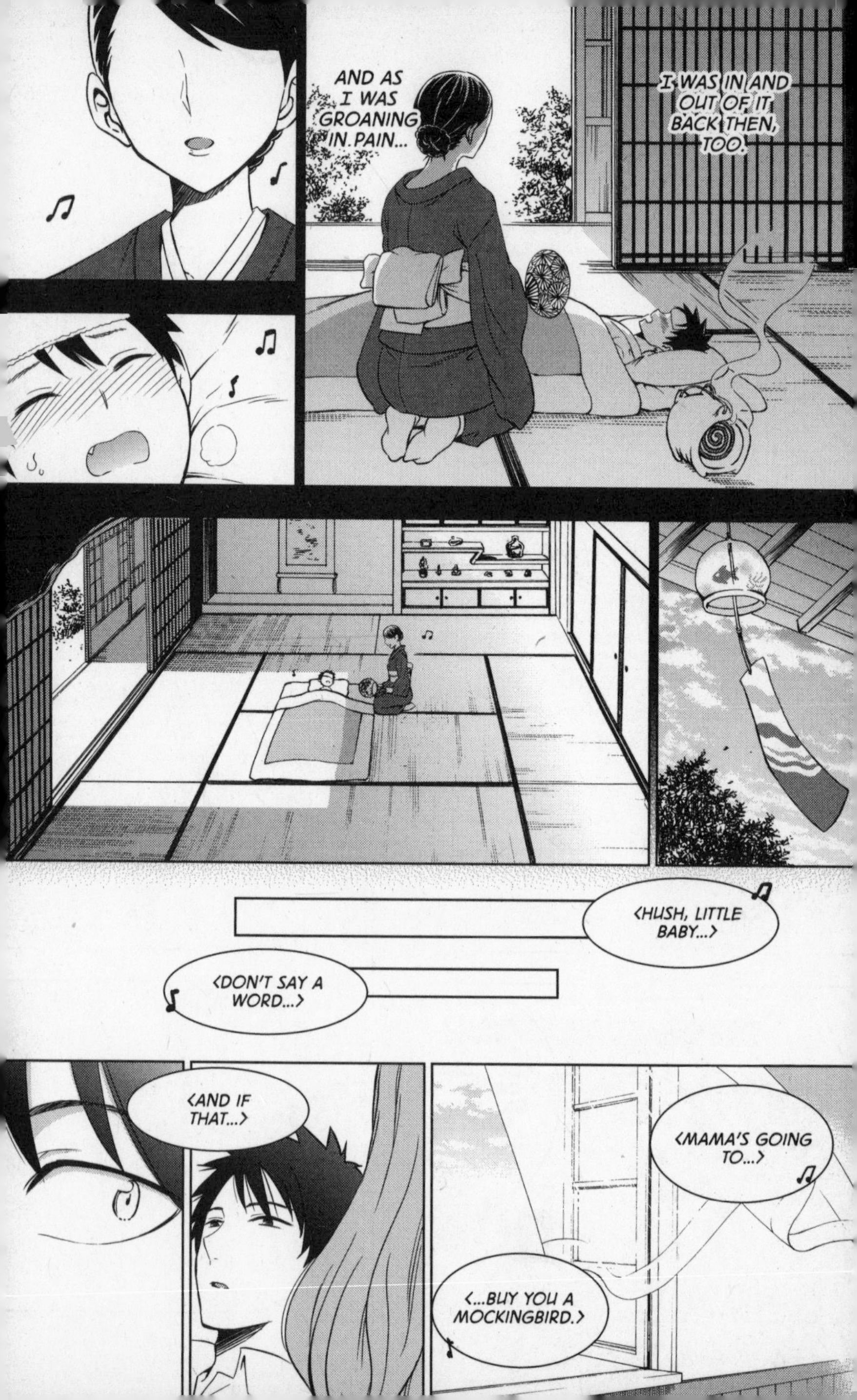
I WAS IN AND OUT OF IT BACK THEN, TOO.
AND AS I WAS GROANING IN PAIN...
<HUSH, LITTLE BABY...>
<DON'T SAY A WORD...>
<MAMA'S GOING TO...>
<...BUY YOU A MOCKINGBIRD.>
<AND IF THAT...>

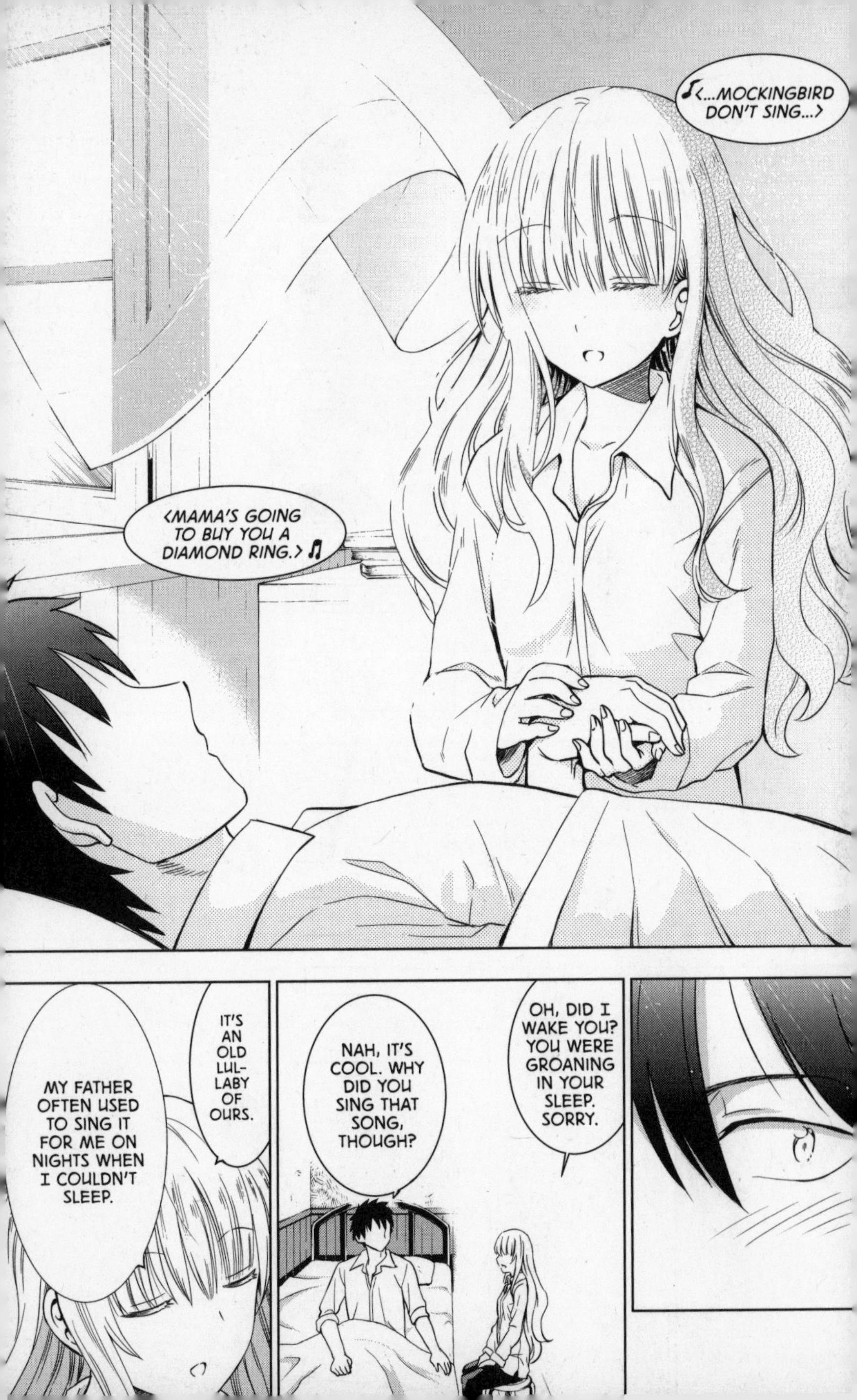
♪‹...MOCKINGBIRD DON'T SING...›
‹MAMA'S GOING TO BUY YOU A DIAMOND RING.› ♫
OH, DID I WAKE YOU? YOU WERE GROANING IN YOUR SLEEP. SORRY.
NAH, IT'S COOL. WHY DID YOU SING THAT SONG, THOUGH?
IT'S AN OLD LUL-LABY OF OURS.
MY FATHER OFTEN USED TO SING IT FOR ME ON NIGHTS WHEN I COULDN'T SLEEP.

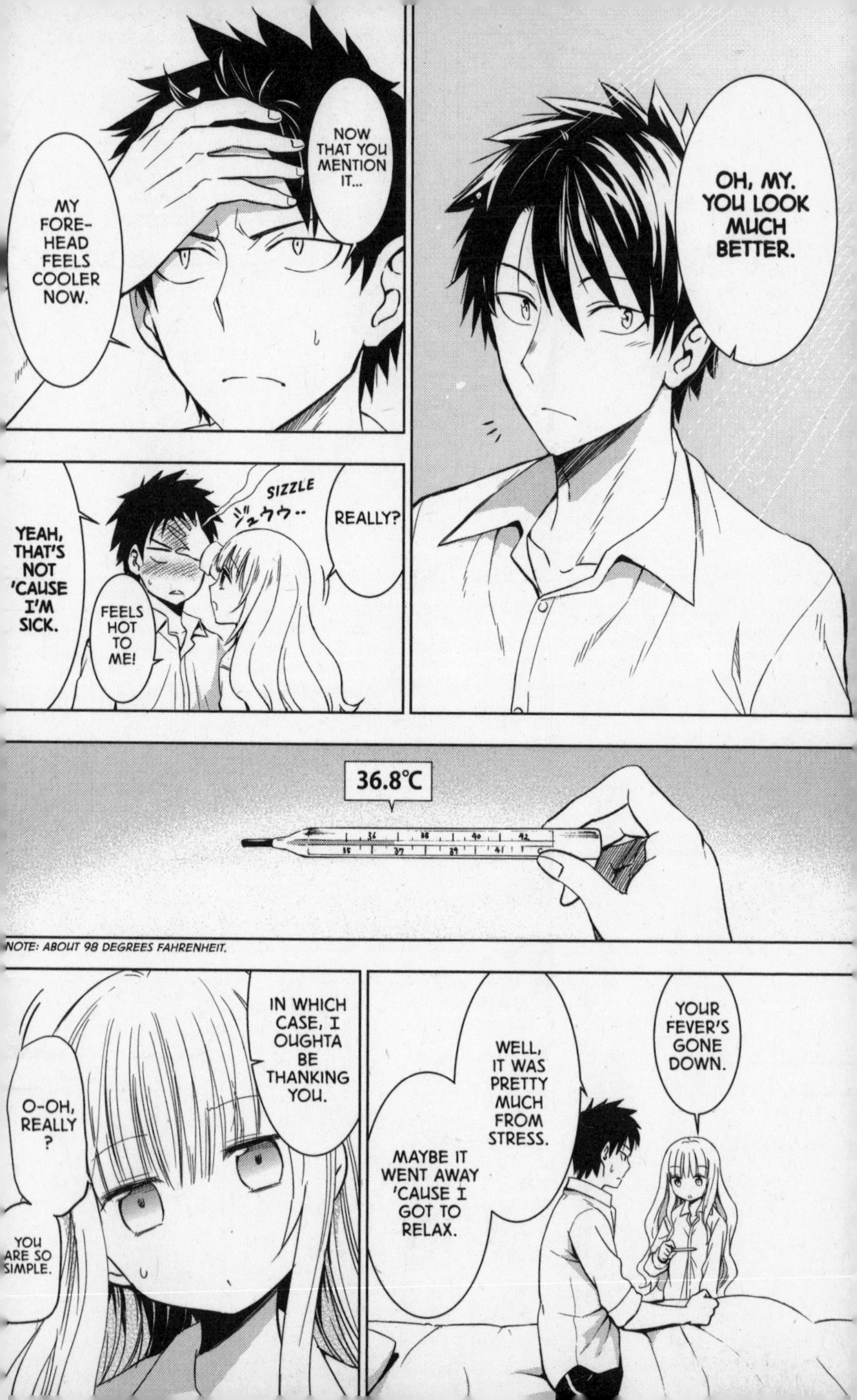
OH, MY. YOU LOOK MUCH BETTER.
NOW THAT YOU MENTION IT...
MY FOREHEAD FEELS COOLER NOW.
REALLY?
SIZZLE
ジュウウ…
YEAH, THAT'S NOT 'CAUSE I'M SICK.
FEELS HOT TO ME!
36.8°C
YOUR FEVER'S GONE DOWN.
WELL, IT WAS PRETTY MUCH FROM STRESS.
MAYBE IT WENT AWAY 'CAUSE I GOT TO RELAX.
IN WHICH CASE, I OUGHTA BE THANKING YOU.
O-OH, REALLY?
YOU ARE SO SIMPLE.
NOTE: ABOUT 98 DEGREES FAHRENHEIT.

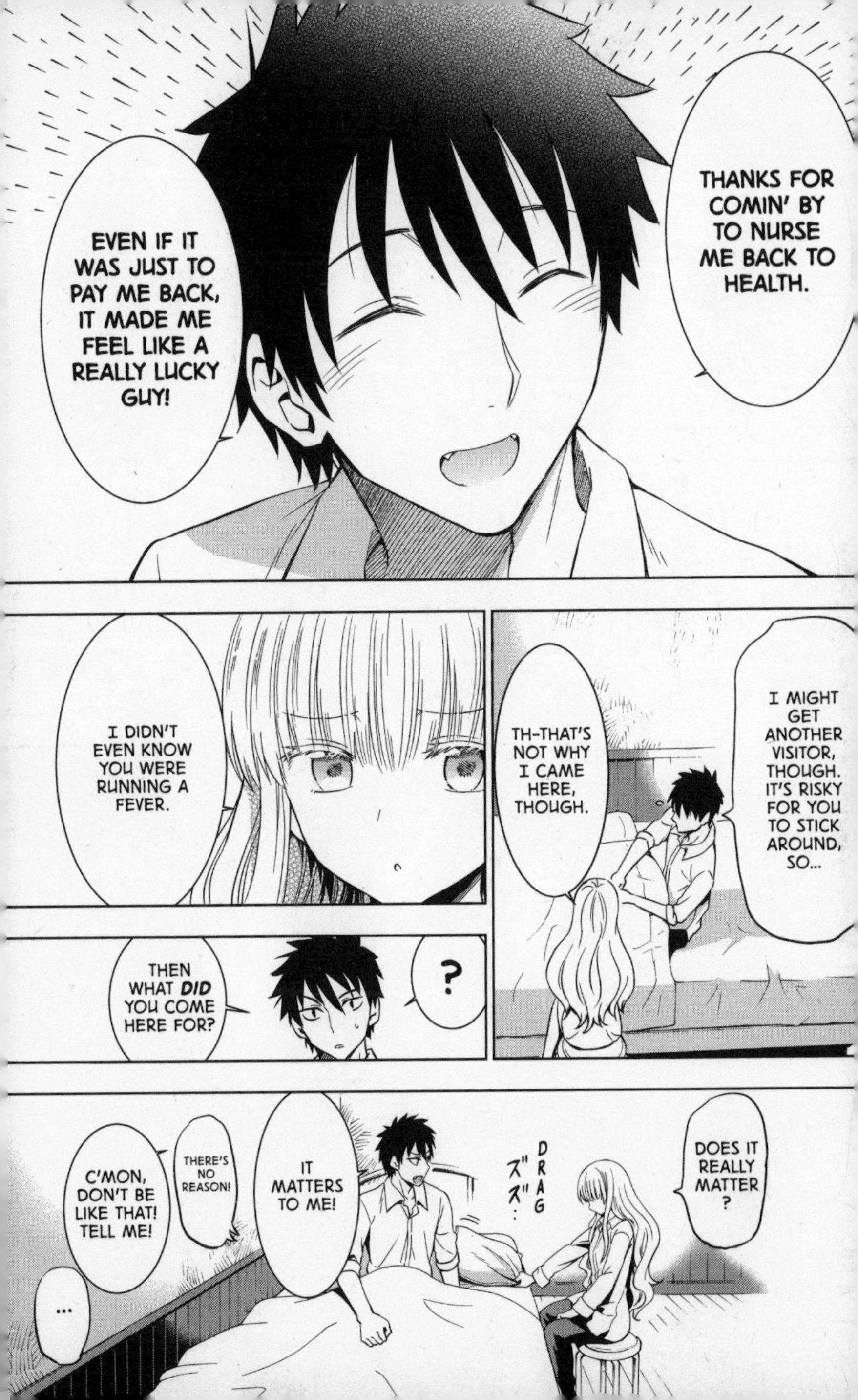
THANKS FOR COMIN' BY TO NURSE ME BACK TO HEALTH.
EVEN IF IT WAS JUST TO PAY ME BACK, IT MADE ME FEEL LIKE A REALLY LUCKY GUY!
I MIGHT GET ANOTHER VISITOR, THOUGH. IT'S RISKY FOR YOU TO STICK AROUND, SO...
TH-THAT'S NOT WHY I CAME HERE, THOUGH.
I DIDN'T EVEN KNOW YOU WERE RUNNING A FEVER.
?
THEN WHAT *DID* YOU COME HERE FOR?
DOES IT REALLY MATTER?
ズズ… DRAG
IT MATTERS TO ME!
THERE'S NO REASON!
C'MON, DON'T BE LIKE THAT! TELL ME!
...

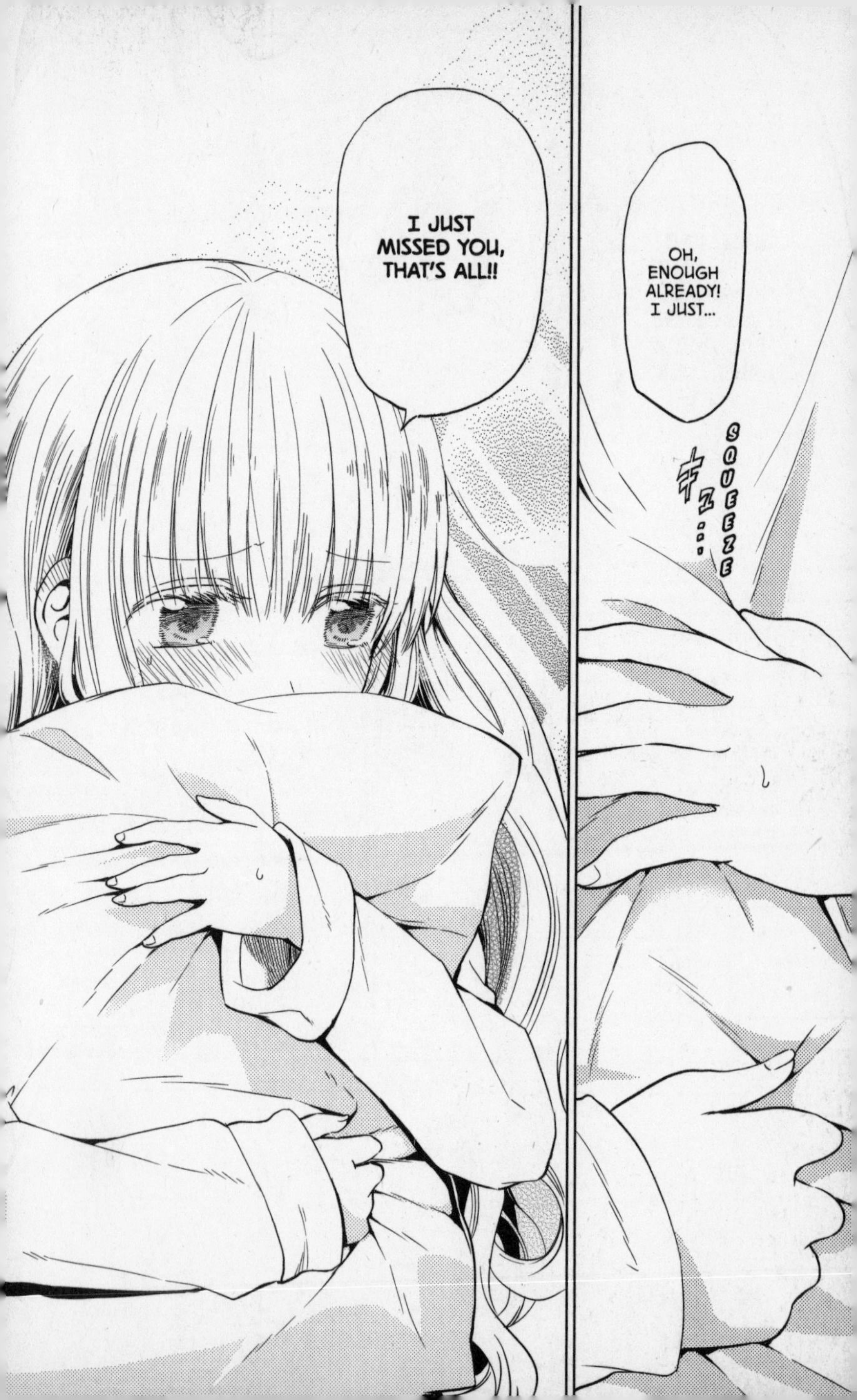
OH, ENOUGH ALREADY! I JUST...
キュ…
SQUEEZE
I JUST MISSED YOU, THAT'S ALL!!

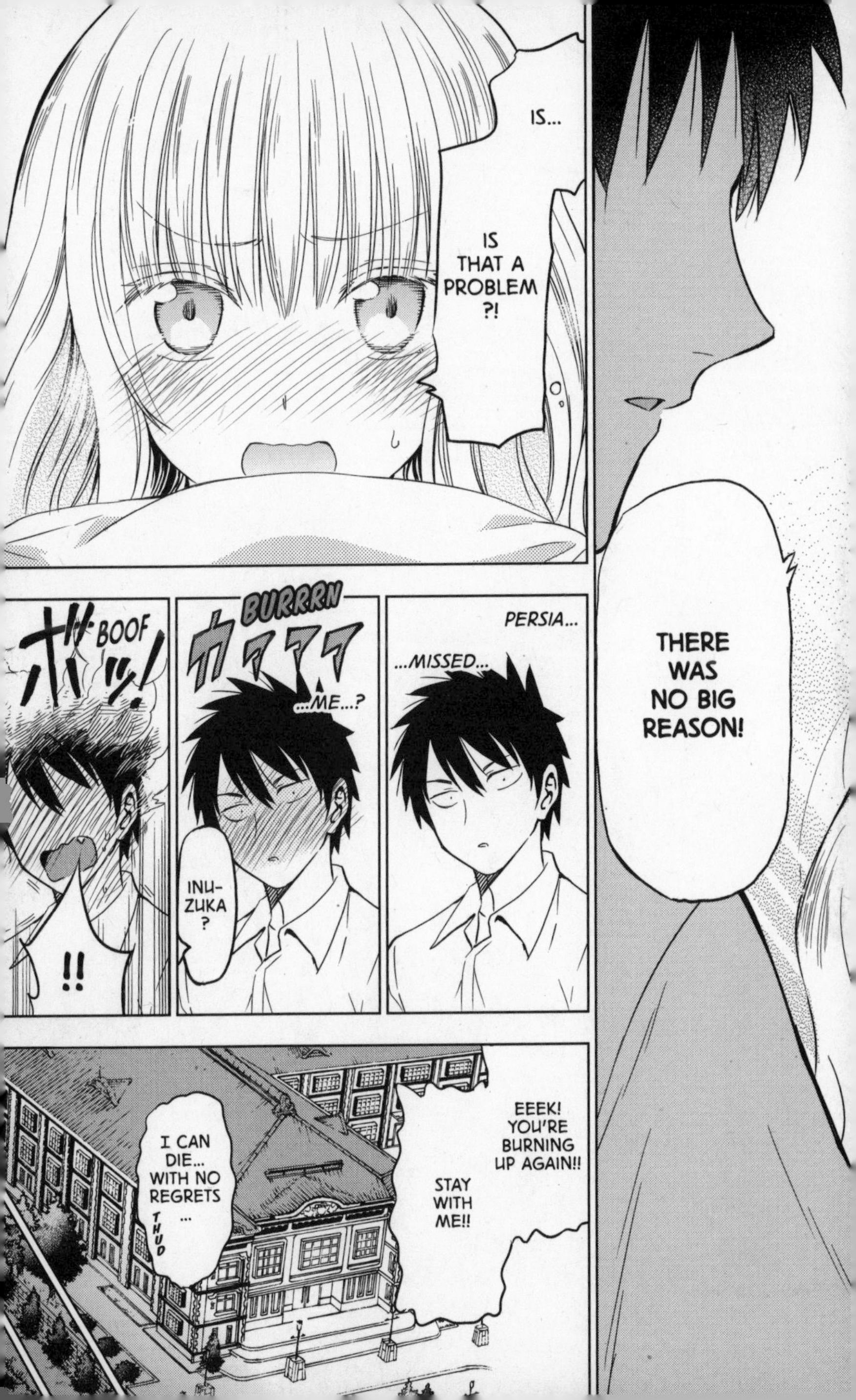
THERE WAS NO BIG REASON!
IS...
IS THAT A PROBLEM ?!
PERSIA...
...MISSED...
カァァァ
BURRRN
...ME...?
INUZUKA ?
ボッ!
BOOF
!!
EEEK! YOU'RE BURNING UP AGAIN!!
STAY WITH ME!!
I CAN DIE... WITH NO REGRETS ...
THUD

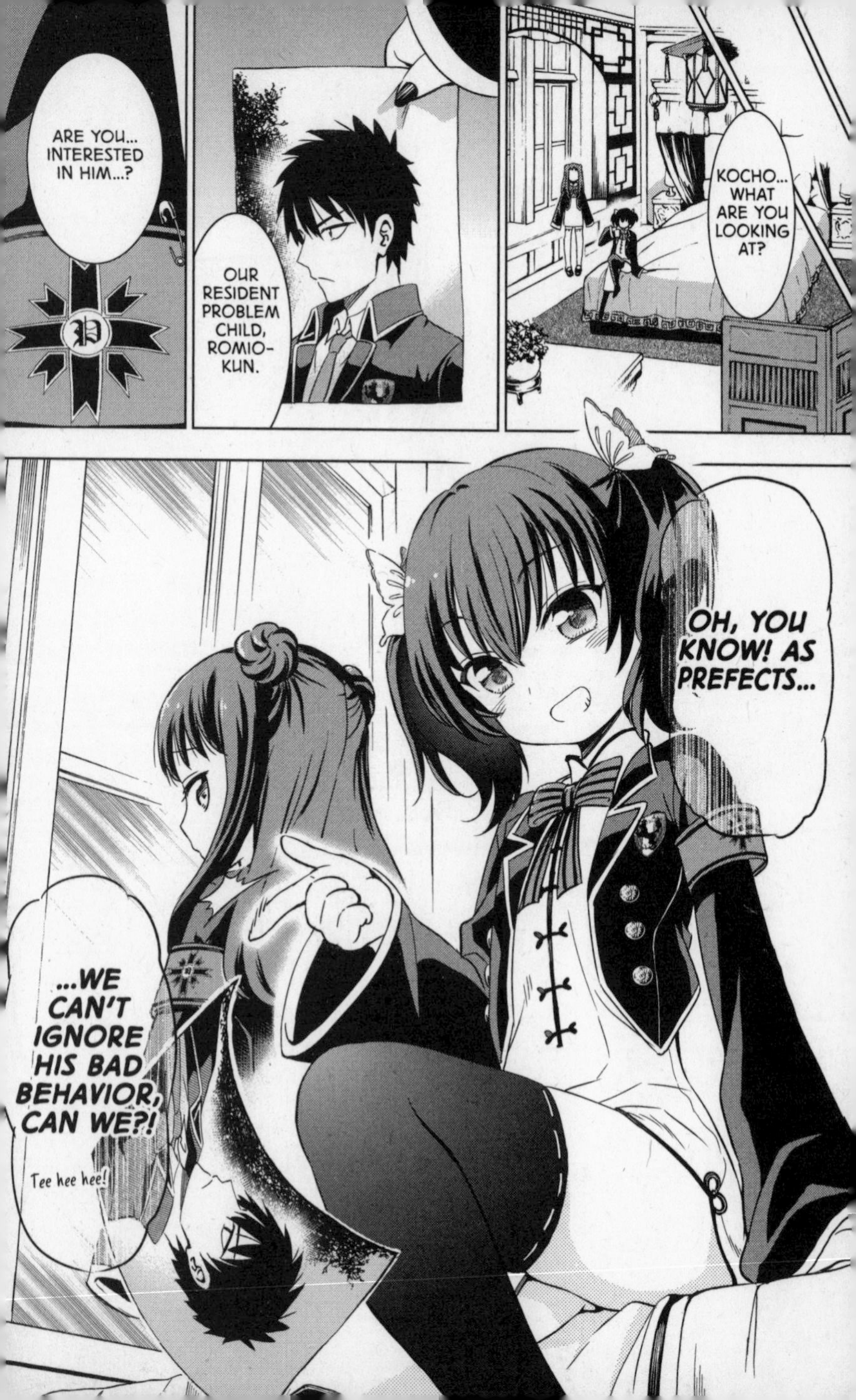
KOCHO... WHAT ARE YOU LOOKING AT?
OUR RESIDENT PROBLEM CHILD, ROMIO-KUN.
ARE YOU... INTERESTED IN HIM...?
OH, YOU KNOW! AS PREFECTS...
...WE CAN'T IGNORE HIS BAD BEHAVIOR, CAN WE?!
Tee hee hee!

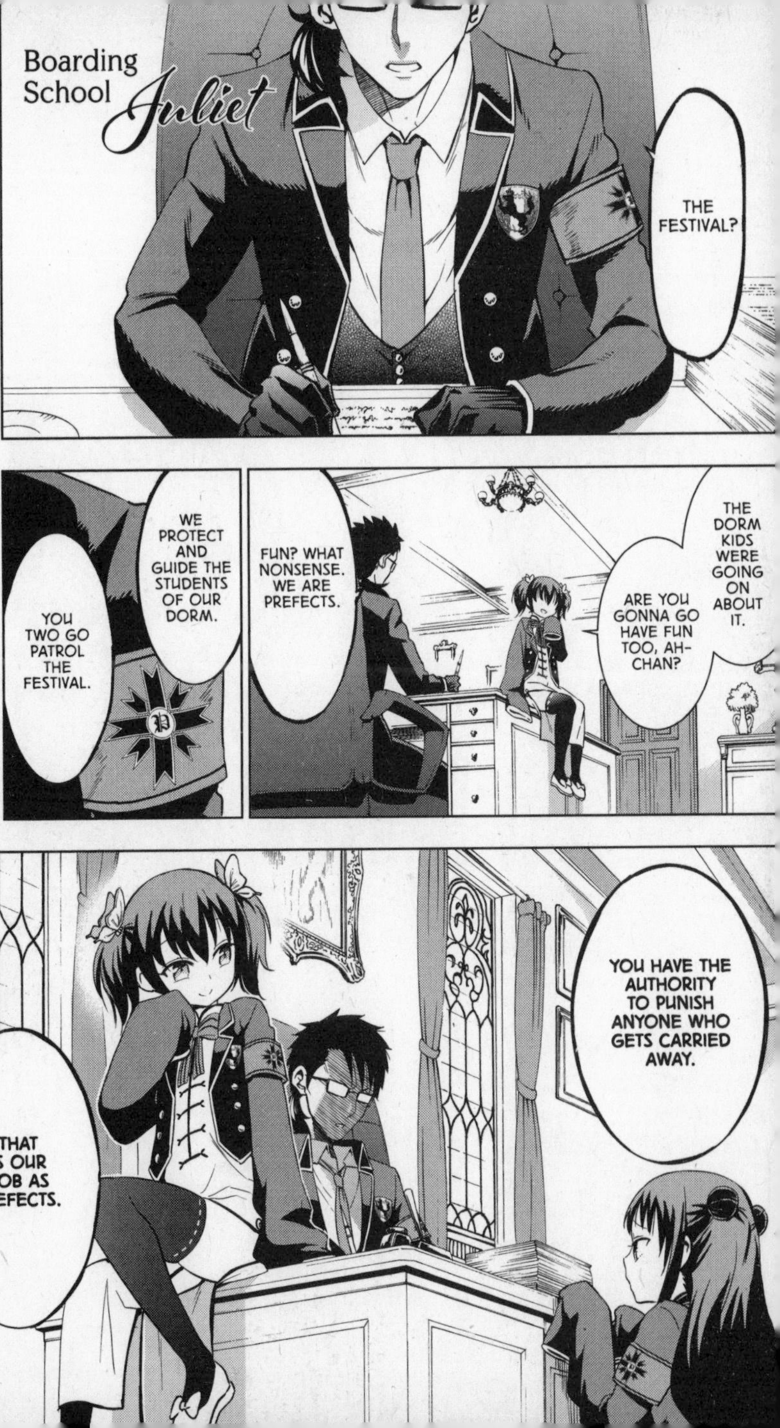
Boarding School Juliet
THE FESTIVAL?
THE DORM KIDS WERE GOING ON ABOUT IT.
ARE YOU GONNA GO HAVE FUN TOO, AH-CHAN?
FUN? WHAT NONSENSE. WE ARE PREFECTS.
WE PROTECT AND GUIDE THE STUDENTS OF OUR DORM.
YOU TWO GO PATROL THE FESTIVAL.
YOU HAVE THE AUTHORITY TO PUNISH ANYONE WHO GETS CARRIED AWAY.
THAT IS OUR JOB AS PREFECTS.

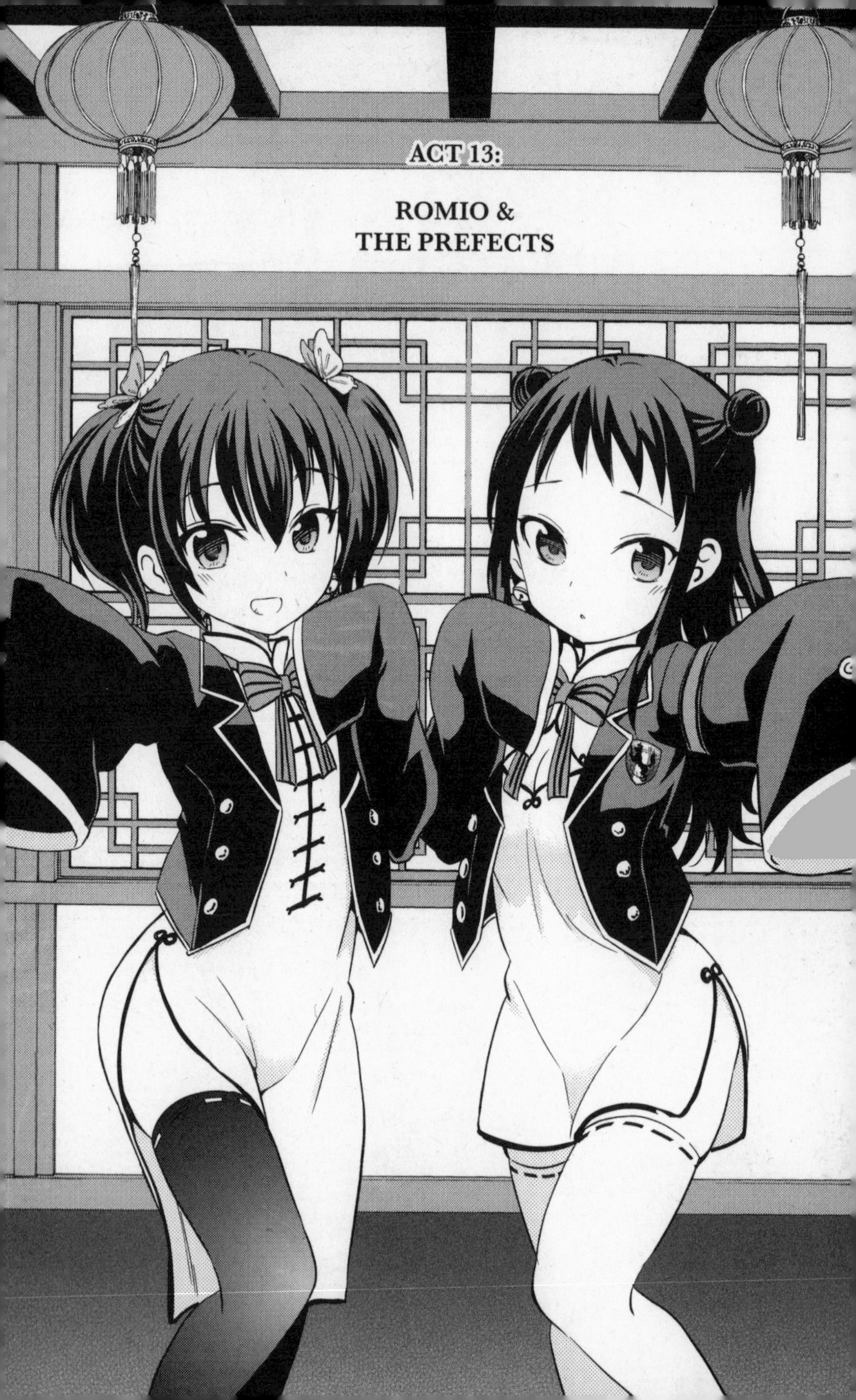
ACT 13:
ROMIO & THE PREFECTS

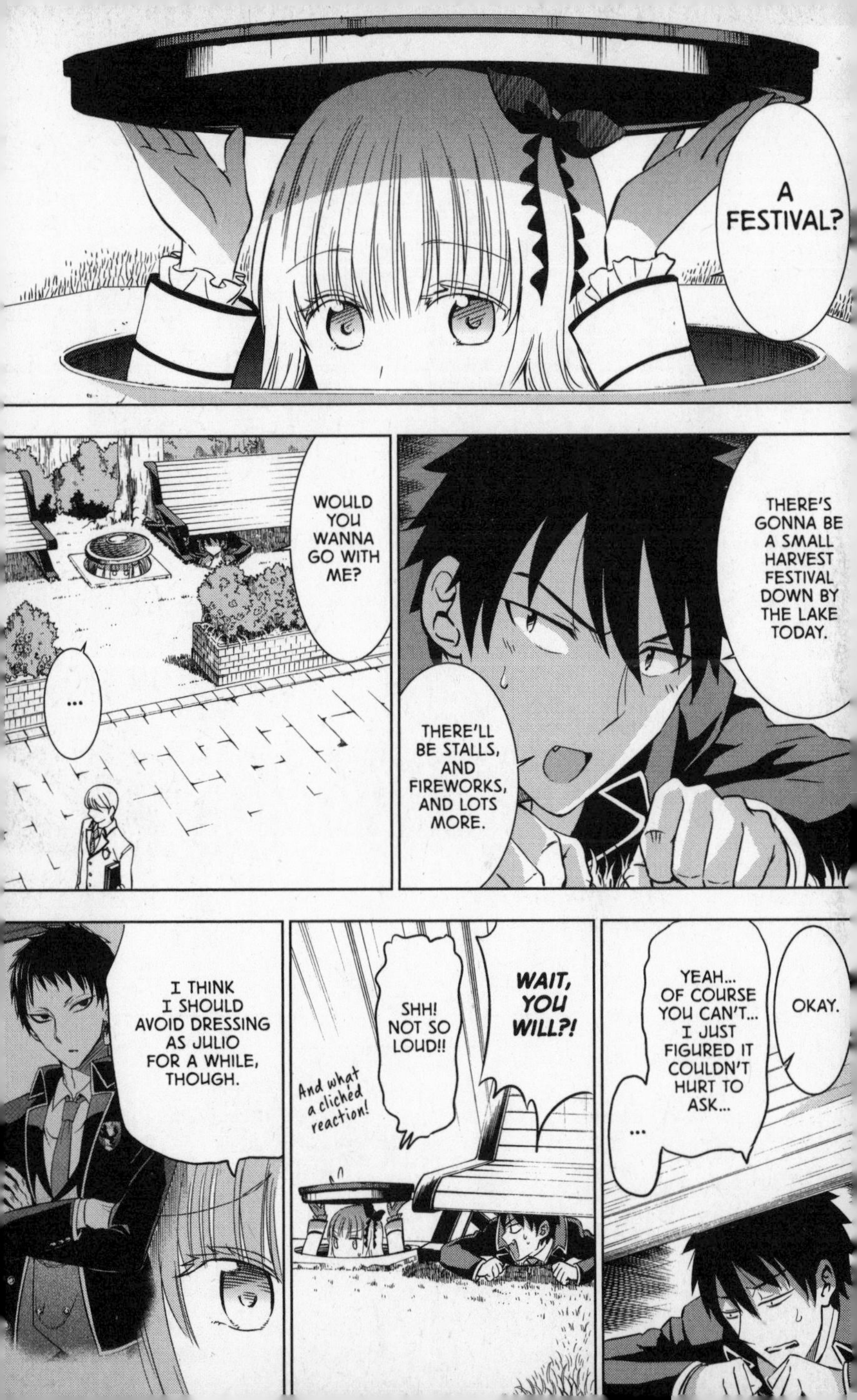
A FESTIVAL?
THERE'S GONNA BE A SMALL HARVEST FESTIVAL DOWN BY THE LAKE TODAY.
THERE'LL BE STALLS, AND FIREWORKS, AND LOTS MORE.
WOULD YOU WANNA GO WITH ME?
...
OKAY.
YEAH... OF COURSE YOU CAN'T... I JUST FIGURED IT COULDN'T HURT TO ASK...
...
WAIT, YOU WILL?!
SHH! NOT SO LOUD!!
And what a cliched reaction!
I THINK I SHOULD AVOID DRESSING AS JULIO FOR A WHILE, THOUGH.

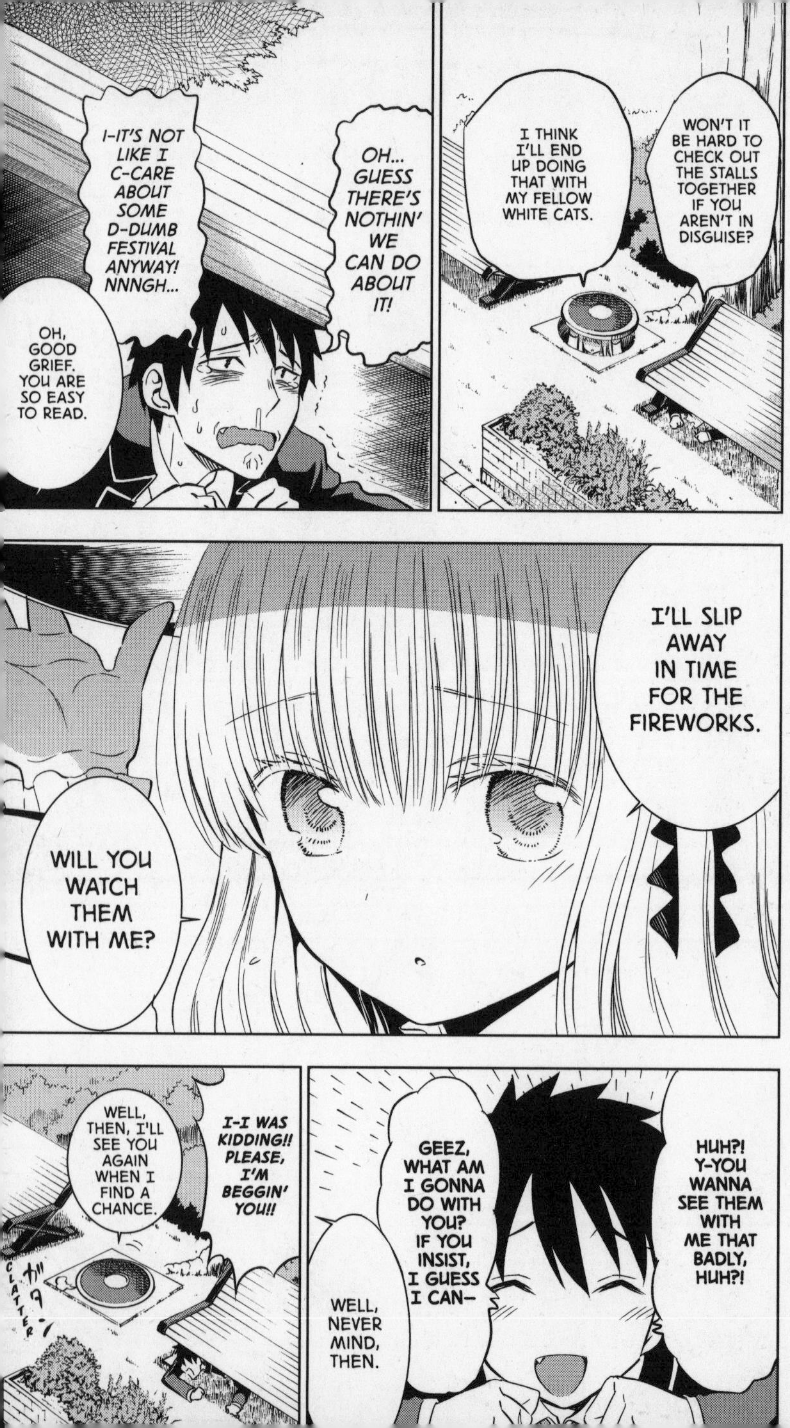
WON'T IT BE HARD TO CHECK OUT THE STALLS TOGETHER IF YOU AREN'T IN DISGUISE?
I THINK I'LL END UP DOING THAT WITH MY FELLOW WHITE CATS.
OH... GUESS THERE'S NOTHIN' WE CAN DO ABOUT IT!
I-IT'S NOT LIKE I C-CARE ABOUT SOME D-DUMB FESTIVAL ANYWAY! NNNGH...
OH, GOOD GRIEF. YOU ARE SO EASY TO READ.
I'LL SLIP AWAY IN TIME FOR THE FIREWORKS.
WILL YOU WATCH THEM WITH ME?
HUH?! Y-YOU WANNA SEE THEM WITH ME THAT BADLY, HUH?!
GEEZ, WHAT AM I GONNA DO WITH YOU? IF YOU INSIST, I GUESS I CAN–
WELL, NEVER MIND, THEN.
I-I WAS KIDDING!! PLEASE, I'M BEGGIN' YOU!!
WELL, THEN, I'LL SEE YOU AGAIN WHEN I FIND A CHANCE.
CLATTER

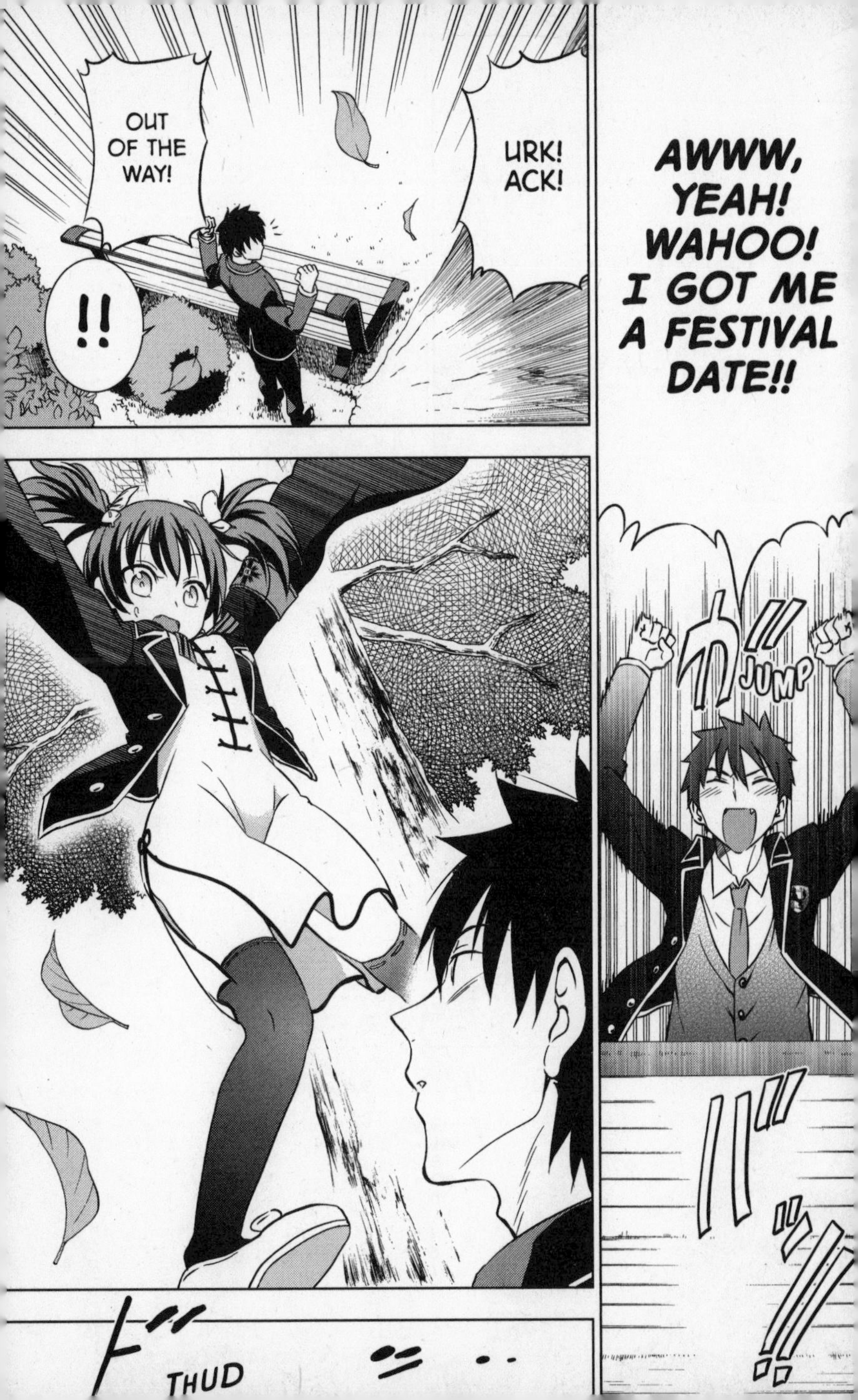
AWWW, YEAH! WAHOO! I GOT ME A FESTIVAL DATE!!
JUMP
URK! ACK!
OUT OF THE WAY!
!!
THUD

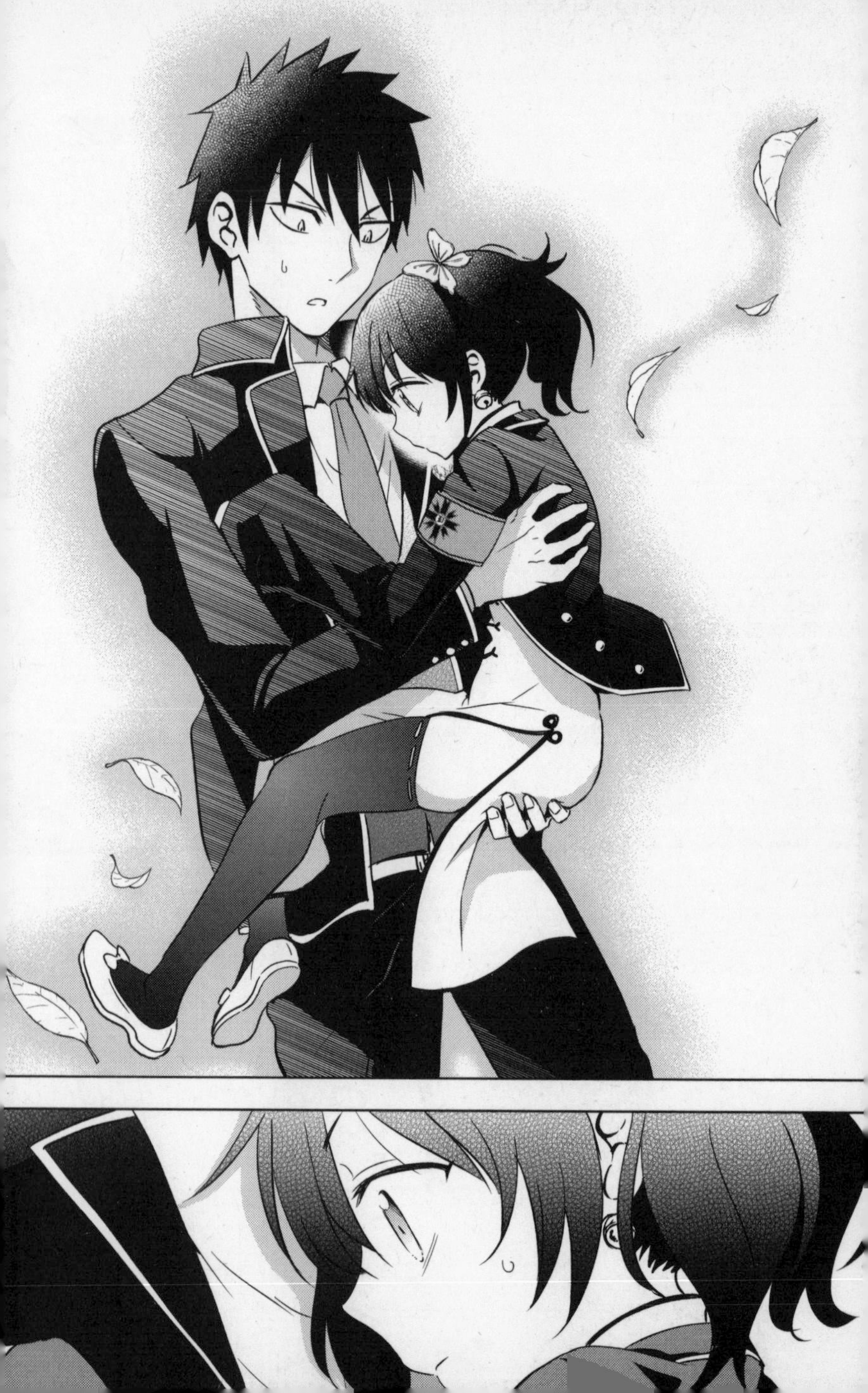

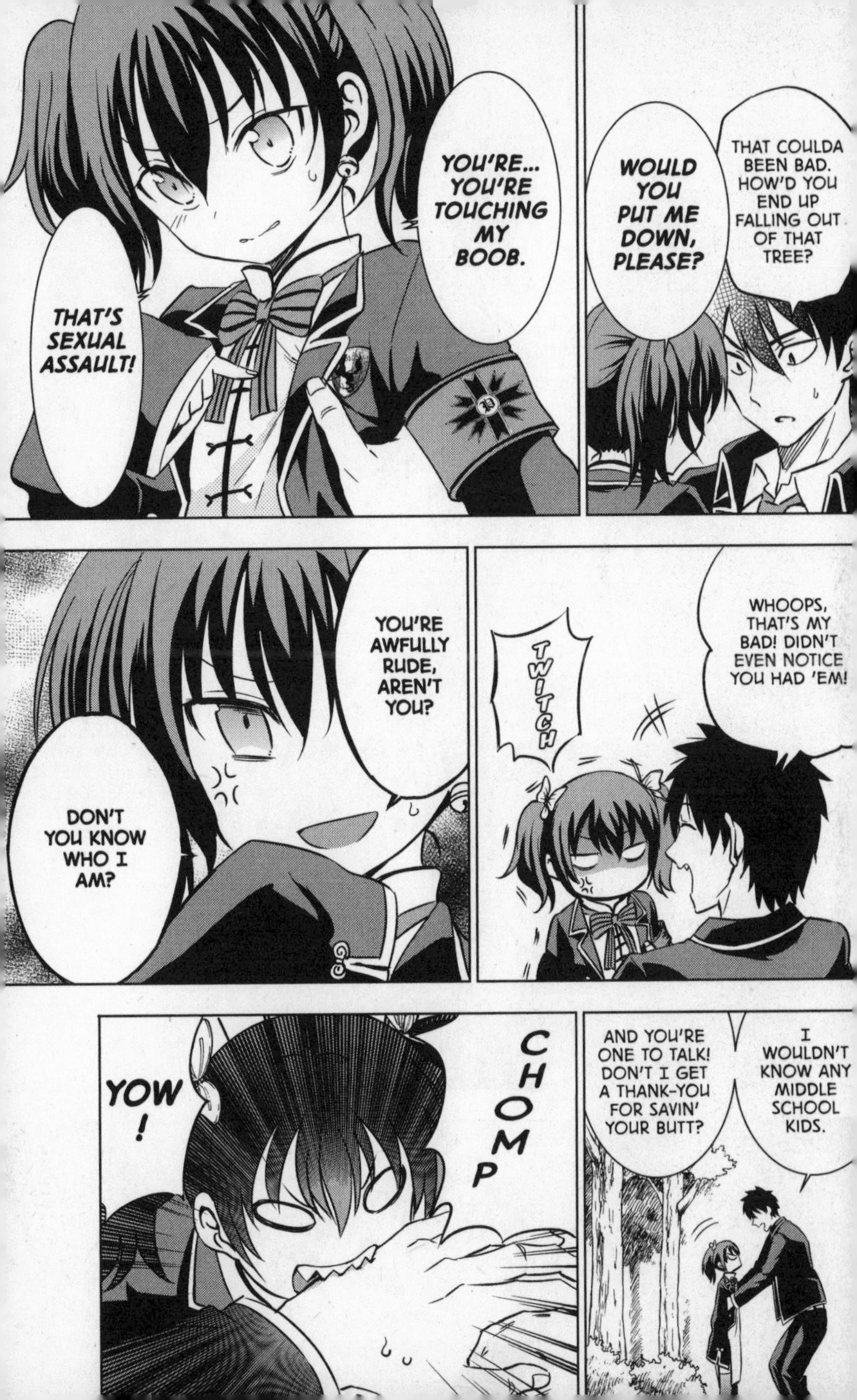
THAT COULDA BEEN BAD. HOW'D YOU END UP FALLING OUT OF THAT TREE?
WOULD YOU PUT ME DOWN, PLEASE?
YOU'RE... YOU'RE TOUCHING MY BOOB.
THAT'S SEXUAL ASSAULT!
WHOOPS, THAT'S MY BAD! DIDN'T EVEN NOTICE YOU HAD 'EM!
TWITCH
YOU'RE AWFULLY RUDE, AREN'T YOU?
DON'T YOU KNOW WHO I AM?
I WOULDN'T KNOW ANY MIDDLE SCHOOL KIDS.
AND YOU'RE ONE TO TALK! DON'T I GET A THANK-YOU FOR SAVIN' YOUR BUTT?
CHOMP
YOW!

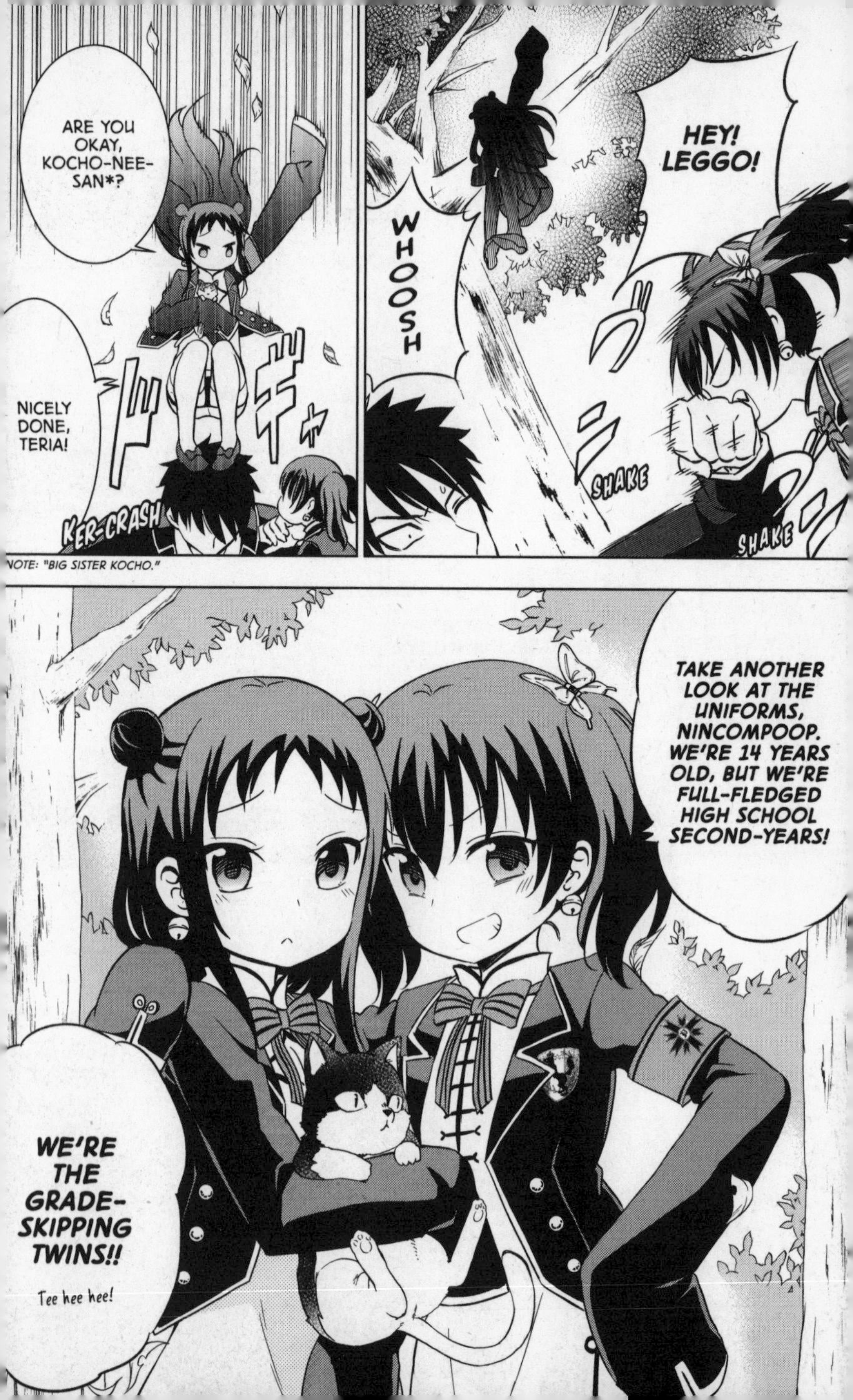
HEY! LEGGO!
WHOOSH
SHAKE
SHAKE
ARE YOU OKAY, KOCHO-NEE-SAN*?
ド
ギャ
NICELY DONE, TERIA!
KER-CRASH
NOTE: "BIG SISTER KOCHO."
TAKE ANOTHER LOOK AT THE UNIFORMS, NINCOMPOOP. WE'RE 14 YEARS OLD, BUT WE'RE FULL-FLEDGED HIGH SCHOOL SECOND-YEARS!
WE'RE THE GRADE-SKIPPING TWINS!!
Tee hee hee!

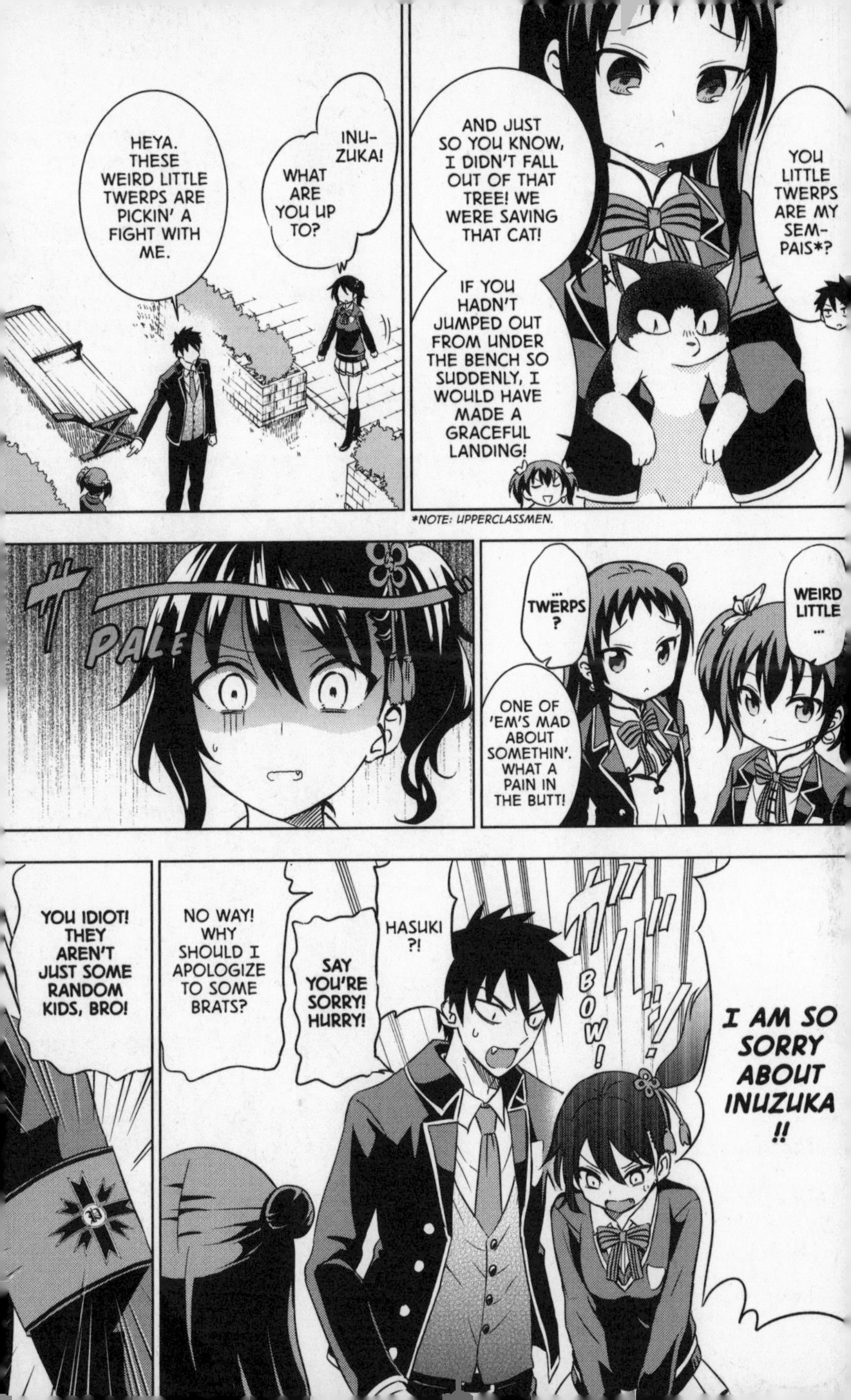
YOU LITTLE TWERPS ARE MY SEMPAIS*?
AND JUST SO YOU KNOW, I DIDN'T FALL OUT OF THAT TREE! WE WERE SAVING THAT CAT!
IF YOU HADN'T JUMPED OUT FROM UNDER THE BENCH SO SUDDENLY, I WOULD HAVE MADE A GRACEFUL LANDING!
INU-ZUKA!
WHAT ARE YOU UP TO?
HEYA. THESE WEIRD LITTLE TWERPS ARE PICKIN' A FIGHT WITH ME.
*NOTE: UPPERCLASSMEN.
WEIRD LITTLE ...
... TWERPS ?
ONE OF 'EM'S MAD ABOUT SOMETHIN'. WHAT A PAIN IN THE BUTT!
PALE
I AM SO SORRY ABOUT INUZUKA !!
BOW!
HASUKI ?!
SAY YOU'RE SORRY! HURRY!
NO WAY! WHY SHOULD I APOLOGIZE TO SOME BRATS?
YOU IDIOT! THEY AREN'T JUST SOME RANDOM KIDS, BRO!

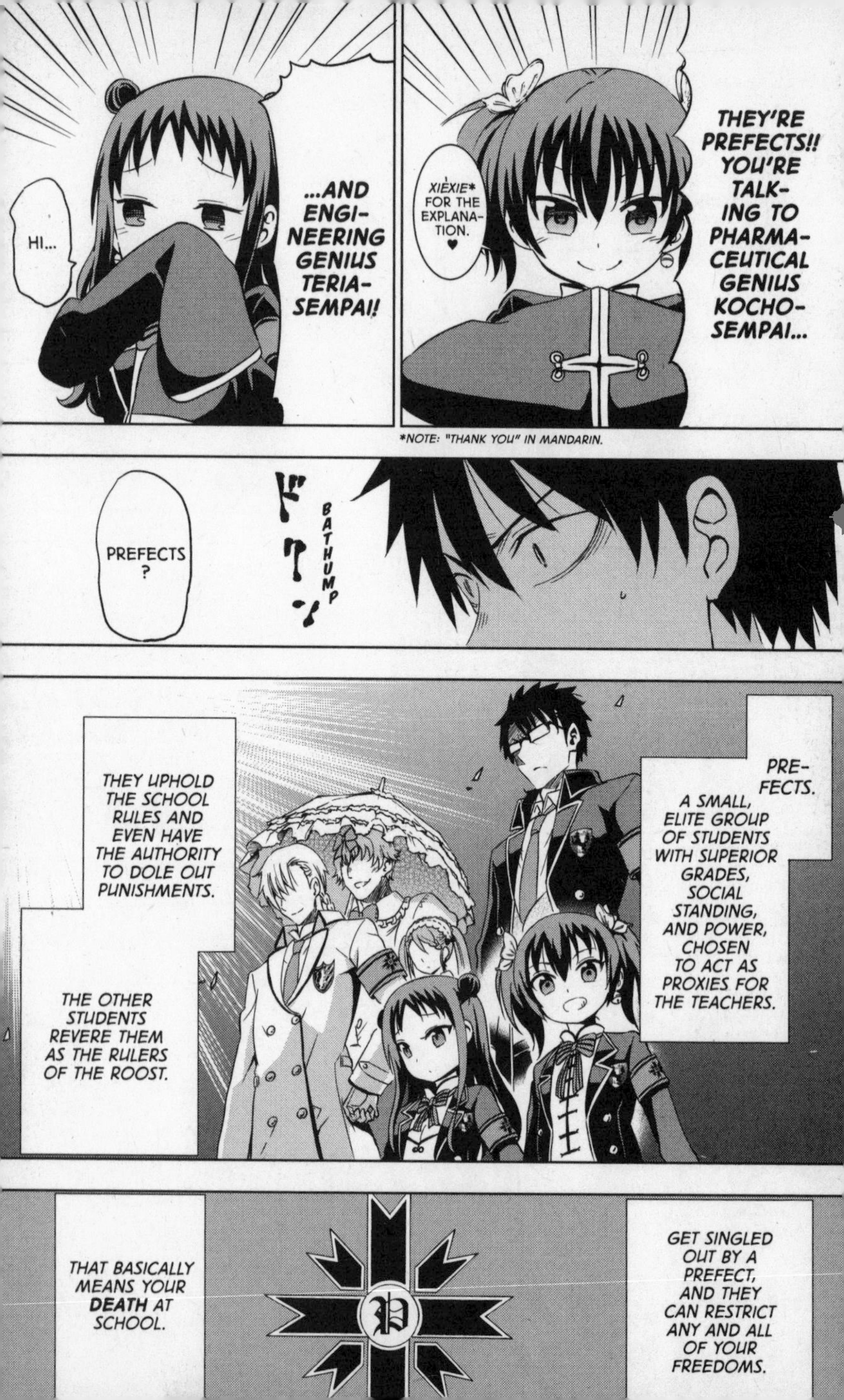
THEY'RE PREFECTS!! YOU'RE TALKING TO PHARMACEUTICAL GENIUS KOCHO-SEMPAI...
XIEXIE* FOR THE EXPLANATION. ♥
...AND ENGINEERING GENIUS TERIA-SEMPAI!
HI...
*NOTE: "THANK YOU" IN MANDARIN.
BATHUMP
PREFECTS?
PREFECTS. A SMALL, ELITE GROUP OF STUDENTS WITH SUPERIOR GRADES, SOCIAL STANDING, AND POWER, CHOSEN TO ACT AS PROXIES FOR THE TEACHERS.
THEY UPHOLD THE SCHOOL RULES AND EVEN HAVE THE AUTHORITY TO DOLE OUT PUNISHMENTS.
THE OTHER STUDENTS REVERE THEM AS THE RULERS OF THE ROOST.
GET SINGLED OUT BY A PREFECT, AND THEY CAN RESTRICT ANY AND ALL OF YOUR FREEDOMS.
THAT BASICALLY MEANS YOUR **DEATH** AT SCHOOL.

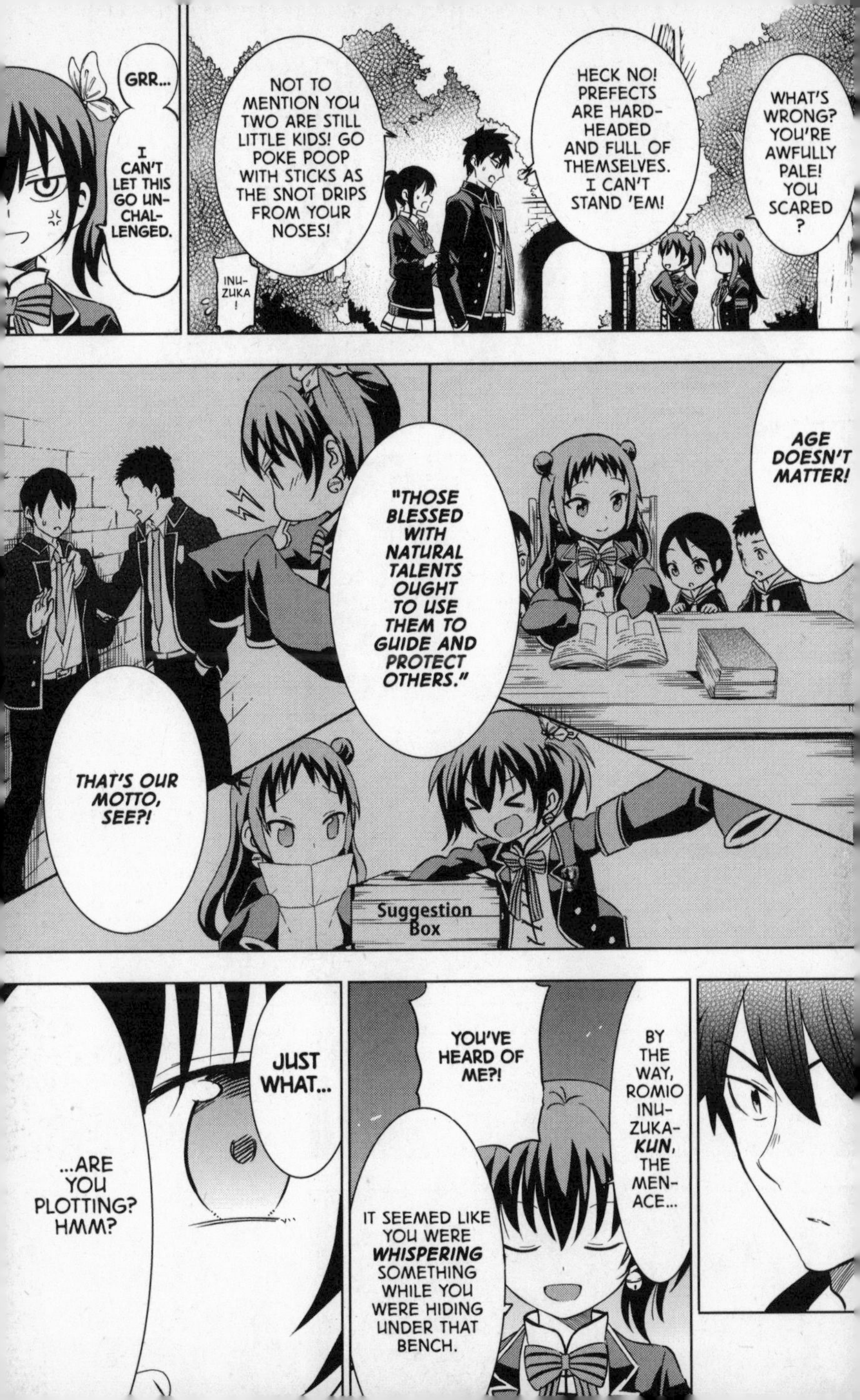
WHAT'S WRONG? YOU'RE AWFULLY PALE! YOU SCARED?
HECK NO! PREFECTS ARE HARD-HEADED AND FULL OF THEMSELVES. I CAN'T STAND 'EM!
NOT TO MENTION YOU TWO ARE STILL LITTLE KIDS! GO POKE POOP WITH STICKS AS THE SNOT DRIPS FROM YOUR NOSES!
INU-ZUKA!
GRR...
I CAN'T LET THIS GO UN-CHAL-LENGED.
AGE DOESN'T MATTER!
"THOSE BLESSED WITH NATURAL TALENTS OUGHT TO USE THEM TO GUIDE AND PROTECT OTHERS."
THAT'S OUR MOTTO, SEE?!
Suggestion Box
BY THE WAY, ROMIO INU-ZUKA-KUN, THE MEN-ACE...
YOU'VE HEARD OF ME?!
IT SEEMED LIKE YOU WERE WHISPERING SOMETHING WHILE YOU WERE HIDING UNDER THAT BENCH.
JUST WHAT...
...ARE YOU PLOTTING? HMM?

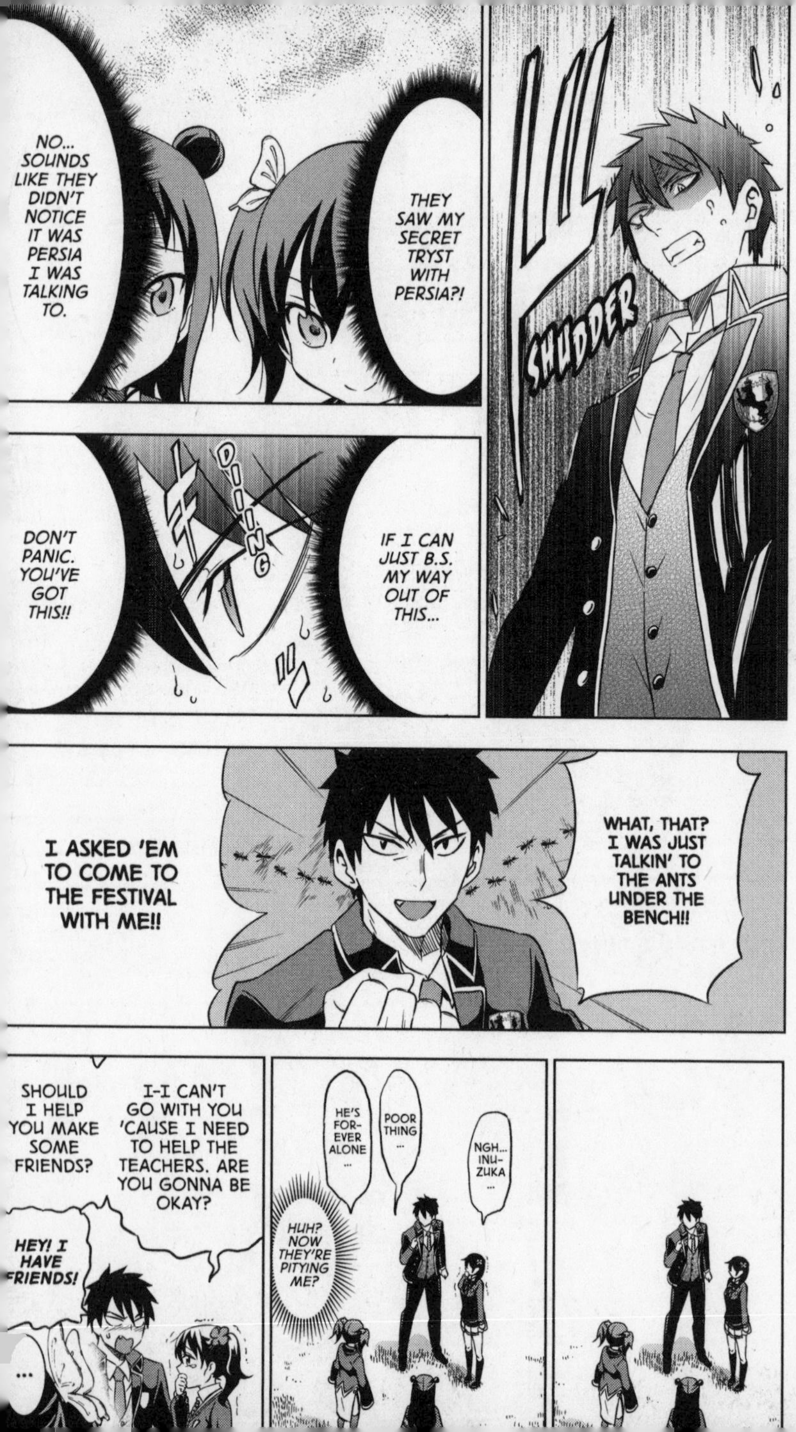

SHUDDER
THEY SAW MY SECRET TRYST WITH PERSIA?!
NO... SOUNDS LIKE THEY DIDN'T NOTICE IT WAS PERSIA I WAS TALKING TO.
IF I CAN JUST B.S. MY WAY OUT OF THIS...
DIIING
DON'T PANIC. YOU'VE GOT THIS!!
WHAT, THAT? I WAS JUST TALKIN' TO THE ANTS UNDER THE BENCH!!
I ASKED 'EM TO COME TO THE FESTIVAL WITH ME!!
NGH... INUZUKA ...
POOR THING ...
HE'S FOREVER ALONE ...
HUH? NOW THEY'RE PITYING ME?
I-I CAN'T GO WITH YOU 'CAUSE I NEED TO HELP THE TEACHERS. ARE YOU GONNA BE OKAY?
SHOULD I HELP YOU MAKE SOME FRIENDS?
HEY! I HAVE FRIENDS!
...

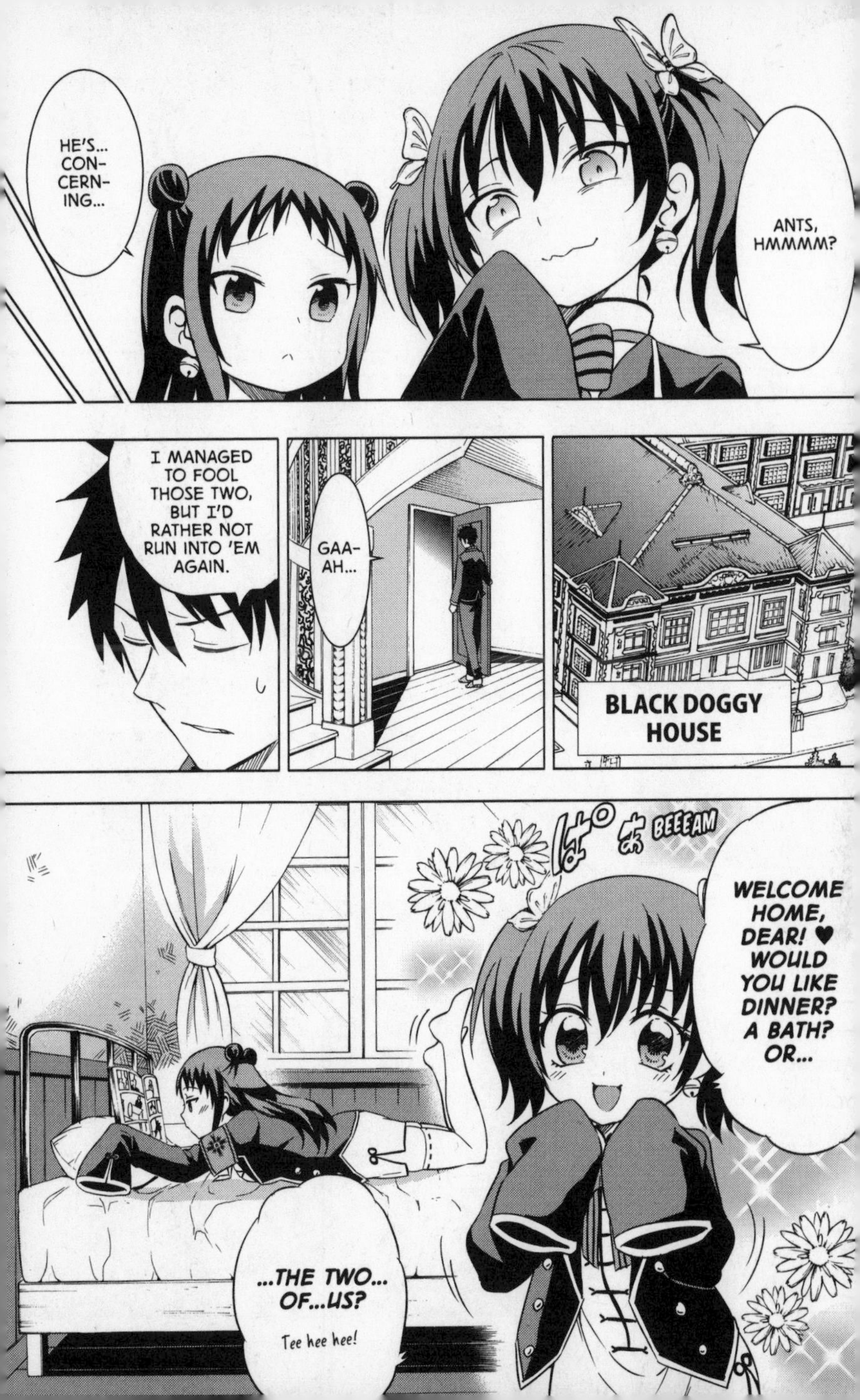
ANTS, HMMMM?
HE'S... CON-CERN-ING...
BLACK DOGGY HOUSE
GAA-AH...
I MANAGED TO FOOL THOSE TWO, BUT I'D RATHER NOT RUN INTO 'EM AGAIN.
ぱぁ BEEEAM
WELCOME HOME, DEAR! ♥ WOULD YOU LIKE DINNER? A BATH? OR...
...THE TWO... OF...US?
Tee hee hee!

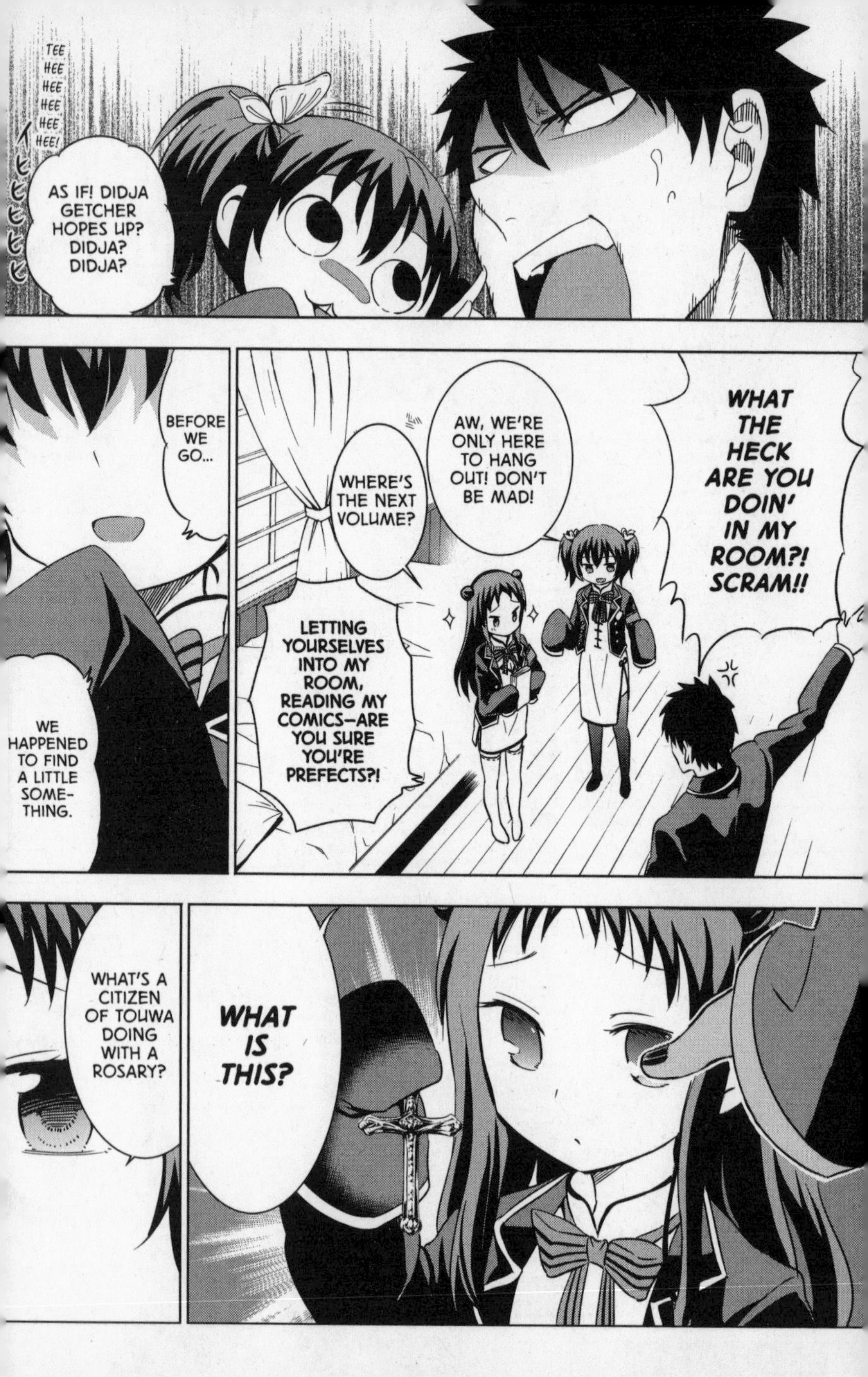
TEE HEE HEE HEE HEE HEE!
AS IF! DIDJA GETCHER HOPES UP? DIDJA? DIDJA?
WHAT THE HECK ARE YOU DOIN' IN MY ROOM?! SCRAM!!
AW, WE'RE ONLY HERE TO HANG OUT! DON'T BE MAD!
WHERE'S THE NEXT VOLUME?
LETTING YOURSELVES INTO MY ROOM, READING MY COMICS—ARE YOU SURE YOU'RE PREFECTS?!
BEFORE WE GO...
WE HAPPENED TO FIND A LITTLE SOMETHING.
WHAT IS THIS?
WHAT'S A CITIZEN OF TOUWA DOING WITH A ROSARY?

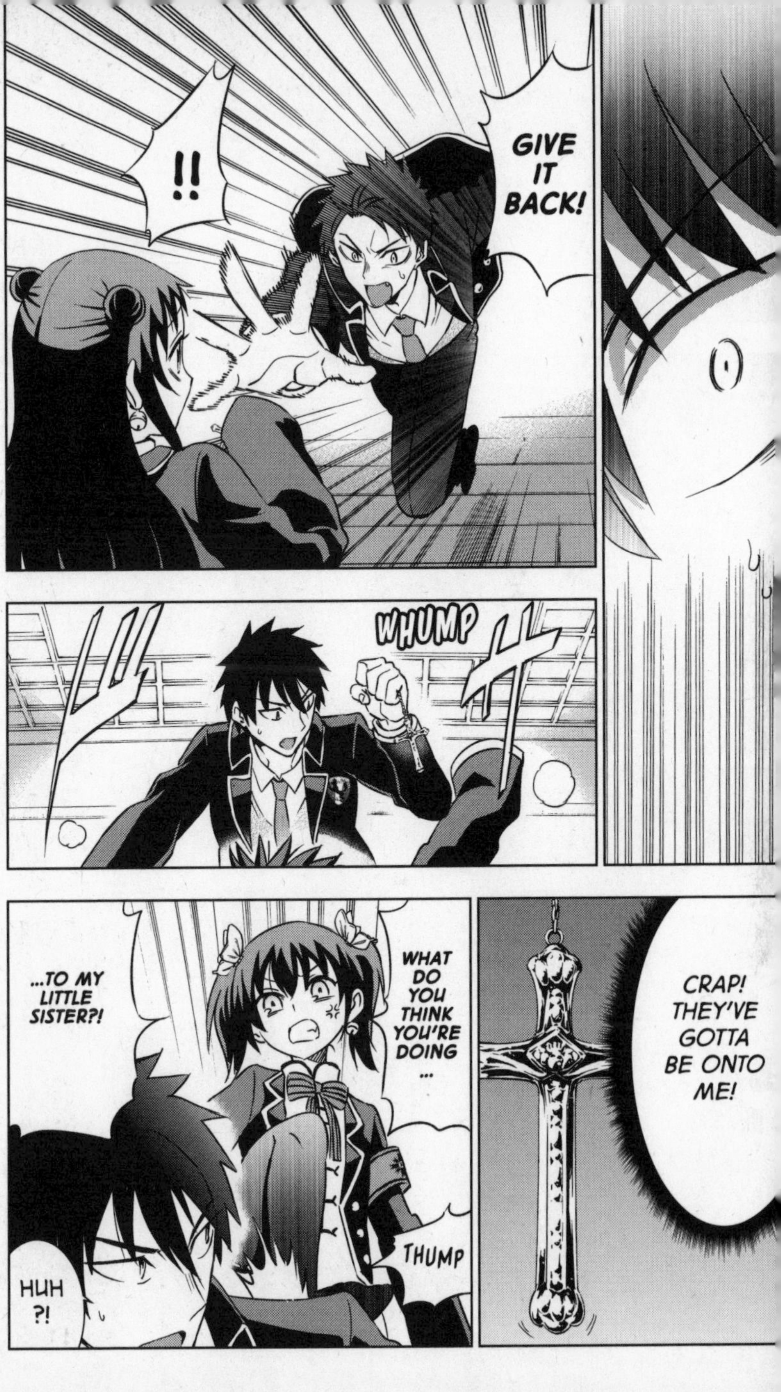
GIVE IT BACK!
!!
WHUMP
CRAP! THEY'VE GOTTA BE ONTO ME!
WHAT DO YOU THINK YOU'RE DOING ...
...TO MY LITTLE SISTER?!
THUMP
HUH ?!

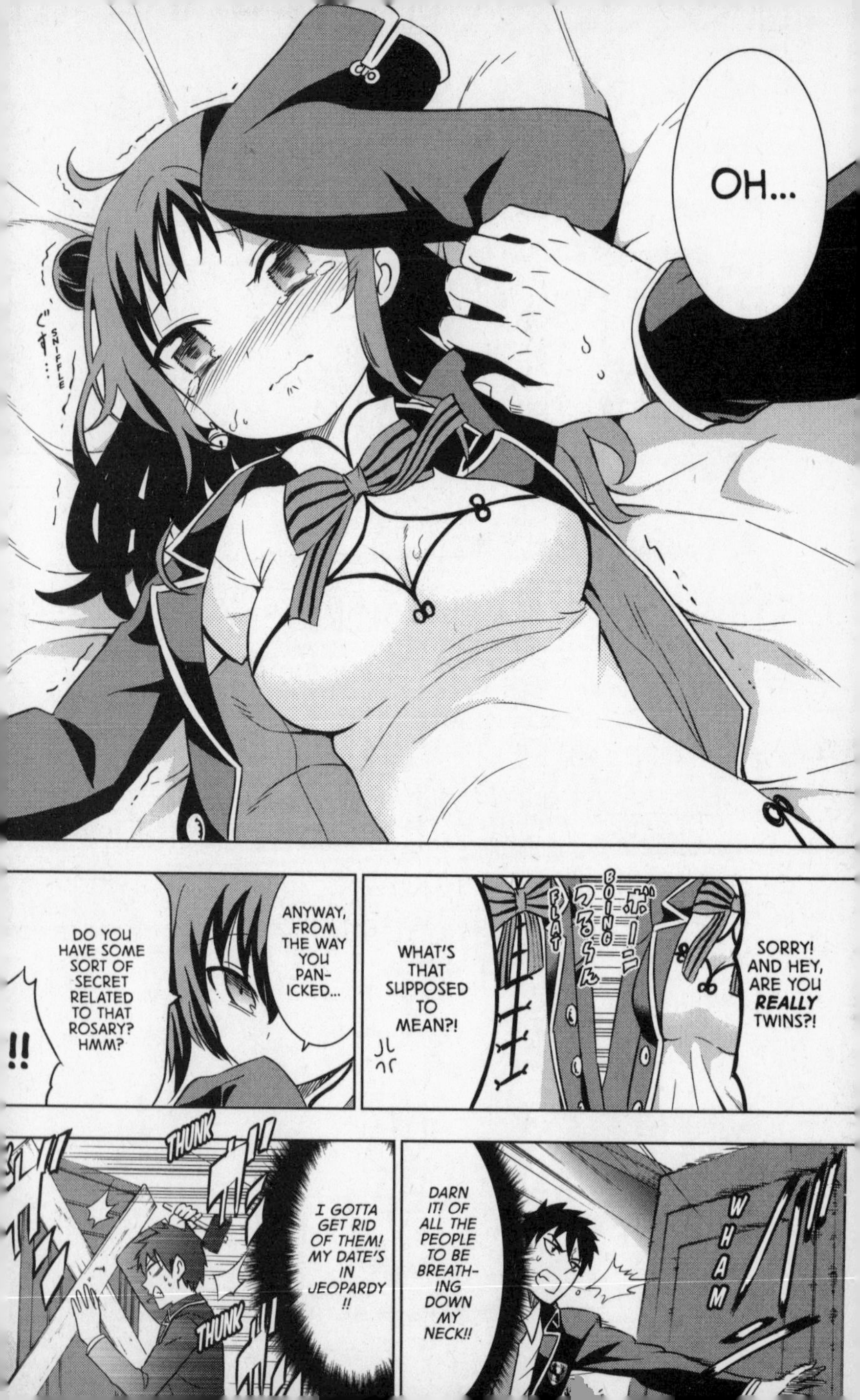

OH...
ぐす…
SNIFFLE
SORRY! AND HEY, ARE YOU *REALLY* TWINS?!
BOING
FLAT
WHAT'S THAT SUPPOSED TO MEAN?!
ANYWAY, FROM THE WAY YOU PAN-ICKED...
DO YOU HAVE SOME SORT OF SECRET RELATED TO THAT ROSARY? HMM?
!!
WHAM
DARN IT! OF ALL THE PEOPLE TO BE BREATH-ING DOWN MY NECK!!
I GOTTA GET RID OF THEM! MY DATE'S IN JEOPARDY !!
THUNK
THUNK

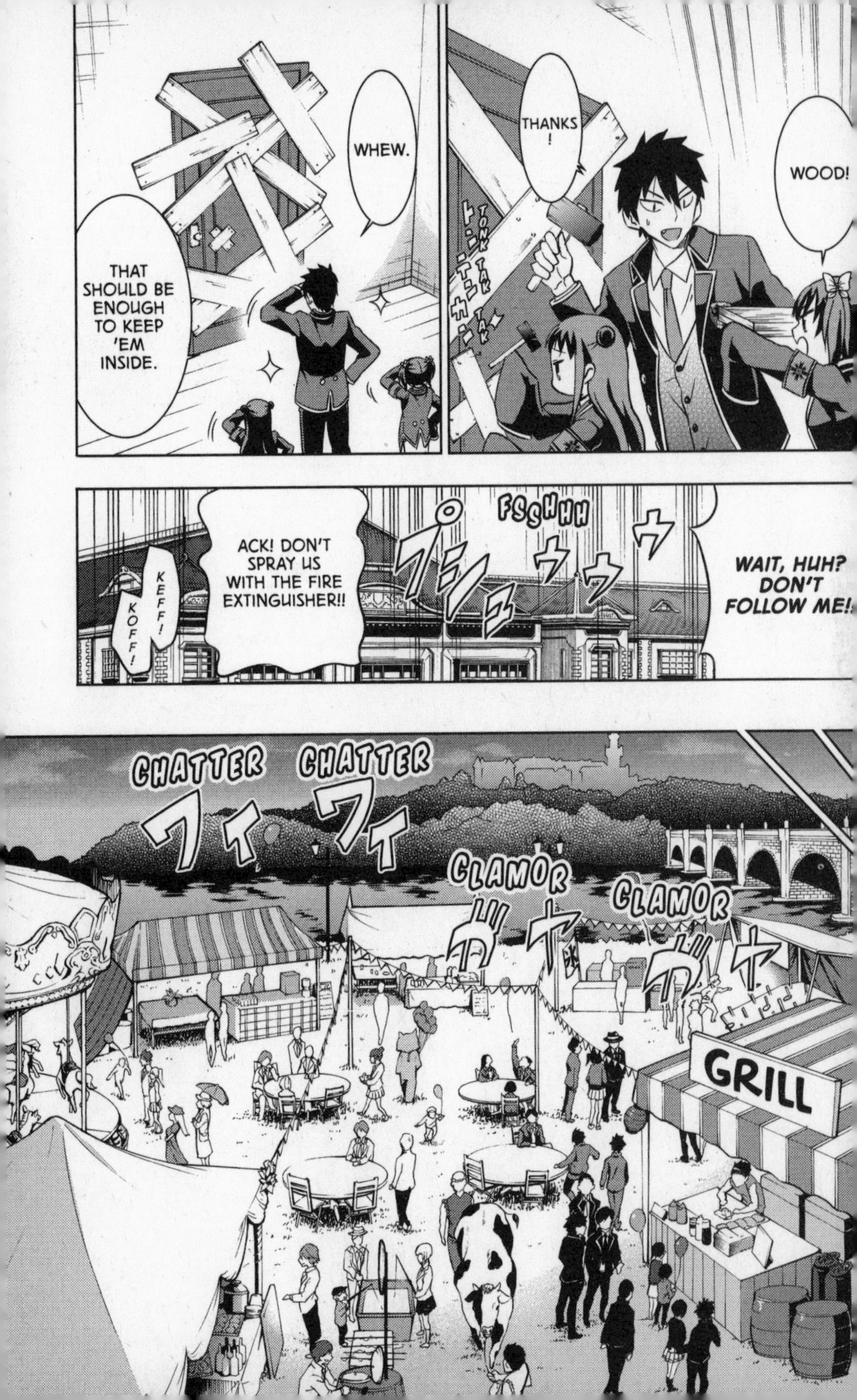
WOOD!
THANKS!
TONK TAK TAK
WHEW.
THAT SHOULD BE ENOUGH TO KEEP 'EM INSIDE.
WAIT, HUH? DON'T FOLLOW ME!!
FSSHHH
ACK! DON'T SPRAY US WITH THE FIRE EXTINGUISHER!!
KEFF! KOFF!
CHATTER CHATTER
CLAMOR CLAMOR
GRILL

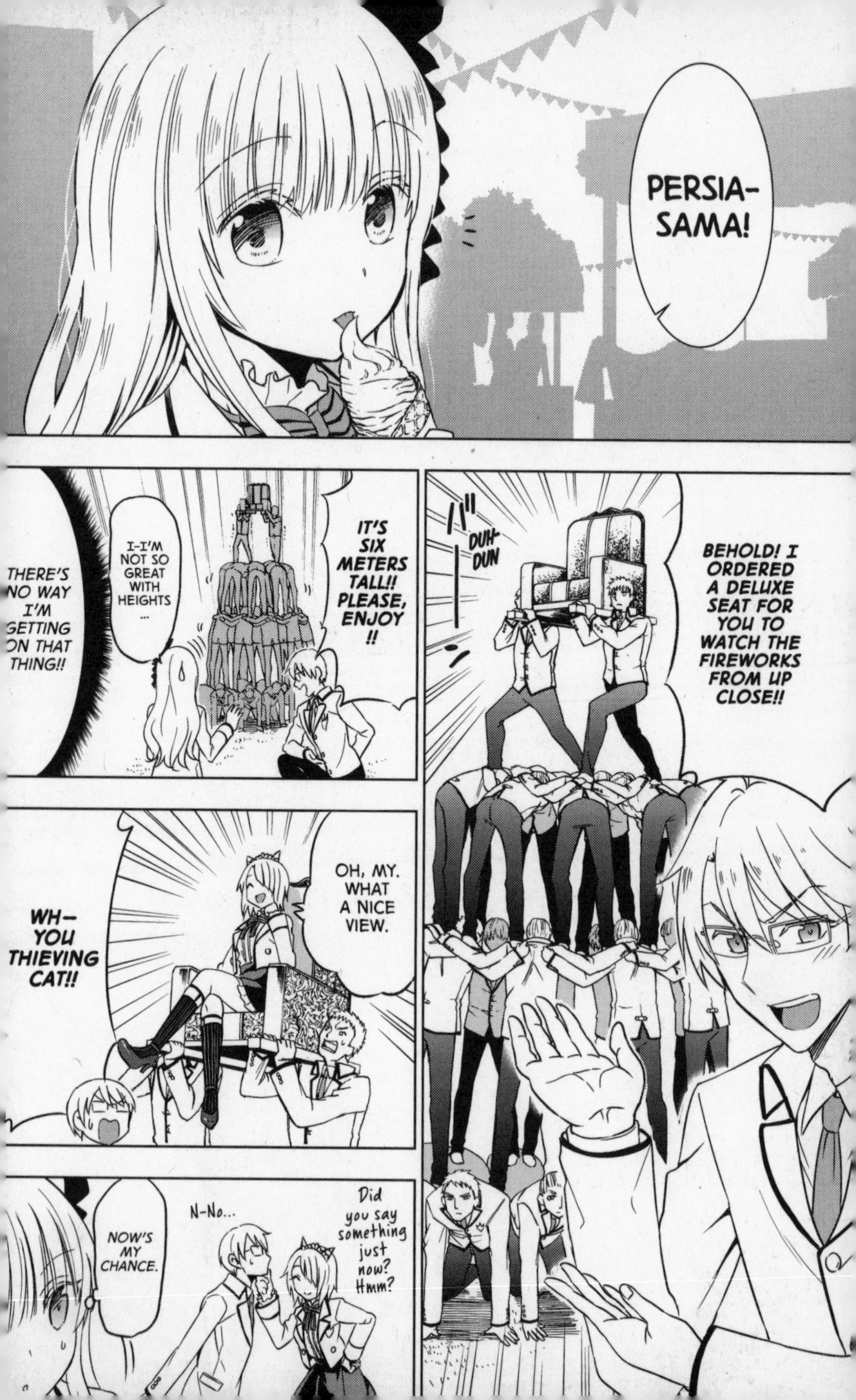
PERSIA-SAMA!
DUH-DUN
BEHOLD! I ORDERED A DELUXE SEAT FOR YOU TO WATCH THE FIREWORKS FROM UP CLOSE!!
IT'S SIX METERS TALL!! PLEASE, ENJOY!!
I-I'M NOT SO GREAT WITH HEIGHTS...
THERE'S NO WAY I'M GETTING ON THAT THING!!
OH, MY. WHAT A NICE VIEW.
WH— YOU THIEVING CAT!!
Did you say something just now? Hmm?
N-No...
NOW'S MY CHANCE.

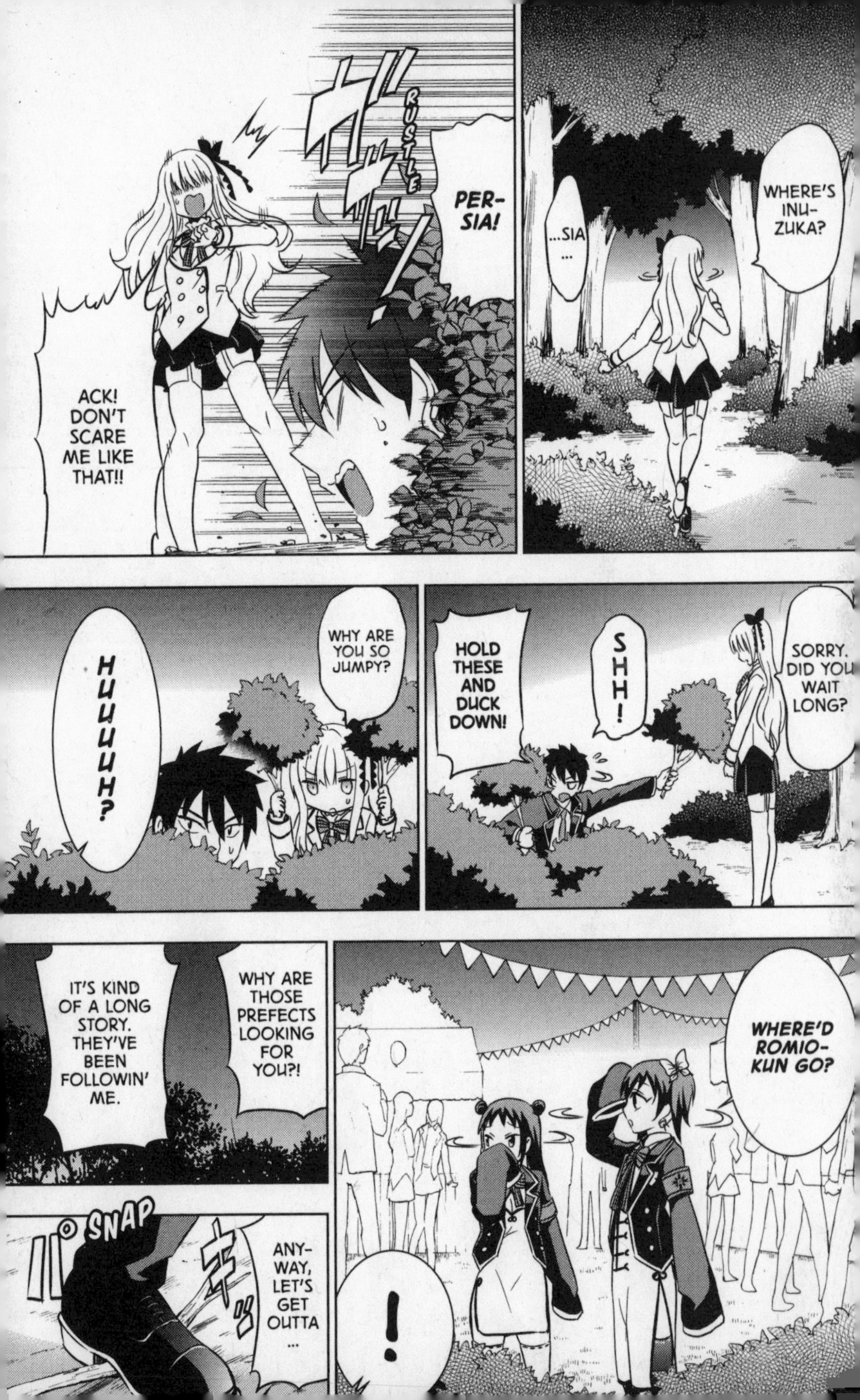

WHERE'S INU-ZUKA?
...SIA ...
PER-SIA!
RUSTLE
ACK! DON'T SCARE ME LIKE THAT!!
SORRY. DID YOU WAIT LONG?
SHH!
HOLD THESE AND DUCK DOWN!
WHY ARE YOU SO JUMPY?
HUUUUUH?
WHERE'D ROMIO-KUN GO?
!
WHY ARE THOSE PREFECTS LOOKING FOR YOU?!
IT'S KIND OF A LONG STORY. THEY'VE BEEN FOLLOWIN' ME.
ANY-WAY, LET'S GET OUTTA ...
SNAP

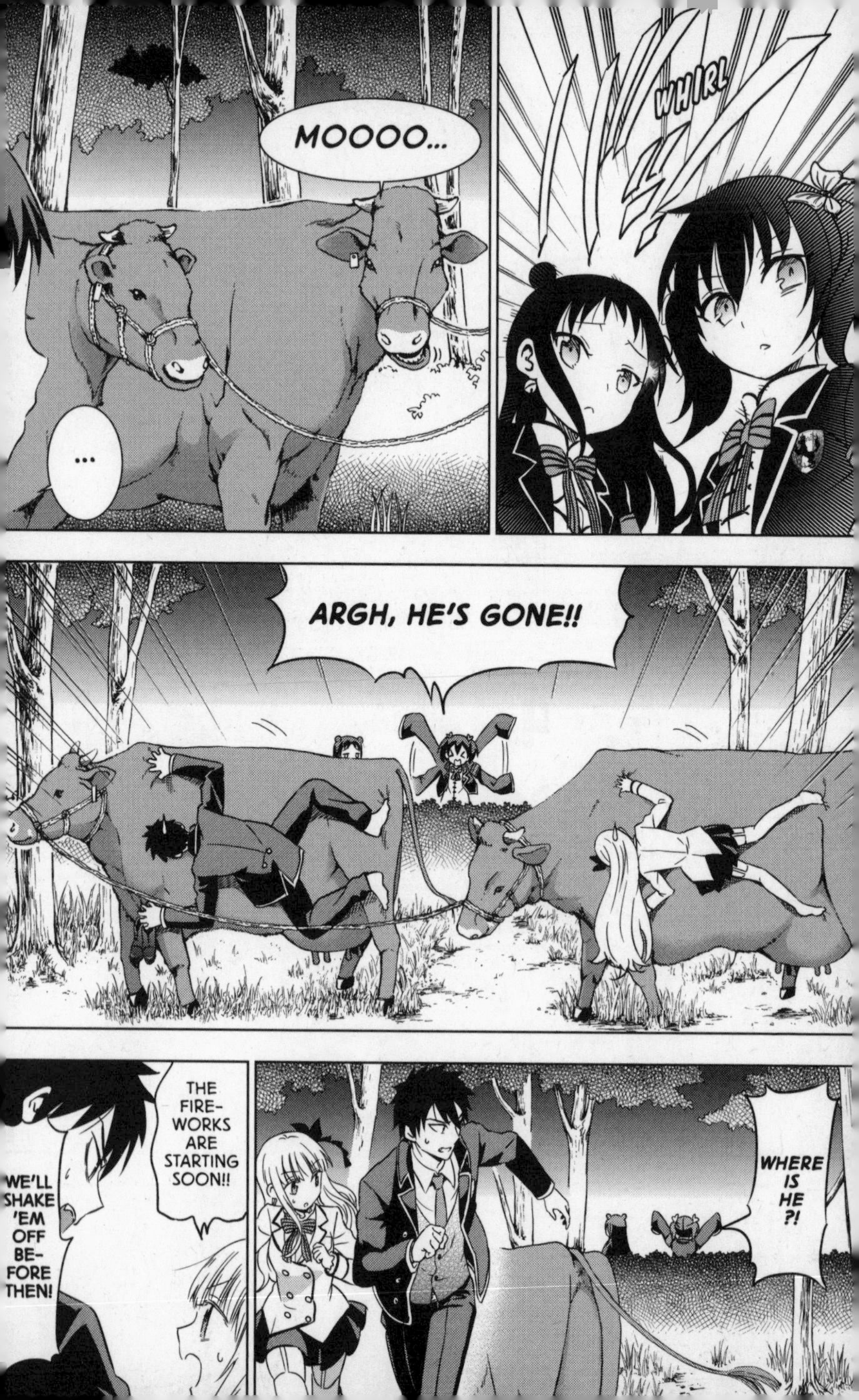
WHIRL
MOOOO...
...
ARGH, HE'S GONE!!
WHERE IS HE?!
THE FIRE-WORKS ARE STARTING SOON!!
WE'LL SHAKE 'EM OFF BE-FORE THEN!

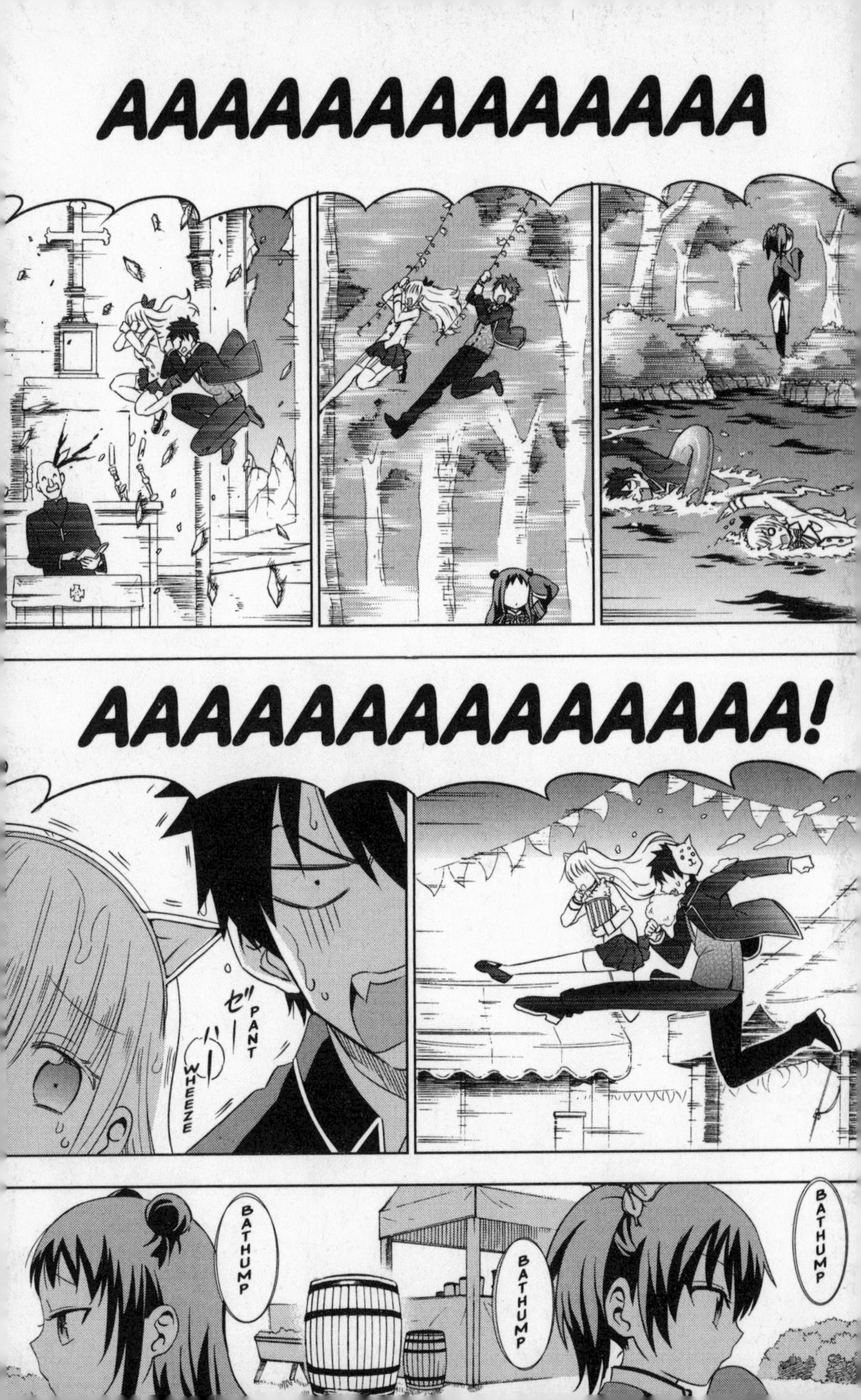
AAAAAAAAAAAAA
AAAAAAAAAAAAAA!
ゼ" PANT
ハ WHEEZE
BATHUMP
BATHUMP
BATHUMP

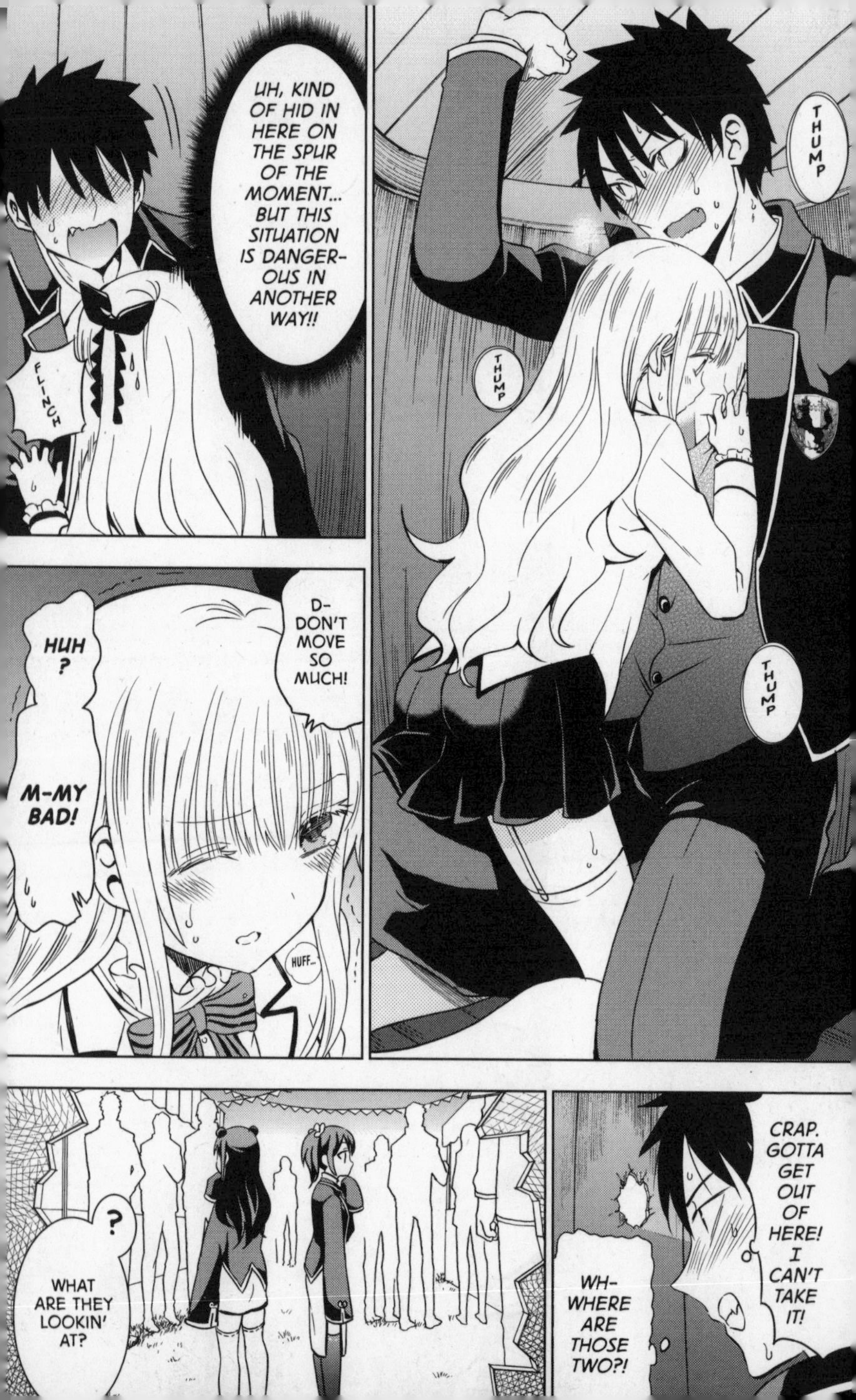
THUMP
THUMP
THUMP
UH, KIND OF HID IN HERE ON THE SPUR OF THE MOMENT... BUT THIS SITUATION IS DANGER-OUS IN ANOTHER WAY!!
FLINCH
D-DON'T MOVE SO MUCH!
HUH?
M-MY BAD!
HUFF...
CRAP. GOTTA GET OUT OF HERE! I CAN'T TAKE IT!
WH-WHERE ARE THOSE TWO?!
?
WHAT ARE THEY LOOKIN' AT?

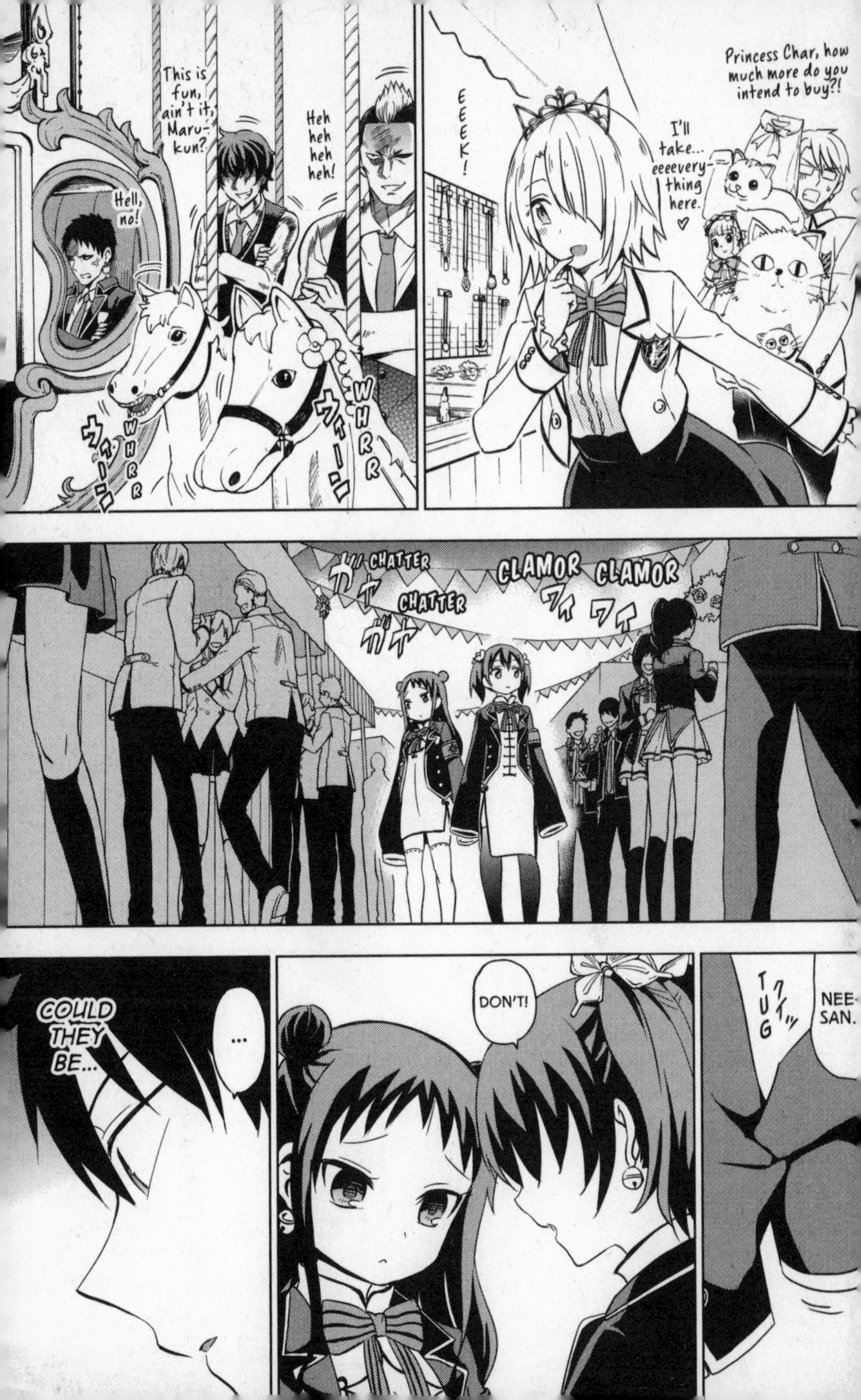
Princess Char, how much more do you intend to buy?!
I'll take... eeeevery-thing here. ♡
EEEEK!
Heh heh heh heh!
This is fun, ain't it, Maru-kun?
Hell, no!
WHRR
WHRR
CLAMOR CLAMOR
CHATTER
CHATTER
NEE-SAN.
TUG
DON'T!
...
COULD THEY BE...

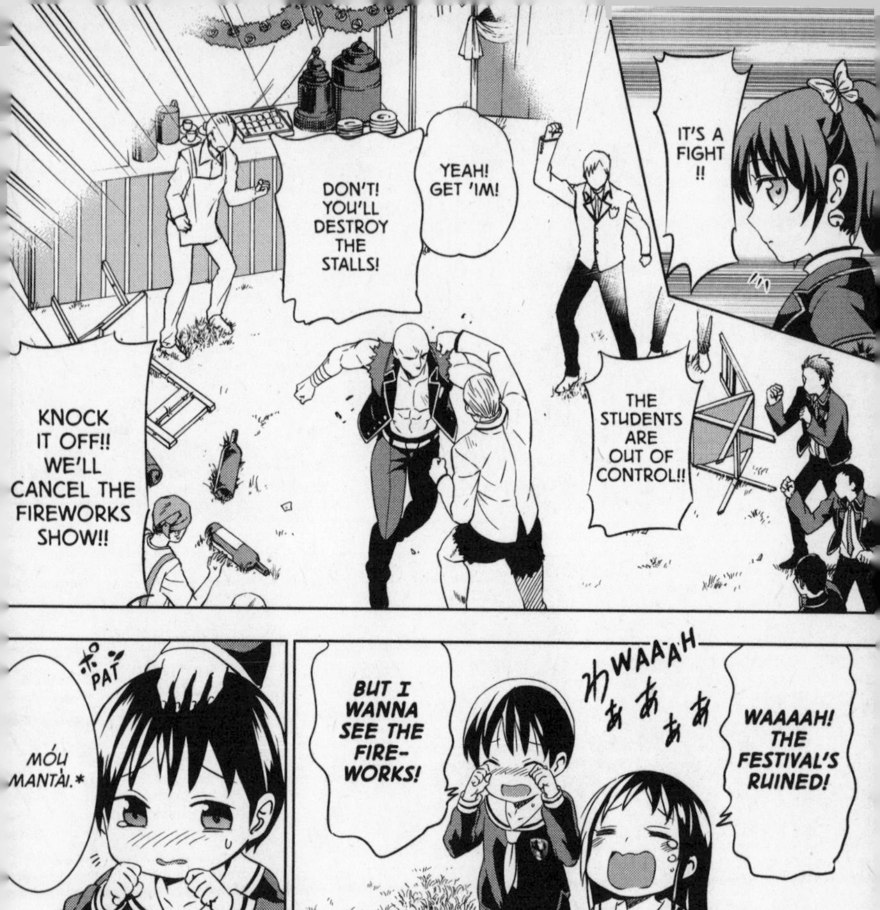
IT'S A FIGHT !!
YEAH! GET 'IM!
DON'T! YOU'LL DESTROY THE STALLS!
THE STUDENTS ARE OUT OF CONTROL!!
KNOCK IT OFF!! WE'LL CANCEL THE FIREWORKS SHOW!!
WAAAAH! THE FESTIVAL'S RUINED!
わあああ
WAAAH
BUT I WANNA SEE THE FIRE-WORKS!
PAT
MÓU MANTÀI.*

TRANSLATOR'S NOTE: "NO PROBLEM" OR "DON'T WORRY" IN CANTONESE.

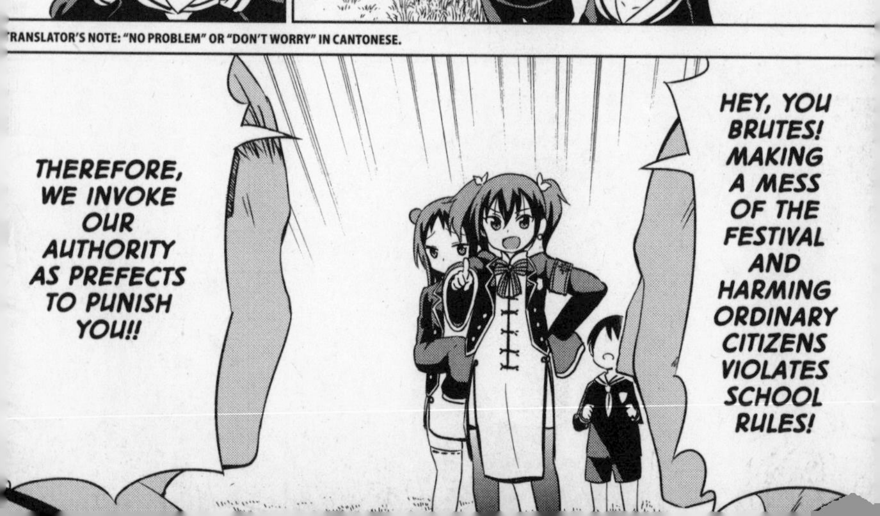
HEY, YOU BRUTES! MAKING A MESS OF THE FESTIVAL AND HARMING ORDINARY CITIZENS VIOLATES SCHOOL RULES!
THEREFORE, WE INVOKE OUR AUTHORITY AS PREFECTS TO PUNISH YOU!!

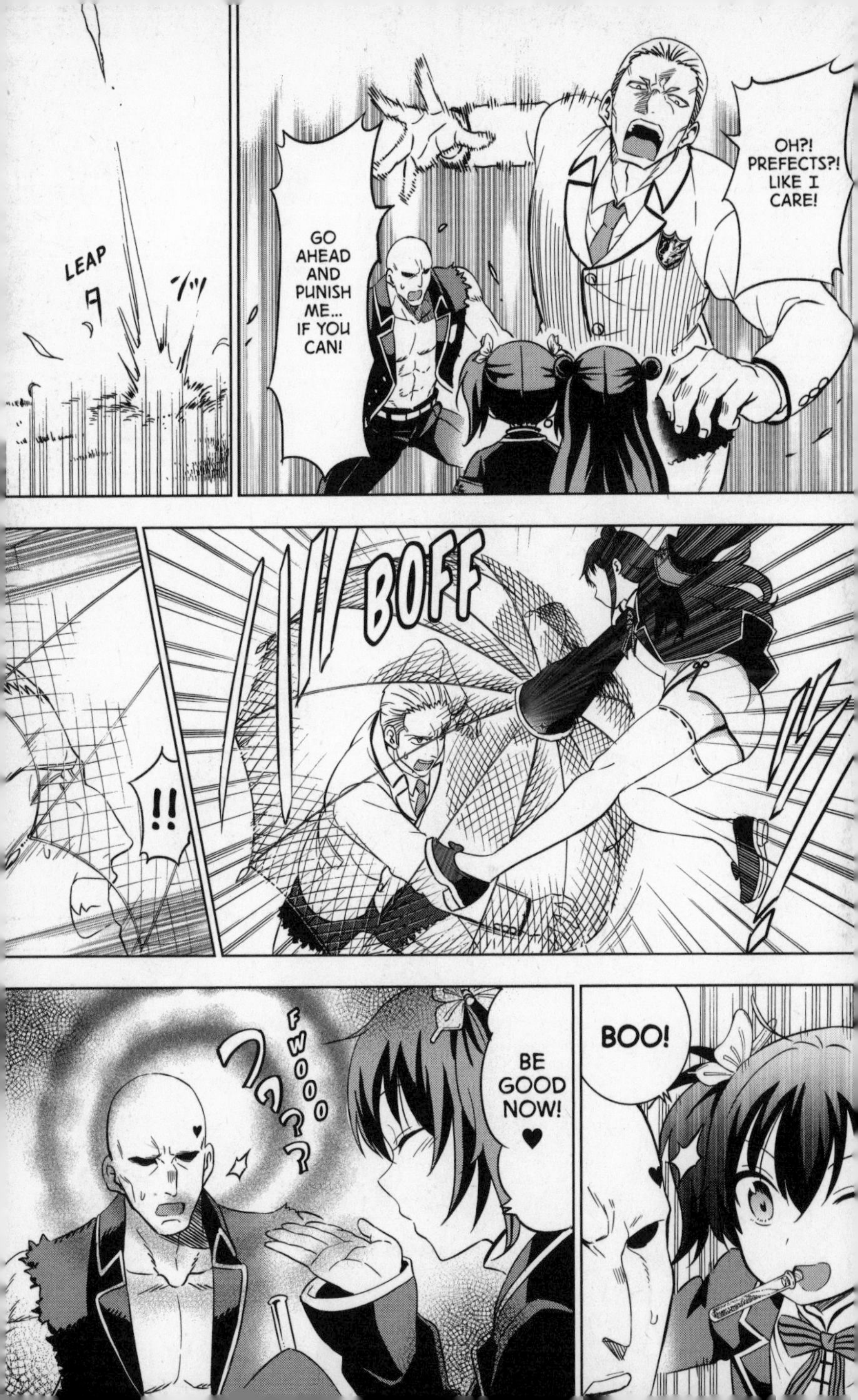
OH?! PREFECTS?! LIKE I CARE!
GO AHEAD AND PUNISH ME... IF YOU CAN!
LEAP
BOFF
!!
BOO!
BE GOOD NOW! ♥
FWOOO

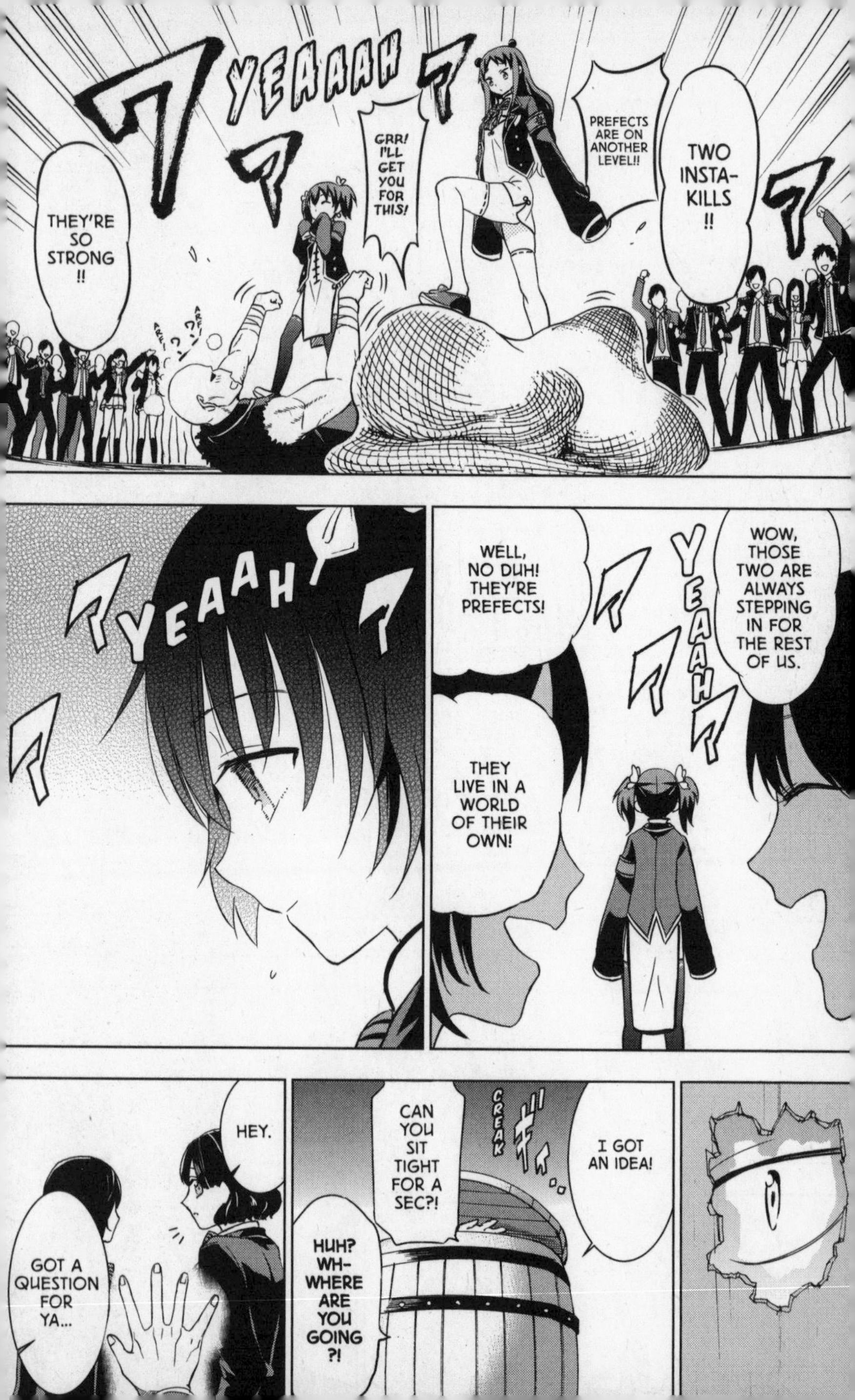
TWO INSTA-KILLS !!
PREFECTS ARE ON ANOTHER LEVEL!!
YEAAAH
GRR! I'LL GET YOU FOR THIS!
THEY'RE SO STRONG !!
WOW, THOSE TWO ARE ALWAYS STEPPING IN FOR THE REST OF US.
YEAAH
WELL, NO DUH! THEY'RE PREFECTS!
THEY LIVE IN A WORLD OF THEIR OWN!
YEAAH
I GOT AN IDEA!
CREAK
CAN YOU SIT TIGHT FOR A SEC?!
HUH? WH- WHERE ARE YOU GOING ?!
HEY.
GOT A QUESTION FOR YA...

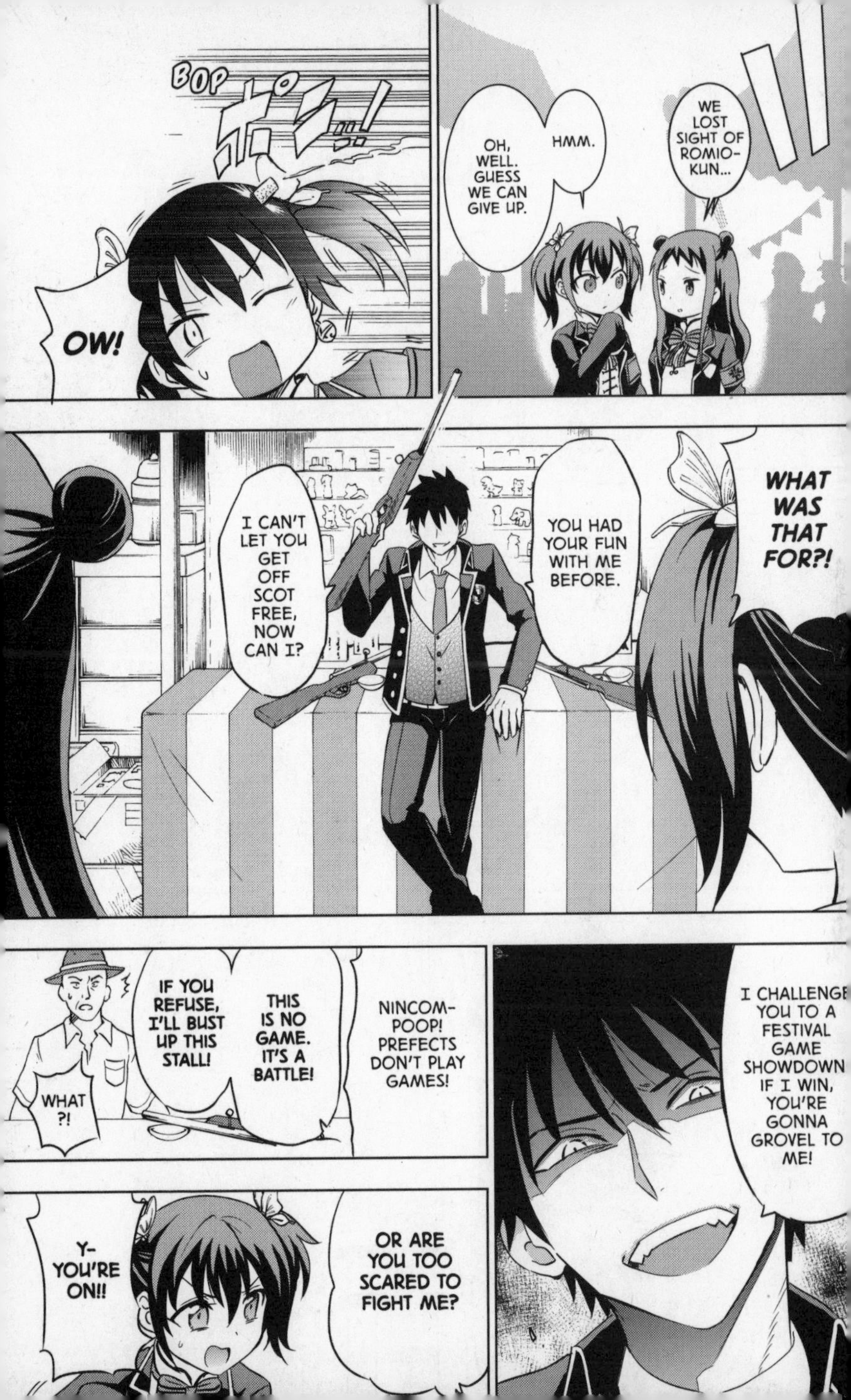
WE LOST SIGHT OF ROMIO-KUN...
HMM.
OH, WELL. GUESS WE CAN GIVE UP.
BOP
OW!
WHAT WAS THAT FOR?!
YOU HAD YOUR FUN WITH ME BEFORE.
I CAN'T LET YOU GET OFF SCOT FREE, NOW CAN I?
I CHALLENGE YOU TO A FESTIVAL GAME SHOWDOWN IF I WIN, YOU'RE GONNA GROVEL TO ME!
NINCOM-POOP! PREFECTS DON'T PLAY GAMES!
THIS IS NO GAME. IT'S A BATTLE!
IF YOU REFUSE, I'LL BUST UP THIS STALL!
WHAT ?!
OR ARE YOU TOO SCARED TO FIGHT ME?
Y- YOU'RE ON!!

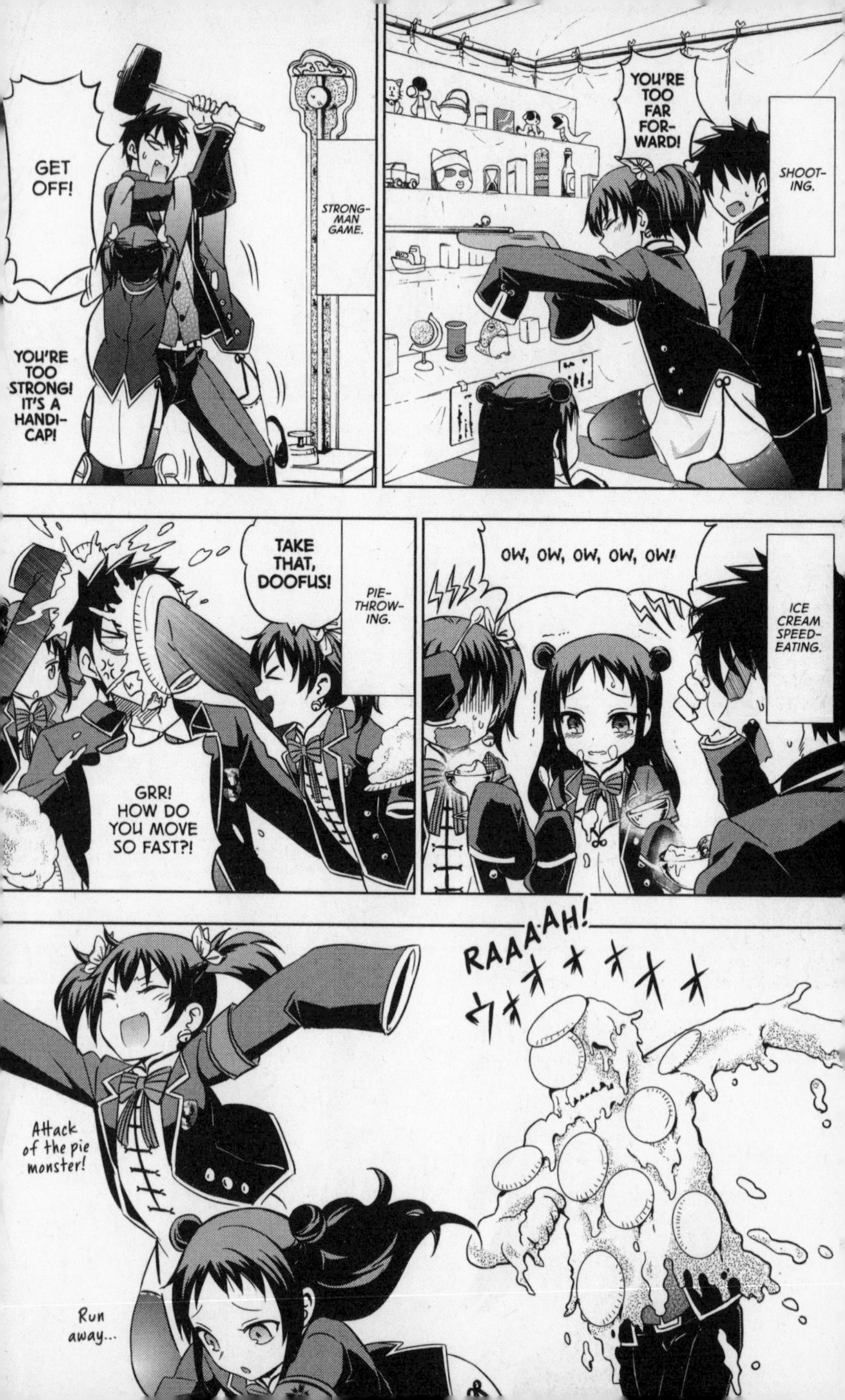
SHOOTING.
YOU'RE TOO FAR FORWARD!
STRONGMAN GAME.
GET OFF!
YOU'RE TOO STRONG! IT'S A HANDICAP!
ICE CREAM SPEED-EATING.
OW, OW, OW, OW, OW!
PIE-THROWING.
TAKE THAT, DOOFUS!
GRR! HOW DO YOU MOVE SO FAST?!
RAAAAH!
Attack of the pie monster!
Run away...

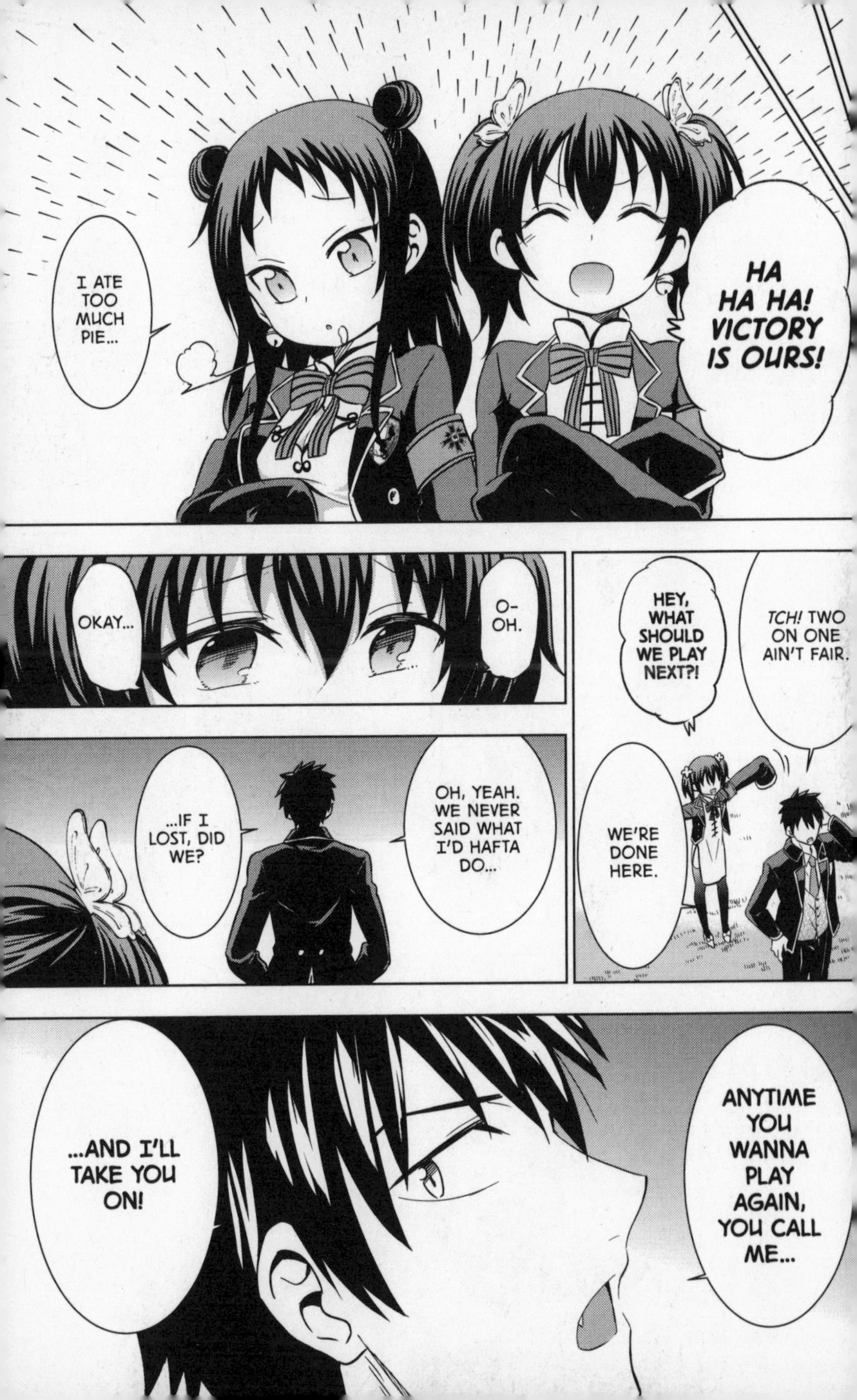
HA HA HA! VICTORY IS OURS!
I ATE TOO MUCH PIE...
TCH! TWO ON ONE AIN'T FAIR.
HEY, WHAT SHOULD WE PLAY NEXT?!
WE'RE DONE HERE.
O-OH.
OKAY...
OH, YEAH. WE NEVER SAID WHAT I'D HAFTA DO...
...IF I LOST, DID WE?
ANYTIME YOU WANNA PLAY AGAIN, YOU CALL ME...
...AND I'LL TAKE YOU ON!

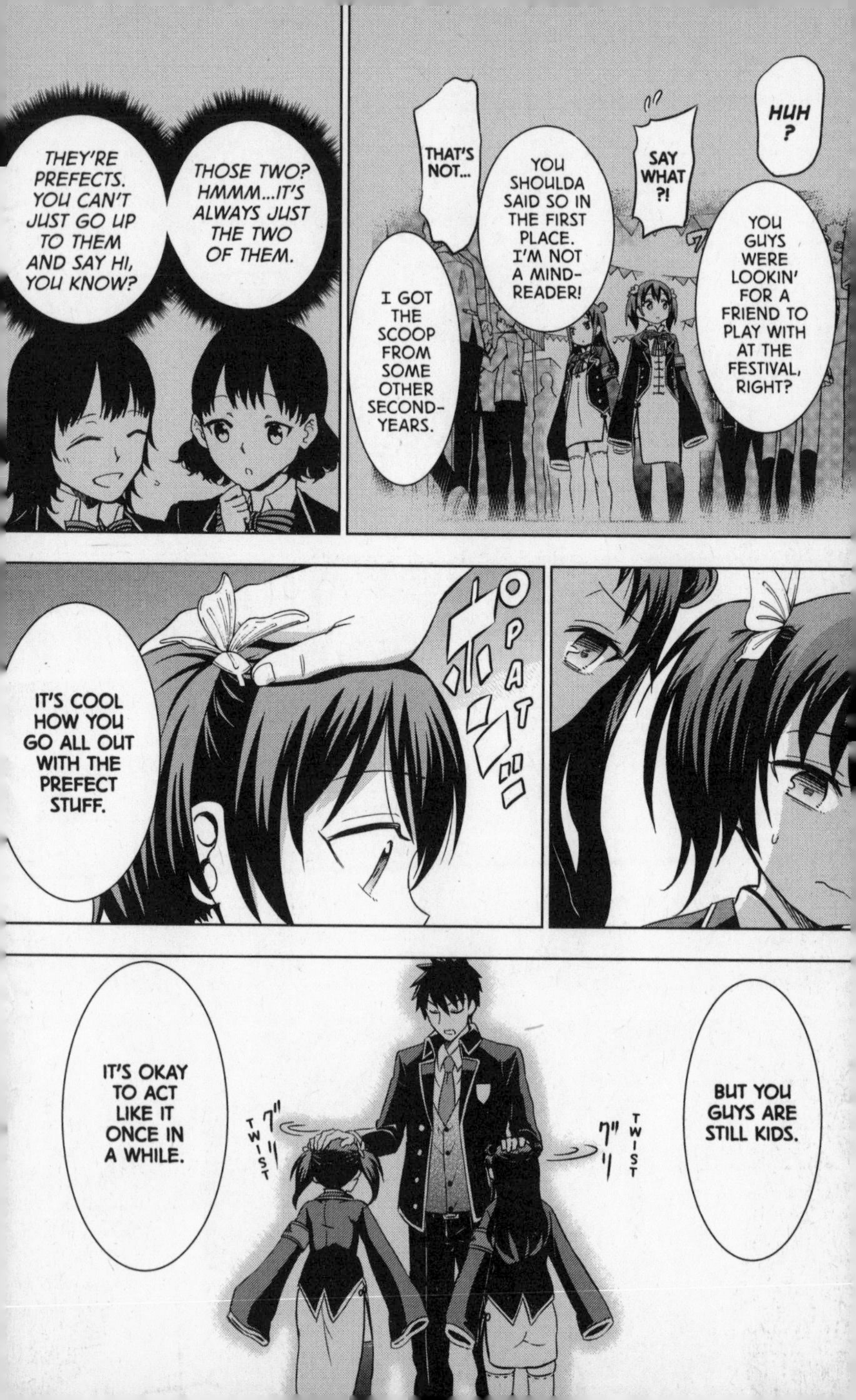
HUH?
SAY WHAT?!
YOU GUYS WERE LOOKIN' FOR A FRIEND TO PLAY WITH AT THE FESTIVAL, RIGHT?
YOU SHOULDA SAID SO IN THE FIRST PLACE. I'M NOT A MIND-READER!
THAT'S NOT...
I GOT THE SCOOP FROM SOME OTHER SECOND-YEARS.
THOSE TWO? HMMM...IT'S ALWAYS JUST THE TWO OF THEM.
THEY'RE PREFECTS. YOU CAN'T JUST GO UP TO THEM AND SAY HI, YOU KNOW?
PAT
IT'S COOL HOW YOU GO ALL OUT WITH THE PREFECT STUFF.
BUT YOU GUYS ARE STILL KIDS.
TWIST
TWIST
IT'S OKAY TO ACT LIKE IT ONCE IN A WHILE.

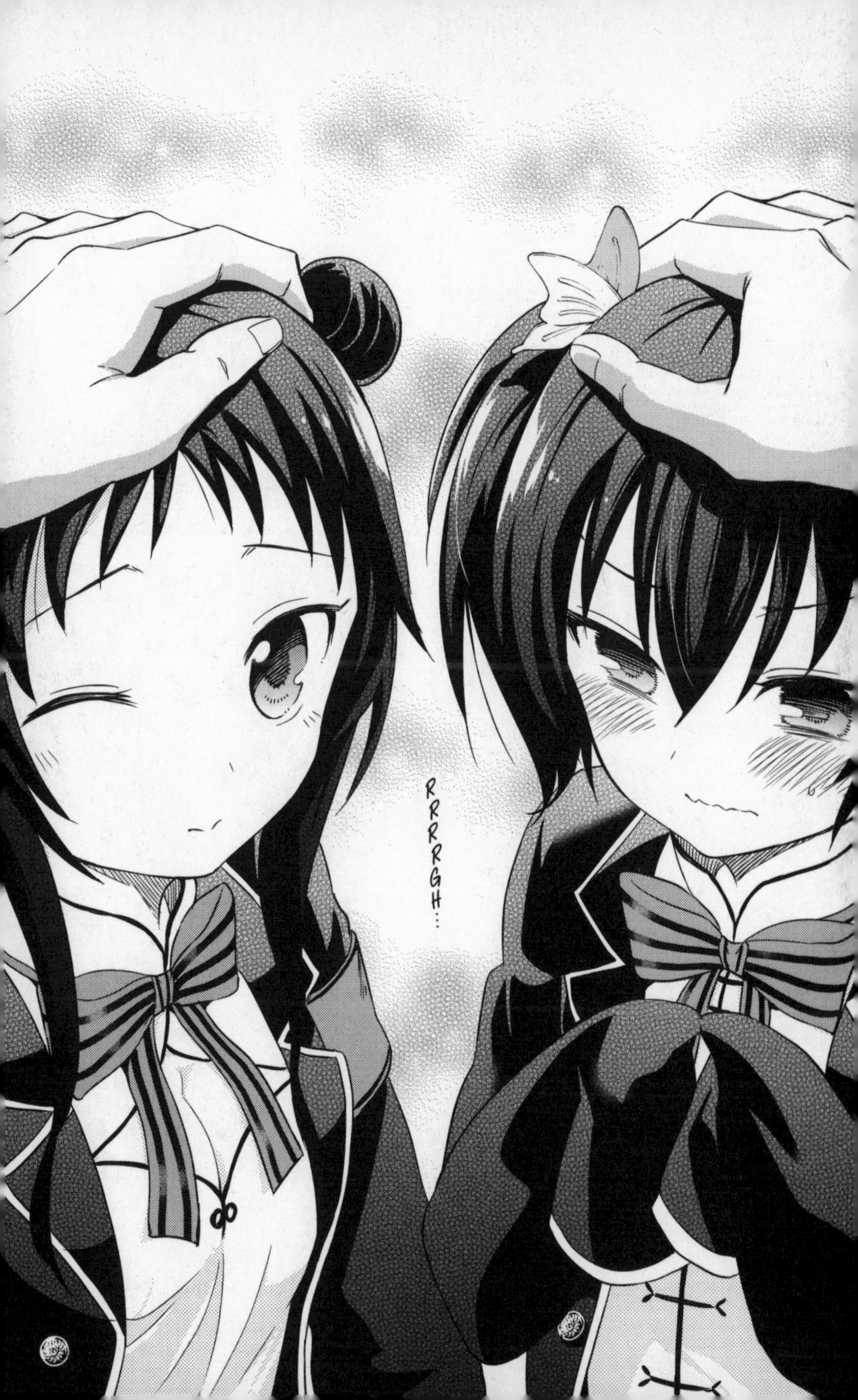
RRRRGH...

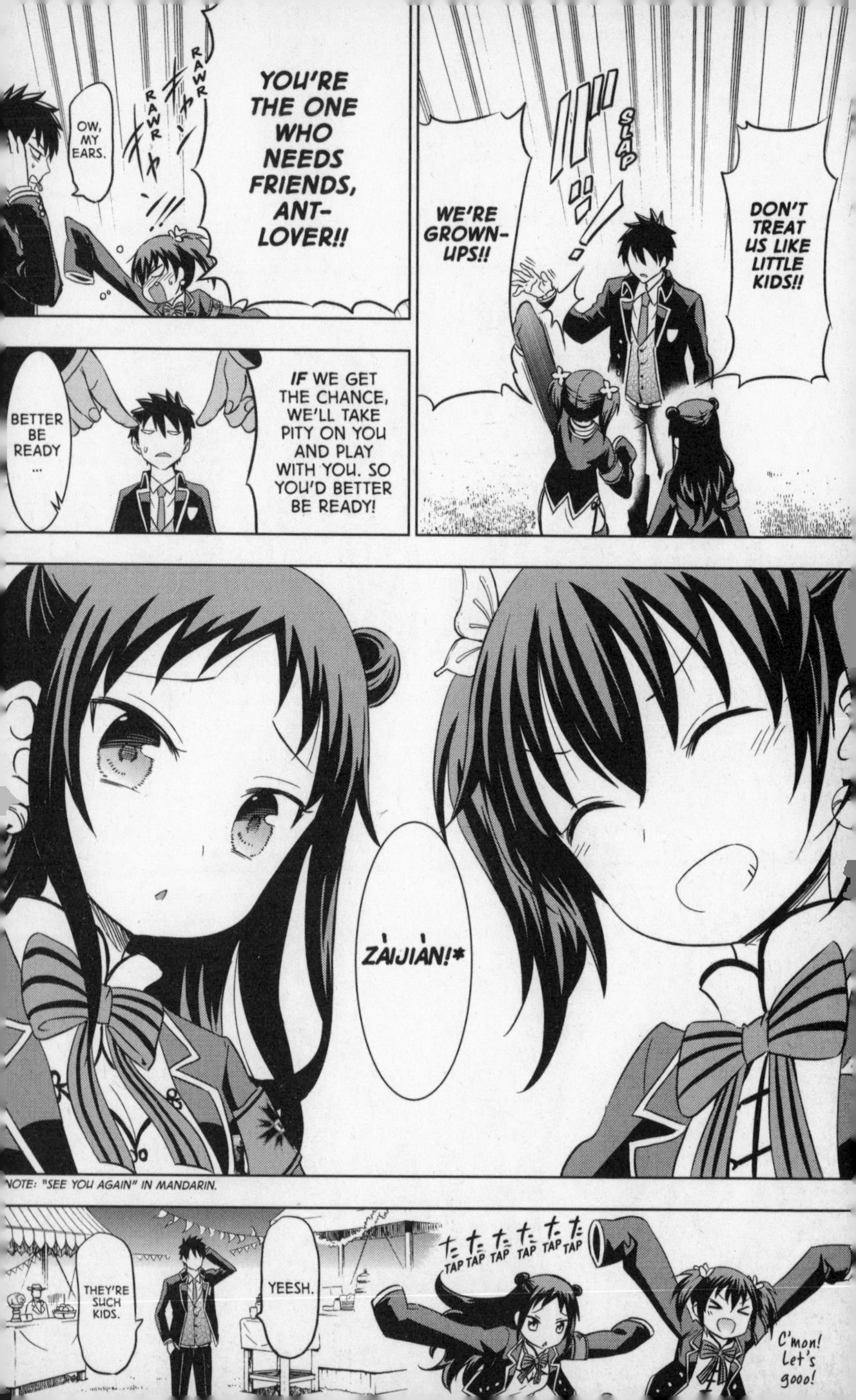
DON'T TREAT US LIKE LITTLE KIDS!!
SLAP
WE'RE GROWN-UPS!!
YOU'RE THE ONE WHO NEEDS FRIENDS, ANT-LOVER!!
RAWR
RAWR
OW, MY EARS.
IF WE GET THE CHANCE, WE'LL TAKE PITY ON YOU AND PLAY WITH YOU. SO YOU'D BETTER BE READY!
BETTER BE READY ...
ZÀIJIÀN!*
C'mon! Let's gooo!
TAP TAP TAP TAP TAP TAP
YEESH.
THEY'RE SUCH KIDS.

NOTE: "SEE YOU AGAIN" IN MANDARIN.

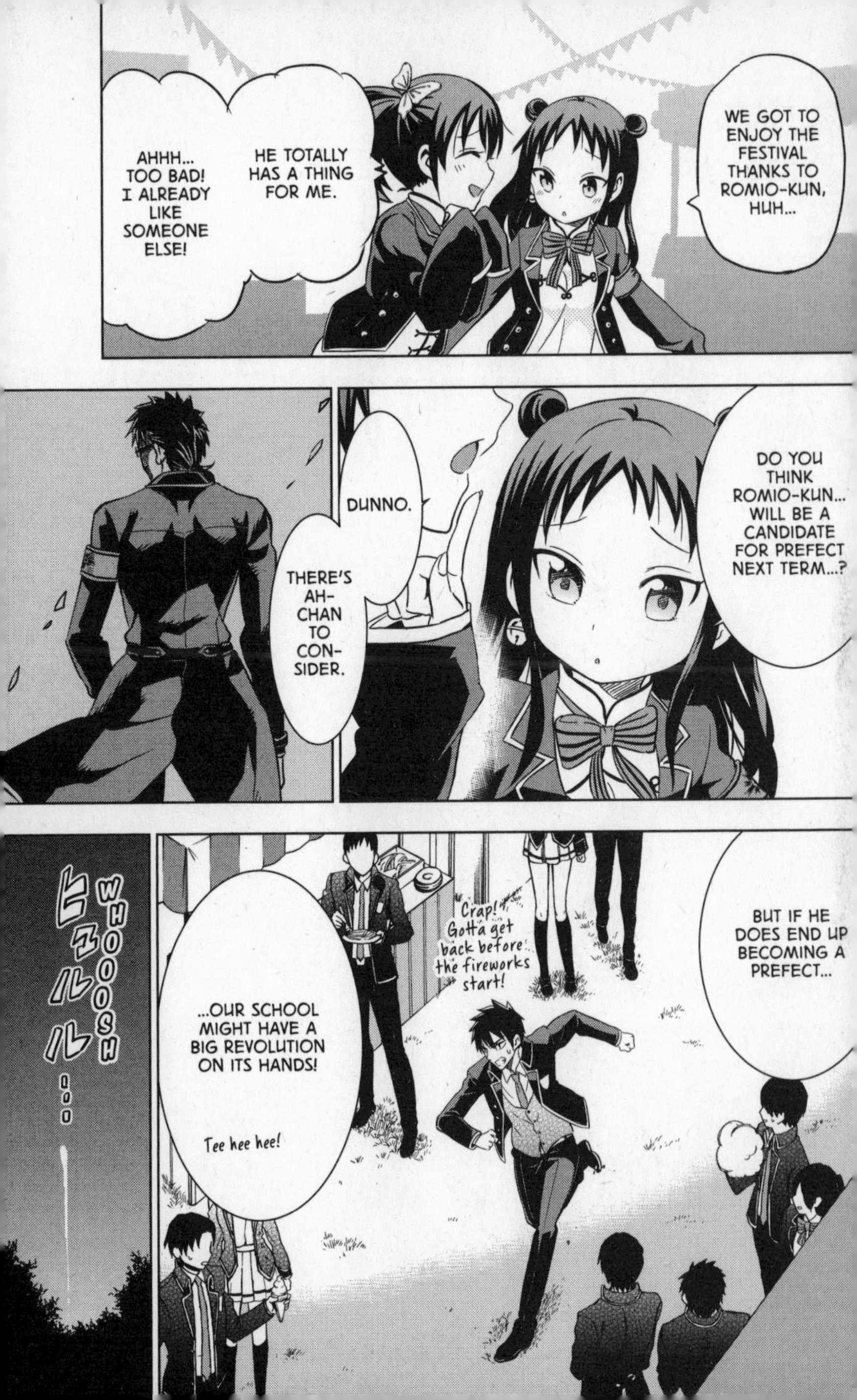
WE GOT TO ENJOY THE FESTIVAL THANKS TO ROMIO-KUN, HUH...
HE TOTALLY HAS A THING FOR ME.
AHHH... TOO BAD! I ALREADY LIKE SOMEONE ELSE!
DO YOU THINK ROMIO-KUN... WILL BE A CANDIDATE FOR PREFECT NEXT TERM...?
DUNNO.
THERE'S AH-CHAN TO CONSIDER.
BUT IF HE DOES END UP BECOMING A PREFECT...
Crap! Gotta get back before the fireworks start!
...OUR SCHOOL MIGHT HAVE A BIG REVOLUTION ON ITS HANDS!
Tee hee hee!
WHOOOOSH
ヒュルル…

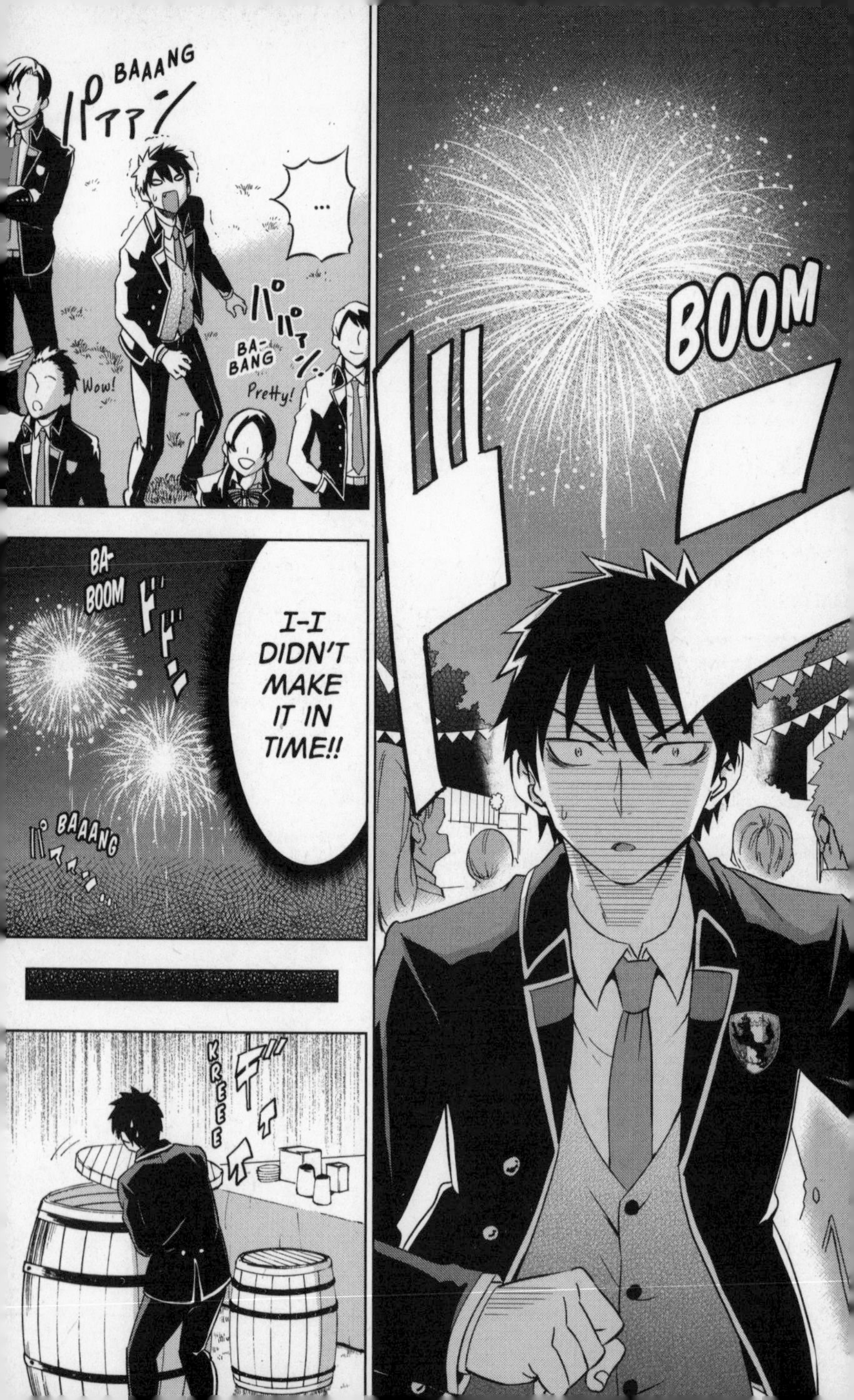
BOOM
BAAANG
パァァン
...
BA-BANG
パパァン
Wow!
Pretty!
BA-BOOM
ドドン
I-I DIDN'T MAKE IT IN TIME!!
BAAANG
KREEE

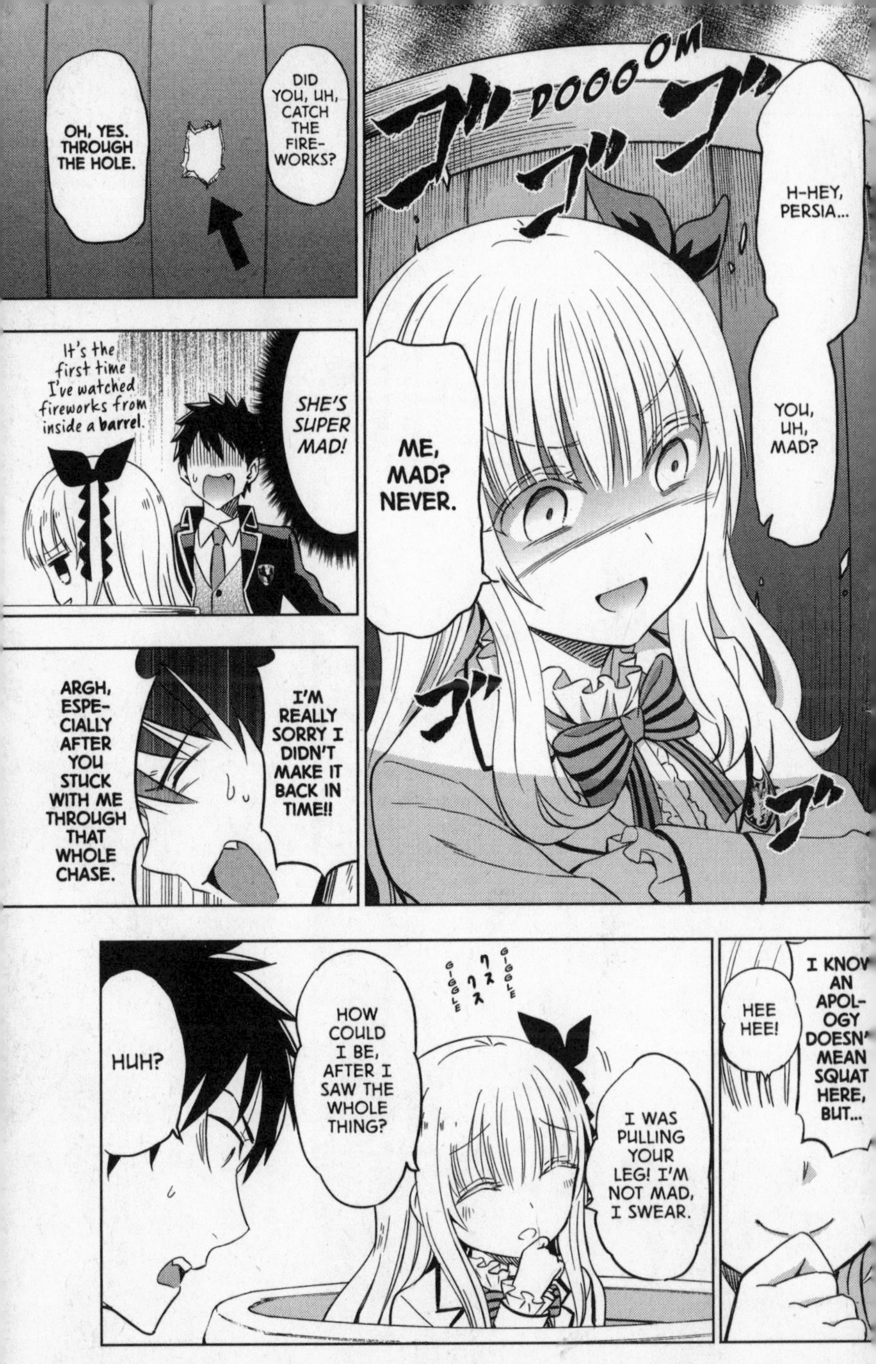
H-HEY, PERSIA...
DOOOOM
YOU, UH, MAD?
ME, MAD? NEVER.
DID YOU, UH, CATCH THE FIRE-WORKS?
OH, YES. THROUGH THE HOLE.
SHE'S SUPER MAD!
It's the first time I've watched fireworks from inside a barrel.
I'M REALLY SORRY I DIDN'T MAKE IT BACK IN TIME!!
ARGH, ESPE-CIALLY AFTER YOU STUCK WITH ME THROUGH THAT WHOLE CHASE.
I KNOW AN APOL-OGY DOESN' MEAN SQUAT HERE, BUT...
HEE HEE!
I WAS PULLING YOUR LEG! I'M NOT MAD, I SWEAR.
GIGGLE GIGGLE
HOW COULD I BE, AFTER I SAW THE WHOLE THING?
HUH?

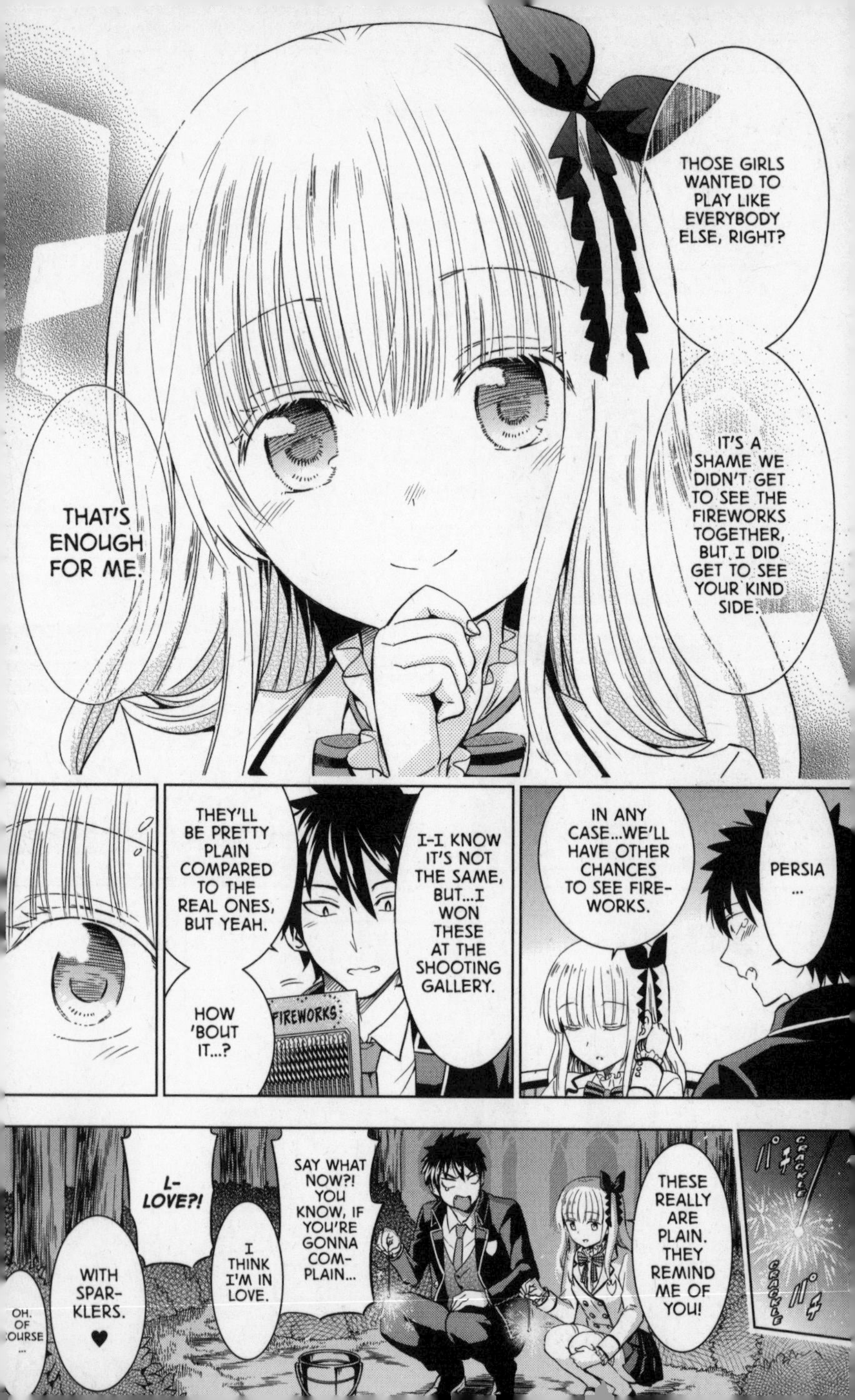

THOSE GIRLS WANTED TO PLAY LIKE EVERYBODY ELSE, RIGHT?
IT'S A SHAME WE DIDN'T GET TO SEE THE FIREWORKS TOGETHER, BUT I DID GET TO SEE YOUR KIND SIDE.
THAT'S ENOUGH FOR ME.
PERSIA ...
IN ANY CASE...WE'LL HAVE OTHER CHANCES TO SEE FIRE-WORKS.
I-I KNOW IT'S NOT THE SAME, BUT...I WON THESE AT THE SHOOTING GALLERY.
THEY'LL BE PRETTY PLAIN COMPARED TO THE REAL ONES, BUT YEAH.
HOW 'BOUT IT...?
FIREWORKS
CRACKLE
CRACKLE
THESE REALLY ARE PLAIN. THEY REMIND ME OF YOU!
SAY WHAT NOW?! YOU KNOW, IF YOU'RE GONNA COM-PLAIN...
I THINK I'M IN LOVE.
L-LOVE?!
WITH SPAR-KLERS. ♥
OH. OF OURSE ...

BONUS MANGA 1: MARU-KUN & THE FESTIVAL

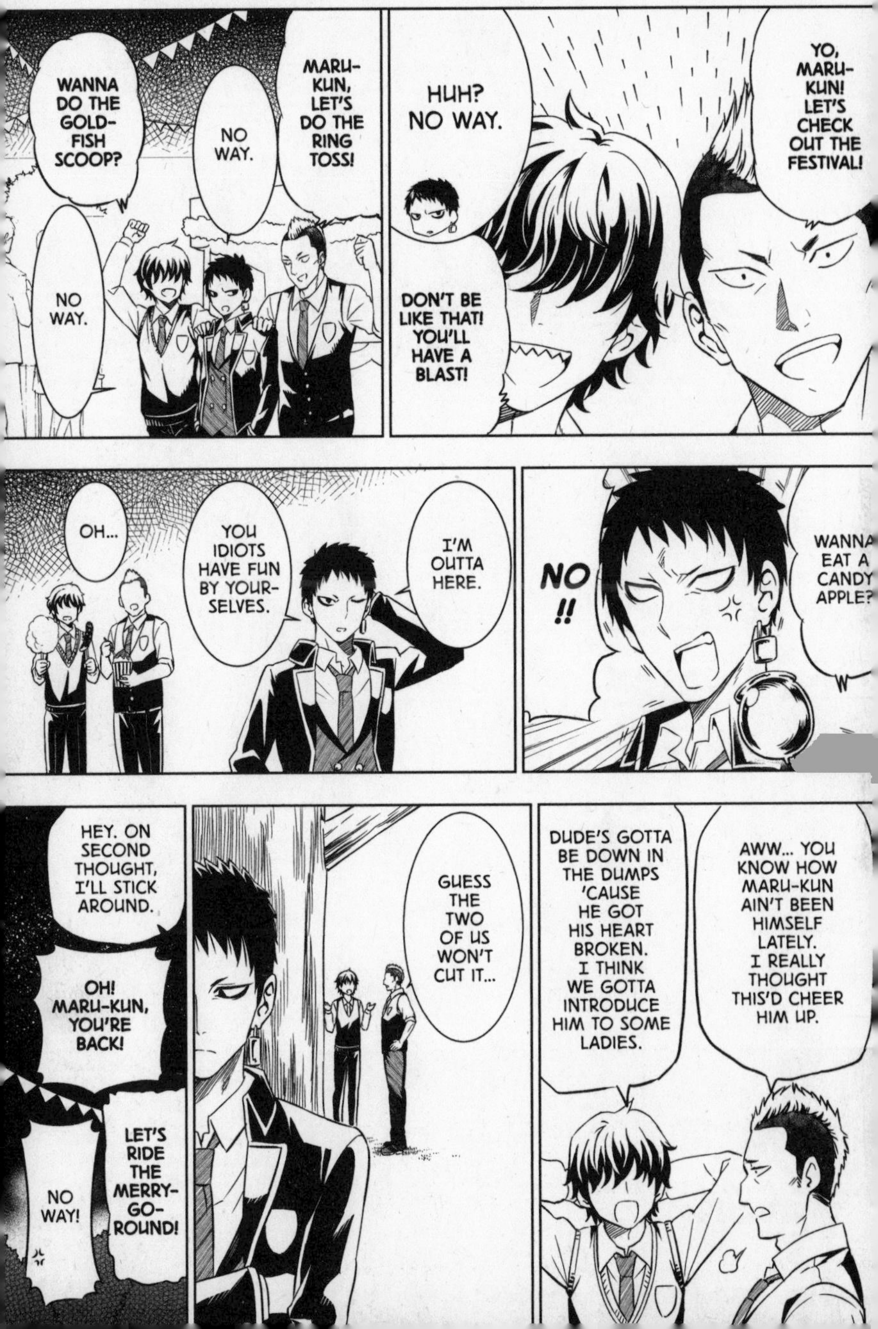
YO, MARU-KUN! LET'S CHECK OUT THE FESTIVAL!
HUH? NO WAY.
DON'T BE LIKE THAT! YOU'LL HAVE A BLAST!
MARU-KUN, LET'S DO THE RING TOSS!
NO WAY.
WANNA DO THE GOLD-FISH SCOOP?
NO WAY.
WANNA EAT A CANDY APPLE?
NO !!
I'M OUTTA HERE.
YOU IDIOTS HAVE FUN BY YOUR-SELVES.
OH...
AWW... YOU KNOW HOW MARU-KUN AIN'T BEEN HIMSELF LATELY. I REALLY THOUGHT THIS'D CHEER HIM UP.
DUDE'S GOTTA BE DOWN IN THE DUMPS 'CAUSE HE GOT HIS HEART BROKEN. I THINK WE GOTTA INTRODUCE HIM TO SOME LADIES.
GUESS THE TWO OF US WON'T CUT IT...
HEY. ON SECOND THOUGHT, I'LL STICK AROUND.
OH! MARU-KUN, YOU'RE BACK!
LET'S RIDE THE MERRY-GO-ROUND!
NO WAY!

BONUS MANGA 2: A TALE FROM THE TWINS' PAST

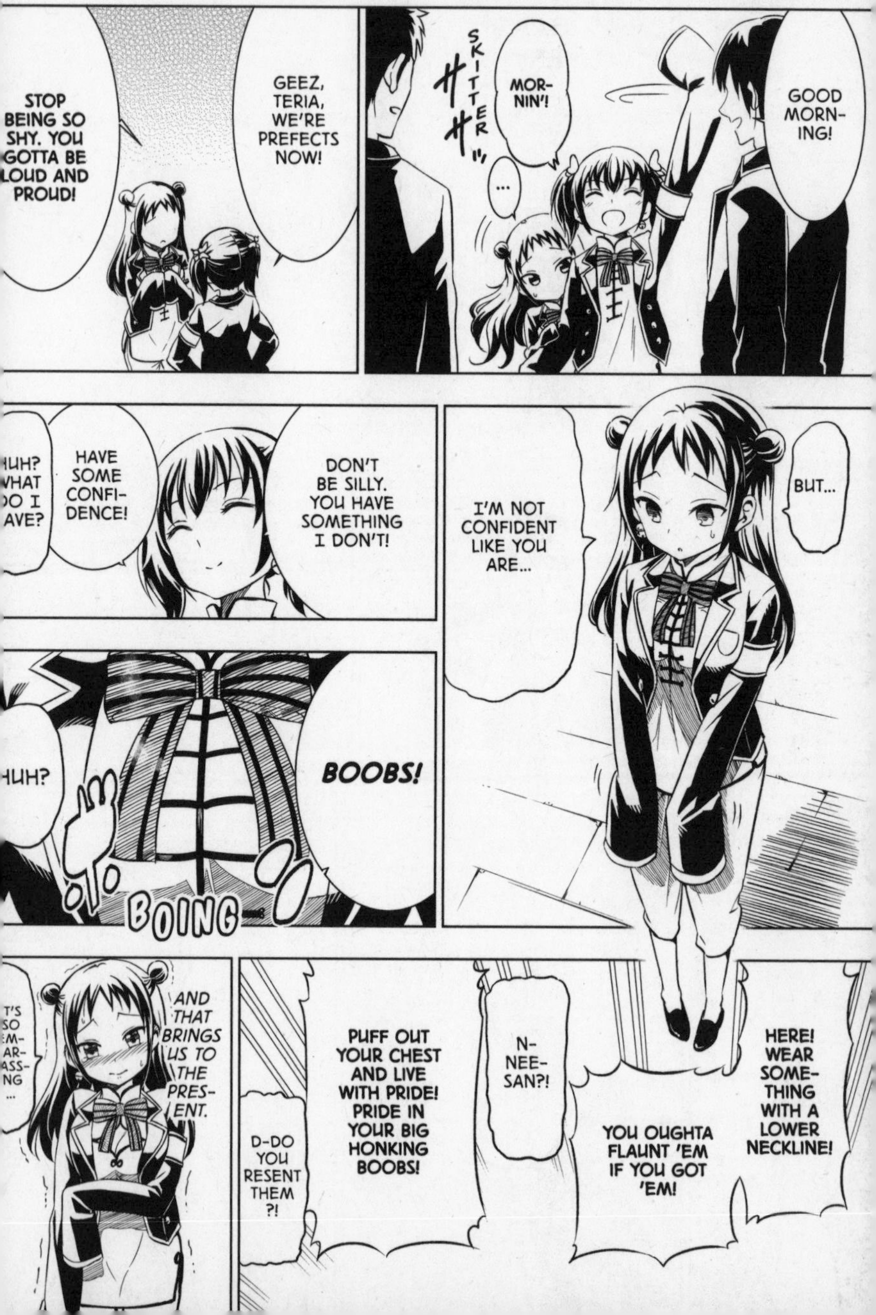
GOOD MORNING!
MOR-NIN'!
SKITTER
...
GEEZ, TERIA, WE'RE PREFECTS NOW!
STOP BEING SO SHY. YOU GOTTA BE LOUD AND PROUD!
BUT...
I'M NOT CONFIDENT LIKE YOU ARE...
DON'T BE SILLY. YOU HAVE SOMETHING I DON'T!
HAVE SOME CONFIDENCE!
UH? VHAT O I AVE?
BOOBS!
UH?
BOING
HERE! WEAR SOME-THING WITH A LOWER NECKLINE!
YOU OUGHTA FLAUNT 'EM IF YOU GOT 'EM!
N-NEE-SAN?!
PUFF OUT YOUR CHEST AND LIVE WITH PRIDE! PRIDE IN YOUR BIG HONKING BOOBS!
D-DO YOU RESENT THEM?!
AND THAT BRINGS US TO THE PRES-ENT.
T'S SO EM-AR-ASS-NG ...

ACT 14:

ROMIO & CHAR & THE PRESENT

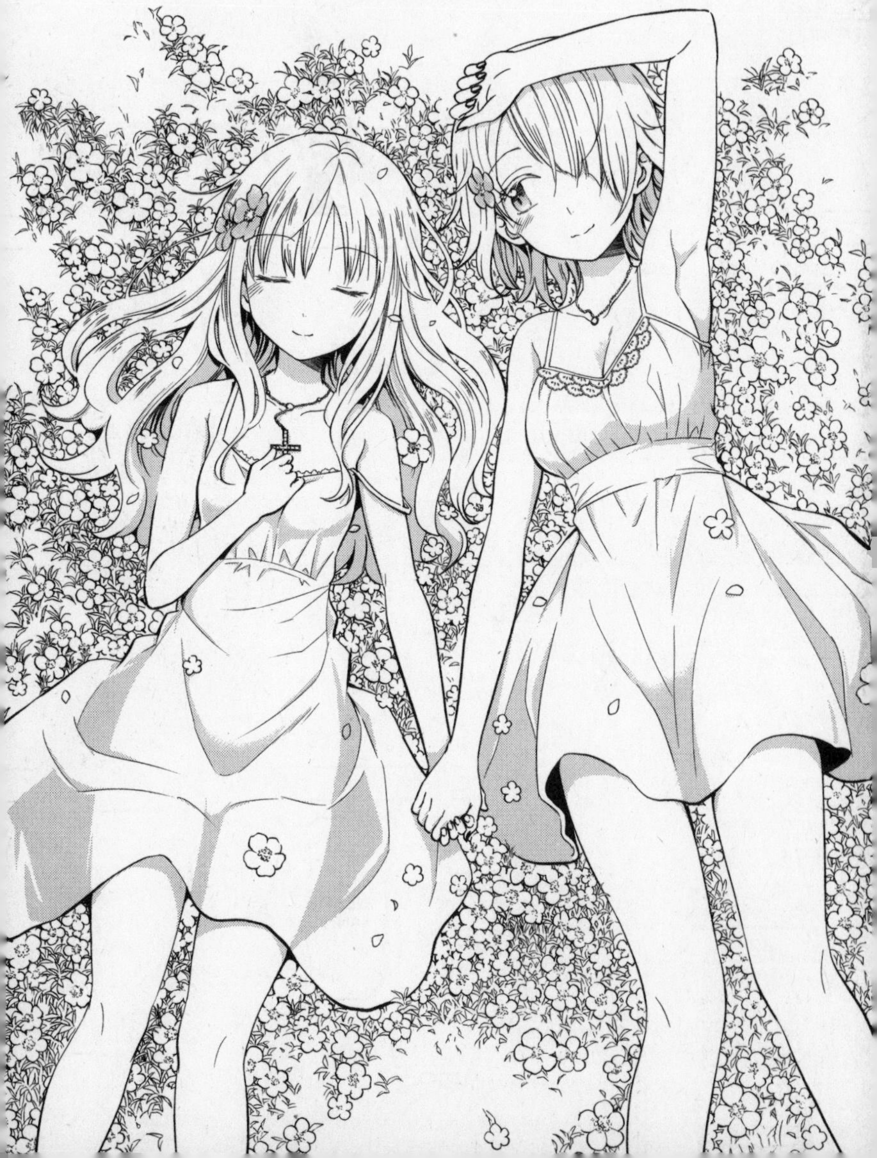

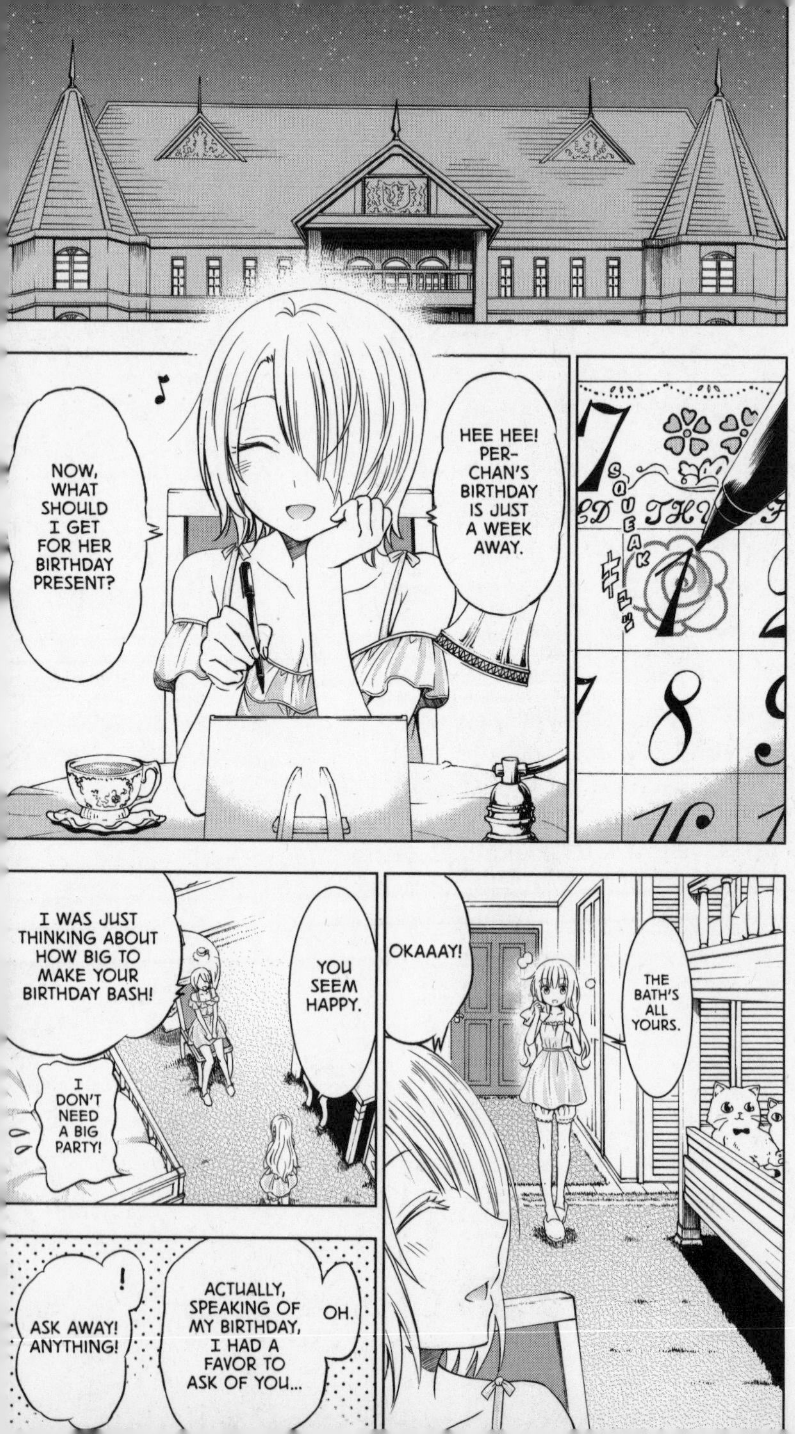
SQUEAK
キュッ
HEE HEE! PER-CHAN'S BIRTHDAY IS JUST A WEEK AWAY.
NOW, WHAT SHOULD I GET FOR HER BIRTHDAY PRESENT?
THE BATH'S ALL YOURS.
OKAAAY!
YOU SEEM HAPPY.
I WAS JUST THINKING ABOUT HOW BIG TO MAKE YOUR BIRTHDAY BASH!
I DON'T NEED A BIG PARTY!
OH.
ACTUALLY, SPEAKING OF MY BIRTHDAY, I HAD A FAVOR TO ASK OF YOU...
!
ASK AWAY! ANYTHING!

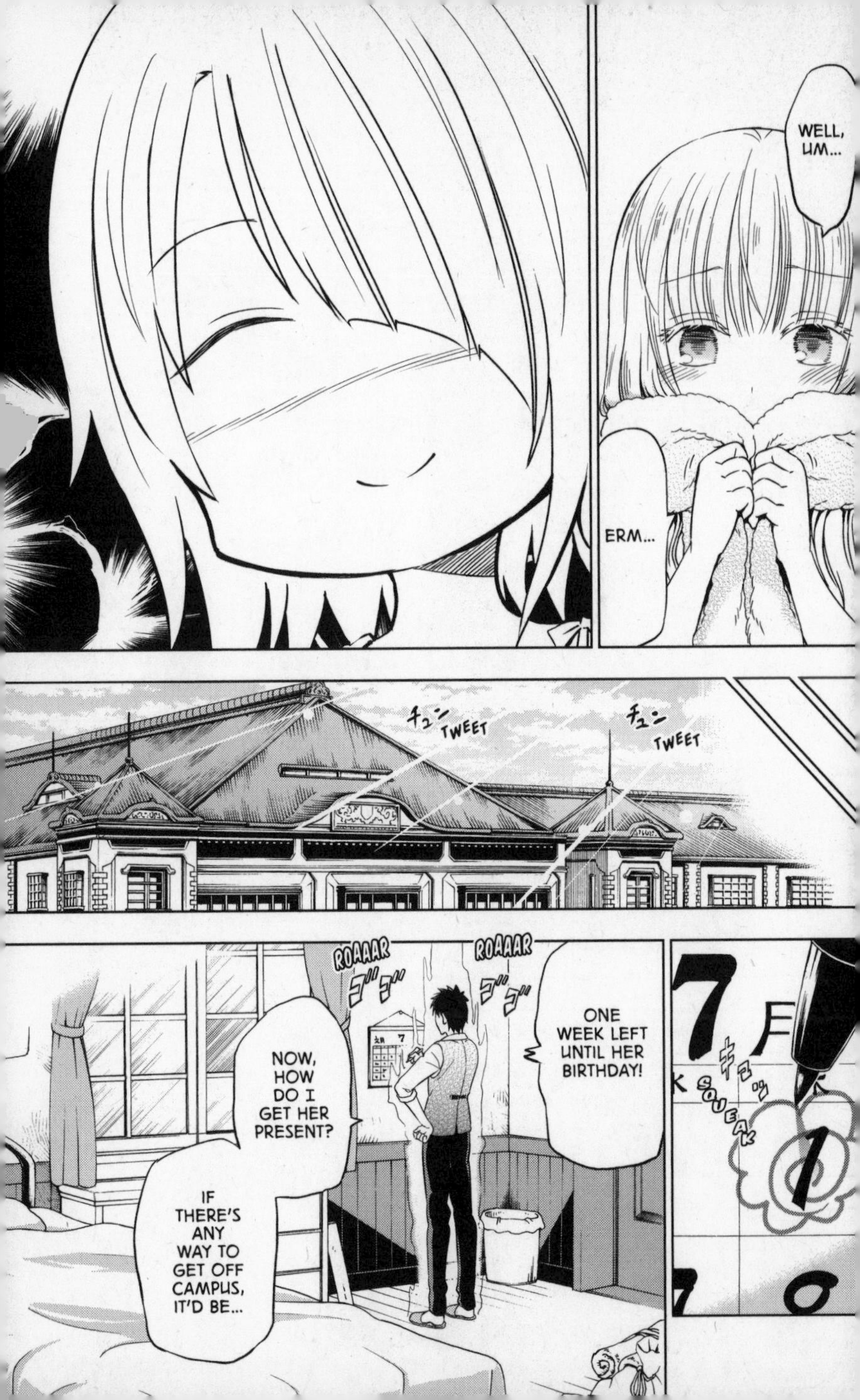
WELL, UM...
ERM...
チュン TWEET
チュン TWEET
7月
キュッ SQUEAK
ROAAAR ゴゴ
ROAAAR ゴゴ
ONE WEEK LEFT UNTIL HER BIRTHDAY!
NOW, HOW DO I GET HER PRESENT?
IF THERE'S ANY WAY TO GET OFF CAMPUS, IT'D BE...

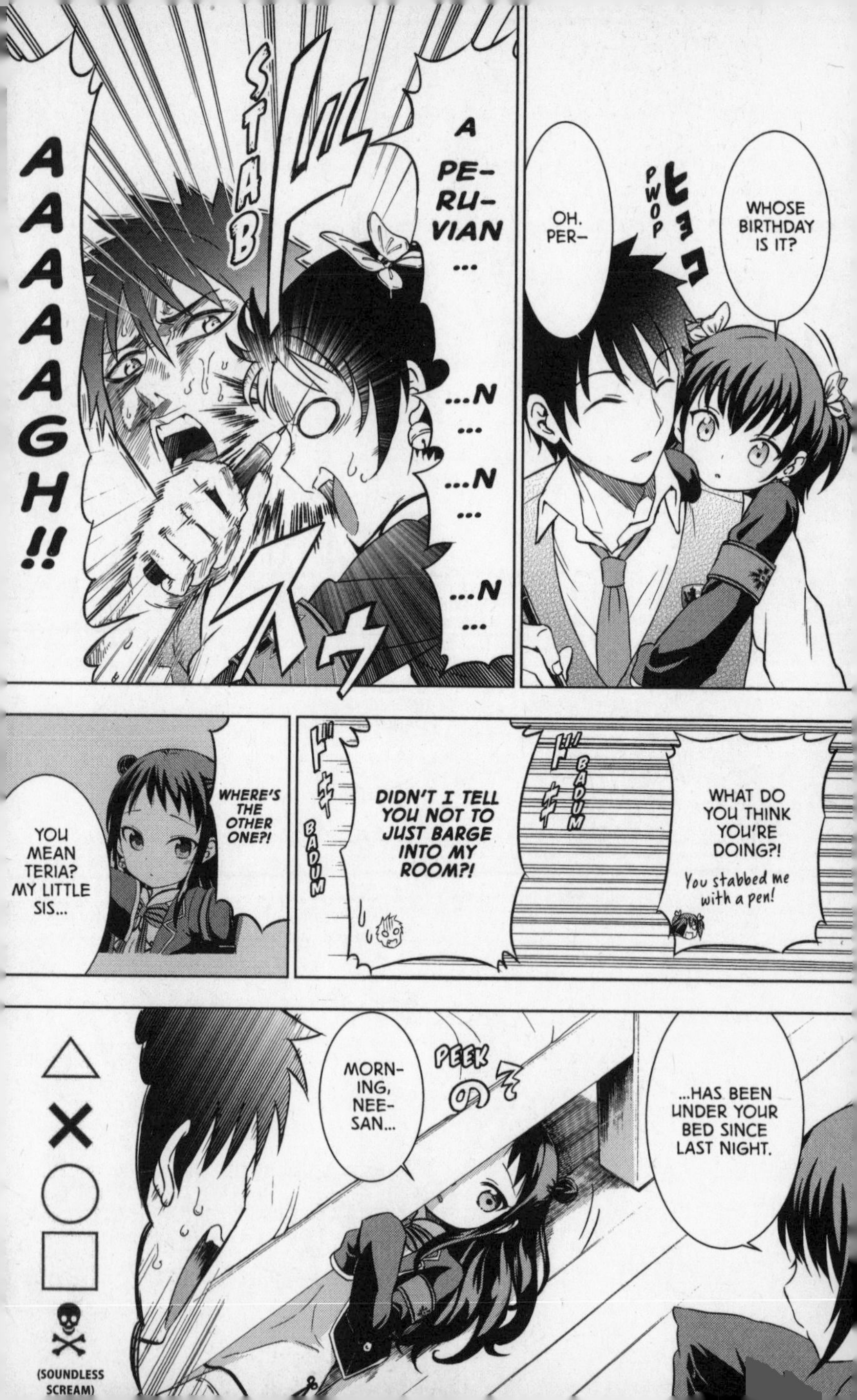
WHOSE BIRTHDAY IS IT?
PWOP
OH. PER–
A PERUVIAN...
...N ...
...N ...
...N ...
STAB
AAAAAAAGH!!
WHAT DO YOU THINK YOU'RE DOING?!
You stabbed me with a pen!
BADUM
DIDN'T I TELL YOU NOT TO JUST BARGE INTO MY ROOM?!
BADUM
WHERE'S THE OTHER ONE?!
YOU MEAN TERIA? MY LITTLE SIS...
...HAS BEEN UNDER YOUR BED SINCE LAST NIGHT.
PEEK
MORNING, NEE-SAN...
(SOUNDLESS SCREAM)

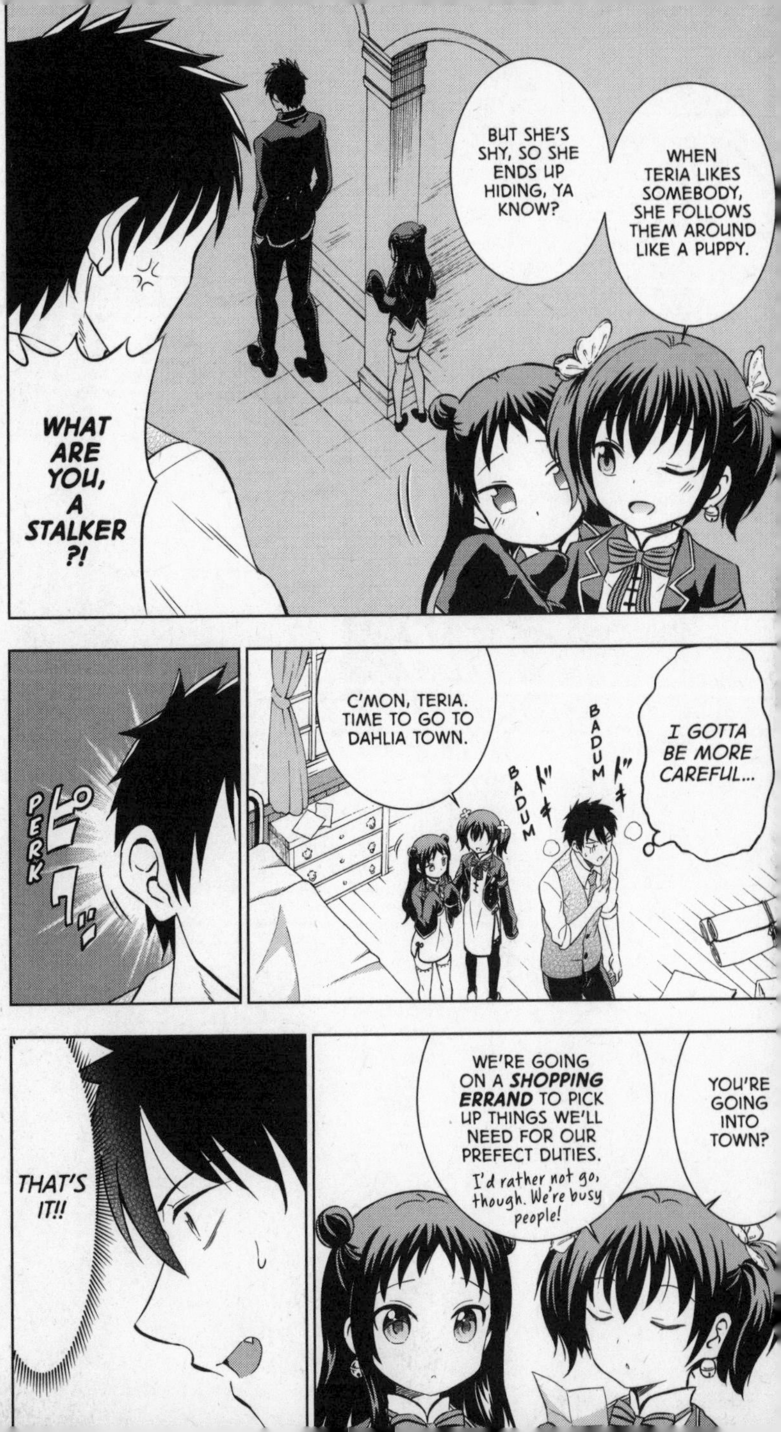

WHEN TERIA LIKES SOMEBODY, SHE FOLLOWS THEM AROUND LIKE A PUPPY.
BUT SHE'S SHY, SO SHE ENDS UP HIDING, YA KNOW?
WHAT ARE YOU, A STALKER?!
I GOTTA BE MORE CAREFUL...
BADUM
BADUM
C'MON, TERIA. TIME TO GO TO DAHLIA TOWN.
PERK
YOU'RE GOING INTO TOWN?
WE'RE GOING ON A SHOPPING ERRAND TO PICK UP THINGS WE'LL NEED FOR OUR PREFECT DUTIES.
I'd rather not go, though. We're busy people!
THAT'S IT!!

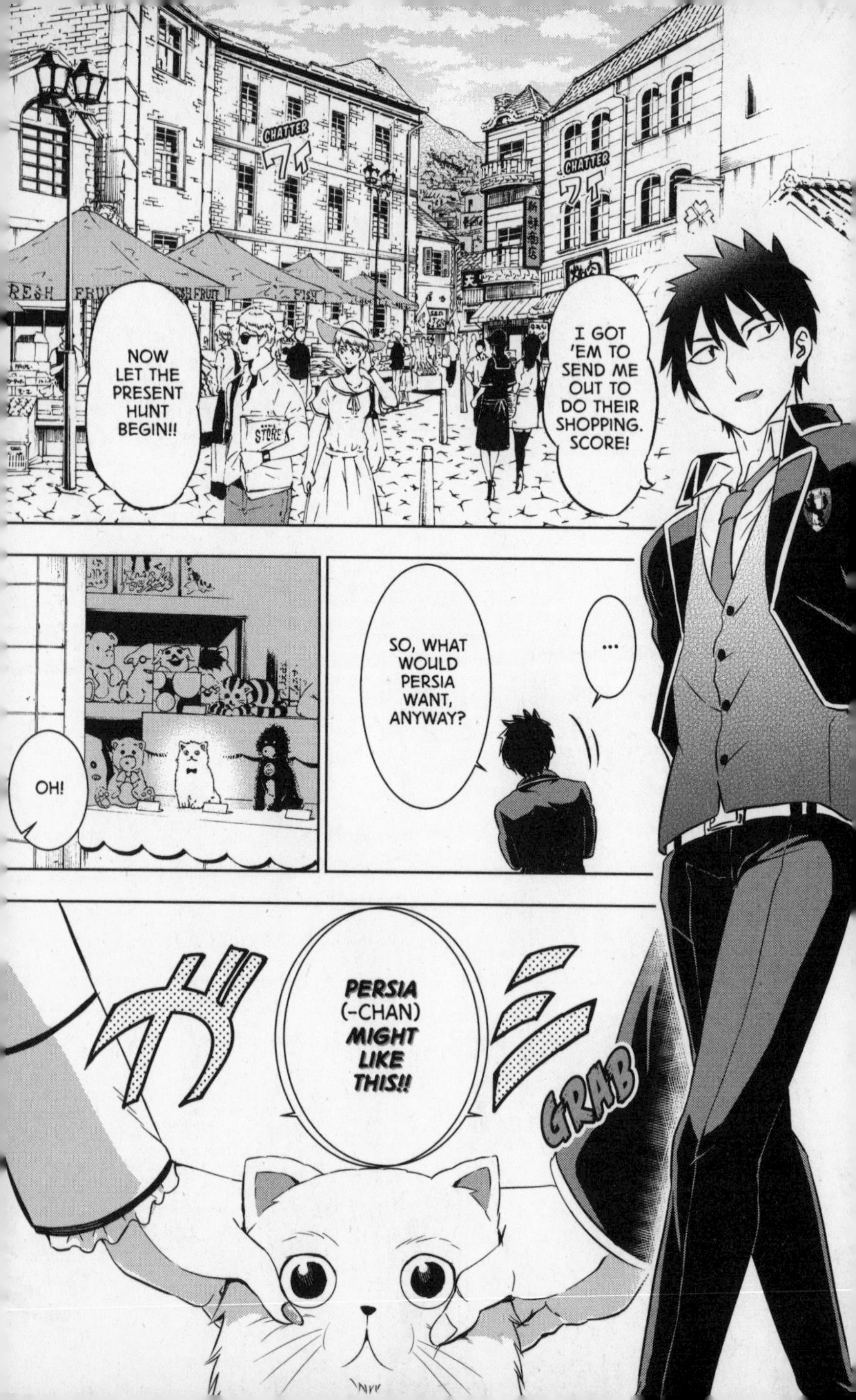
CHATTER
CHATTER
I GOT 'EM TO SEND ME OUT TO DO THEIR SHOPPING. SCORE!
NOW LET THE PRESENT HUNT BEGIN!!
...
SO, WHAT WOULD PERSIA WANT, ANYWAY?
OH!
GRAB
PERSIA (-CHAN) MIGHT LIKE THIS!!

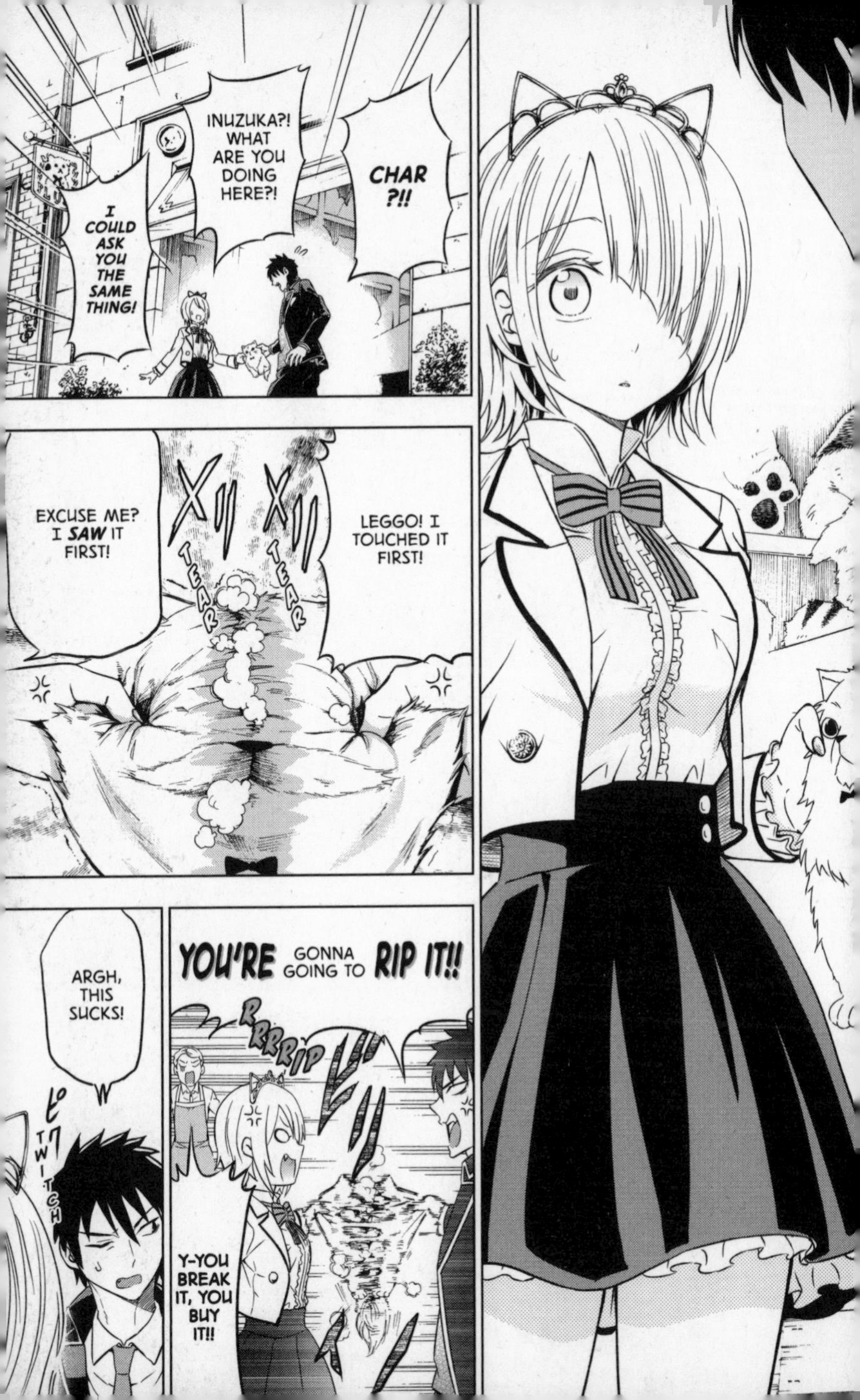
CHAR ?!!
INUZUKA?! WHAT ARE YOU DOING HERE?!
I COULD ASK YOU THE SAME THING!
LEGGO! I TOUCHED IT FIRST!
TEAR
TEAR
EXCUSE ME? I SAW IT FIRST!
YOU'RE GONNA GOING TO RIP IT!!
RRRRIP
Y-YOU BREAK IT, YOU BUY IT!!
ARGH, THIS SUCKS!
TWITCH

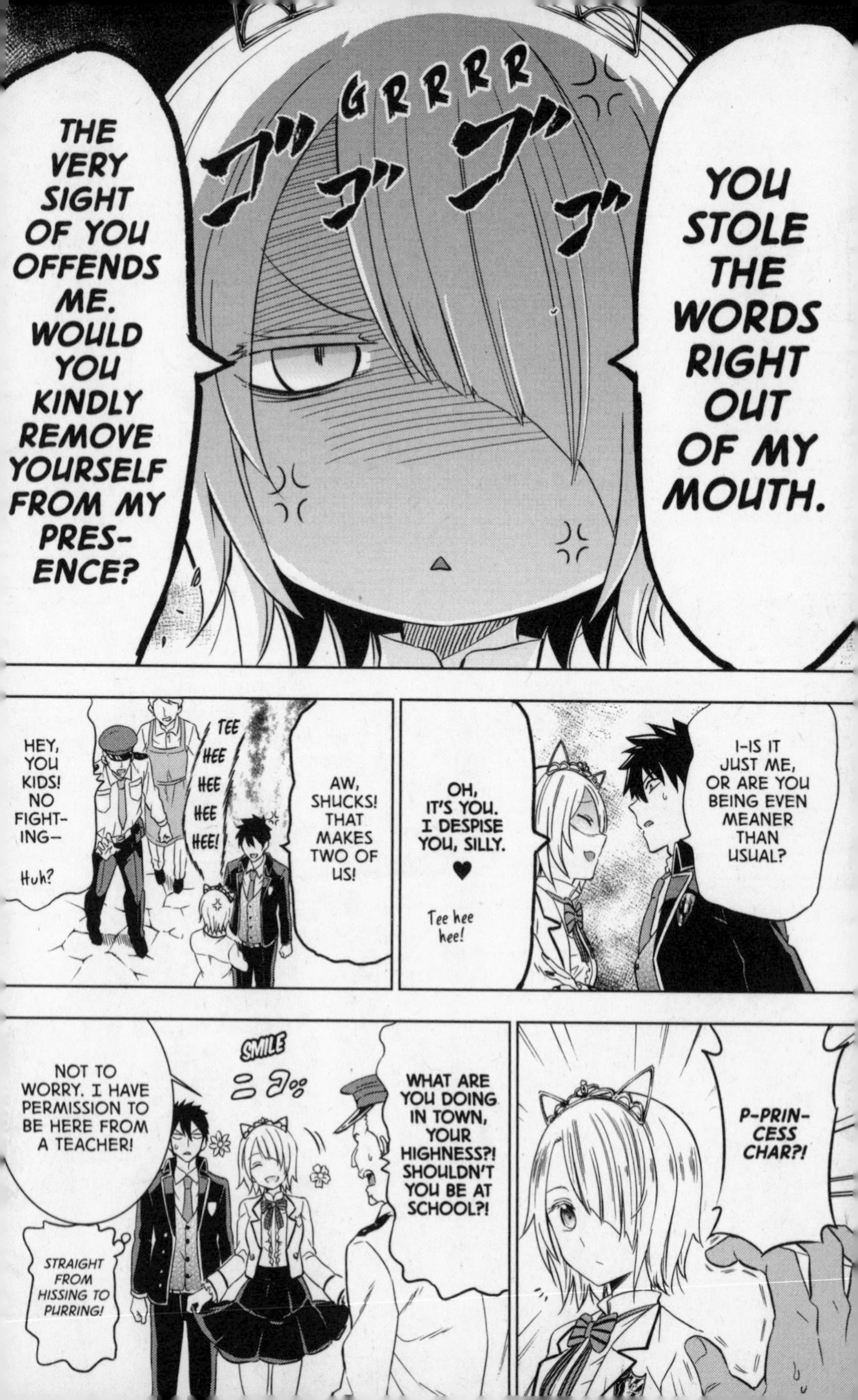
GRRRR
YOU STOLE THE WORDS RIGHT OUT OF MY MOUTH.
THE VERY SIGHT OF YOU OFFENDS ME. WOULD YOU KINDLY REMOVE YOURSELF FROM MY PRES-ENCE?
I-IS IT JUST ME, OR ARE YOU BEING EVEN MEANER THAN USUAL?
OH, IT'S YOU. I DESPISE YOU, SILLY. ♥
Tee hee hee!
AW, SHUCKS! THAT MAKES TWO OF US!
TEE HEE HEE HEE HEE!
HEY, YOU KIDS! NO FIGHT-ING—
Huh?
P-PRIN-CESS CHAR?!
WHAT ARE YOU DOING IN TOWN, YOUR HIGHNESS?! SHOULDN'T YOU BE AT SCHOOL?!
SMILE
NOT TO WORRY. I HAVE PERMISSION TO BE HERE FROM A TEACHER!
STRAIGHT FROM HISSING TO PURRING!

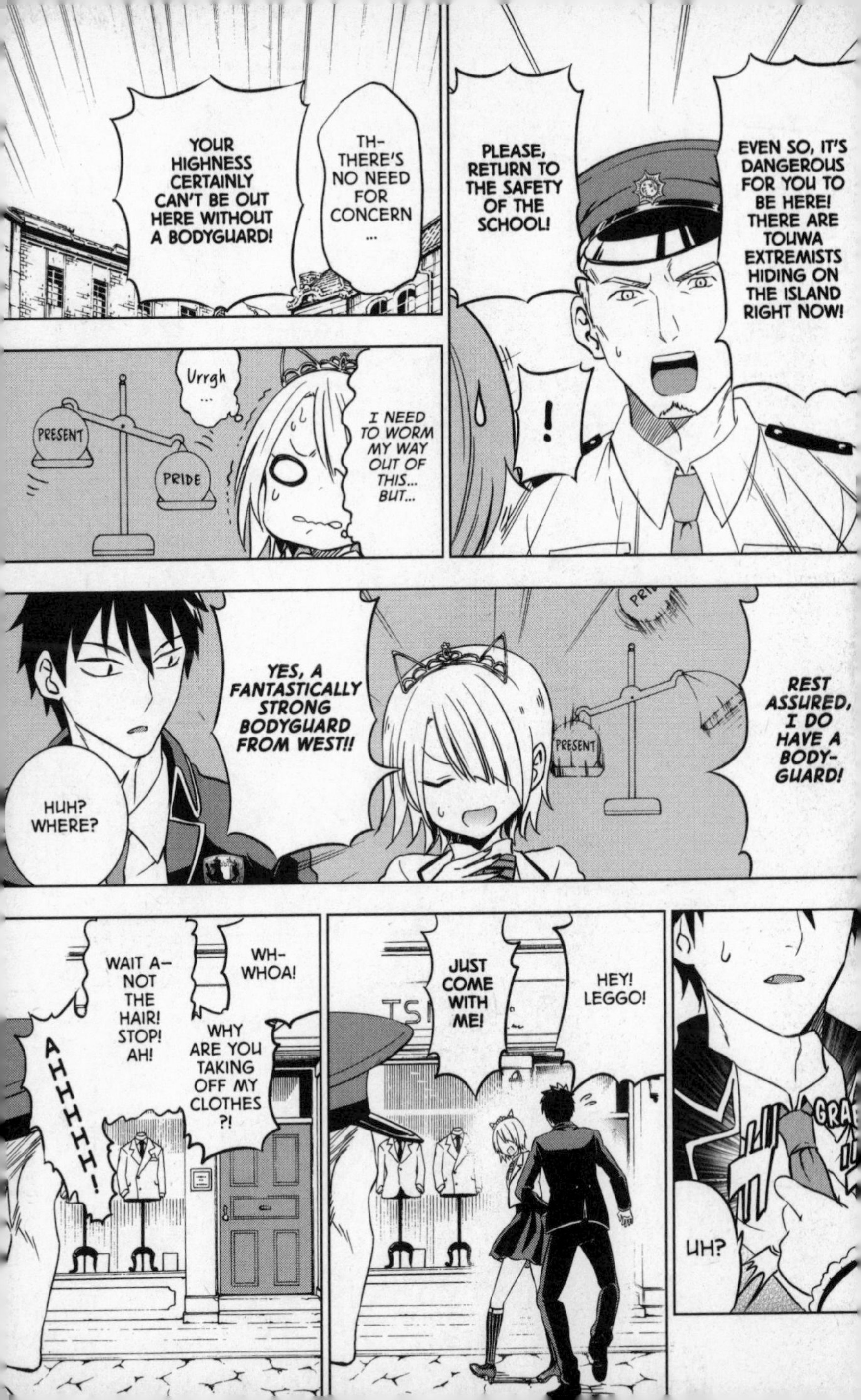
EVEN SO, IT'S DANGEROUS FOR YOU TO BE HERE! THERE ARE TOUWA EXTREMISTS HIDING ON THE ISLAND RIGHT NOW!
PLEASE, RETURN TO THE SAFETY OF THE SCHOOL!
!
TH- THERE'S NO NEED FOR CONCERN ...
YOUR HIGHNESS CERTAINLY CAN'T BE OUT HERE WITHOUT A BODYGUARD!
I NEED TO WORM MY WAY OUT OF THIS... BUT...
Urrgh ...
PRESENT
PRIDE
REST ASSURED, I DO HAVE A BODY-GUARD!
YES, A FANTASTICALLY STRONG BODYGUARD FROM WEST!!
PRESENT
HUH? WHERE?
GRA
UH?
HEY! LEGGO!
JUST COME WITH ME!
WH- WHOA!
WAIT A- NOT THE HAIR! STOP! AH!
WHY ARE YOU TAKING OFF MY CLOTHES ?!
AHHHHH!

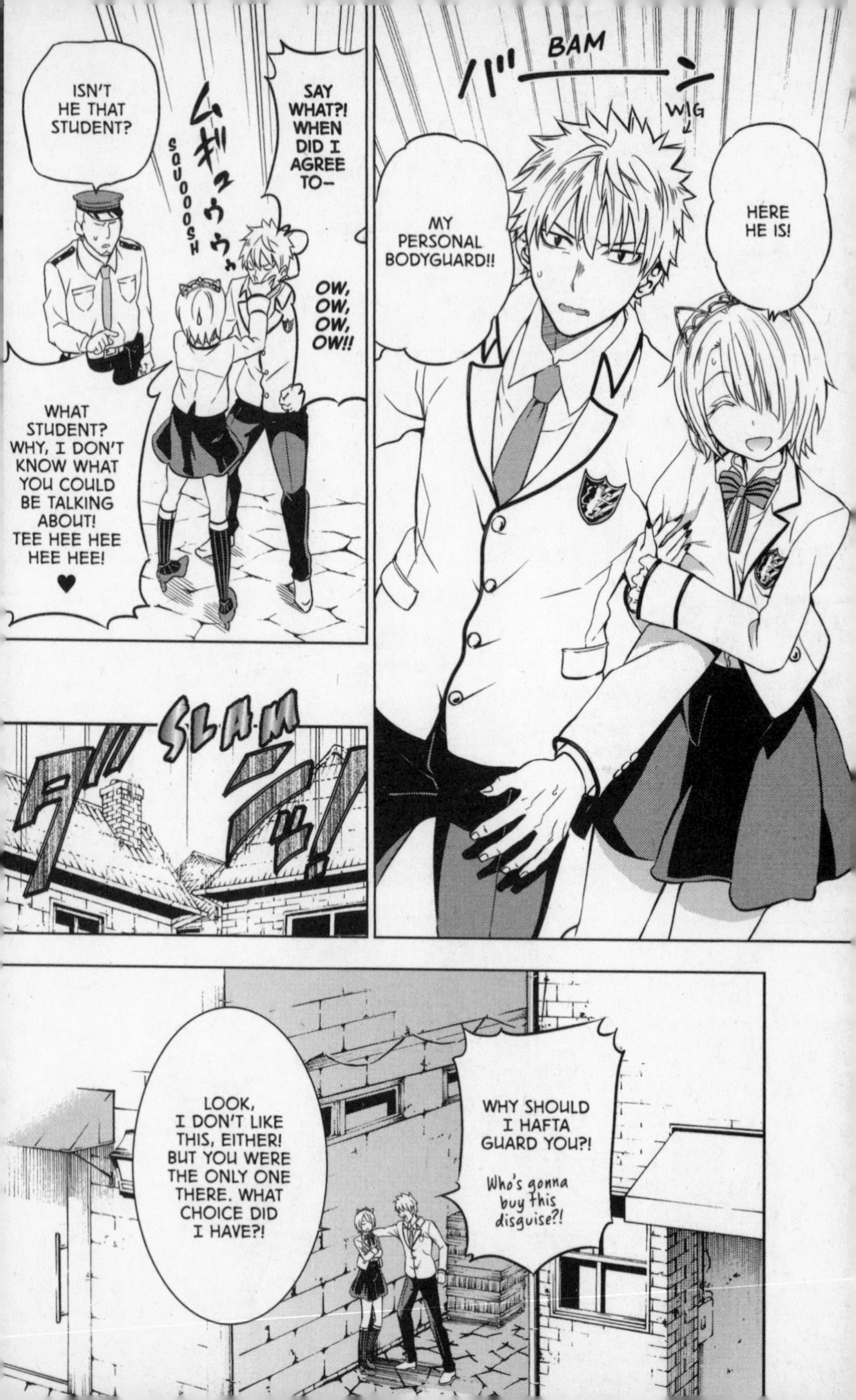
BAM
WIG
HERE HE IS!
MY PERSONAL BODYGUARD!!
SAY WHAT?! WHEN DID I AGREE TO—
SQUOOOOSH
ISN'T HE THAT STUDENT?
OW, OW, OW, OW!!
WHAT STUDENT? WHY, I DON'T KNOW WHAT YOU COULD BE TALKING ABOUT! TEE HEE HEE HEE HEE! ♥
SLAM
WHY SHOULD I HAFTA GUARD YOU?!
Who's gonna buy this disguise?!
LOOK, I DON'T LIKE THIS, EITHER! BUT YOU WERE THE ONLY ONE THERE. WHAT CHOICE DID I HAVE?!

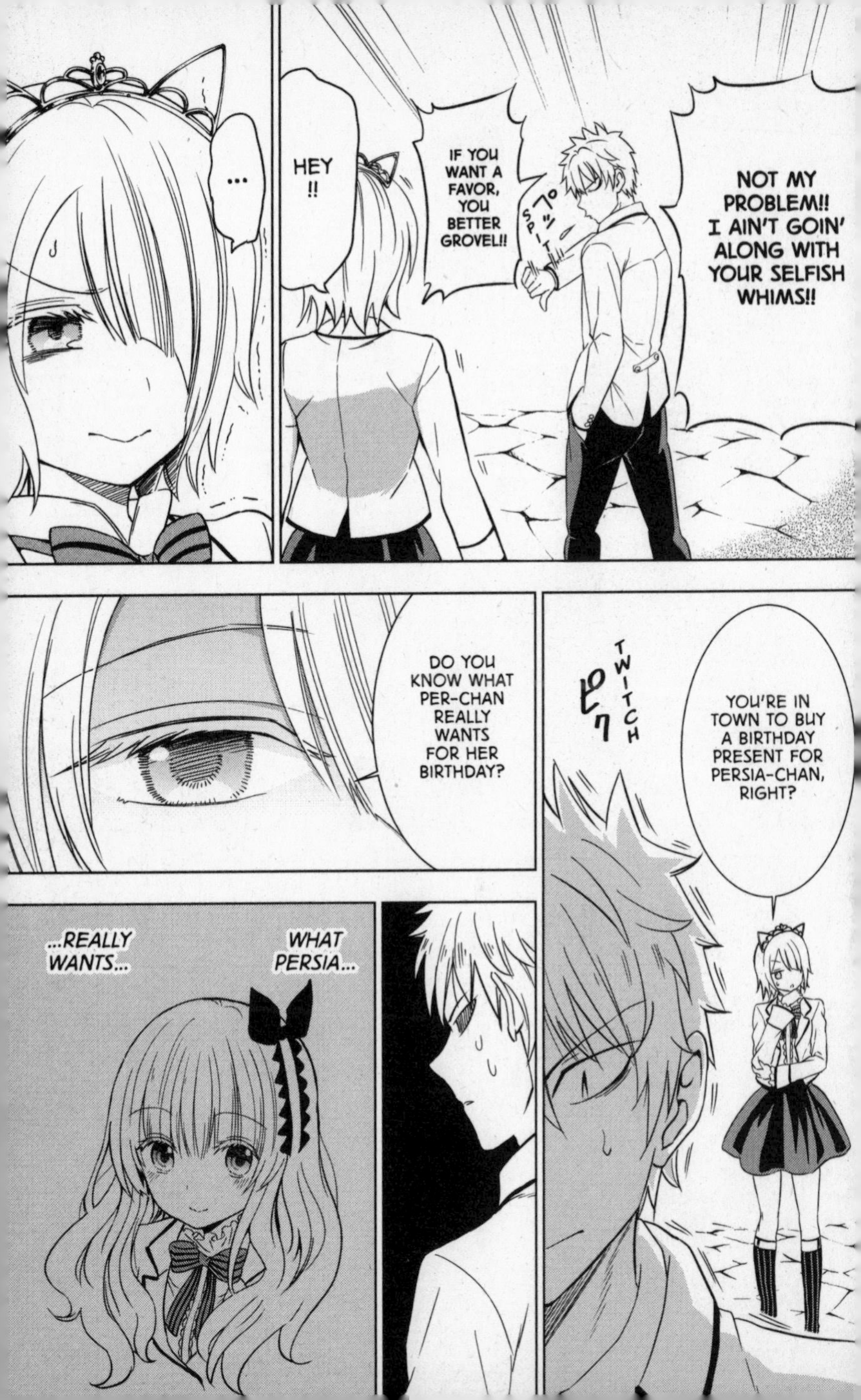
NOT MY PROBLEM!! I AIN'T GOIN' ALONG WITH YOUR SELFISH WHIMS!!
SPIT
IF YOU WANT A FAVOR, YOU BETTER GROVEL!!
HEY !!
...
YOU'RE IN TOWN TO BUY A BIRTHDAY PRESENT FOR PERSIA-CHAN, RIGHT?
TWITCH
DO YOU KNOW WHAT PER-CHAN REALLY WANTS FOR HER BIRTHDAY?
WHAT PERSIA...
...REALLY WANTS...

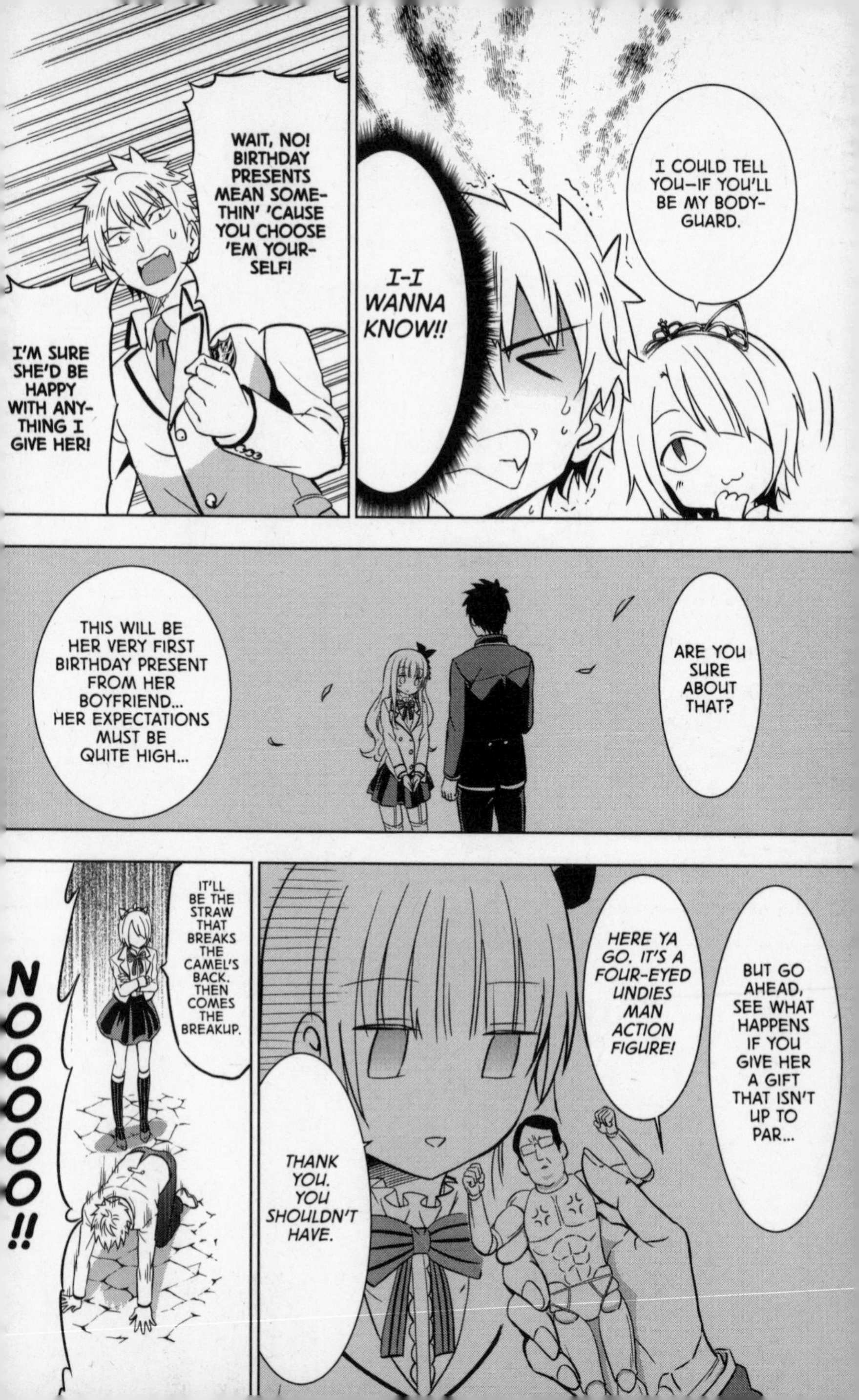
I COULD TELL YOU—IF YOU'LL BE MY BODYGUARD.
I-I WANNA KNOW!!
WAIT, NO! BIRTHDAY PRESENTS MEAN SOMETHIN' 'CAUSE YOU CHOOSE 'EM YOURSELF!
I'M SURE SHE'D BE HAPPY WITH ANYTHING I GIVE HER!
ARE YOU SURE ABOUT THAT?
THIS WILL BE HER VERY FIRST BIRTHDAY PRESENT FROM HER BOYFRIEND... HER EXPECTATIONS MUST BE QUITE HIGH...
BUT GO AHEAD, SEE WHAT HAPPENS IF YOU GIVE HER A GIFT THAT ISN'T UP TO PAR...
HERE YA GO. IT'S A FOUR-EYED UNDIES MAN ACTION FIGURE!
THANK YOU. YOU SHOULDN'T HAVE.
IT'LL BE THE STRAW THAT BREAKS THE CAMEL'S BACK. THEN COMES THE BREAKUP.
NOOOOOOO!!

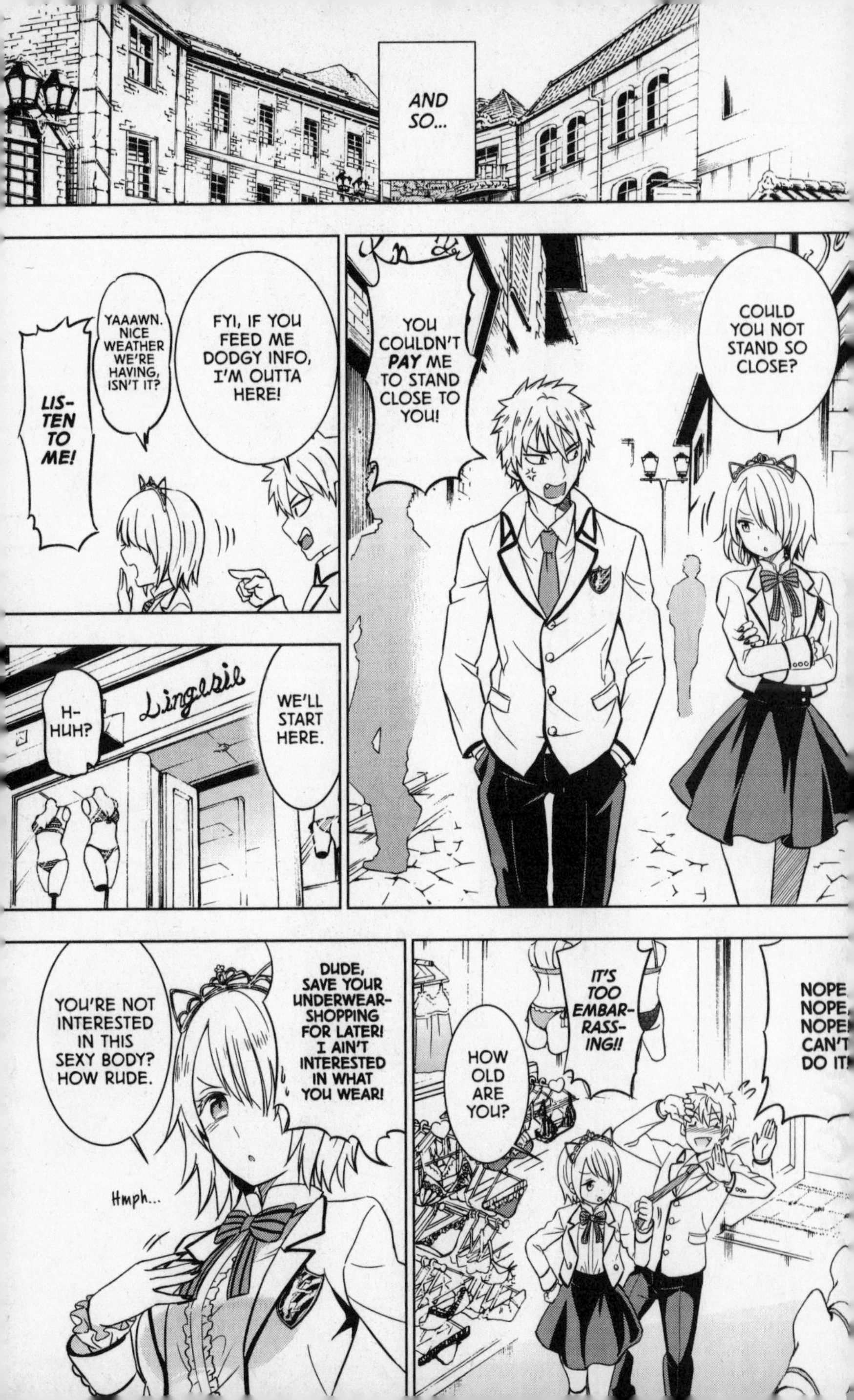
AND SO...
COULD YOU NOT STAND SO CLOSE?
YOU COULDN'T *PAY* ME TO STAND CLOSE TO YOU!
FYI, IF YOU FEED ME DODGY INFO, I'M OUTTA HERE!
YAAAWN. NICE WEATHER WE'RE HAVING, ISN'T IT?
LIS-TEN TO ME!
WE'LL START HERE.
H-HUH?
Lingerie
NOPE, NOPE, NOPE! CAN'T DO IT!
IT'S TOO EMBAR-RASS-ING!!
HOW OLD ARE YOU?
DUDE, SAVE YOUR UNDERWEAR-SHOPPING FOR LATER! I AIN'T INTERESTED IN WHAT YOU WEAR!
YOU'RE NOT INTERESTED IN THIS SEXY BODY? HOW RUDE.
Hmph...

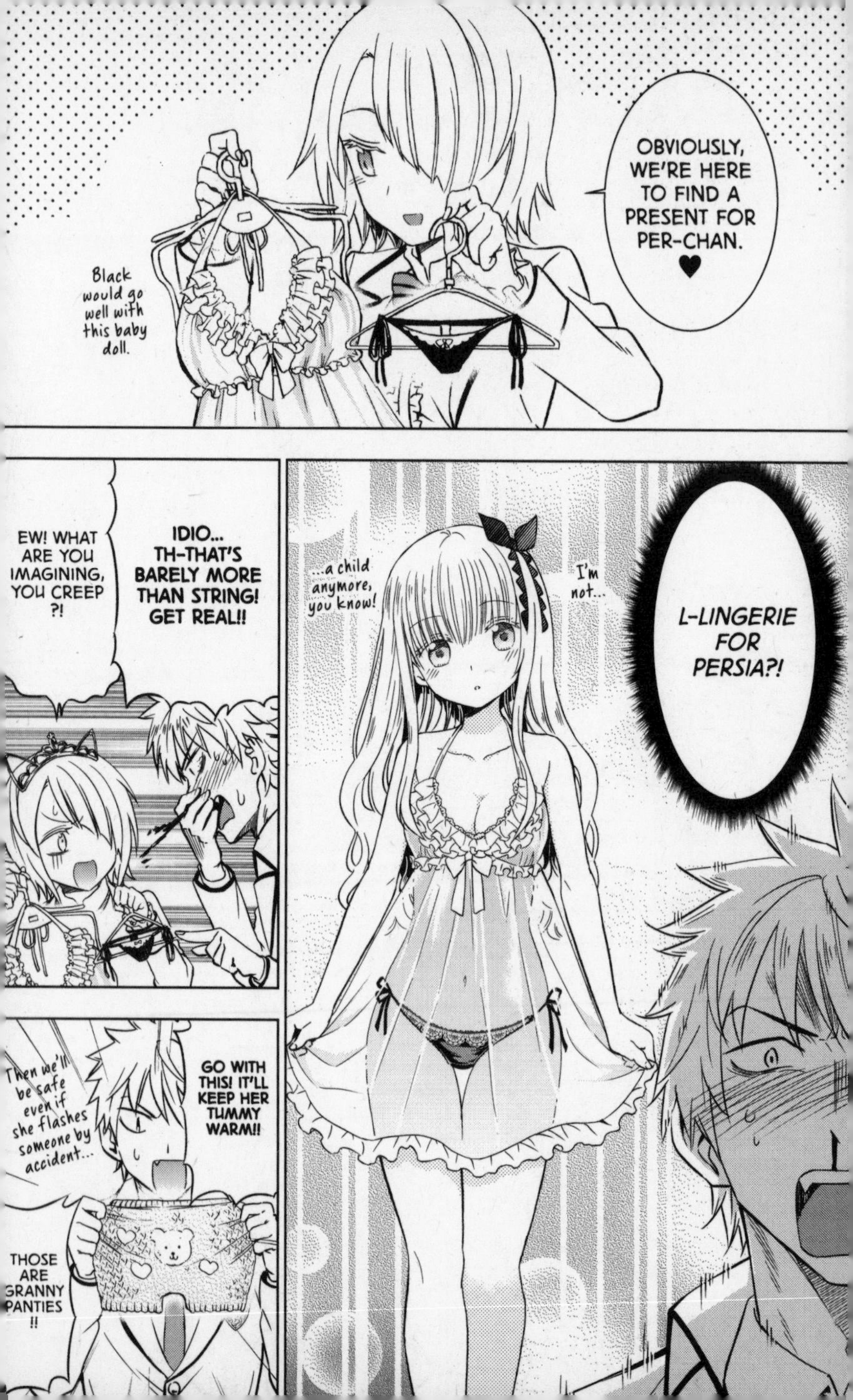
OBVIOUSLY, WE'RE HERE TO FIND A PRESENT FOR PER-CHAN. ♥
Black would go well with this baby doll.
L-LINGERIE FOR PERSIA?!
I'm not...
...a child anymore, you know!
IDIO... TH-THAT'S BARELY MORE THAN STRING! GET REAL!!
EW! WHAT ARE YOU IMAGINING, YOU CREEP ?!
GO WITH THIS! IT'LL KEEP HER TUMMY WARM!!
Then we'll be safe even if she flashes someone by accident...
THOSE ARE GRANNY PANTIES !!

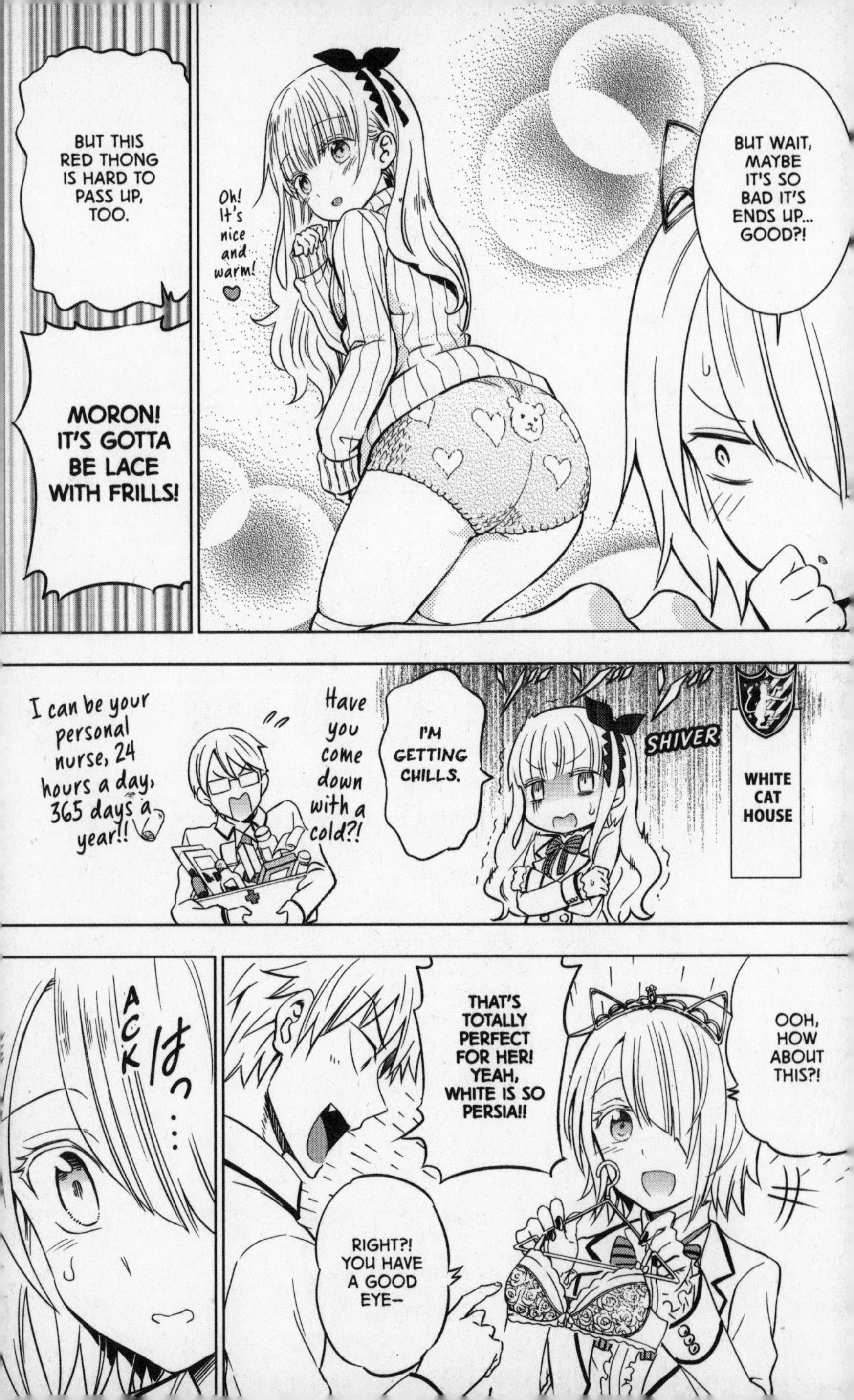

BUT WAIT, MAYBE IT'S SO BAD IT'S ENDS UP... GOOD?!
Oh! It's nice and warm!
BUT THIS RED THONG IS HARD TO PASS UP, TOO.
MORON! IT'S GOTTA BE LACE WITH FRILLS!
WHITE CAT HOUSE
SHIVER
I'M GETTING CHILLS.
Have you come down with a cold?!
I can be your personal nurse, 24 hours a day, 365 days a year!!
OOH, HOW ABOUT THIS?!
THAT'S TOTALLY PERFECT FOR HER! YEAH, WHITE IS SO PERSIA!!
RIGHT?! YOU HAVE A GOOD EYE–
ACK
はっ
...

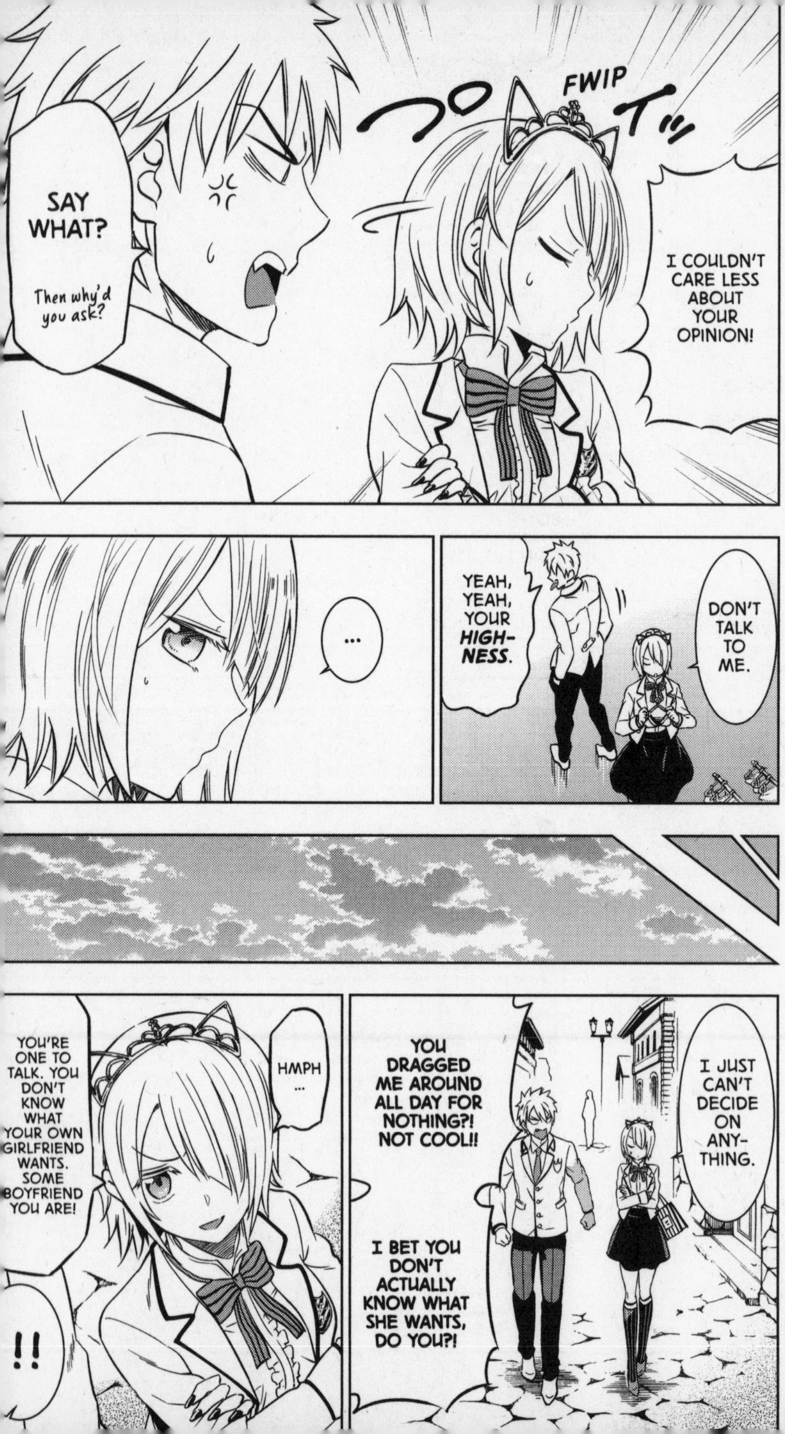
FWIP
I COULDN'T CARE LESS ABOUT YOUR OPINION!
SAY WHAT?
Then why'd you ask?
DON'T TALK TO ME.
YEAH, YEAH, YOUR *HIGHNESS*.
...
I JUST CAN'T DECIDE ON ANYTHING.
YOU DRAGGED ME AROUND ALL DAY FOR NOTHING?! NOT COOL!!
I BET YOU DON'T ACTUALLY KNOW WHAT SHE WANTS, DO YOU?!
HMPH ...
YOU'RE ONE TO TALK. YOU DON'T KNOW WHAT YOUR OWN GIRLFRIEND WANTS. SOME BOYFRIEND YOU ARE!
!!

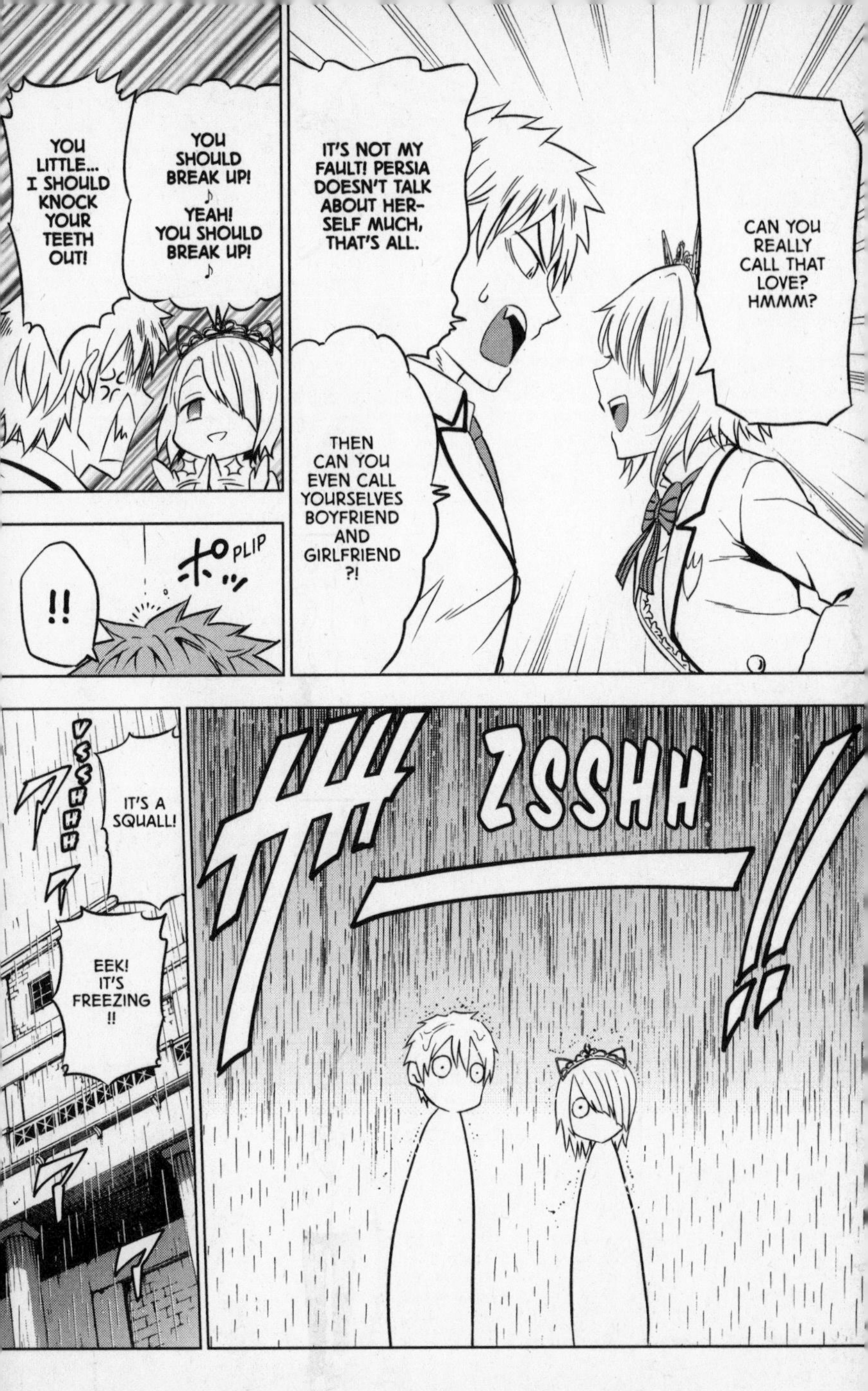
CAN YOU REALLY CALL THAT LOVE? HMMM?
IT'S NOT MY FAULT! PERSIA DOESN'T TALK ABOUT HER-SELF MUCH, THAT'S ALL.
THEN CAN YOU EVEN CALL YOURSELVES BOYFRIEND AND GIRLFRIEND ?!
YOU SHOULD BREAK UP! ♪ YEAH! YOU SHOULD BREAK UP! ♪
YOU LITTLE... I SHOULD KNOCK YOUR TEETH OUT!
PLIP
!!
ZSSHH
VSSHHH
IT'S A SQUALL!
EEK! IT'S FREEZING !!

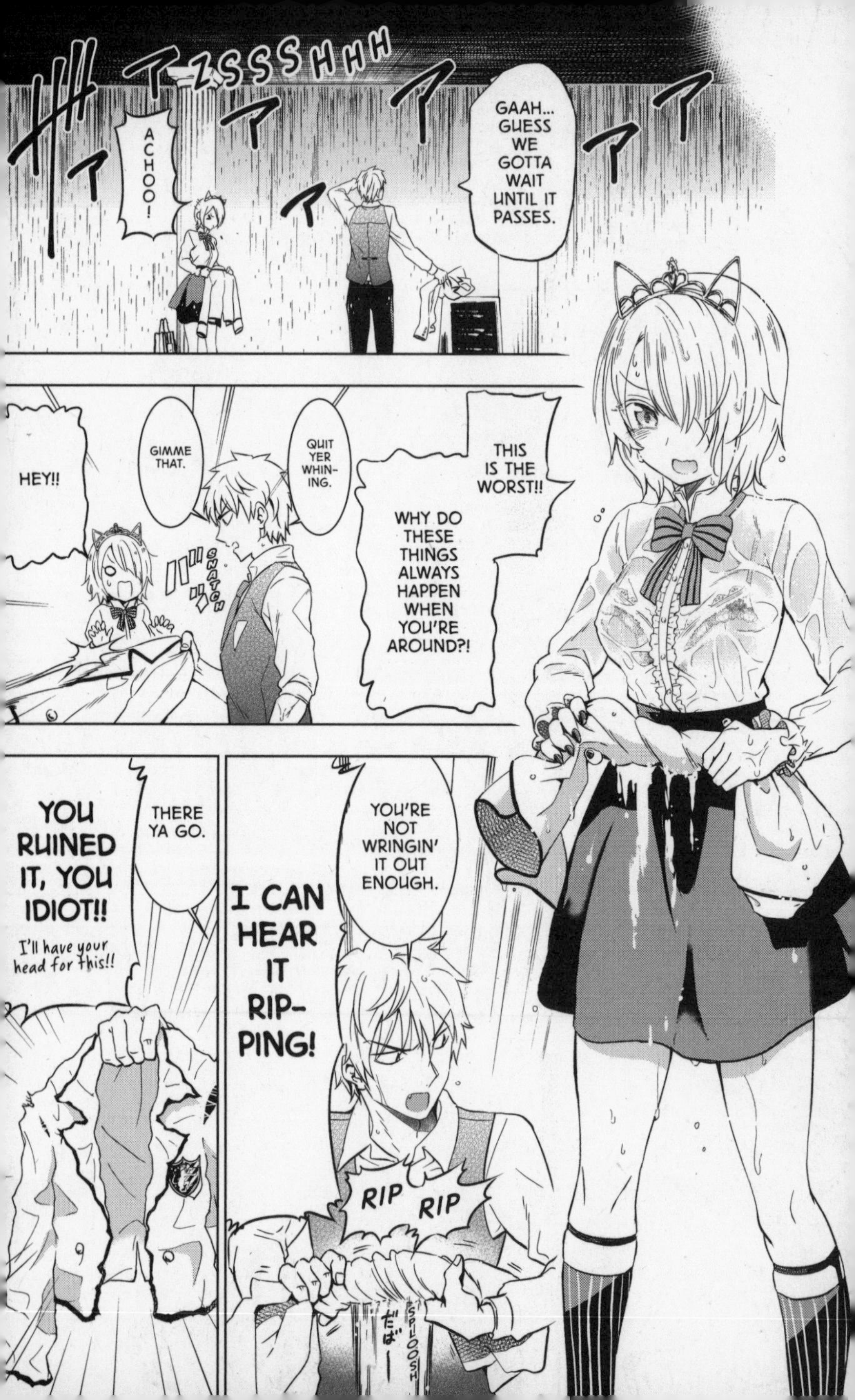
ZSSSSHHH
GAAH... GUESS WE GOTTA WAIT UNTIL IT PASSES.
ACHOO!
THIS IS THE WORST!!
WHY DO THESE THINGS ALWAYS HAPPEN WHEN YOU'RE AROUND?!
QUIT YER WHINING.
GIMME THAT.
SNATCH
HEY!!
YOU'RE NOT WRINGIN' IT OUT ENOUGH.
RIP RIP
SPLOOSH
I CAN HEAR IT RIPPING!
THERE YA GO.
YOU RUINED IT, YOU IDIOT!!
I'll have your head for this!!

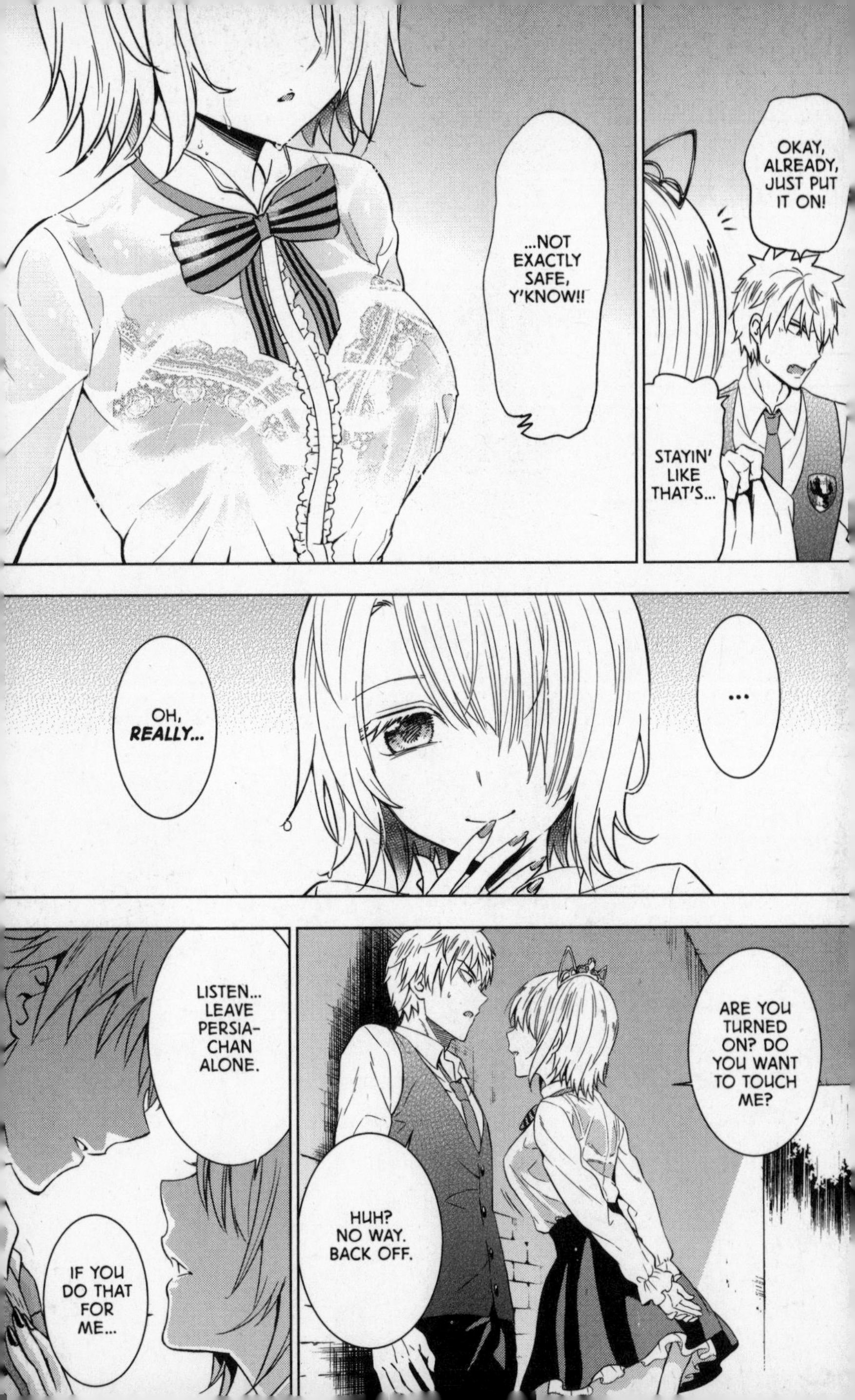
OKAY, ALREADY, JUST PUT IT ON!
STAYIN' LIKE THAT'S...
...NOT EXACTLY SAFE, Y'KNOW!!
...
OH, *REALLY*...
ARE YOU TURNED ON? DO YOU WANT TO TOUCH ME?
HUH? NO WAY. BACK OFF.
LISTEN... LEAVE PERSIA-CHAN ALONE.
IF YOU DO THAT FOR ME...

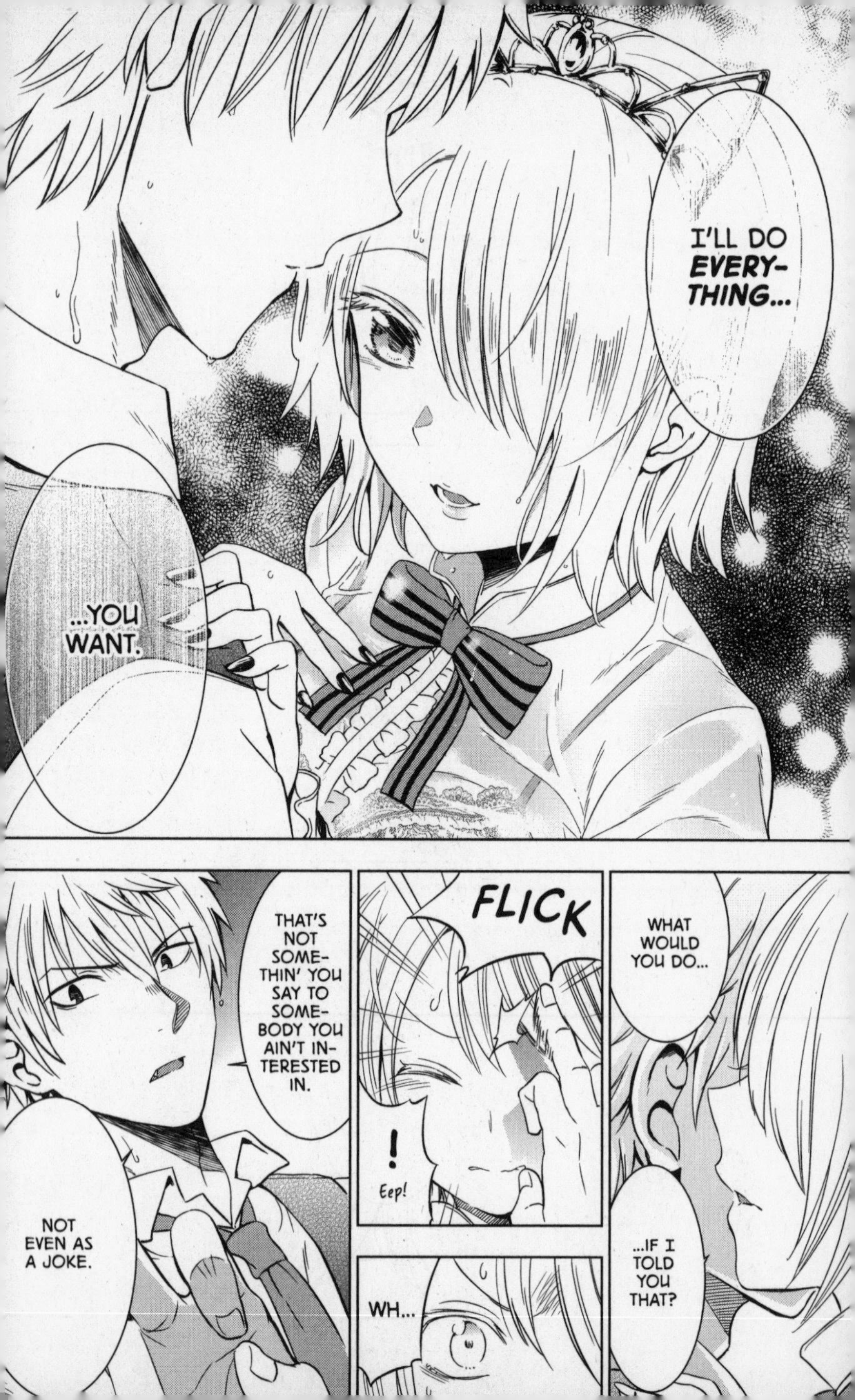

I'LL DO EVERY-THING...
...YOU WANT.
WHAT WOULD YOU DO...
...IF I TOLD YOU THAT?
FLICK
!
Eep!
WH...
THAT'S NOT SOME-THIN' YOU SAY TO SOME-BODY YOU AIN'T IN-TERESTED IN.
NOT EVEN AS A JOKE.

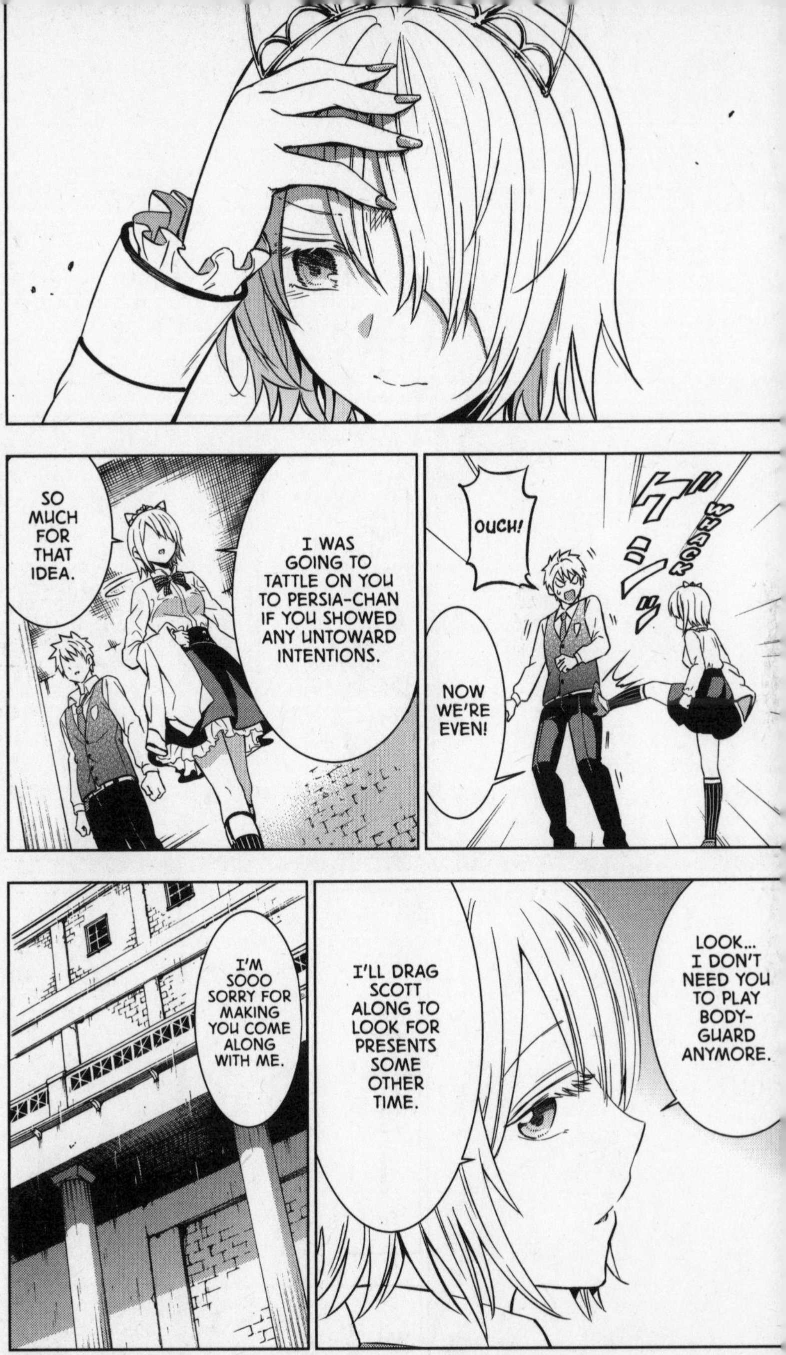
WHACK
OUCH!
NOW WE'RE EVEN!
I WAS GOING TO TATTLE ON YOU TO PERSIA-CHAN IF YOU SHOWED ANY UNTOWARD INTENTIONS.
SO MUCH FOR THAT IDEA.
LOOK... I DON'T NEED YOU TO PLAY BODY-GUARD ANYMORE.
I'LL DRAG SCOTT ALONG TO LOOK FOR PRESENTS SOME OTHER TIME.
I'M SOOO SORRY FOR MAKING YOU COME ALONG WITH ME.

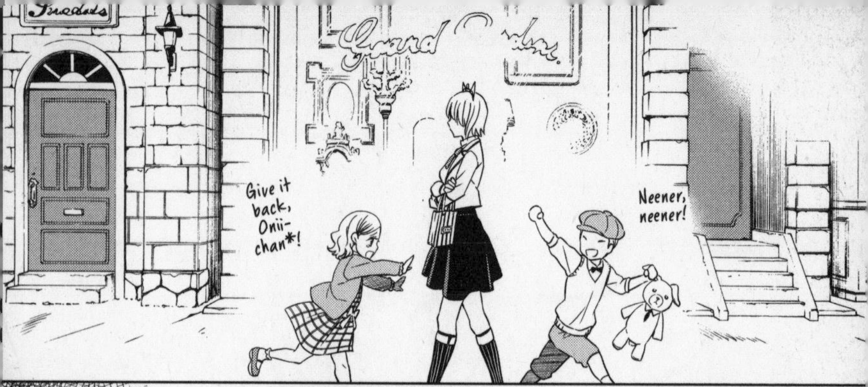
Neener, neener!
Give it back, Onii-chan*!

TRANSLATOR'S NOTE: "BIG BRO."

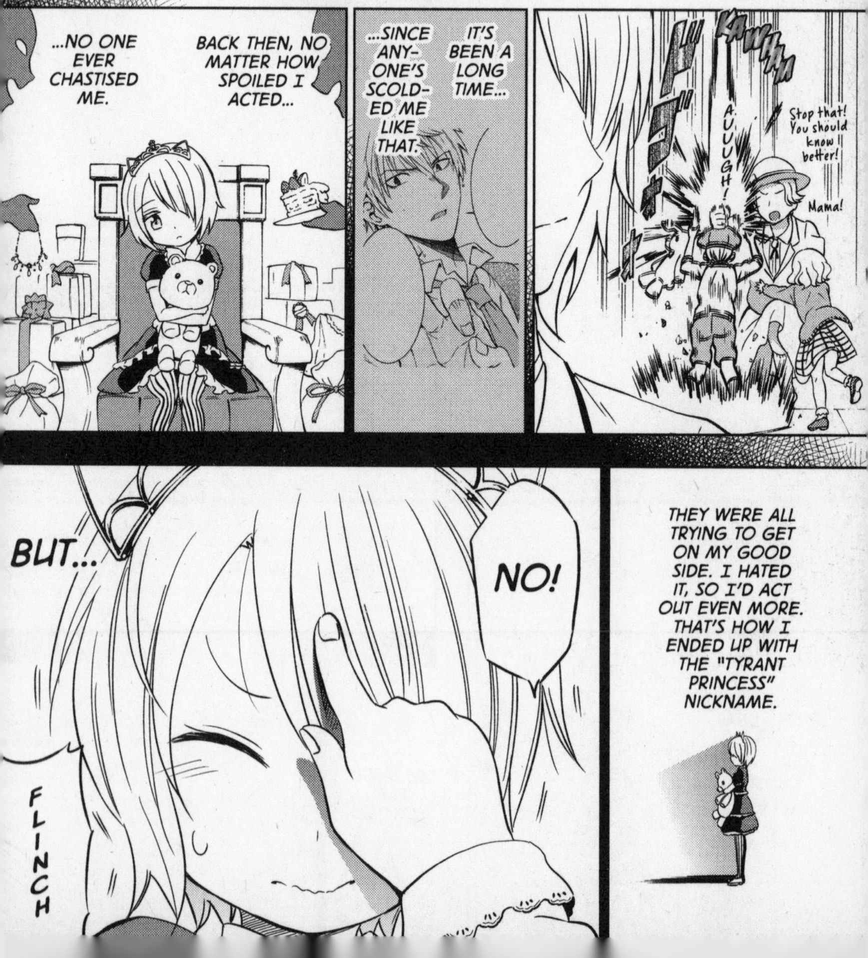
KAWHAM
Stop that! You should know better!
AUUUGH!
Mama!
IT'S BEEN A LONG TIME...
...SINCE ANYONE'S SCOLDED ME LIKE THAT.
BACK THEN, NO MATTER HOW SPOILED I ACTED...
...NO ONE EVER CHASTISED ME.
THEY WERE ALL TRYING TO GET ON MY GOOD SIDE. I HATED IT, SO I'D ACT OUT EVEN MORE. THAT'S HOW I ENDED UP WITH THE "TYRANT PRINCESS" NICKNAME.
NO!
BUT...
FLINCH

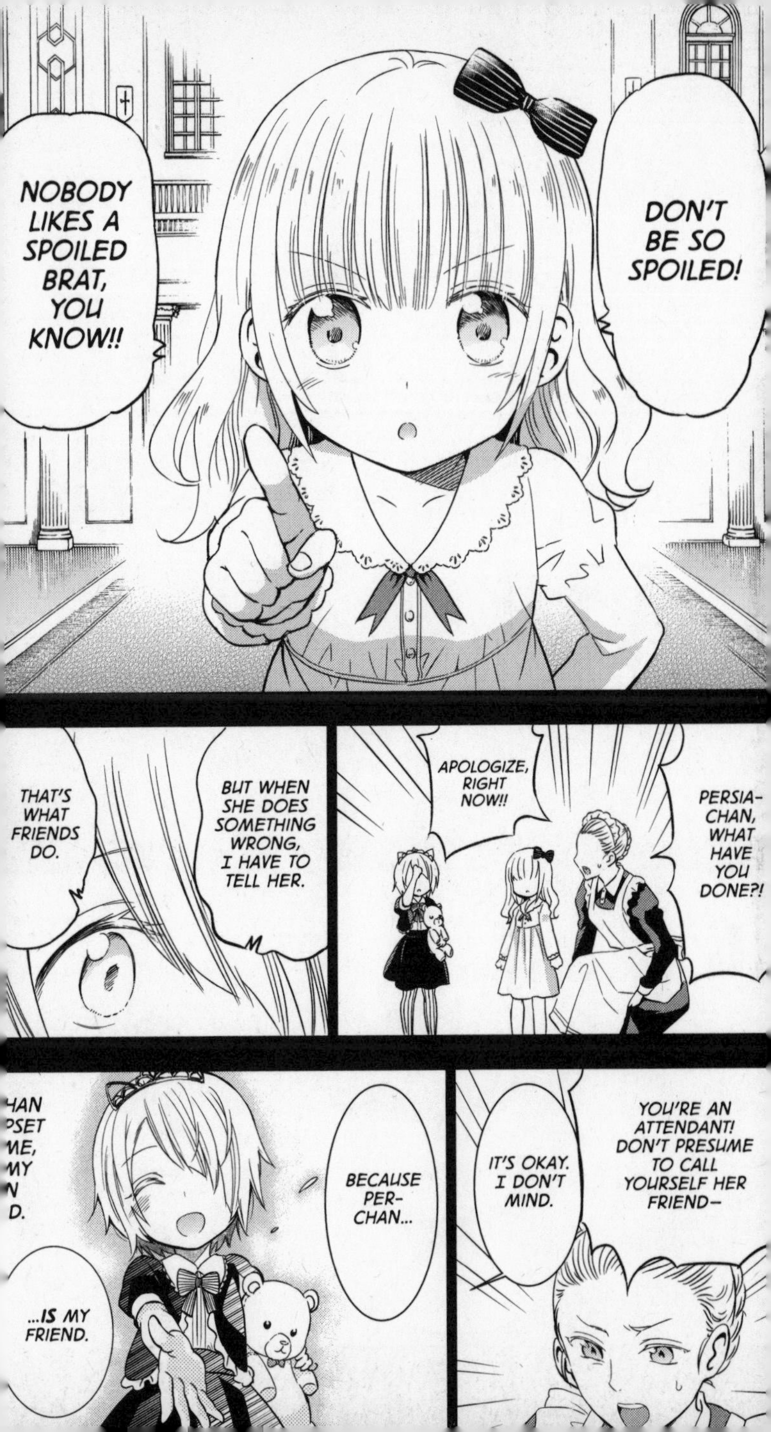
DON'T BE SO SPOILED!
NOBODY LIKES A SPOILED BRAT, YOU KNOW!!
PERSIA-CHAN, WHAT HAVE YOU DONE?!
APOLOGIZE, RIGHT NOW!!
BUT WHEN SHE DOES SOMETHING WRONG, I HAVE TO TELL HER.
THAT'S WHAT FRIENDS DO.
YOU'RE AN ATTENDANT! DON'T PRESUME TO CALL YOURSELF HER FRIEND—
IT'S OKAY. I DON'T MIND.
BECAUSE PER-CHAN...
...IS MY FRIEND.

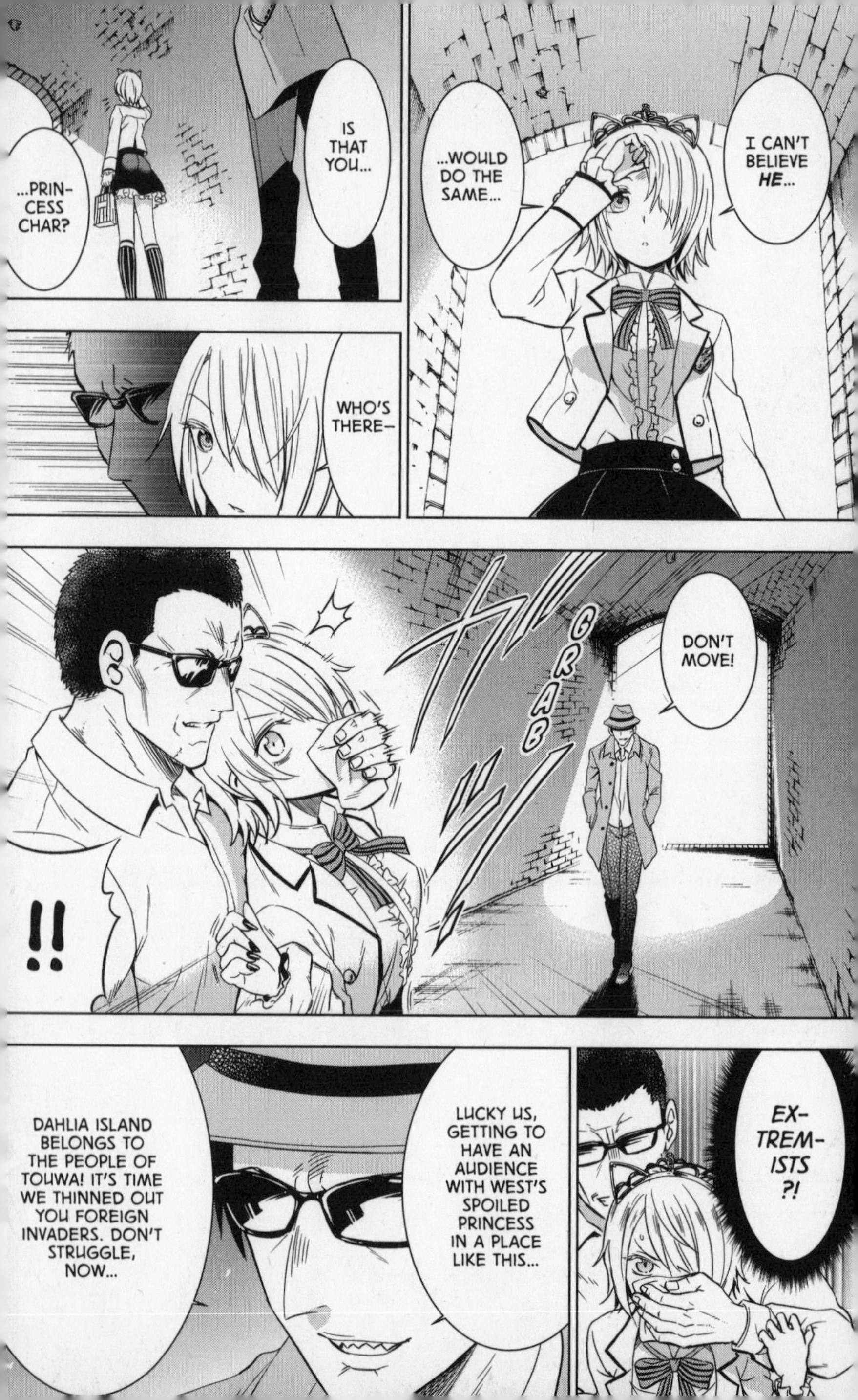
I CAN'T BELIEVE *HE*...
...WOULD DO THE SAME...
IS THAT YOU...
...PRINCESS CHAR?
WHO'S THERE—
DON'T MOVE!
GRAB
!!
EX-TREM-ISTS?!
LUCKY US, GETTING TO HAVE AN AUDIENCE WITH WEST'S SPOILED PRINCESS IN A PLACE LIKE THIS...
DAHLIA ISLAND BELONGS TO THE PEOPLE OF TOUWA! IT'S TIME WE THINNED OUT YOU FOREIGN INVADERS. DON'T STRUGGLE, NOW...

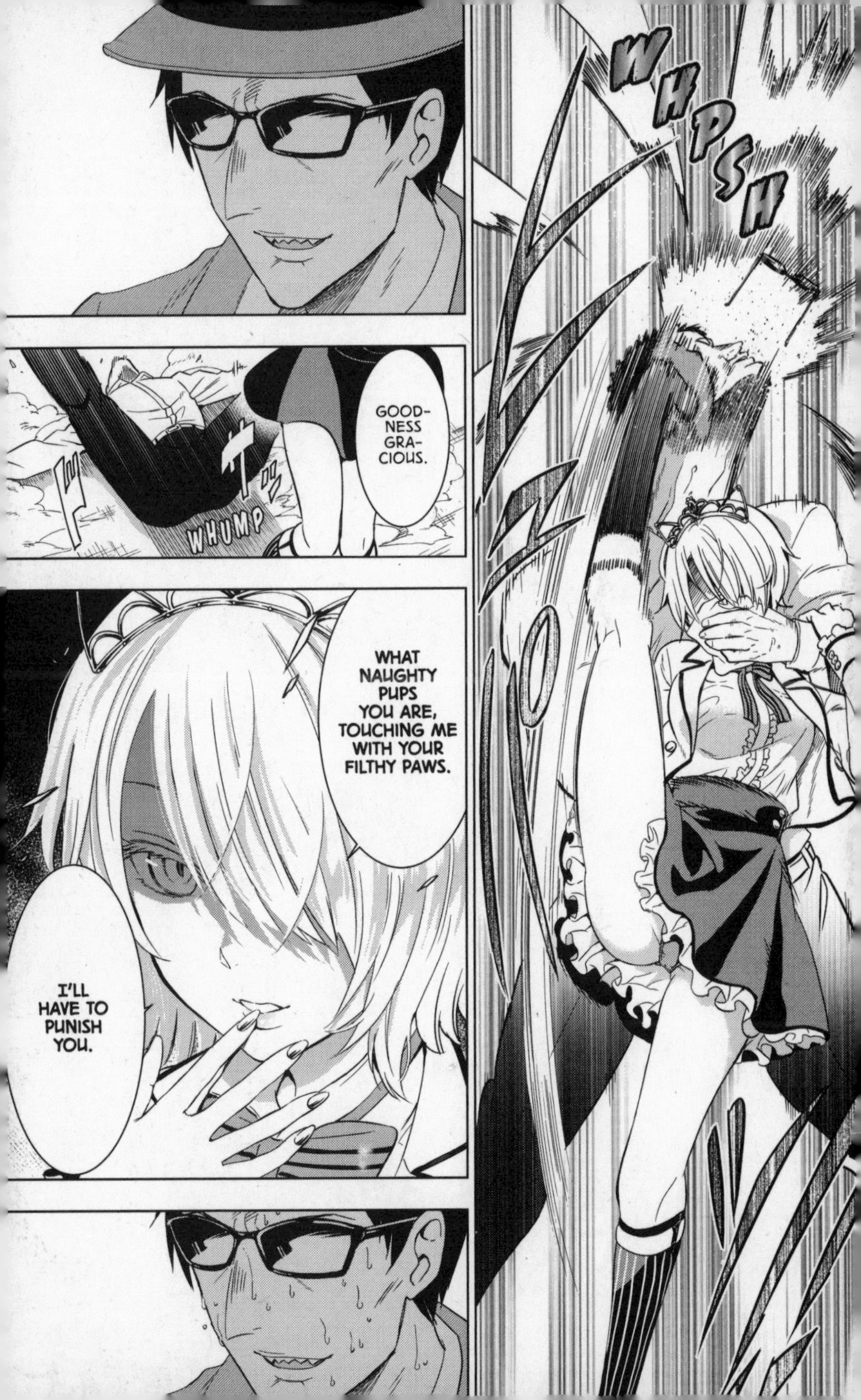
WHPSH
GOODNESS GRACIOUS.
WHUMP
WHAT NAUGHTY PUPS YOU ARE, TOUCHING ME WITH YOUR FILTHY PAWS.
I'LL HAVE TO PUNISH YOU.

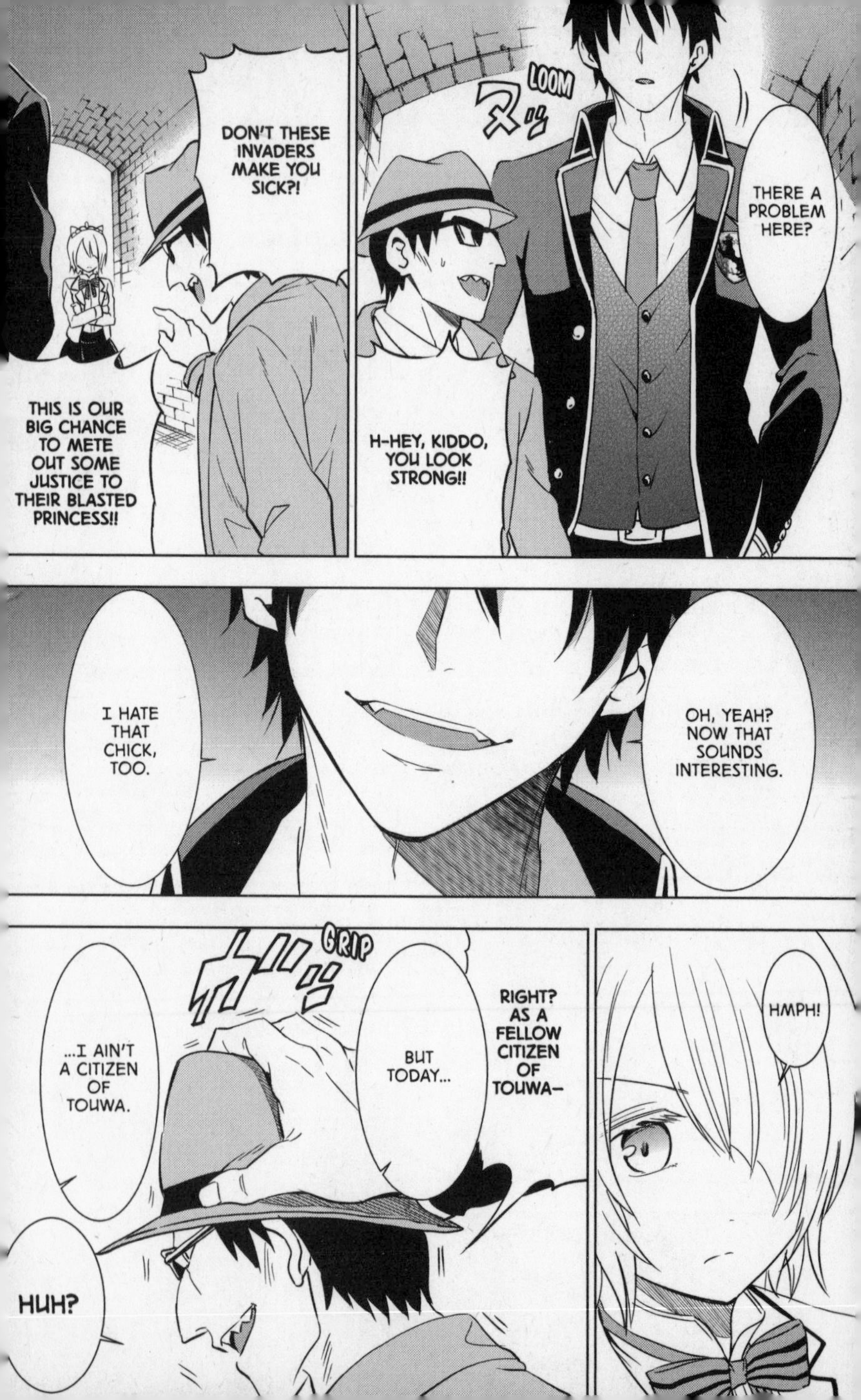
LOOM
THERE A PROBLEM HERE?
H-HEY, KIDDO, YOU LOOK STRONG!!
DON'T THESE INVADERS MAKE YOU SICK?!
THIS IS OUR BIG CHANCE TO METE OUT SOME JUSTICE TO THEIR BLASTED PRINCESS!!
OH, YEAH? NOW THAT SOUNDS INTERESTING.
I HATE THAT CHICK, TOO.
HMPH!
RIGHT? AS A FELLOW CITIZEN OF TOUWA—
GRIP
BUT TODAY...
...I AIN'T A CITIZEN OF TOUWA.
HUH?

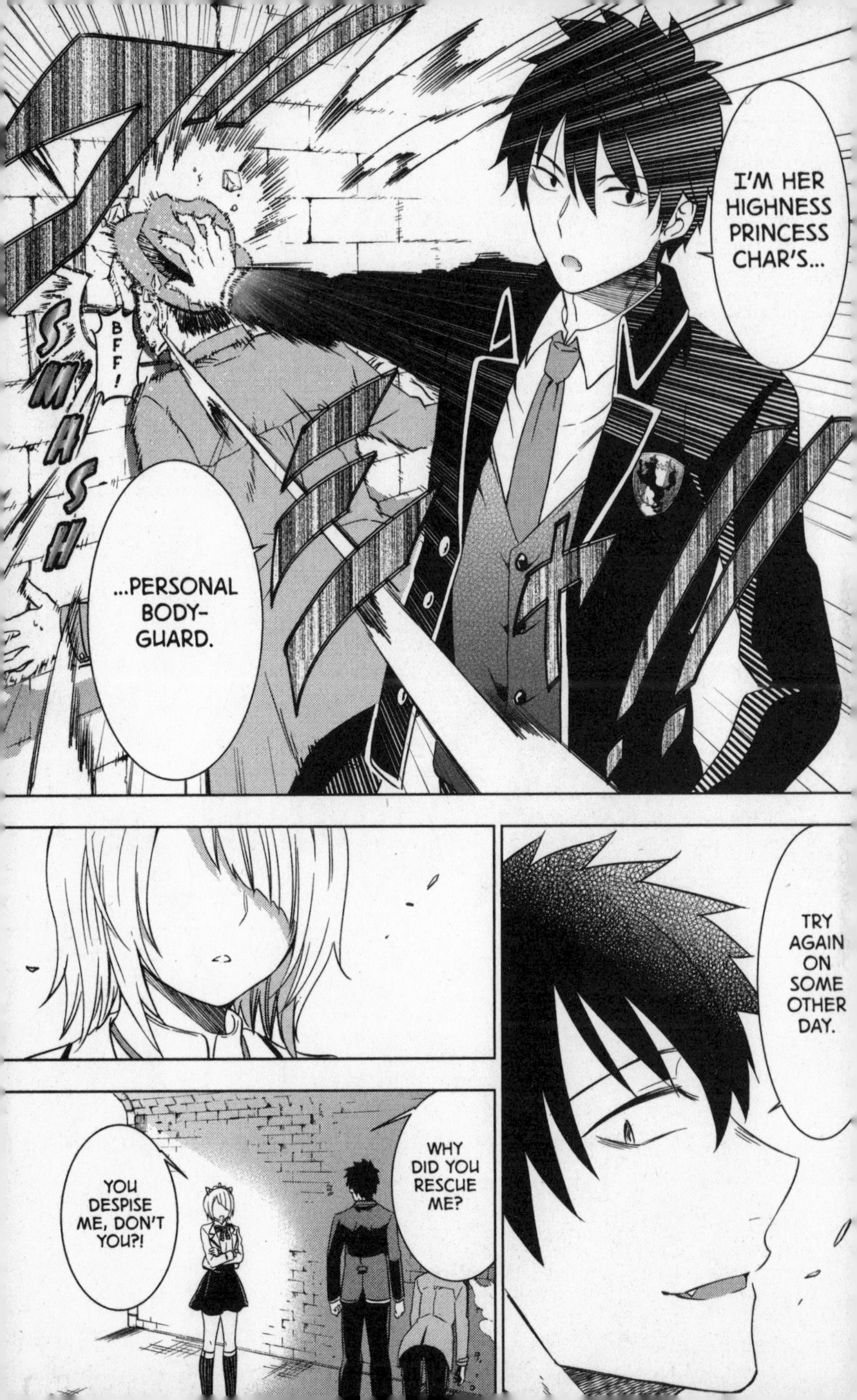
I'M HER HIGHNESS PRINCESS CHAR'S...
SMASH
BFF!
...PERSONAL BODY-GUARD.
TRY AGAIN ON SOME OTHER DAY.
WHY DID YOU RESCUE ME?
YOU DESPISE ME, DON'T YOU?!

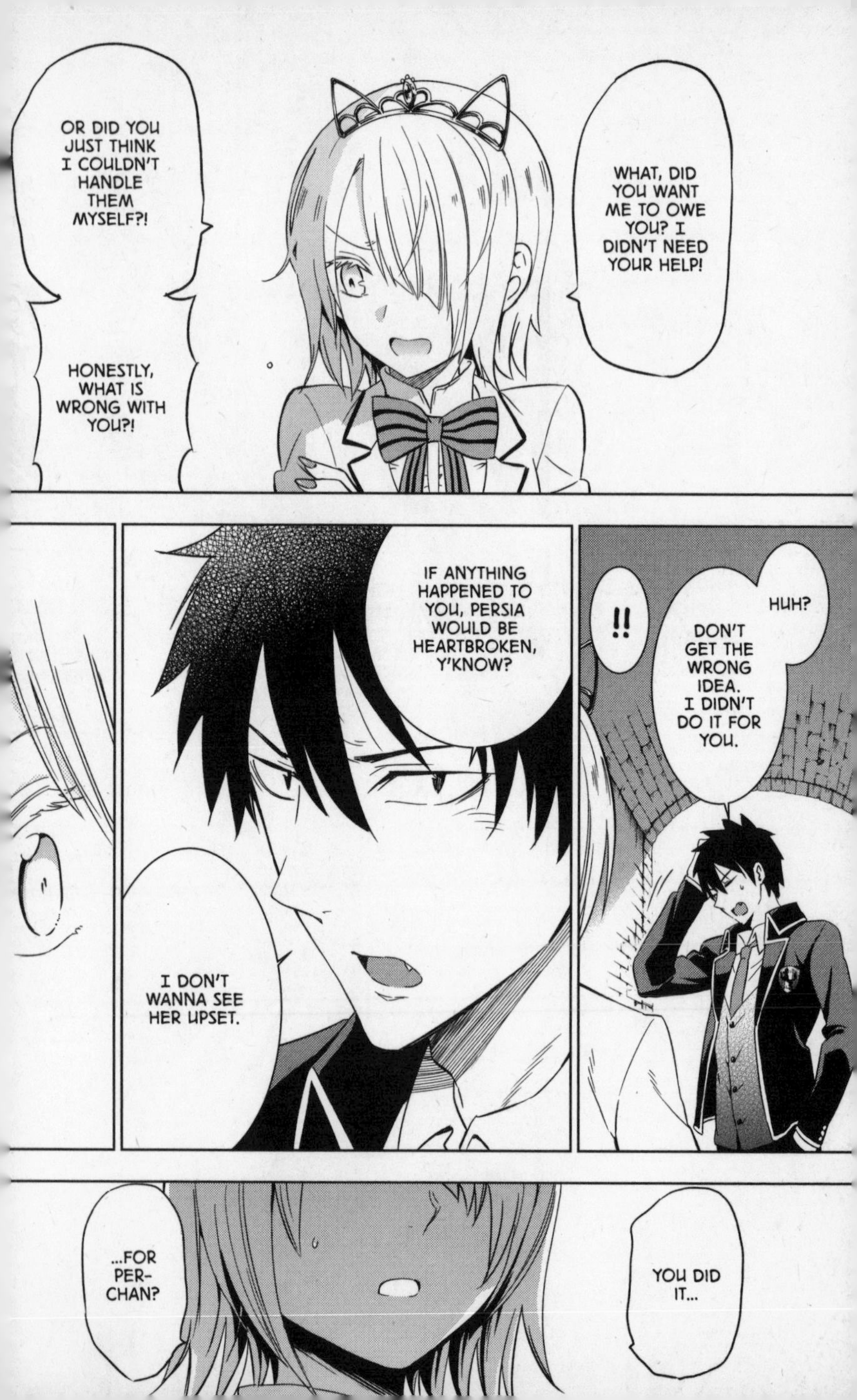
WHAT, DID YOU WANT ME TO OWE YOU? I DIDN'T NEED YOUR HELP!
OR DID YOU JUST THINK I COULDN'T HANDLE THEM MYSELF?!
HONESTLY, WHAT IS WRONG WITH YOU?!
HUH?
DON'T GET THE WRONG IDEA. I DIDN'T DO IT FOR YOU.
!!
IF ANYTHING HAPPENED TO YOU, PERSIA WOULD BE HEARTBROKEN, Y'KNOW?
I DON'T WANNA SEE HER UPSET.
YOU DID IT...
...FOR PER-CHAN?

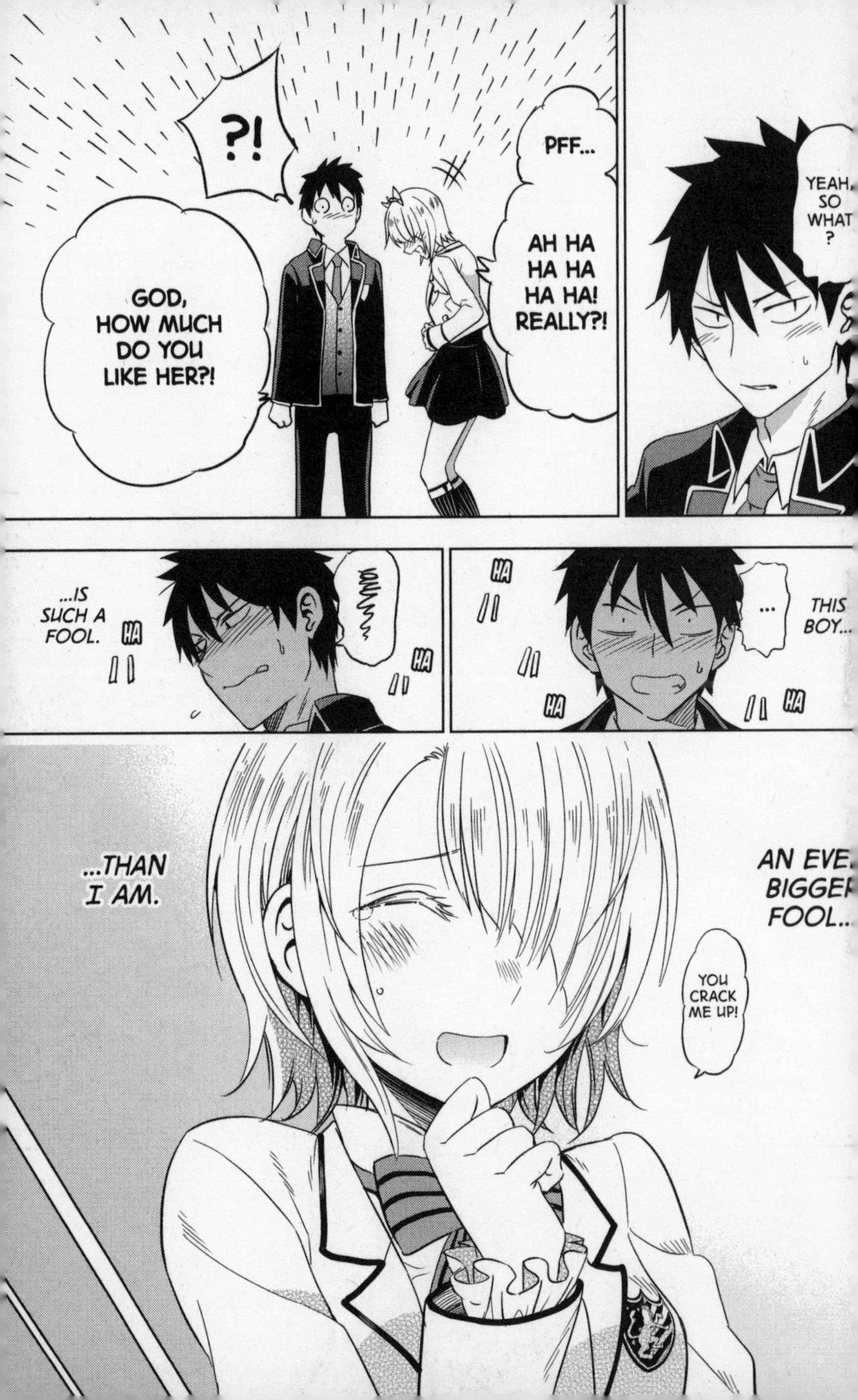
YEAH, SO WHAT?
PFF...
AH HA HA HA HA HA! REALLY?!
?!
GOD, HOW MUCH DO YOU LIKE HER?!
THIS BOY...
...
HA
HA
HA
HA
...IS SUCH A FOOL.
HA
AN EVE
BIGGE
FOOL...
YOU CRACK ME UP!
...THAN I AM.

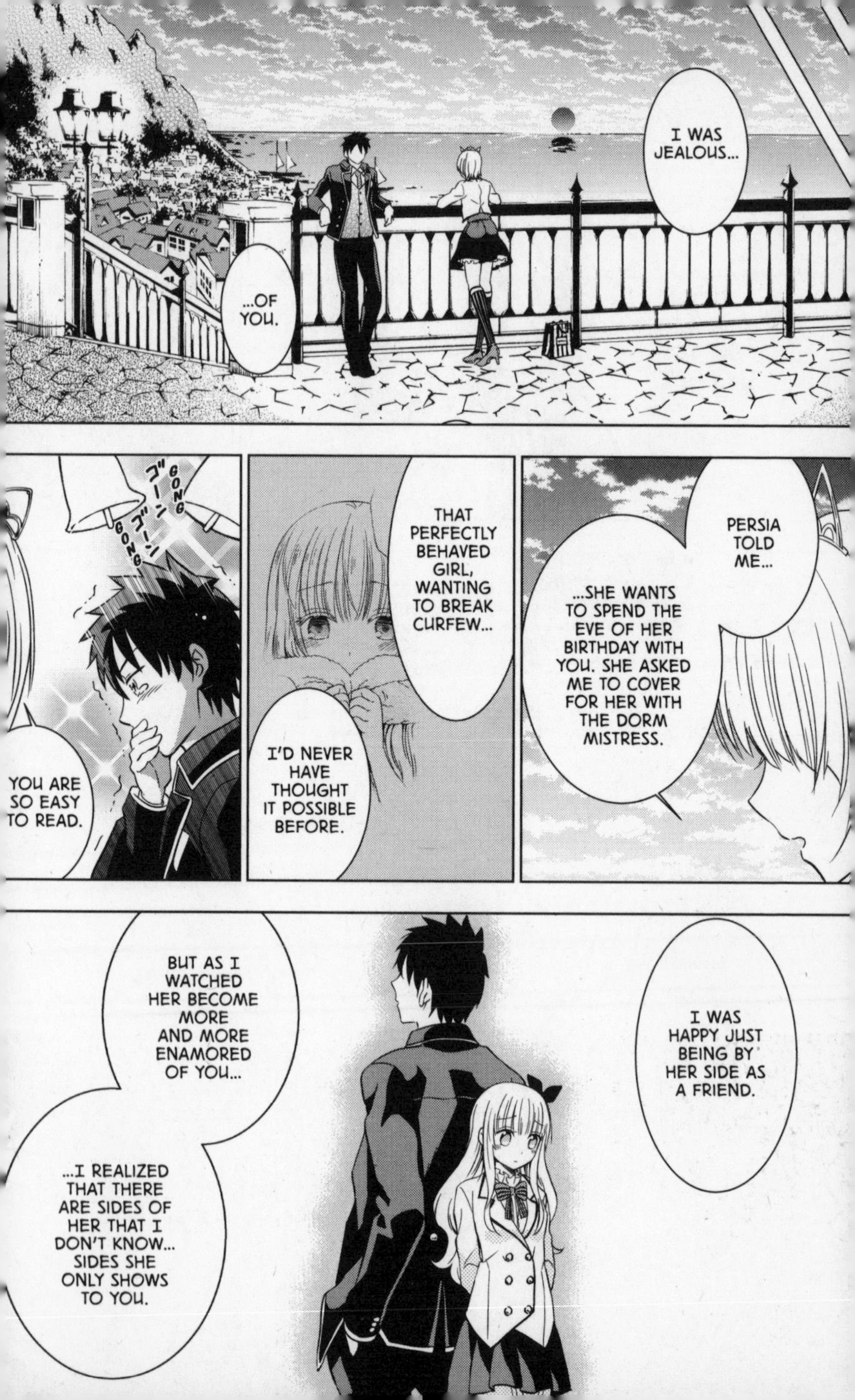
I WAS JEALOUS...
...OF YOU.
PERSIA TOLD ME...
...SHE WANTS TO SPEND THE EVE OF HER BIRTHDAY WITH YOU. SHE ASKED ME TO COVER FOR HER WITH THE DORM MISTRESS.
THAT PERFECTLY BEHAVED GIRL, WANTING TO BREAK CURFEW...
I'D NEVER HAVE THOUGHT IT POSSIBLE BEFORE.
GONG
GONG
YOU ARE SO EASY TO READ.
I WAS HAPPY JUST BEING BY HER SIDE AS A FRIEND.
BUT AS I WATCHED HER BECOME MORE AND MORE ENAMORED OF YOU...
...I REALIZED THAT THERE ARE SIDES OF HER THAT I DON'T KNOW... SIDES SHE ONLY SHOWS TO YOU.

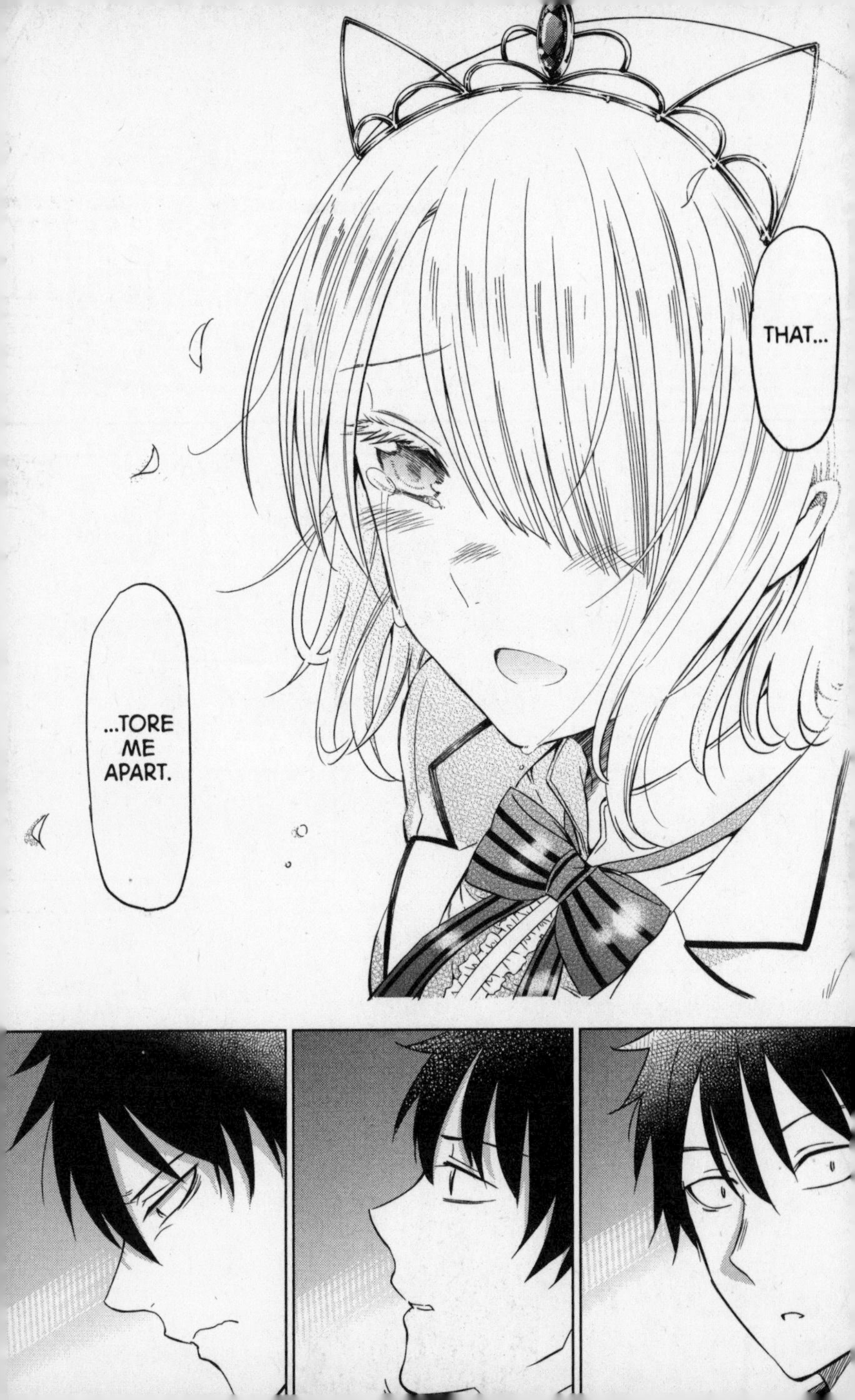
THAT...
...TORE ME APART.

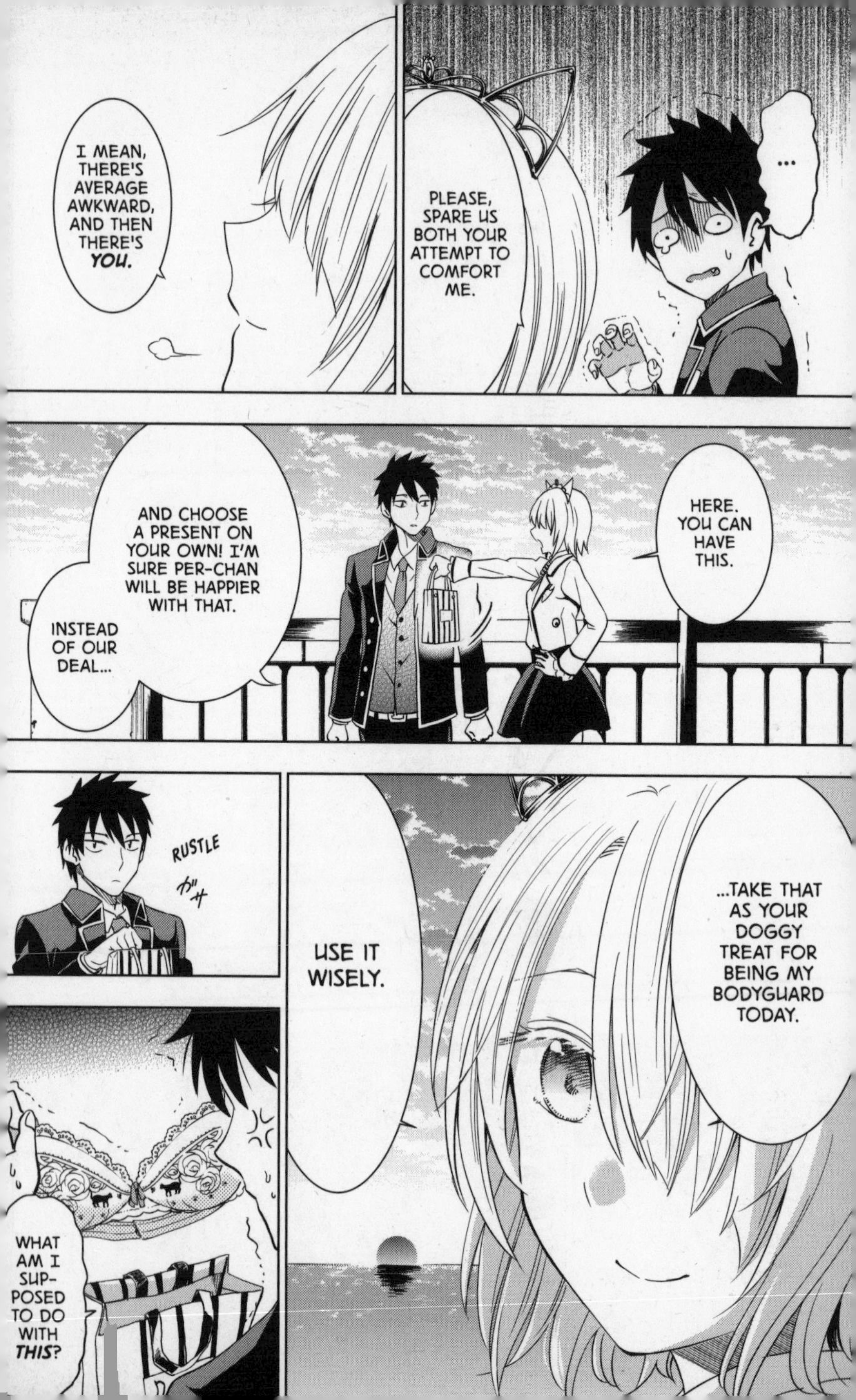
...
PLEASE, SPARE US BOTH YOUR ATTEMPT TO COMFORT ME.
I MEAN, THERE'S AVERAGE AWKWARD, AND THEN THERE'S ***YOU.***
HERE. YOU CAN HAVE THIS.
AND CHOOSE A PRESENT ON YOUR OWN! I'M SURE PER-CHAN WILL BE HAPPIER WITH THAT.
INSTEAD OF OUR DEAL...
...TAKE THAT AS YOUR DOGGY TREAT FOR BEING MY BODYGUARD TODAY.
USE IT WISELY.
RUSTLE
ガサ
WHAT AM I SUP-POSED TO DO WITH ***THIS***?

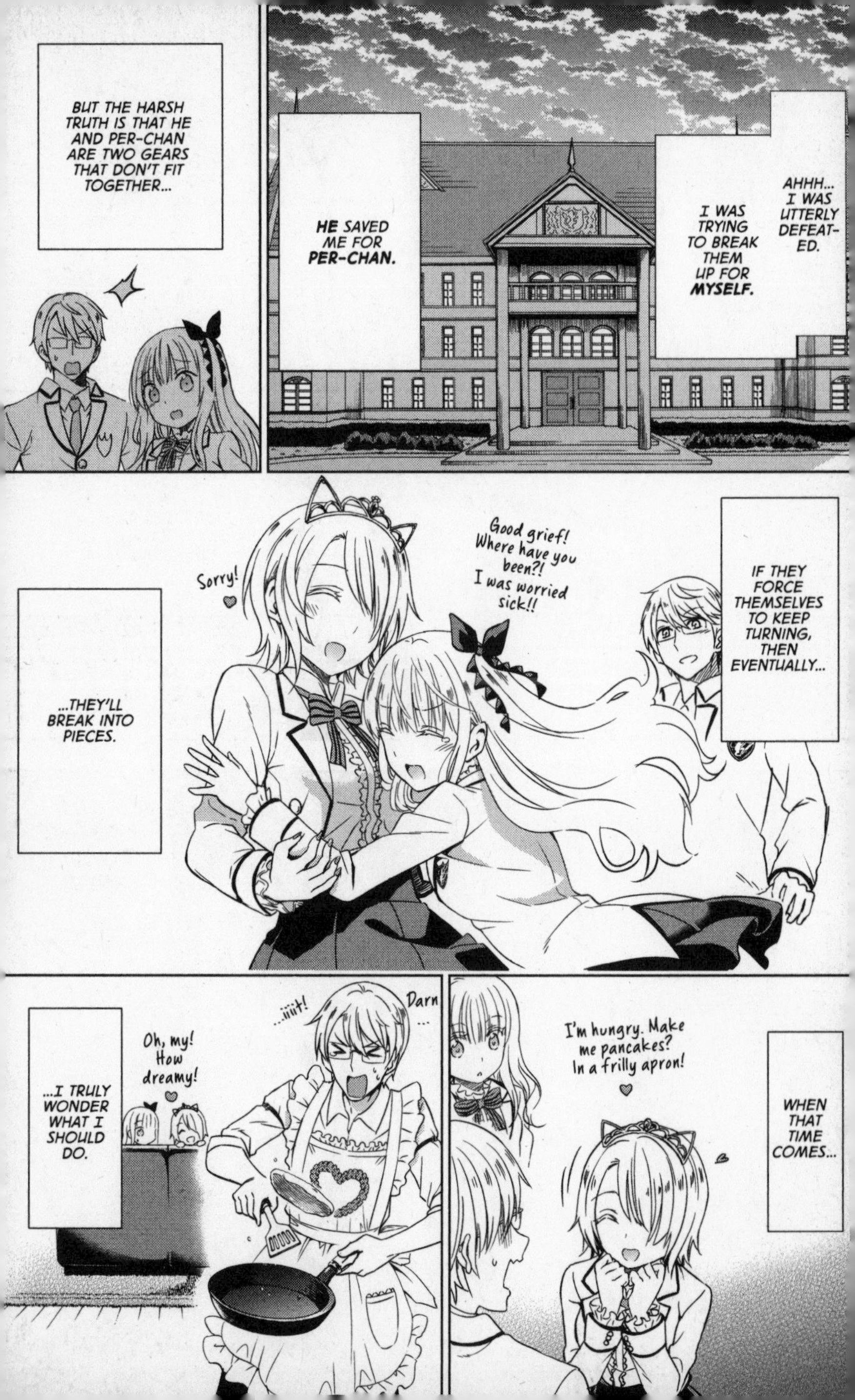
AHHH... I WAS UTTERLY DEFEAT-ED.
I WAS TRYING TO BREAK THEM UP FOR MYSELF.
HE SAVED ME FOR PER-CHAN.
BUT THE HARSH TRUTH IS THAT HE AND PER-CHAN ARE TWO GEARS THAT DON'T FIT TOGETHER...
IF THEY FORCE THEMSELVES TO KEEP TURNING, THEN EVENTUALLY...
Good grief! Where have you been?! I was worried sick!!
Sorry!
...THEY'LL BREAK INTO PIECES.
WHEN THAT TIME COMES...
I'm hungry. Make me pancakes? In a frilly apron!
Darn ...
...iiiit!
Oh, my! How dreamy!
...I TRULY WONDER WHAT I SHOULD DO.

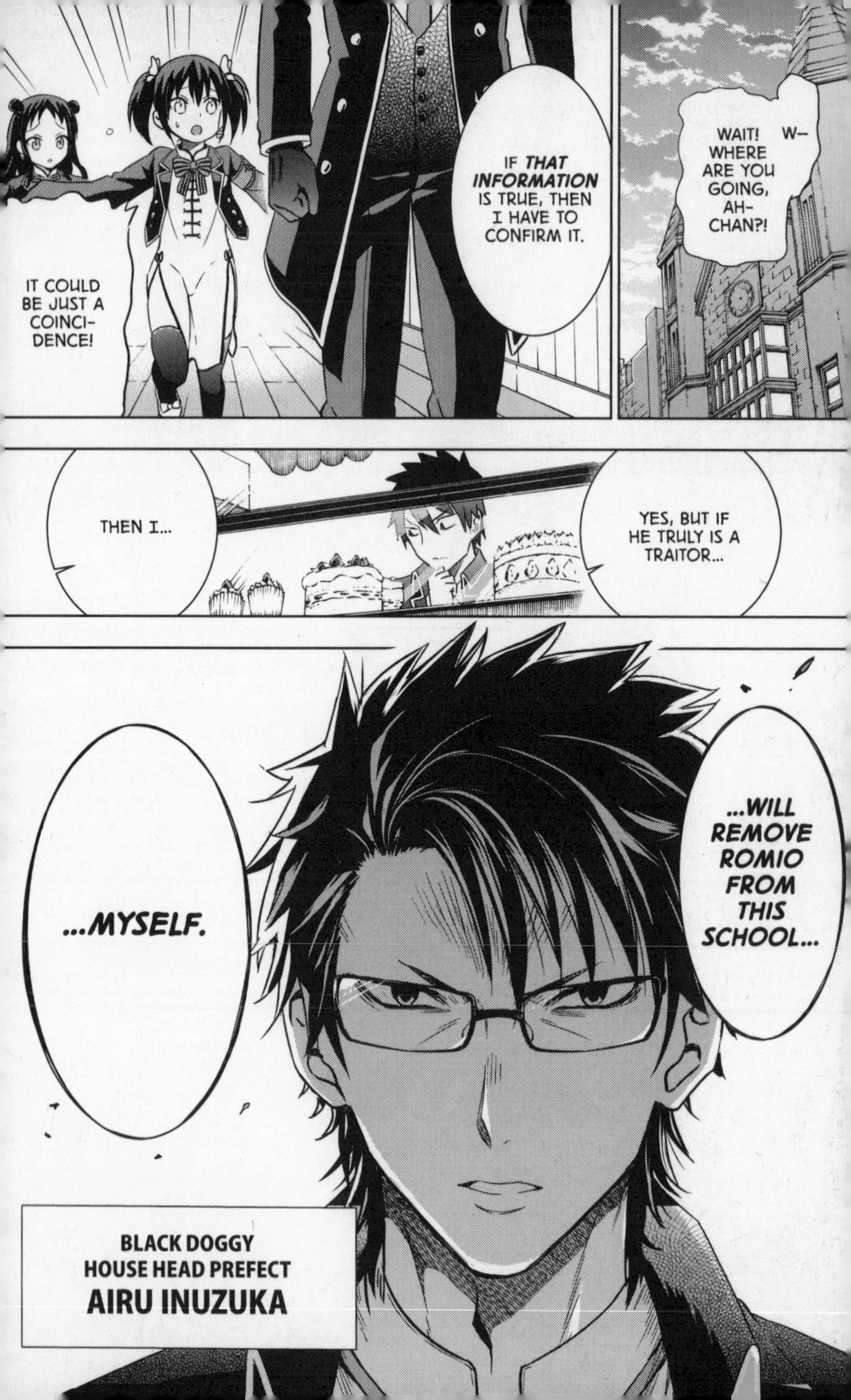
WAIT! W— WHERE ARE YOU GOING, AH-CHAN?!
IF *THAT INFORMATION* IS TRUE, THEN I HAVE TO CONFIRM IT.
IT COULD BE JUST A COINCIDENCE!
YES, BUT IF HE TRULY IS A TRAITOR...
THEN I...
...WILL REMOVE ROMIO FROM THIS SCHOOL...
...MYSELF.
BLACK DOGGY HOUSE HEAD PREFECT
AIRU INUZUKA

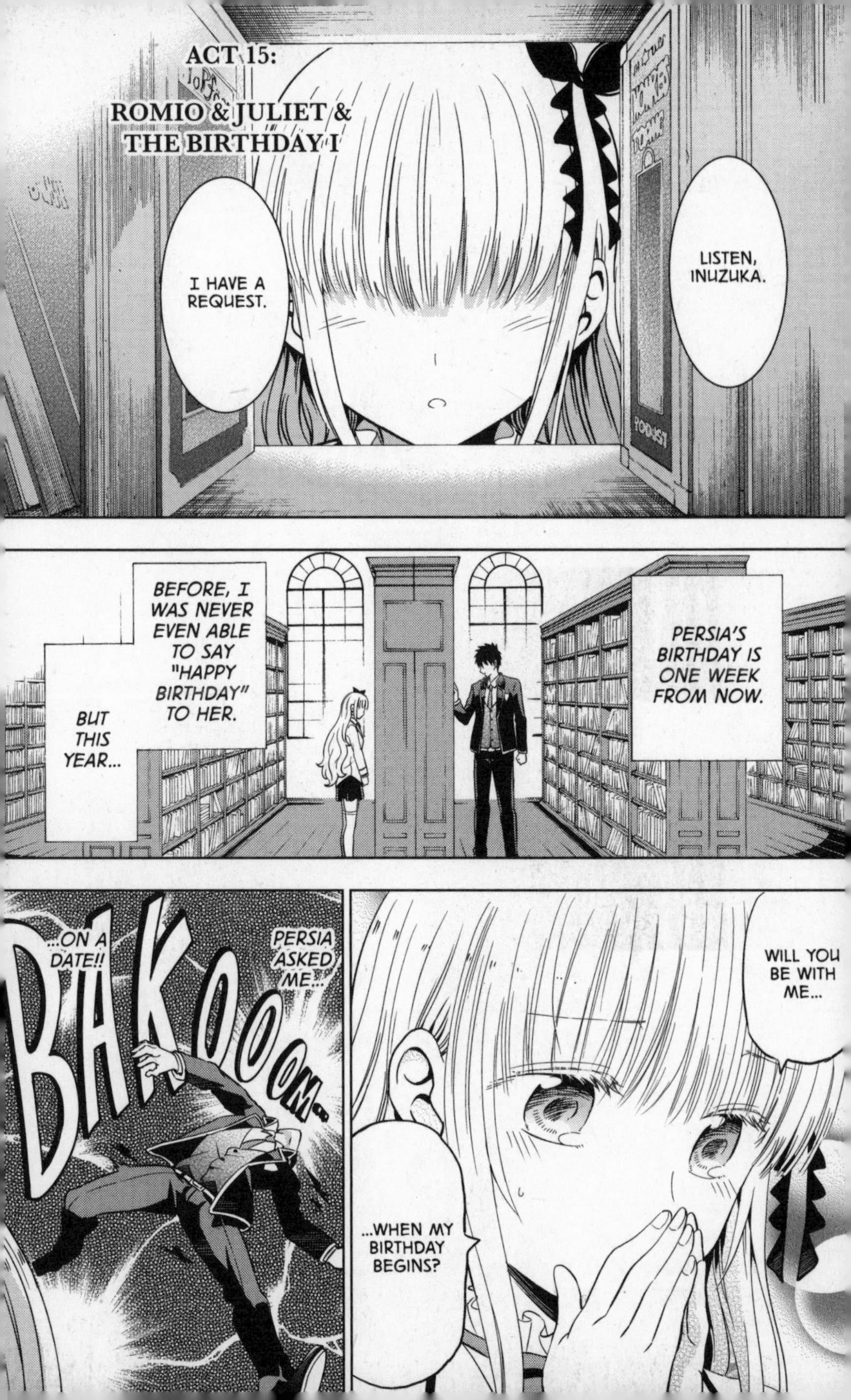
ACT 15:
ROMIO & JULIET & THE BIRTHDAY I
LISTEN, INUZUKA.
I HAVE A REQUEST.
PERSIA'S BIRTHDAY IS ONE WEEK FROM NOW.
BEFORE, I WAS NEVER EVEN ABLE TO SAY "HAPPY BIRTHDAY" TO HER.
BUT THIS YEAR...
WILL YOU BE WITH ME...
...WHEN MY BIRTHDAY BEGINS?
PERSIA ASKED ME...
...ON A DATE!!
BAKOOOM

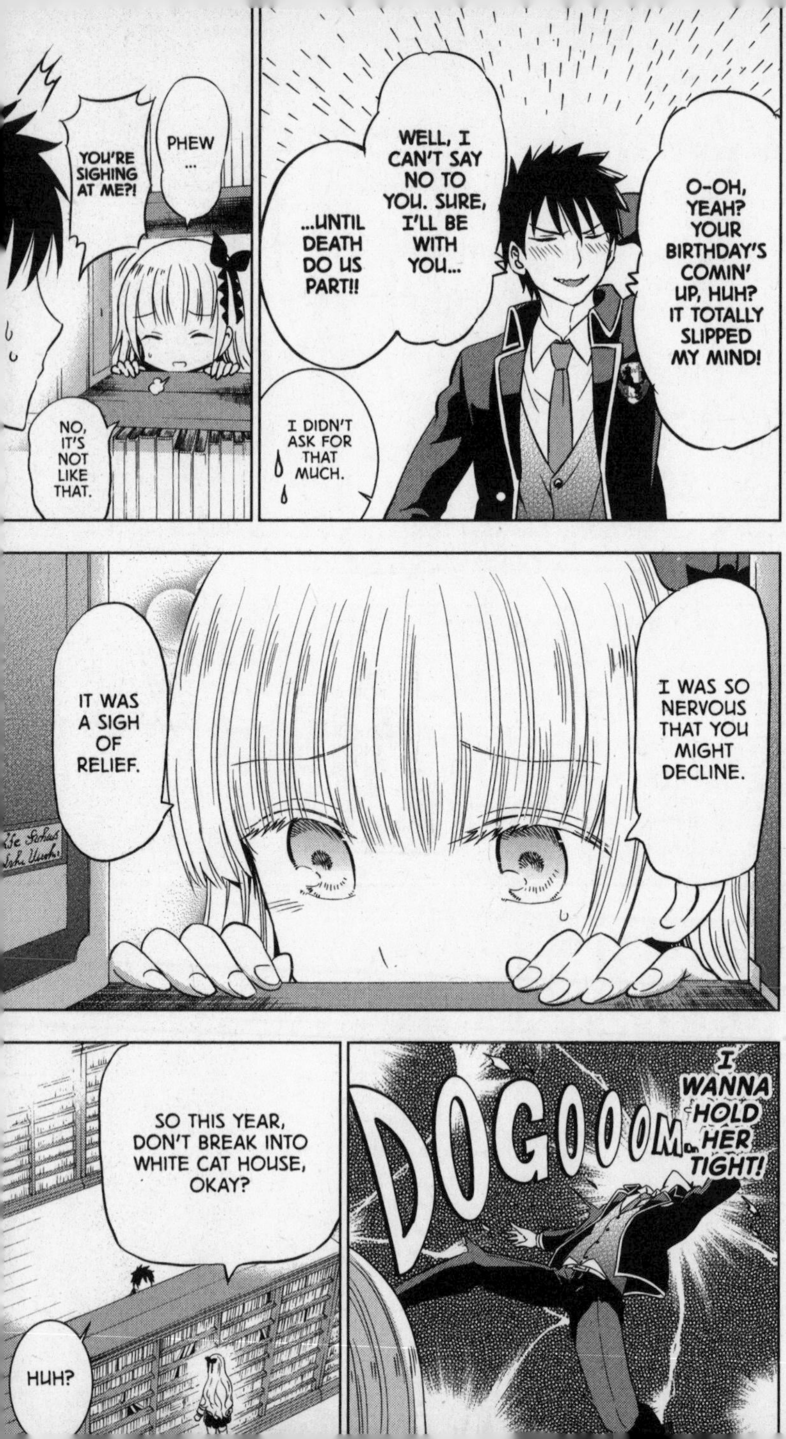
O-OH, YEAH? YOUR BIRTHDAY'S COMIN' UP, HUH? IT TOTALLY SLIPPED MY MIND!
WELL, I CAN'T SAY NO TO YOU. SURE, I'LL BE WITH YOU...
...UNTIL DEATH DO US PART!!
I DIDN'T ASK FOR THAT MUCH.
PHEW ...
YOU'RE SIGHING AT ME?!
NO, IT'S NOT LIKE THAT.
I WAS SO NERVOUS THAT YOU MIGHT DECLINE.
IT WAS A SIGH OF RELIEF.
DOGOOOM
I WANNA HOLD HER TIGHT!
SO THIS YEAR, DON'T BREAK INTO WHITE CAT HOUSE, OKAY?
HUH?

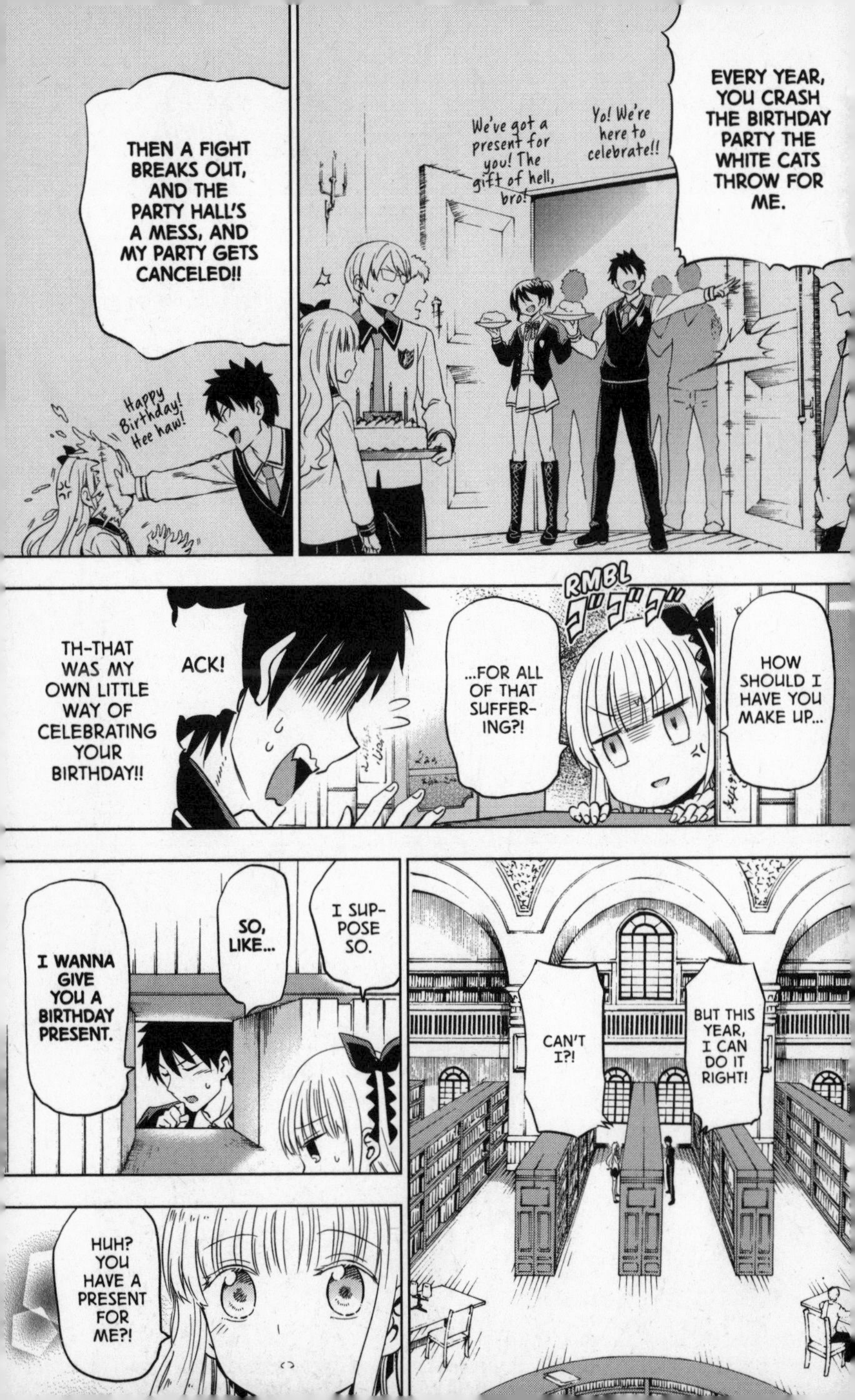
EVERY YEAR, YOU CRASH THE BIRTHDAY PARTY THE WHITE CATS THROW FOR ME.
Yo! We're here to celebrate!!
We've got a present for you! The gift of hell, bro!
THEN A FIGHT BREAKS OUT, AND THE PARTY HALL'S A MESS, AND MY PARTY GETS CANCELED!!
Happy Birthday! Hee haw!
HOW SHOULD I HAVE YOU MAKE UP...
...FOR ALL OF THAT SUFFERING?!
RMBL
ACK!
TH-THAT WAS MY OWN LITTLE WAY OF CELEBRATING YOUR BIRTHDAY!!
BUT THIS YEAR, I CAN DO IT RIGHT!
CAN'T I?!
I SUPPOSE SO.
SO, LIKE...
I WANNA GIVE YOU A BIRTHDAY PRESENT.
HUH? YOU HAVE A PRESENT FOR ME?!

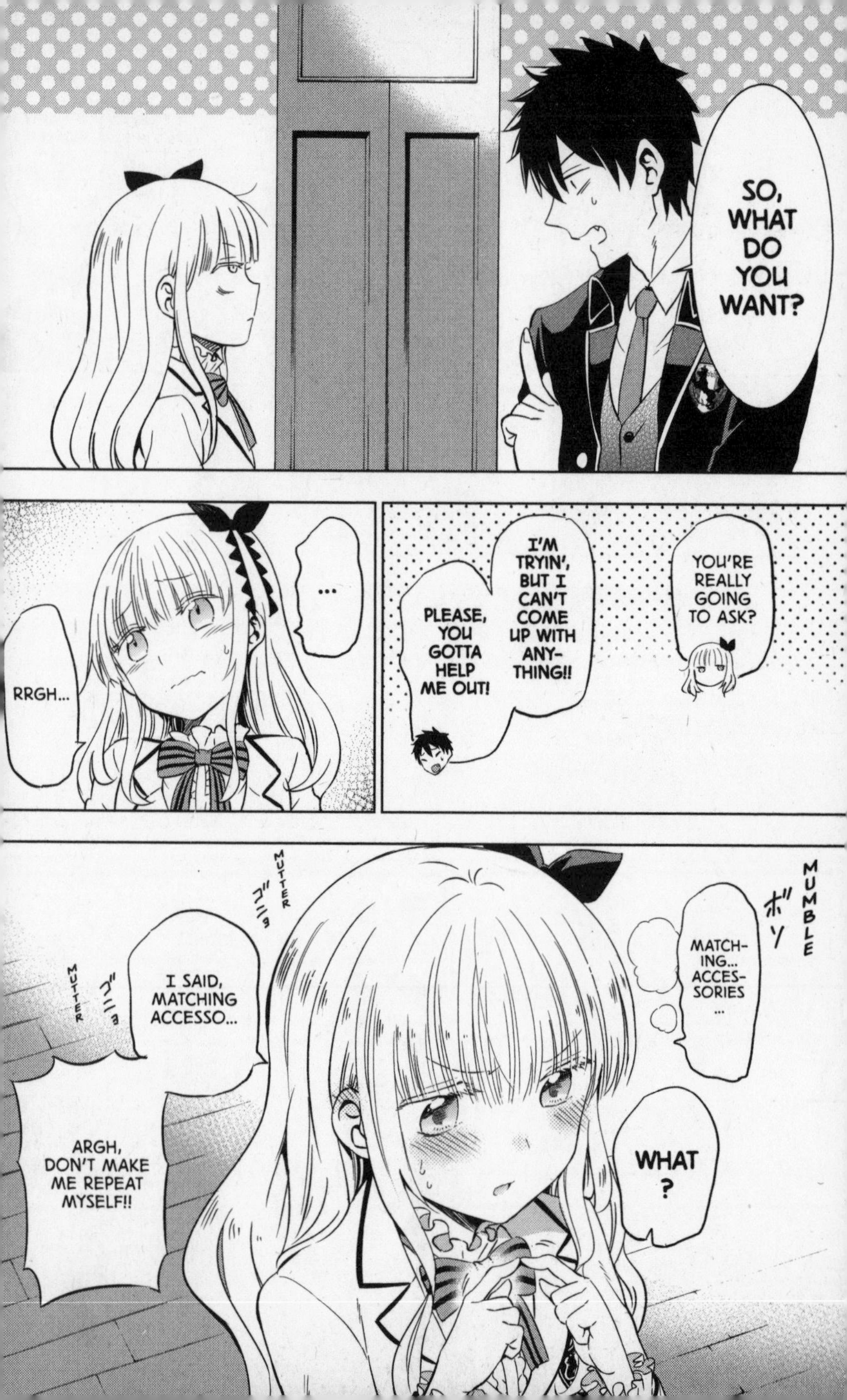
SO, WHAT DO YOU WANT?
YOU'RE REALLY GOING TO ASK?
I'M TRYIN', BUT I CAN'T COME UP WITH ANY-THING!!
PLEASE, YOU GOTTA HELP ME OUT!
...
RRGH...
ボソ MUMBLE
MATCH-ING... ACCES-SORIES ...
WHAT ?
ゴニョ MUTTER
I SAID, MATCHING ACCESSO...
ゴニョ MUTTER
ARGH, DON'T MAKE ME REPEAT MYSELF!!

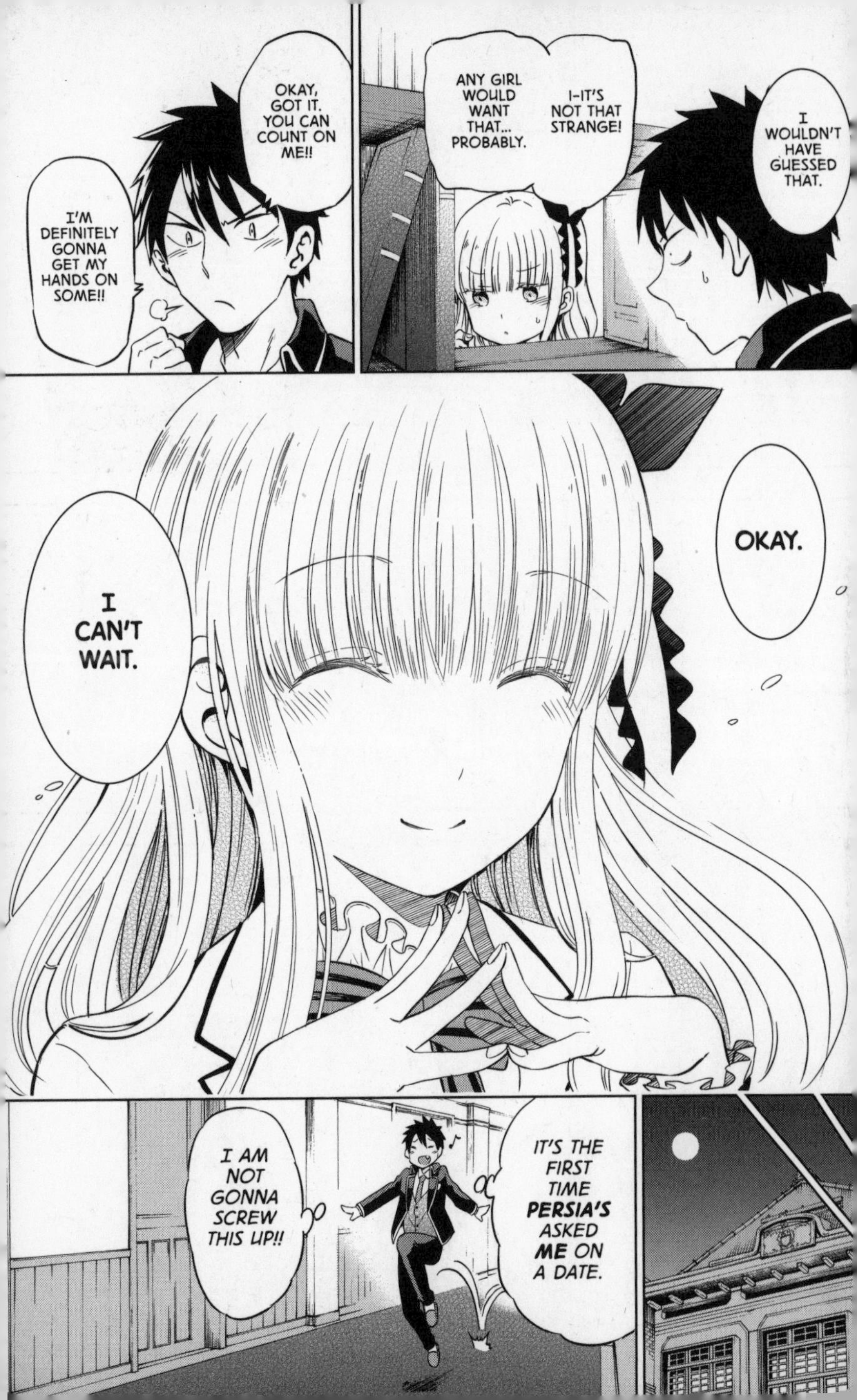
I WOULDN'T HAVE GUESSED THAT.
I-IT'S NOT THAT STRANGE!
ANY GIRL WOULD WANT THAT... PROBABLY.
OKAY, GOT IT. YOU CAN COUNT ON ME!!
I'M DEFINITELY GONNA GET MY HANDS ON SOME!!
OKAY.
I CAN'T WAIT.
IT'S THE FIRST TIME PERSIA'S ASKED ME ON A DATE.
I AM NOT GONNA SCREW THIS UP!!

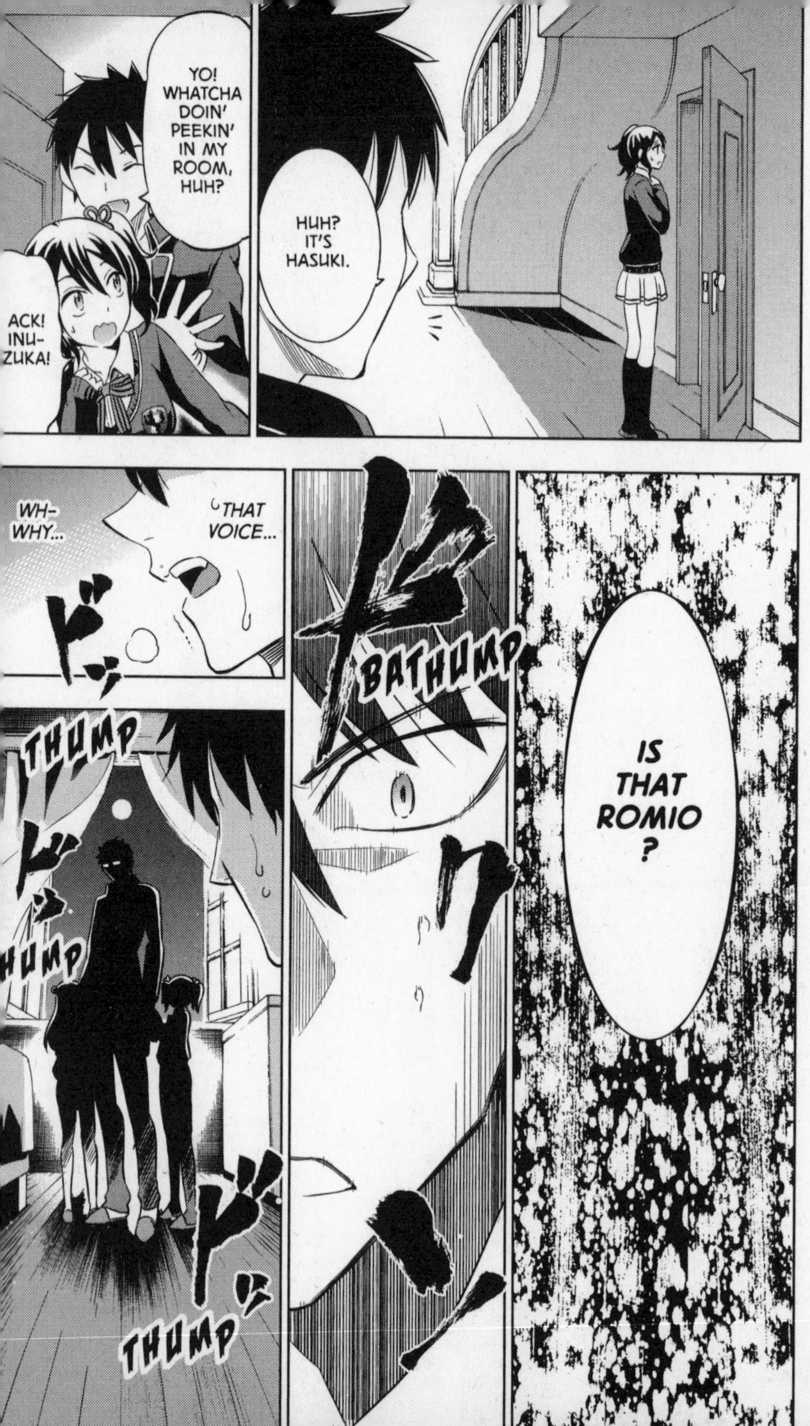
HUH? IT'S HASUKI.
YO! WHATCHA DOIN' PEEKIN' IN MY ROOM, HUH?
ACK! INU-ZUKA!
IS THAT ROMIO ?
BATHUMP
THAT VOICE...
WH- WHY...
THUMP
THUMP
THUMP

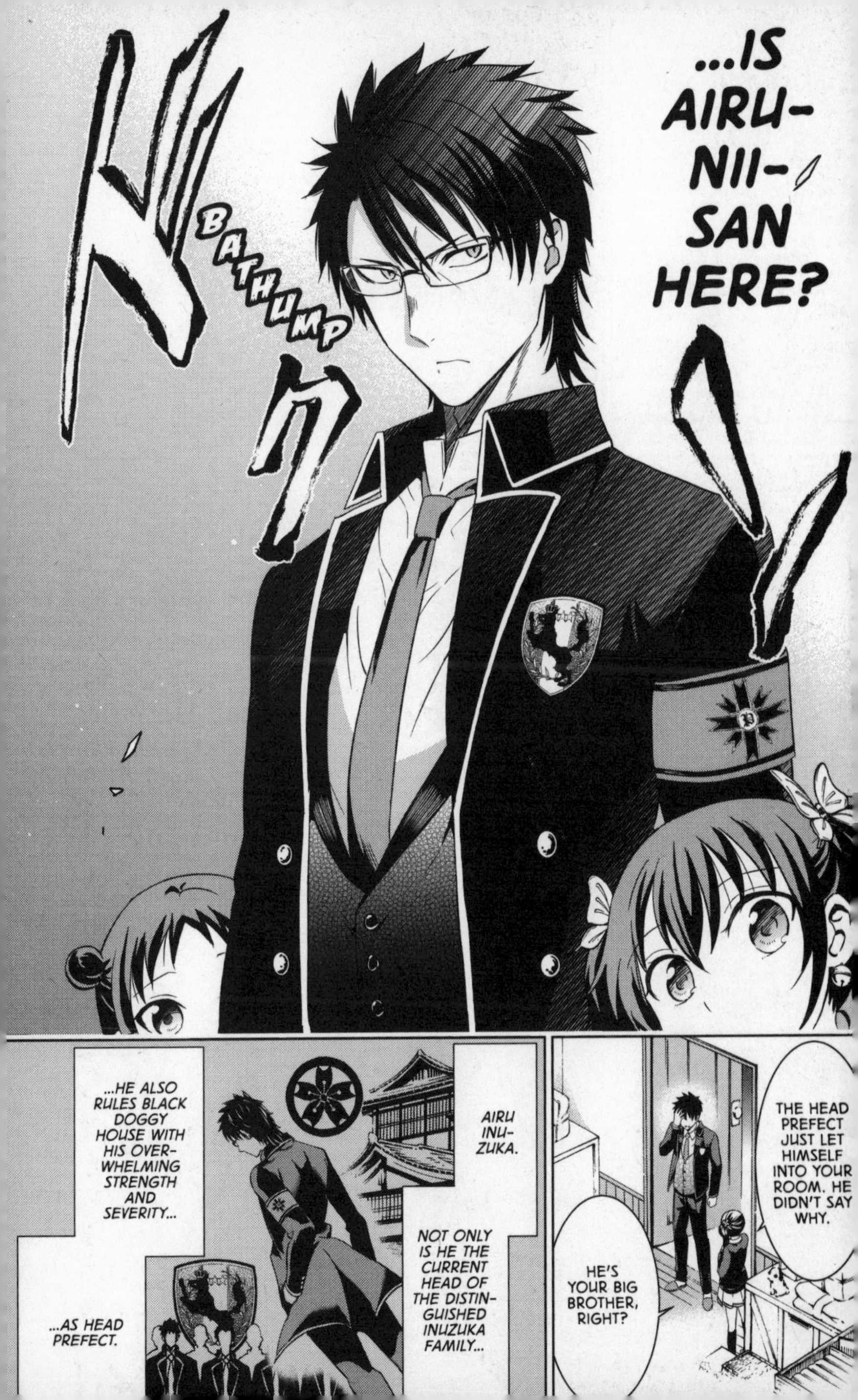
...IS AIRU-NII-SAN HERE?
BATHUMP
THE HEAD PREFECT JUST LET HIMSELF INTO YOUR ROOM. HE DIDN'T SAY WHY.
HE'S YOUR BIG BROTHER, RIGHT?
AIRU INUZUKA.
NOT ONLY IS HE THE CURRENT HEAD OF THE DISTINGUISHED INUZUKA FAMILY...
...HE ALSO RULES BLACK DOGGY HOUSE WITH HIS OVERWHELMING STRENGTH AND SEVERITY...
...AS HEAD PREFECT.

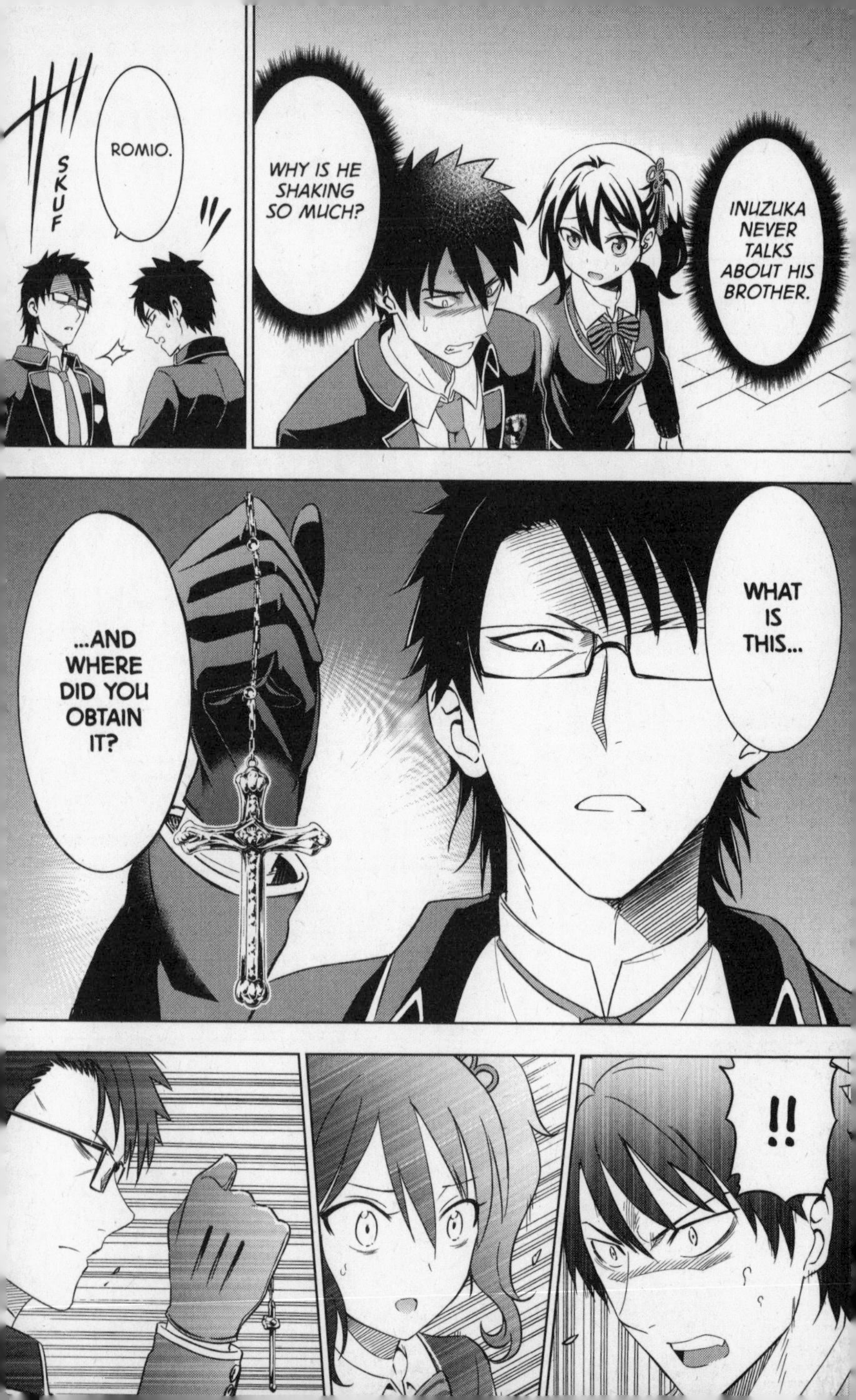
INUZUKA NEVER TALKS ABOUT HIS BROTHER.
WHY IS HE SHAKING SO MUCH?
ROMIO.
SKUF
WHAT IS THIS...
...AND WHERE DID YOU OBTAIN IT?
!!

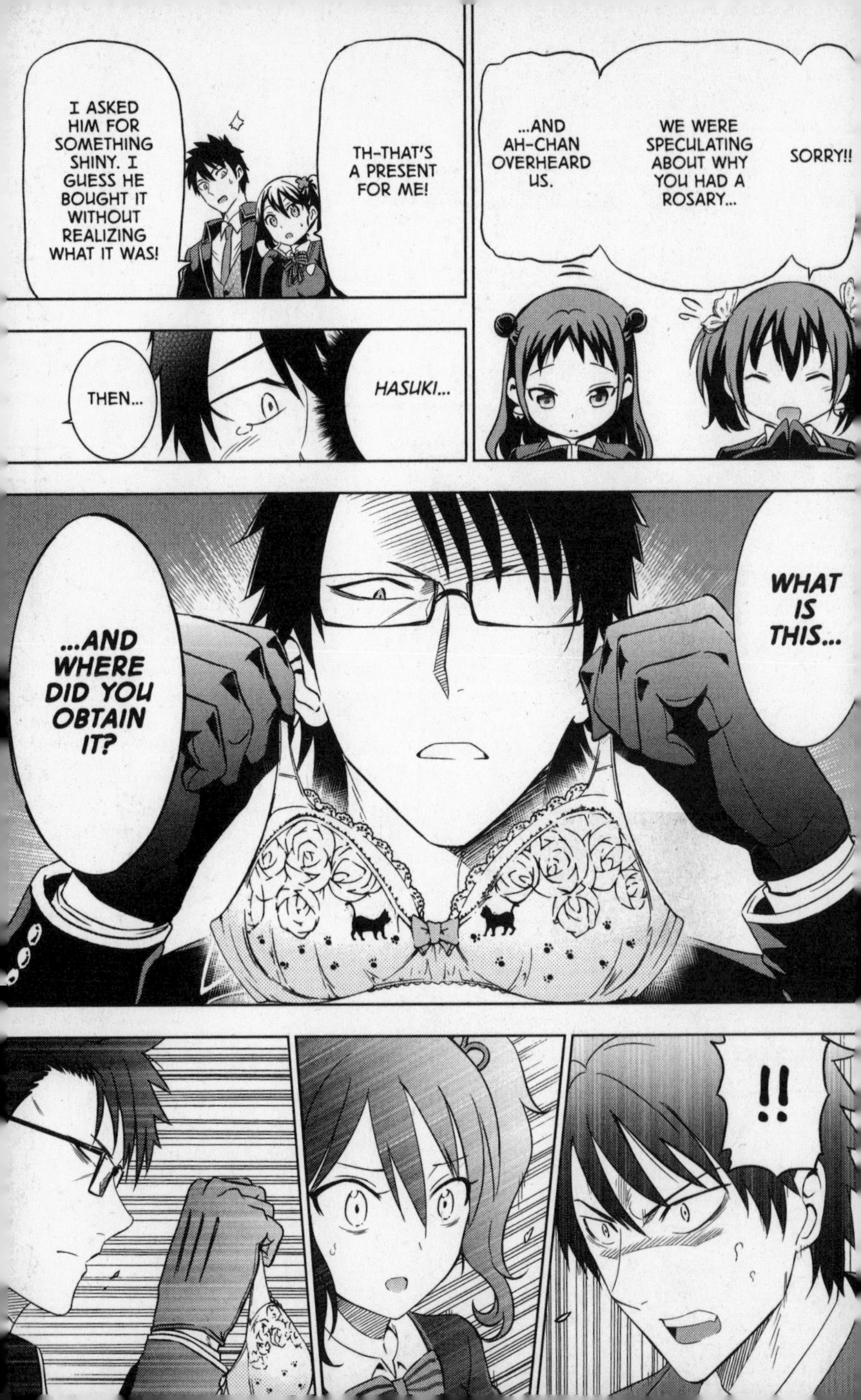
SORRY!!
WE WERE SPECULATING ABOUT WHY YOU HAD A ROSARY...
...AND AH-CHAN OVERHEARD US.
TH-THAT'S A PRESENT FOR ME!
I ASKED HIM FOR SOMETHING SHINY. I GUESS HE BOUGHT IT WITHOUT REALIZING WHAT IT WAS!
HASUKI...
THEN...
WHAT IS THIS...
...AND WHERE DID YOU OBTAIN IT?
!!

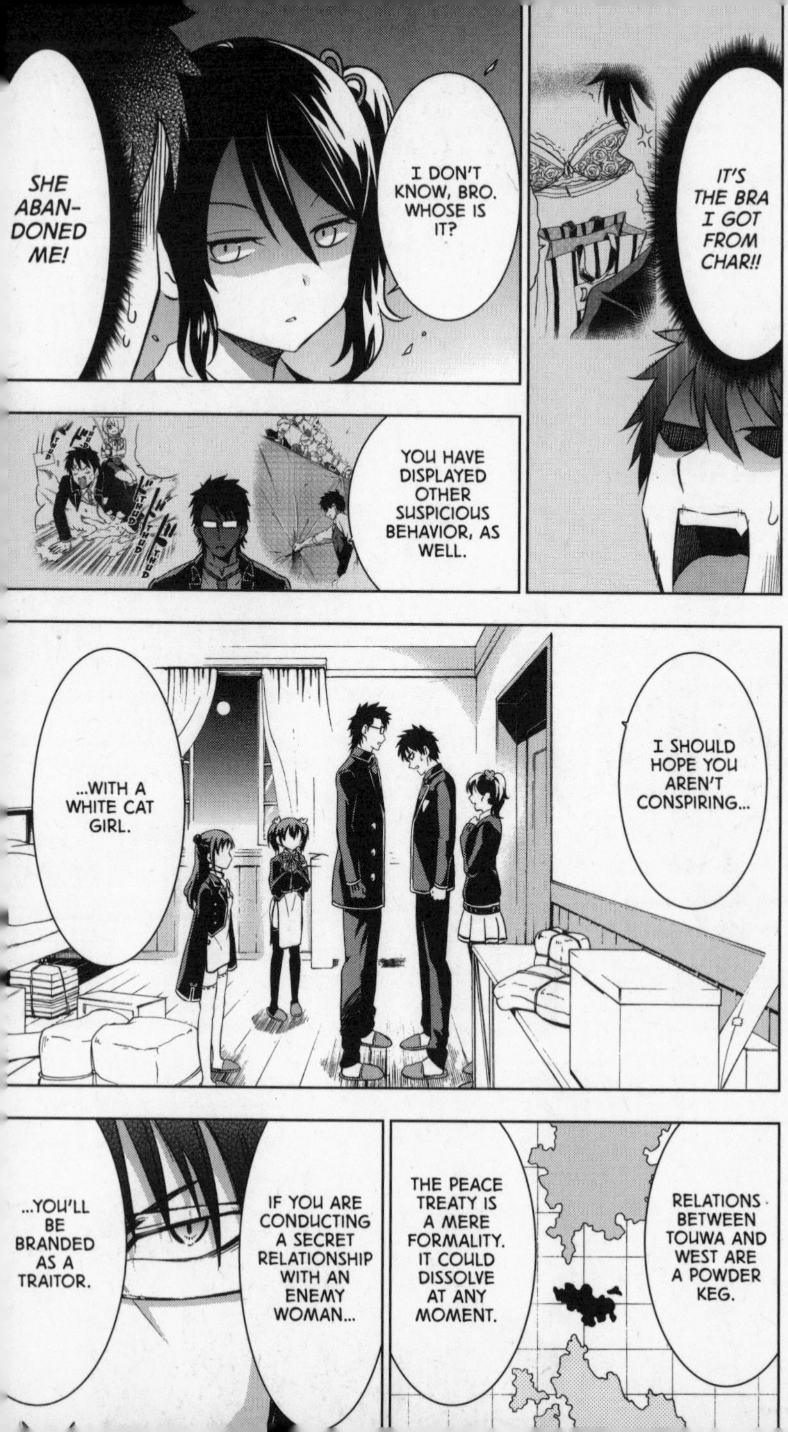
IT'S THE BRA I GOT FROM CHAR!!
I DON'T KNOW, BRO. WHOSE IS IT?
SHE ABAN-DONED ME!
YOU HAVE DISPLAYED OTHER SUSPICIOUS BEHAVIOR, AS WELL.
I SHOULD HOPE YOU AREN'T CONSPIRING...
...WITH A WHITE CAT GIRL.
RELATIONS BETWEEN TOUWA AND WEST ARE A POWDER KEG.
THE PEACE TREATY IS A MERE FORMALITY. IT COULD DISSOLVE AT ANY MOMENT.
IF YOU ARE CONDUCTING A SECRET RELATIONSHIP WITH AN ENEMY WOMAN...
...YOU'LL BE BRANDED AS A TRAITOR.

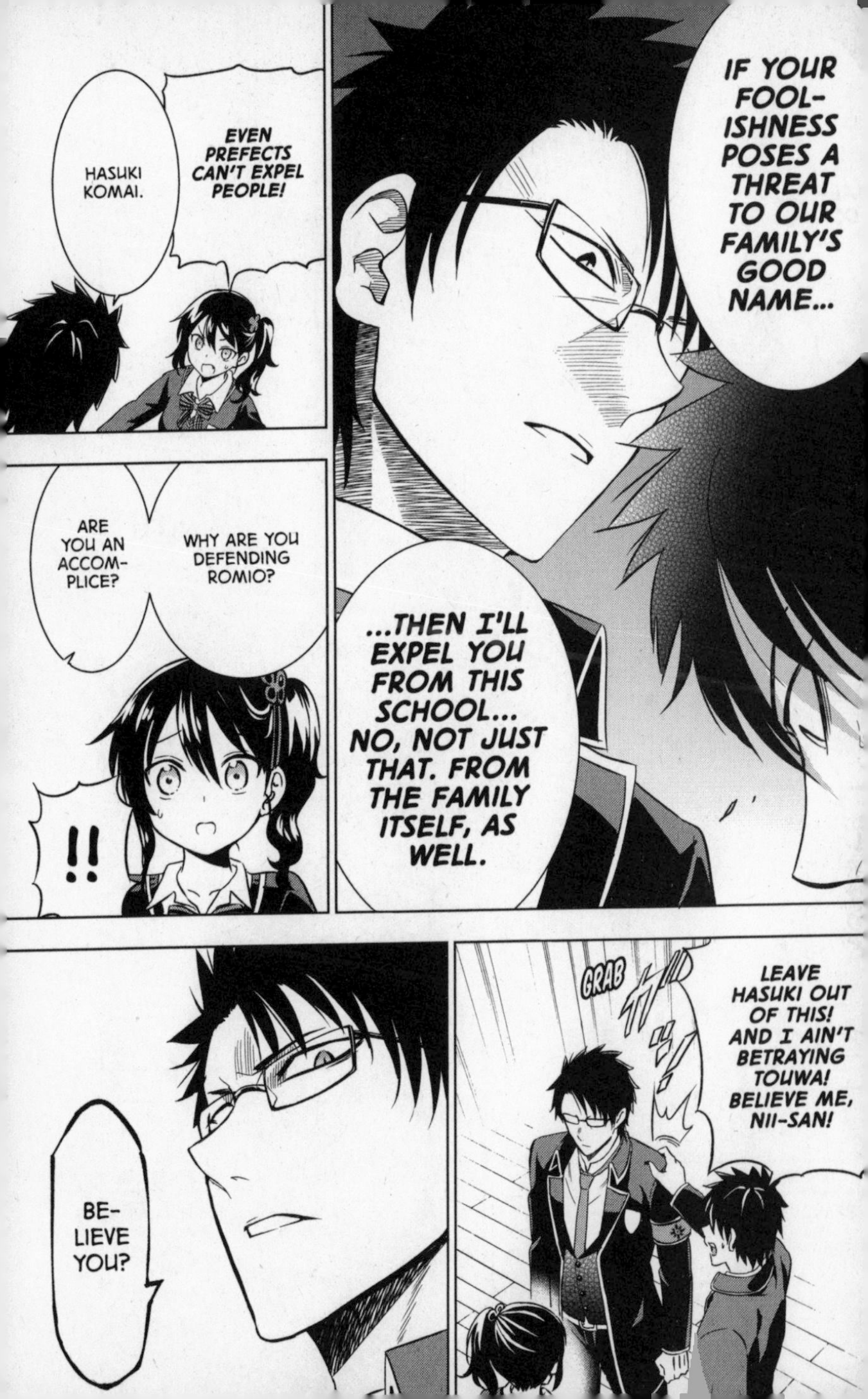
IF YOUR FOOL-ISHNESS POSES A THREAT TO OUR FAMILY'S GOOD NAME...
...THEN I'LL EXPEL YOU FROM THIS SCHOOL... NO, NOT JUST THAT. FROM THE FAMILY ITSELF, AS WELL.
EVEN PREFECTS CAN'T EXPEL PEOPLE!
HASUKI KOMAI.
WHY ARE YOU DEFENDING ROMIO?
ARE YOU AN ACCOM-PLICE?
!!
GRAB
LEAVE HASUKI OUT OF THIS! AND I AIN'T BETRAYING TOUWA! BELIEVE ME, NII-SAN!
BE-LIEVE YOU?

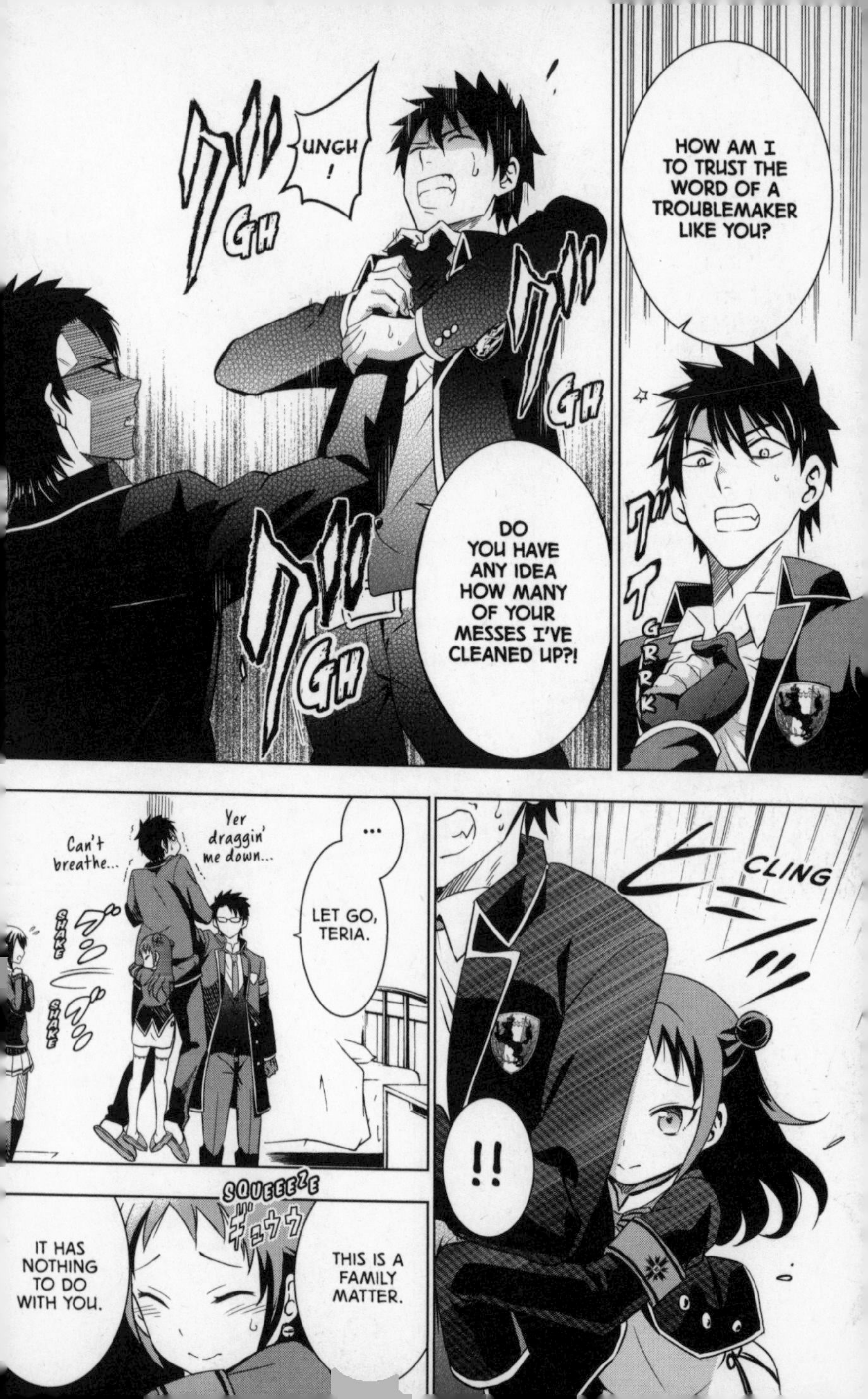
HOW AM I TO TRUST THE WORD OF A TROUBLEMAKER LIKE YOU?
GRRK
UNGH !
GH
DO YOU HAVE ANY IDEA HOW MANY OF YOUR MESSES I'VE CLEANED UP?!
GH
GH
CLING
!!
...
LET GO, TERIA.
Yer draggin' me down...
Can't breathe...
SHAKE
SHAKE
SQUEEEEZE
THIS IS A FAMILY MATTER.
IT HAS NOTHING TO DO WITH YOU.

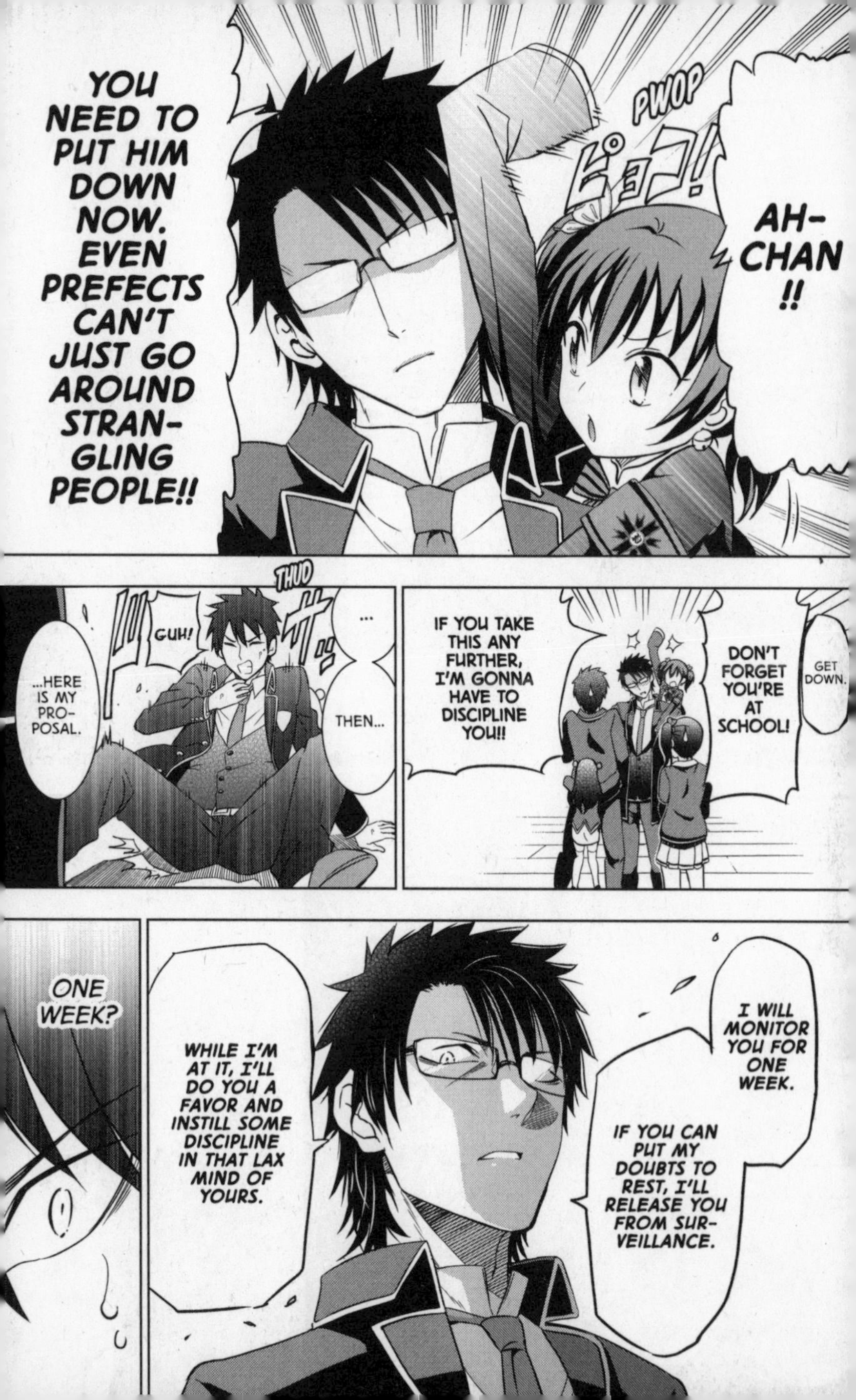
AH-CHAN!!
PWOP
ピョコ!
YOU NEED TO PUT HIM DOWN NOW. EVEN PREFECTS CAN'T JUST GO AROUND STRANGLING PEOPLE!!
GET DOWN.
DON'T FORGET YOU'RE AT SCHOOL!
IF YOU TAKE THIS ANY FURTHER, I'M GONNA HAVE TO DISCIPLINE YOU!!
THUD
...
THEN...
GUH!
...HERE IS MY PROPOSAL.
I WILL MONITOR YOU FOR ONE WEEK.
IF YOU CAN PUT MY DOUBTS TO REST, I'LL RELEASE YOU FROM SURVEILLANCE.
WHILE I'M AT IT, I'LL DO YOU A FAVOR AND INSTILL SOME DISCIPLINE IN THAT LAX MIND OF YOURS.
ONE WEEK?

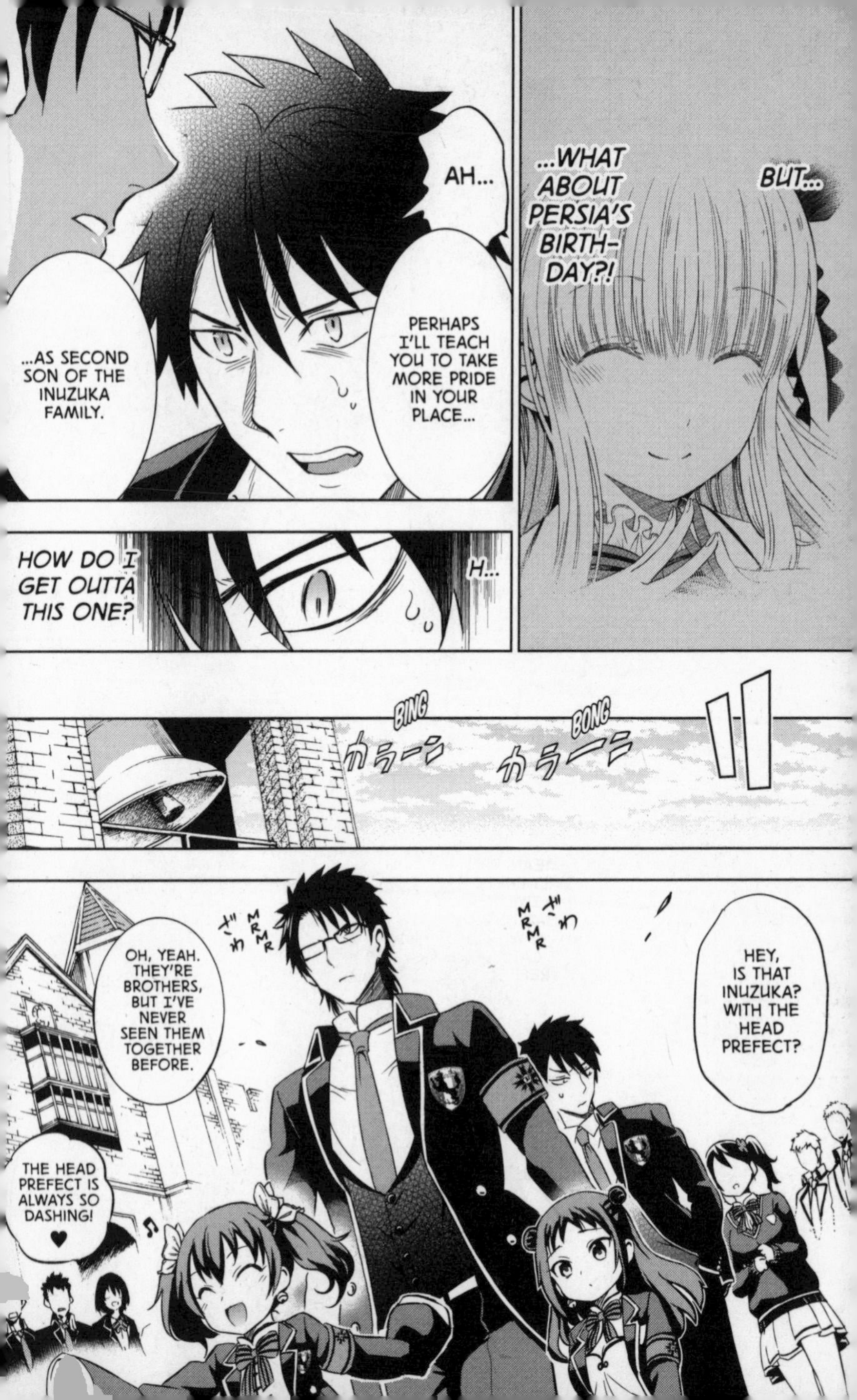
BUT...
...WHAT ABOUT PERSIA'S BIRTH-DAY?!
AH...
PERHAPS I'LL TEACH YOU TO TAKE MORE PRIDE IN YOUR PLACE...
...AS SECOND SON OF THE INUZUKA FAMILY.
H...
HOW DO I GET OUTTA THIS ONE?
BONG
カラーン
BING
カラーン
HEY, IS THAT INUZUKA? WITH THE HEAD PREFECT?
MRMR
ざわ
MRMR
ざわ
OH, YEAH. THEY'RE BROTHERS, BUT I'VE NEVER SEEN THEM TOGETHER BEFORE.
THE HEAD PREFECT IS ALWAYS SO DASHING! ♥

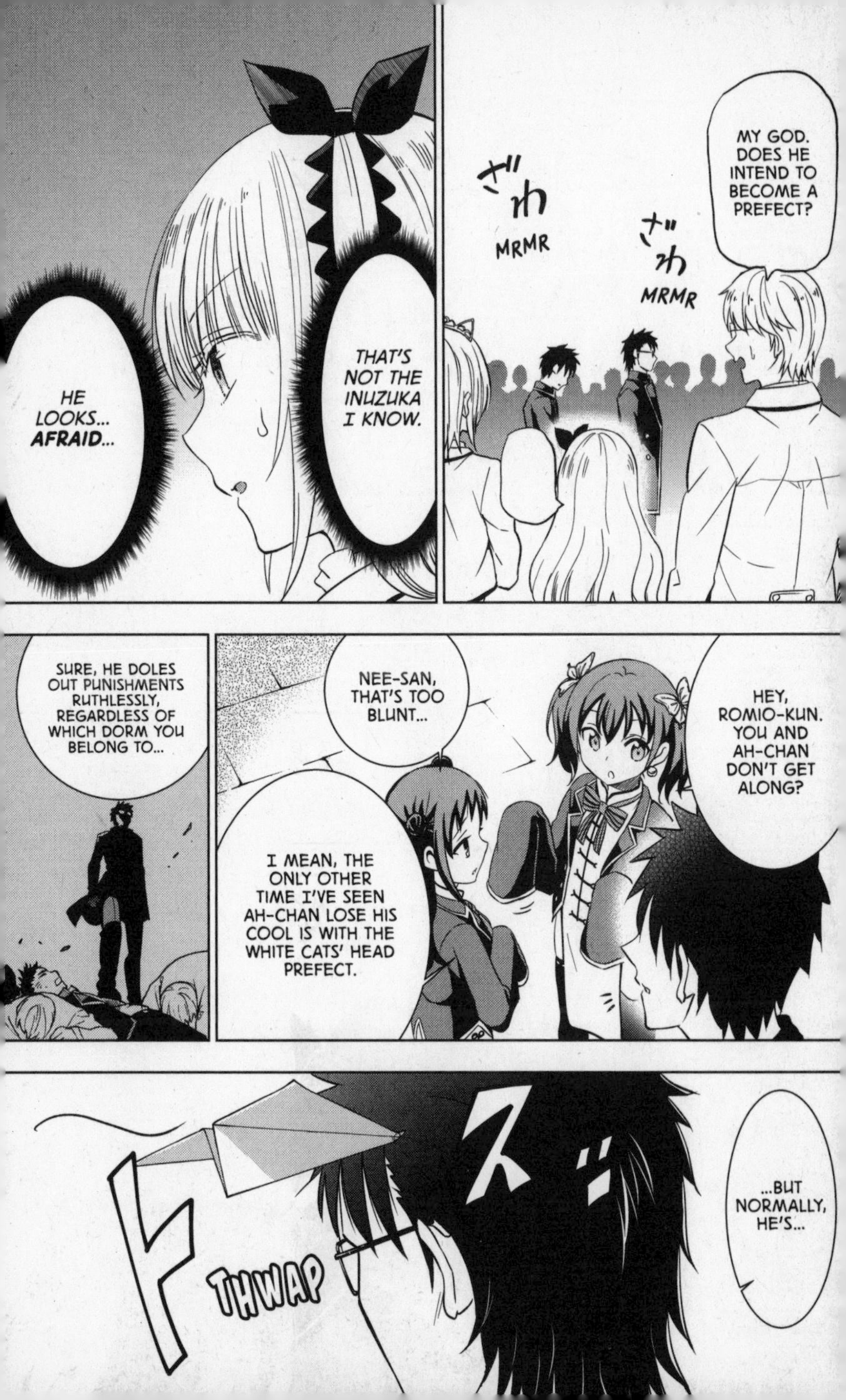
MY GOD. DOES HE INTEND TO BECOME A PREFECT?
ざわ
MRMR
ざわ
MRMR
THAT'S NOT THE INUZUKA I KNOW.
HE LOOKS... **AFRAID**...
HEY, ROMIO-KUN. YOU AND AH-CHAN DON'T GET ALONG?
NEE-SAN, THAT'S TOO BLUNT...
I MEAN, THE ONLY OTHER TIME I'VE SEEN AH-CHAN LOSE HIS COOL IS WITH THE WHITE CATS' HEAD PREFECT.
SURE, HE DOLES OUT PUNISHMENTS RUTHLESSLY, REGARDLESS OF WHICH DORM YOU BELONG TO...
...BUT NORMALLY, HE'S...
THWAP

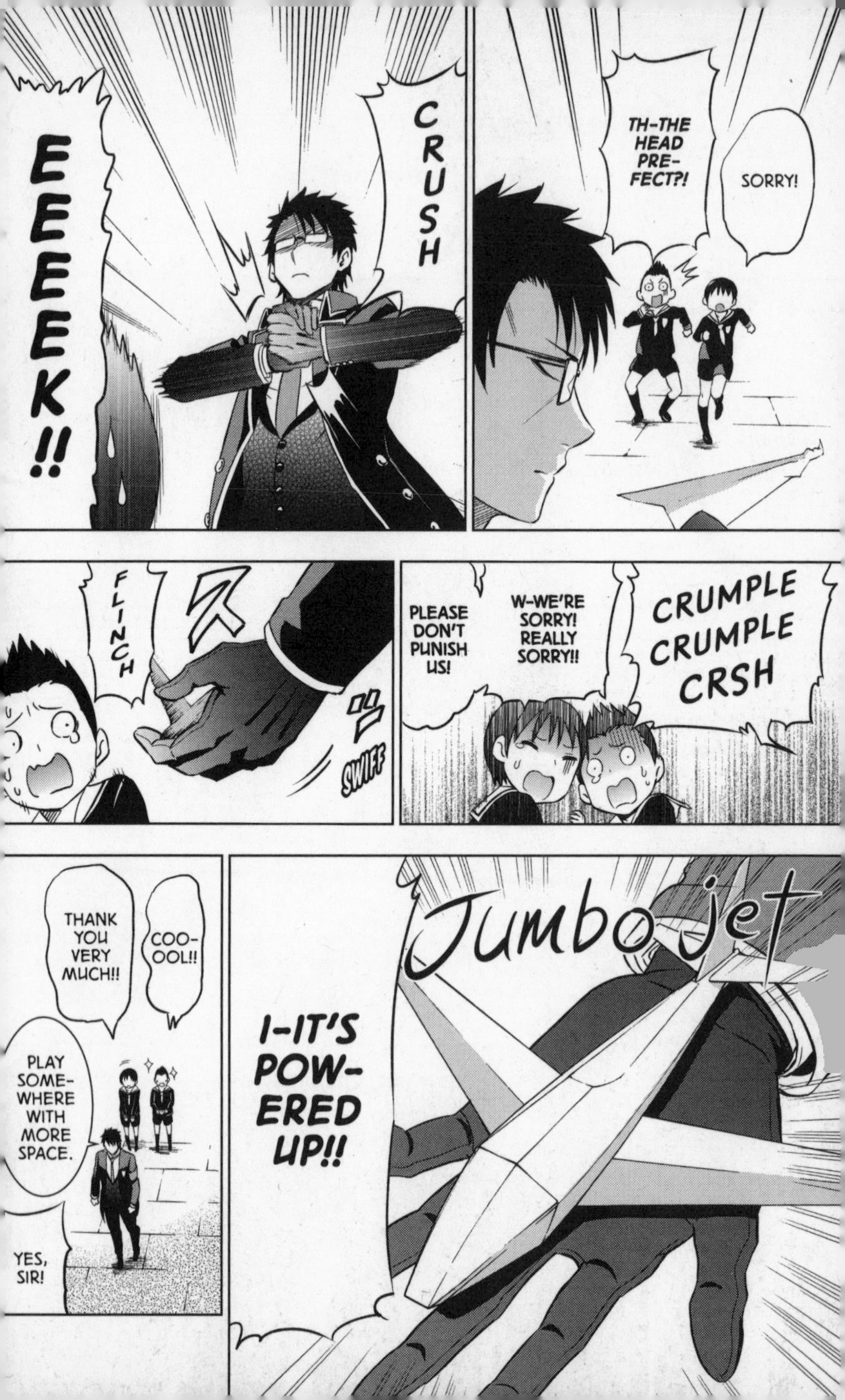
SORRY!
TH-THE HEAD PRE-FECT?!
CRUSH
EEEEEK!!
CRUMPLE CRUMPLE CRSH
W-WE'RE SORRY! REALLY SORRY!!
PLEASE DON'T PUNISH US!
SWIFF
FLINCH
Jumbo jet
I-IT'S POW-ERED UP!!
COO-OOL!!
THANK YOU VERY MUCH!!
PLAY SOME-WHERE WITH MORE SPACE.
YES, SIR!

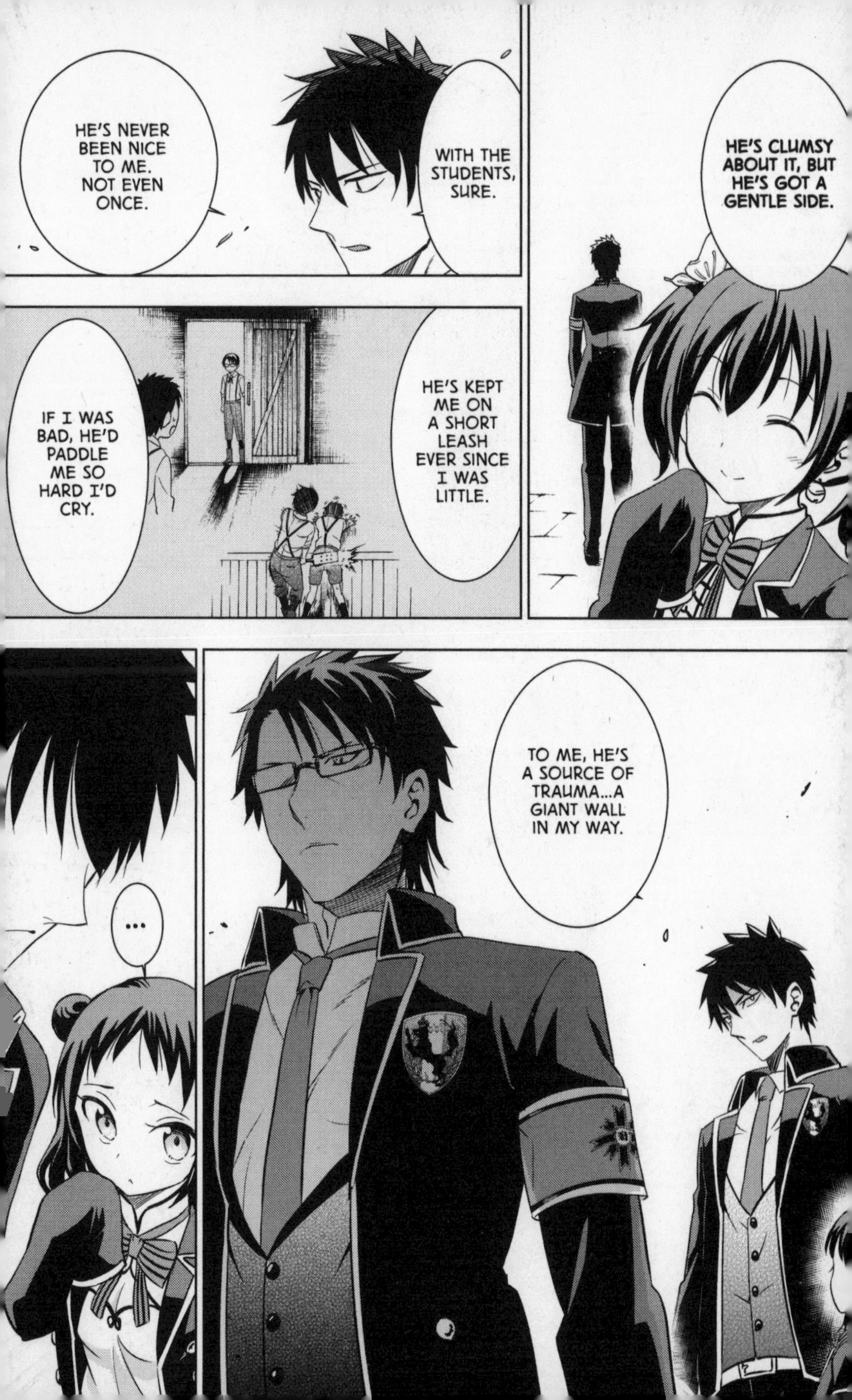
HE'S CLUMSY ABOUT IT, BUT HE'S GOT A GENTLE SIDE.
WITH THE STUDENTS, SURE.
HE'S NEVER BEEN NICE TO ME. NOT EVEN ONCE.
HE'S KEPT ME ON A SHORT LEASH EVER SINCE I WAS LITTLE.
IF I WAS BAD, HE'D PADDLE ME SO HARD I'D CRY.
TO ME, HE'S A SOURCE OF TRAUMA...A GIANT WALL IN MY WAY.
...

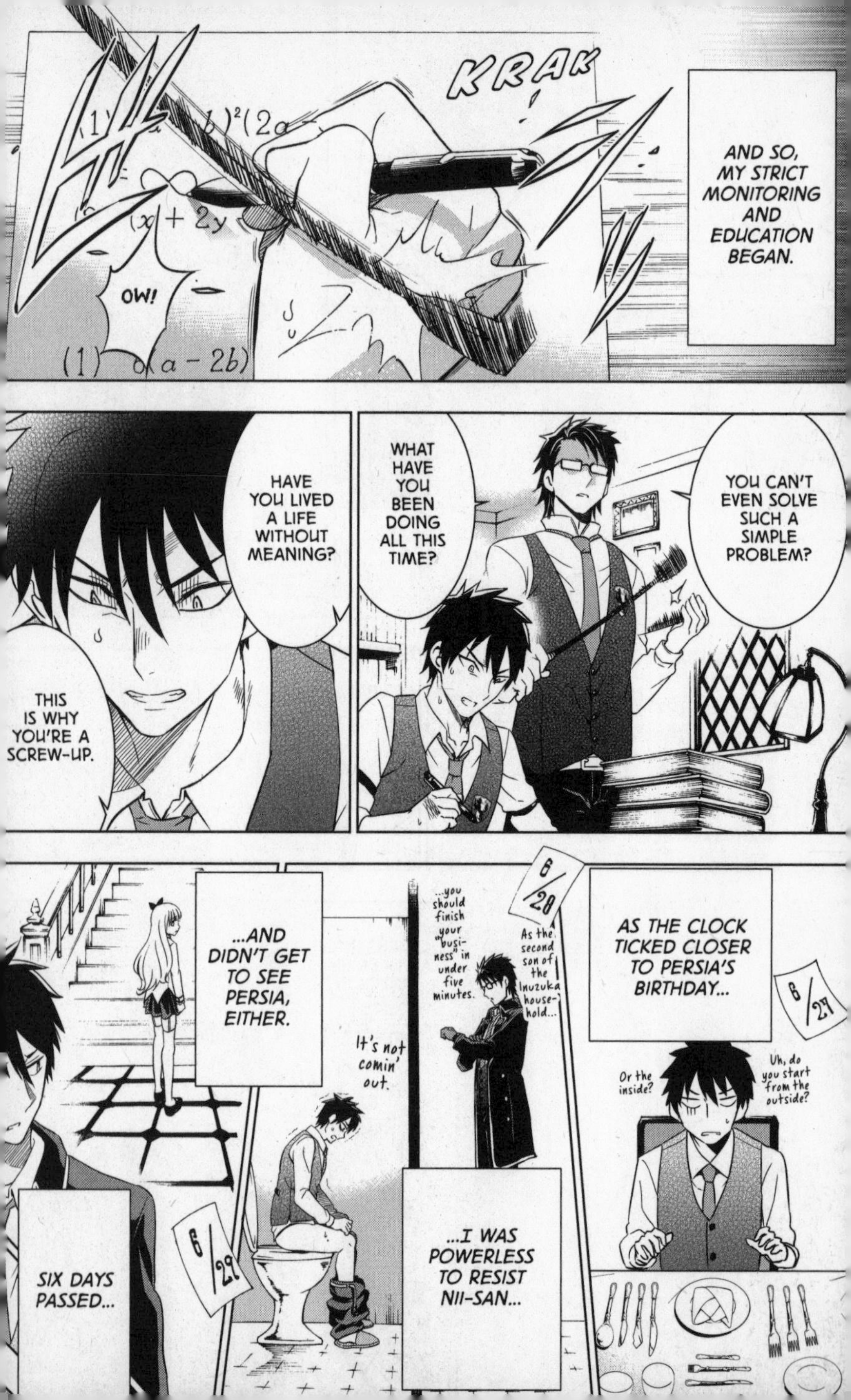
AND SO, MY STRICT MONITORING AND EDUCATION BEGAN.
KRAK
OW!
YOU CAN'T EVEN SOLVE SUCH A SIMPLE PROBLEM?
WHAT HAVE YOU BEEN DOING ALL THIS TIME?
HAVE YOU LIVED A LIFE WITHOUT MEANING?
THIS IS WHY YOU'RE A SCREW-UP.
AS THE CLOCK TICKED CLOSER TO PERSIA'S BIRTHDAY...
6/27
Uh, do you start from the outside?
Or the inside?
As the second son of the Inuzuka household...
...you should finish your "business" in under five minutes.
6/28
It's not comin' out.
...I WAS POWERLESS TO RESIST NII-SAN...
...AND DIDN'T GET TO SEE PERSIA, EITHER.
6/29
SIX DAYS PASSED...

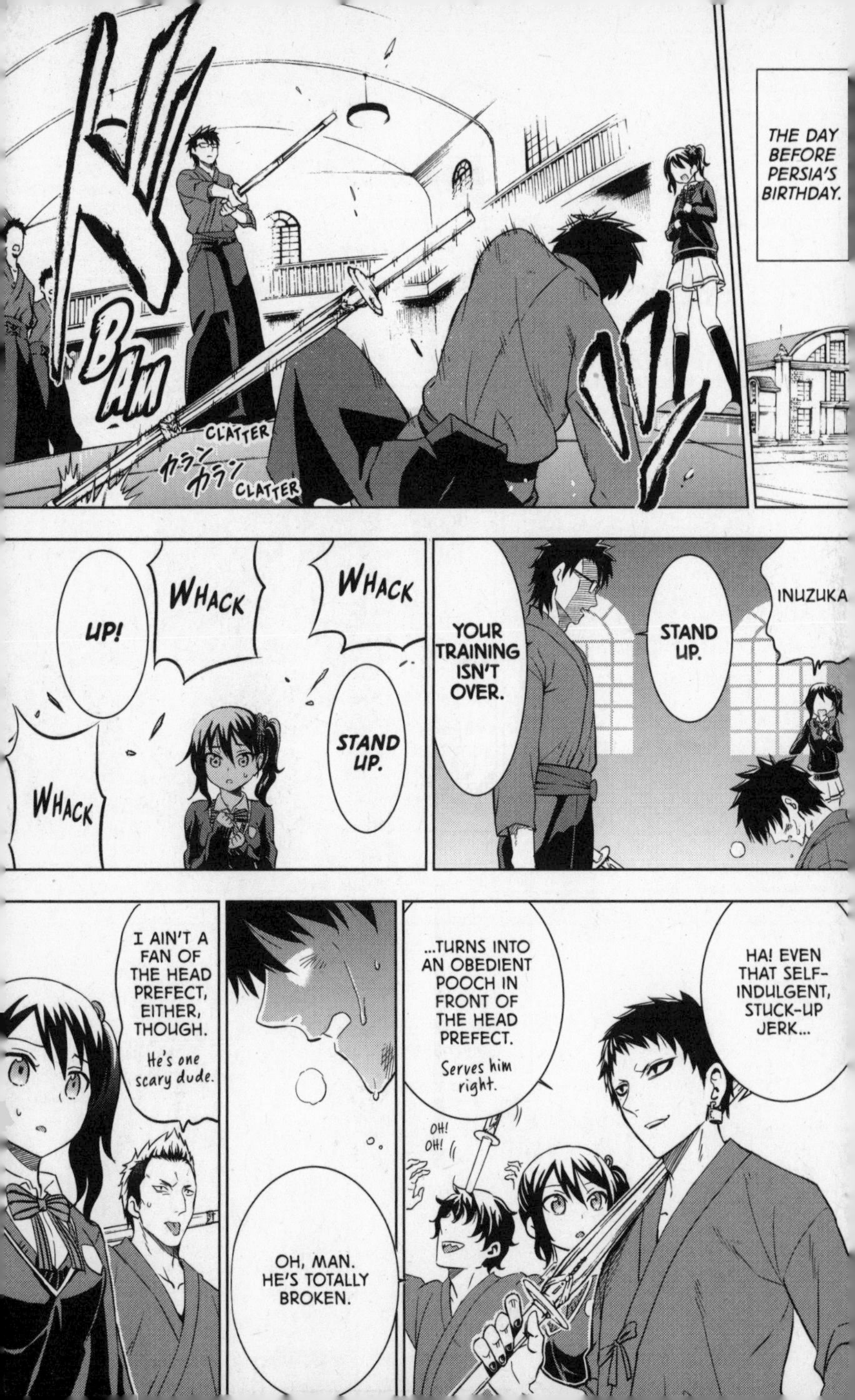
THE DAY BEFORE PERSIA'S BIRTHDAY.
BAM
CLATTER
カラン
カラン
CLATTER
INUZUKA
STAND UP.
YOUR TRAINING ISN'T OVER.
STAND UP.
WHACK
UP!
WHACK
WHACK
HA! EVEN THAT SELF-INDULGENT, STUCK-UP JERK...
...TURNS INTO AN OBEDIENT POOCH IN FRONT OF THE HEAD PREFECT.
Serves him right.
OH! OH!
OH, MAN. HE'S TOTALLY BROKEN.
I AIN'T A FAN OF THE HEAD PREFECT, EITHER, THOUGH.
He's one scary dude.

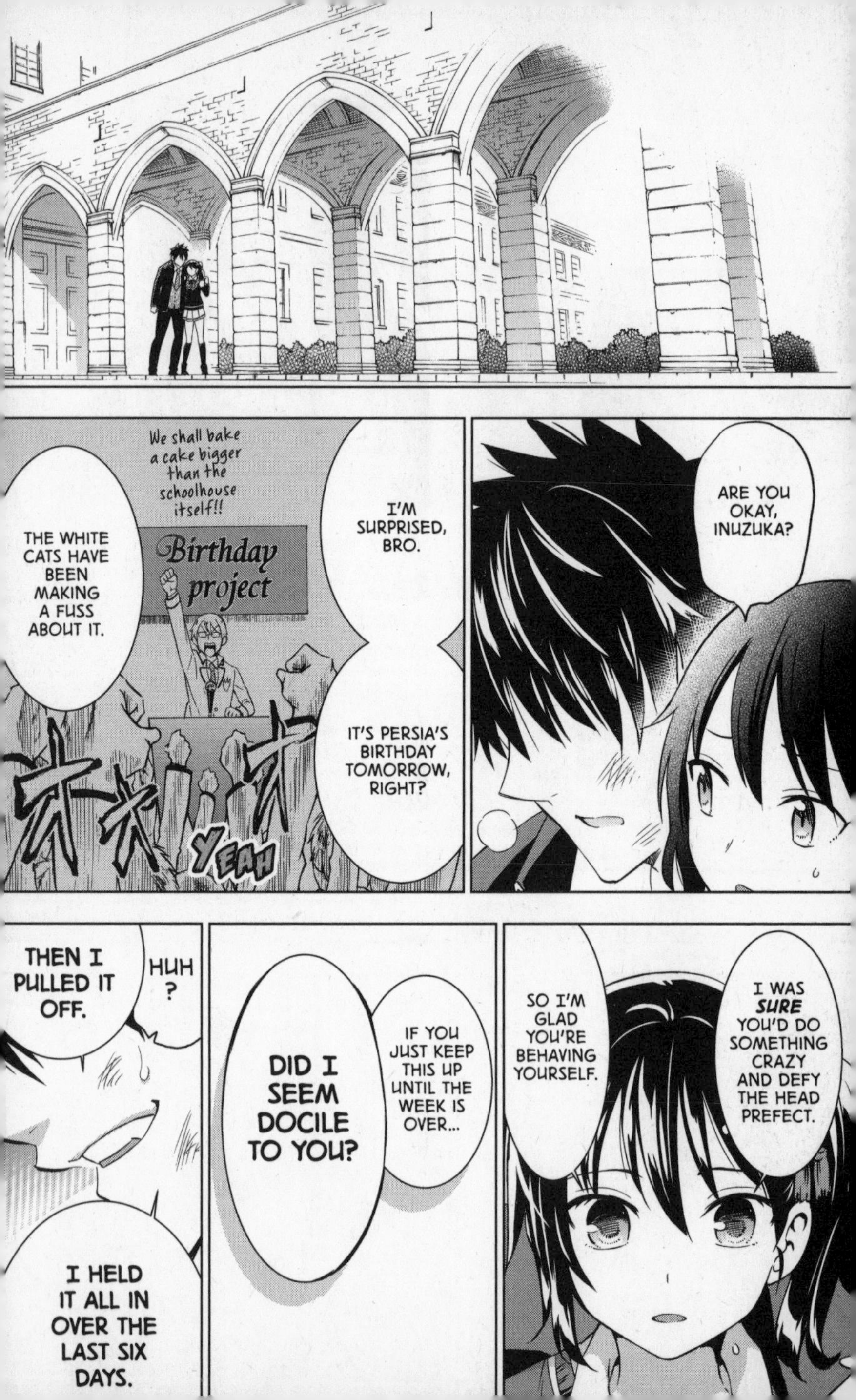
ARE YOU OKAY, INUZUKA?
I'M SURPRISED, BRO.
IT'S PERSIA'S BIRTHDAY TOMORROW, RIGHT?
THE WHITE CATS HAVE BEEN MAKING A FUSS ABOUT IT.
We shall bake a cake bigger than the schoolhouse itself!!
Birthday project
YEAH
I WAS *SURE* YOU'D DO SOMETHING CRAZY AND DEFY THE HEAD PREFECT.
SO I'M GLAD YOU'RE BEHAVING YOURSELF.
IF YOU JUST KEEP THIS UP UNTIL THE WEEK IS OVER...
DID I SEEM DOCILE TO YOU?
HUH?
THEN I PULLED IT OFF.
I HELD IT ALL IN OVER THE LAST SIX DAYS.

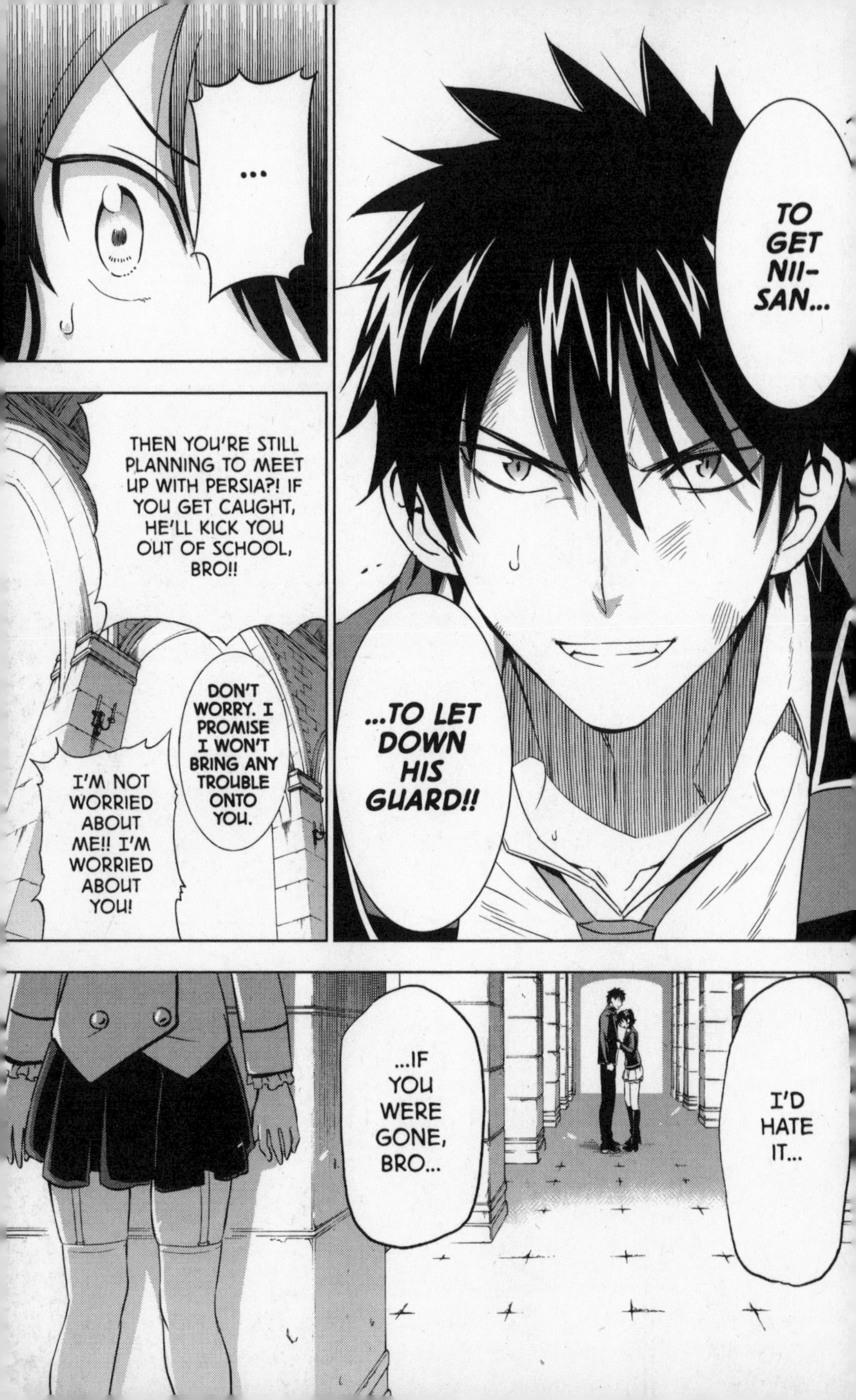

TO GET NII-SAN...
...TO LET DOWN HIS GUARD!!
...
THEN YOU'RE STILL PLANNING TO MEET UP WITH PERSIA?! IF YOU GET CAUGHT, HE'LL KICK YOU OUT OF SCHOOL, BRO!!
DON'T WORRY. I PROMISE I WON'T BRING ANY TROUBLE ONTO YOU.
I'M NOT WORRIED ABOUT ME!! I'M WORRIED ABOUT YOU!
I'D HATE IT...
...IF YOU WERE GONE, BRO...

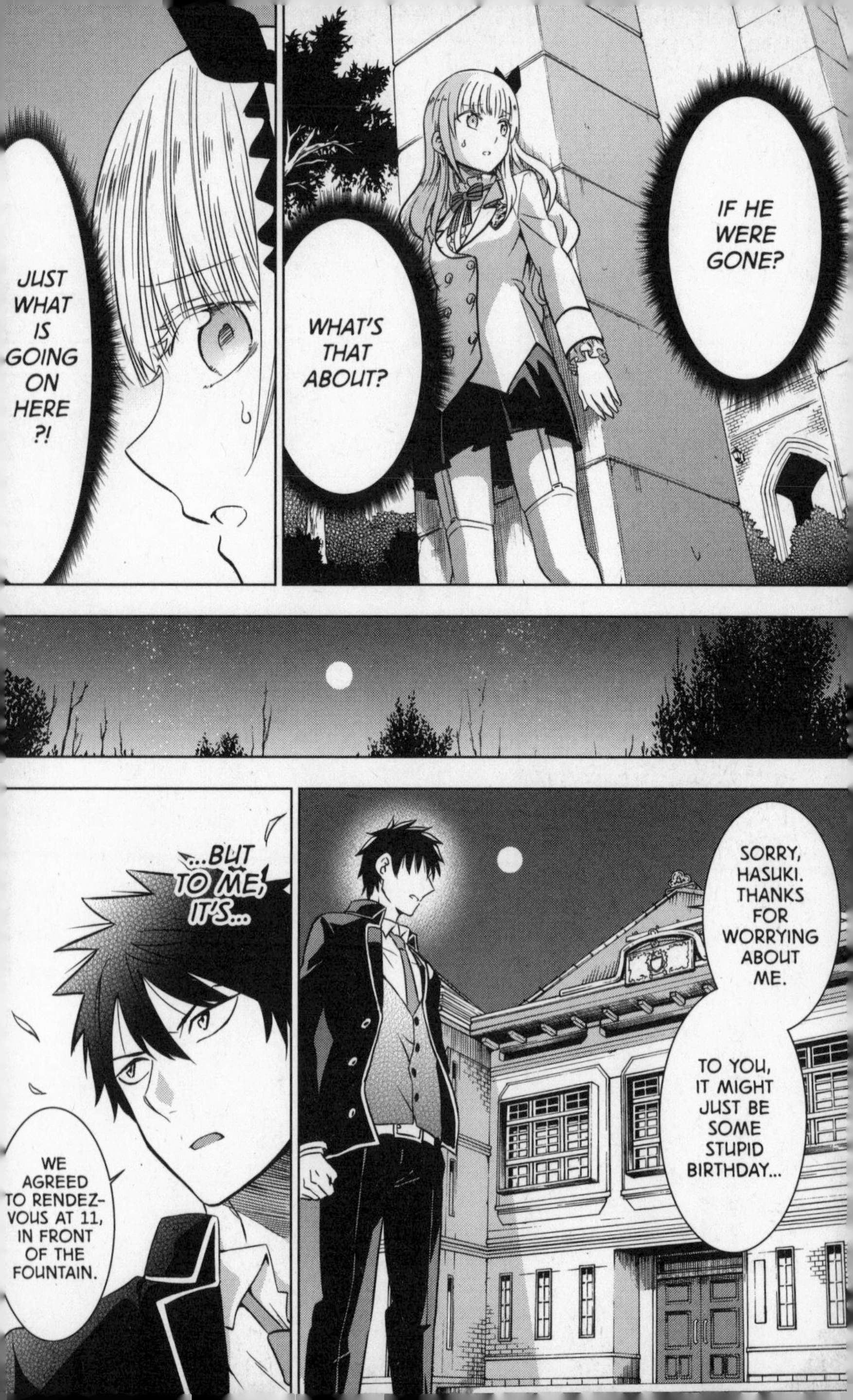
IF HE WERE GONE?
WHAT'S THAT ABOUT?
JUST WHAT IS GOING ON HERE?!
SORRY, HASUKI. THANKS FOR WORRYING ABOUT ME.
TO YOU, IT MIGHT JUST BE SOME STUPID BIRTHDAY...
...BUT TO ME, IT'S...
WE AGREED TO RENDEZ-VOUS AT 11, IN FRONT OF THE FOUNTAIN.

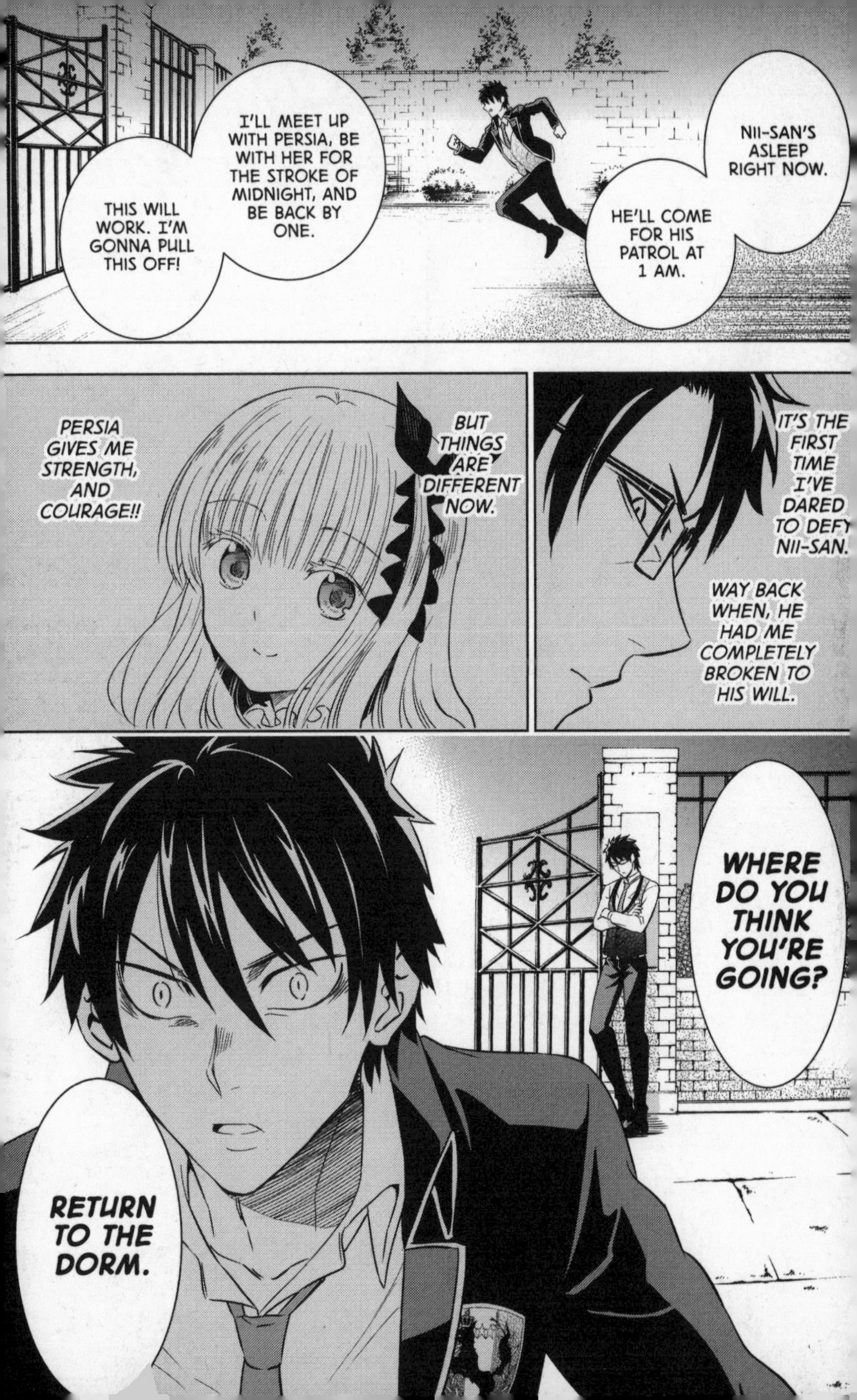
NII-SAN'S ASLEEP RIGHT NOW.
HE'LL COME FOR HIS PATROL AT 1 AM.
I'LL MEET UP WITH PERSIA, BE WITH HER FOR THE STROKE OF MIDNIGHT, AND BE BACK BY ONE.
THIS WILL WORK. I'M GONNA PULL THIS OFF!
IT'S THE FIRST TIME I'VE DARED TO DEFY NII-SAN.
WAY BACK WHEN, HE HAD ME COMPLETELY BROKEN TO HIS WILL.
BUT THINGS ARE DIFFERENT NOW.
PERSIA GIVES ME STRENGTH, AND COURAGE!!
WHERE DO YOU THINK YOU'RE GOING?
RETURN TO THE DORM.

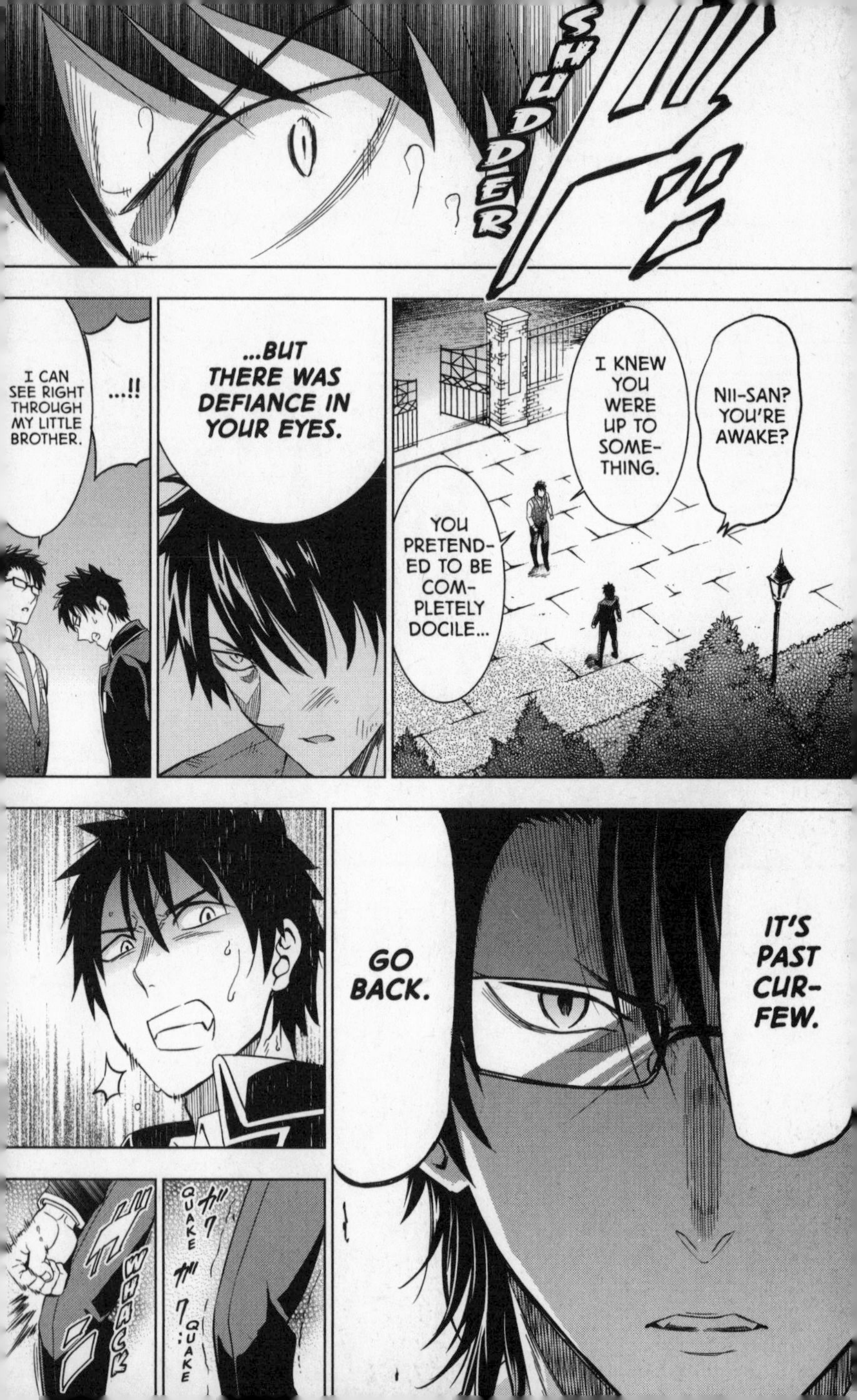
SHUDDER
NII-SAN? YOU'RE AWAKE?
I KNEW YOU WERE UP TO SOME-THING.
YOU PRETEND-ED TO BE COM-PLETELY DOCILE...
...BUT THERE WAS DEFIANCE IN YOUR EYES.
...!!
I CAN SEE RIGHT THROUGH MY LITTLE BROTHER.
IT'S PAST CUR-FEW.
GO BACK.
QUAKE QUAKE
WHACK

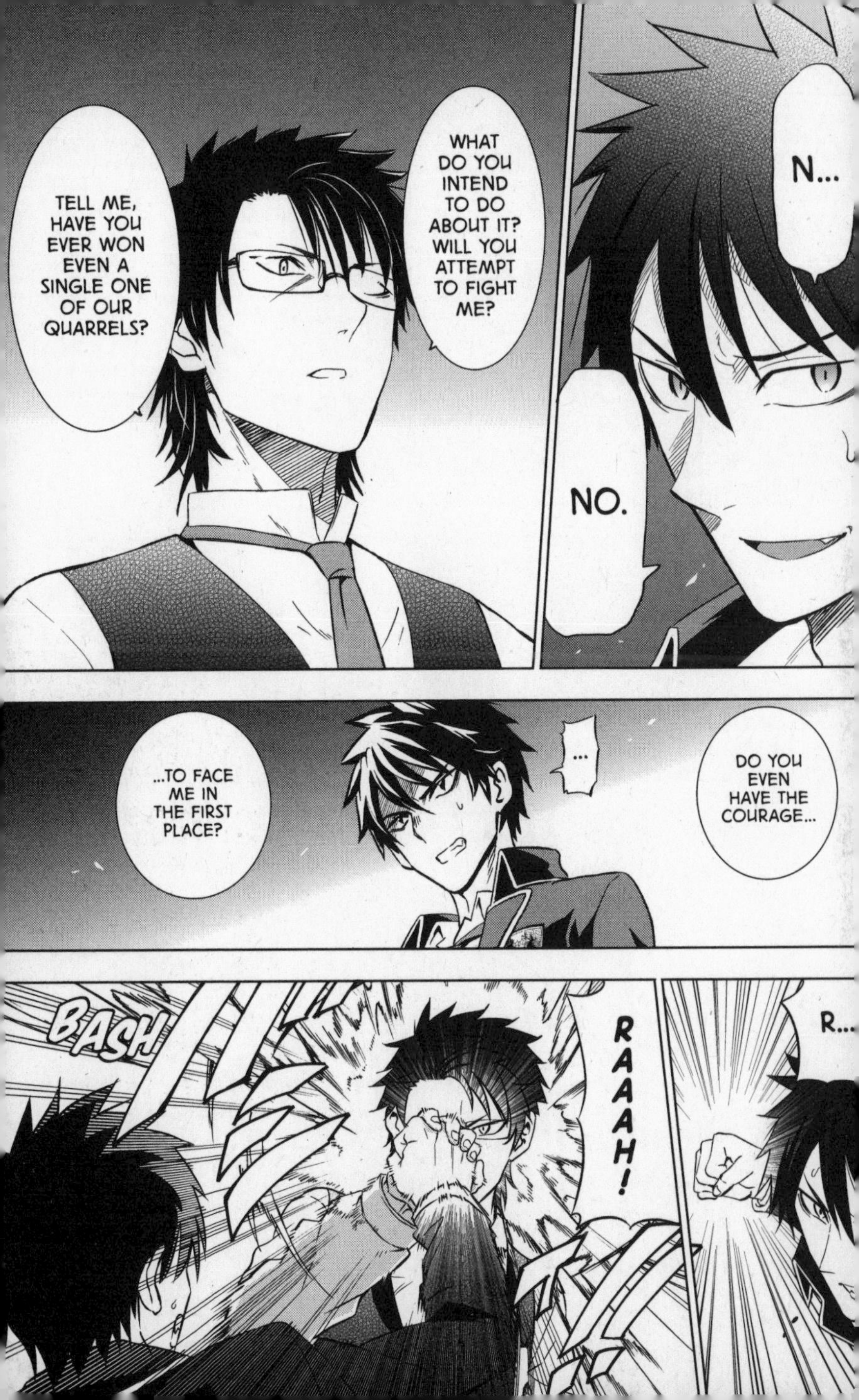
N...
NO.
WHAT DO YOU INTEND TO DO ABOUT IT? WILL YOU ATTEMPT TO FIGHT ME?
TELL ME, HAVE YOU EVER WON EVEN A SINGLE ONE OF OUR QUARRELS?
DO YOU EVEN HAVE THE COURAGE...
...
...TO FACE ME IN THE FIRST PLACE?
R...
RAAAAH!
BASH

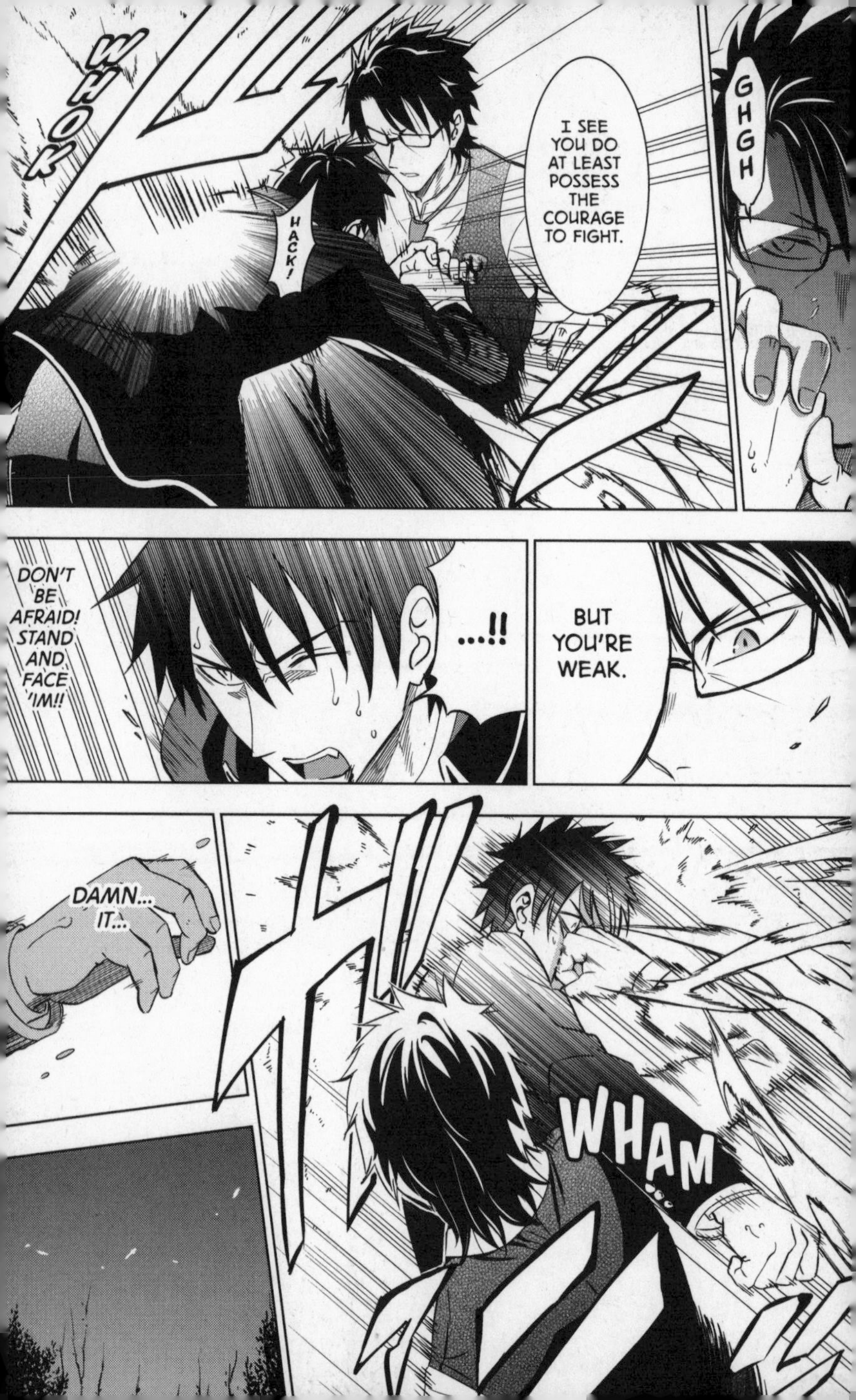
GHGH
I SEE YOU DO AT LEAST POSSESS THE COURAGE TO FIGHT.
WHOK
HACK!
BUT YOU'RE WEAK.
...!!
DON'T BE AFRAID! STAND AND FACE 'IM!!
WHAM
DAMN... IT...

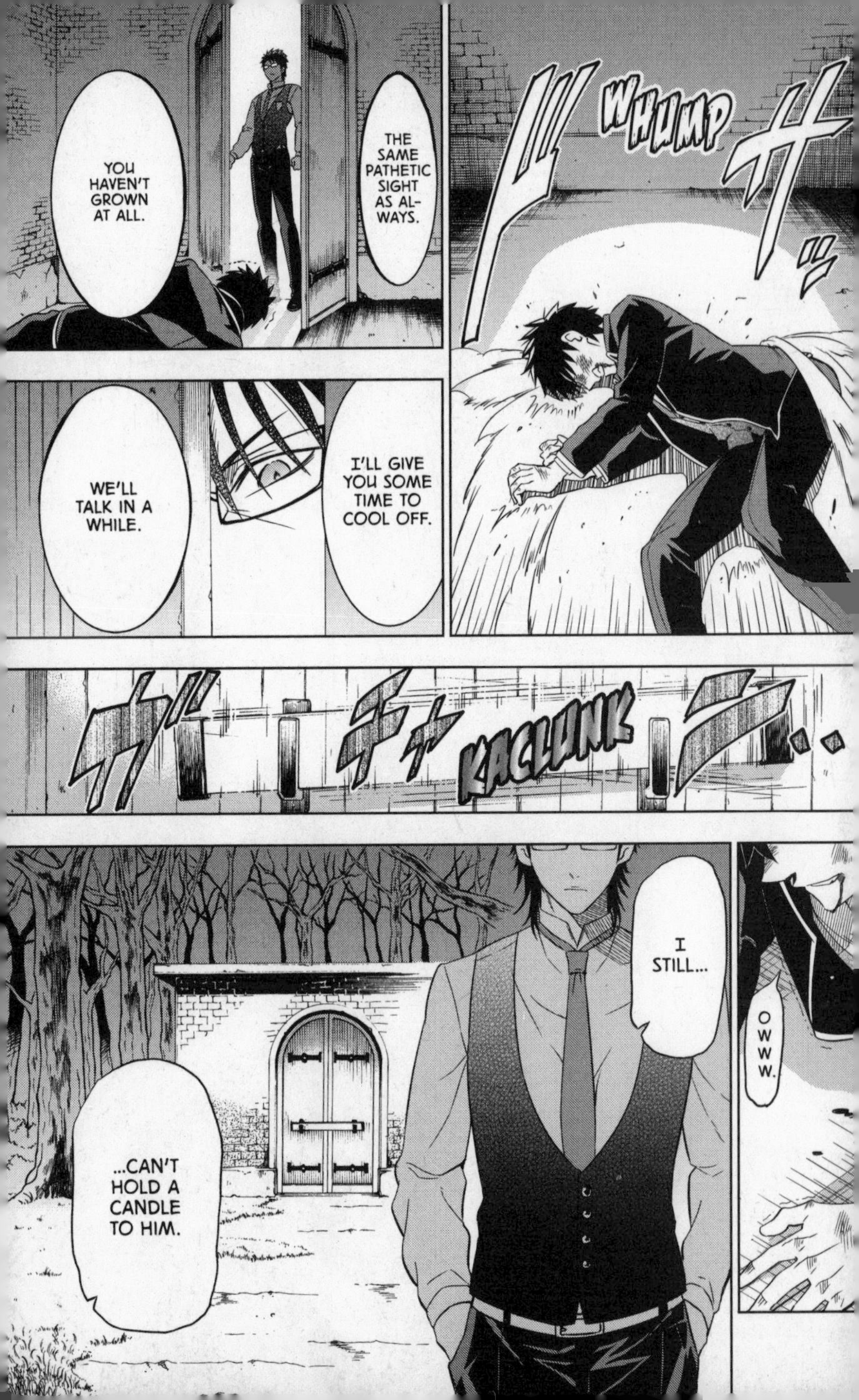
WHUMP
THE SAME PATHETIC SIGHT AS AL-WAYS.
YOU HAVEN'T GROWN AT ALL.
I'LL GIVE YOU SOME TIME TO COOL OFF.
WE'LL TALK IN A WHILE.
KACLUNK
OWWW.
I STILL...
...CAN'T HOLD A CANDLE TO HIM.

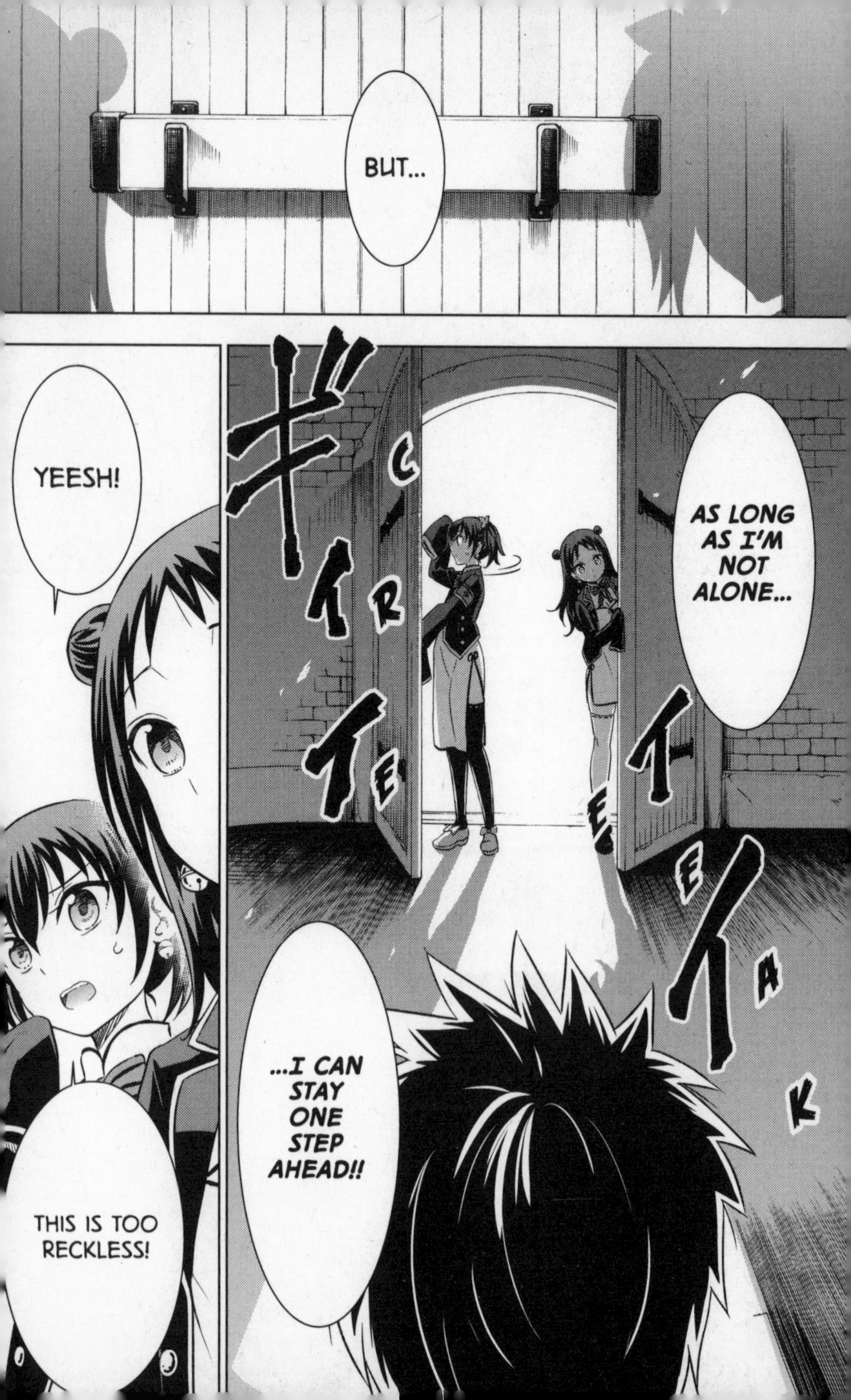
BUT...
AS LONG AS I'M NOT ALONE...
ギイイイ
CREEEAK
...I CAN STAY ONE STEP AHEAD!!
YEESH!
THIS IS TOO RECKLESS!

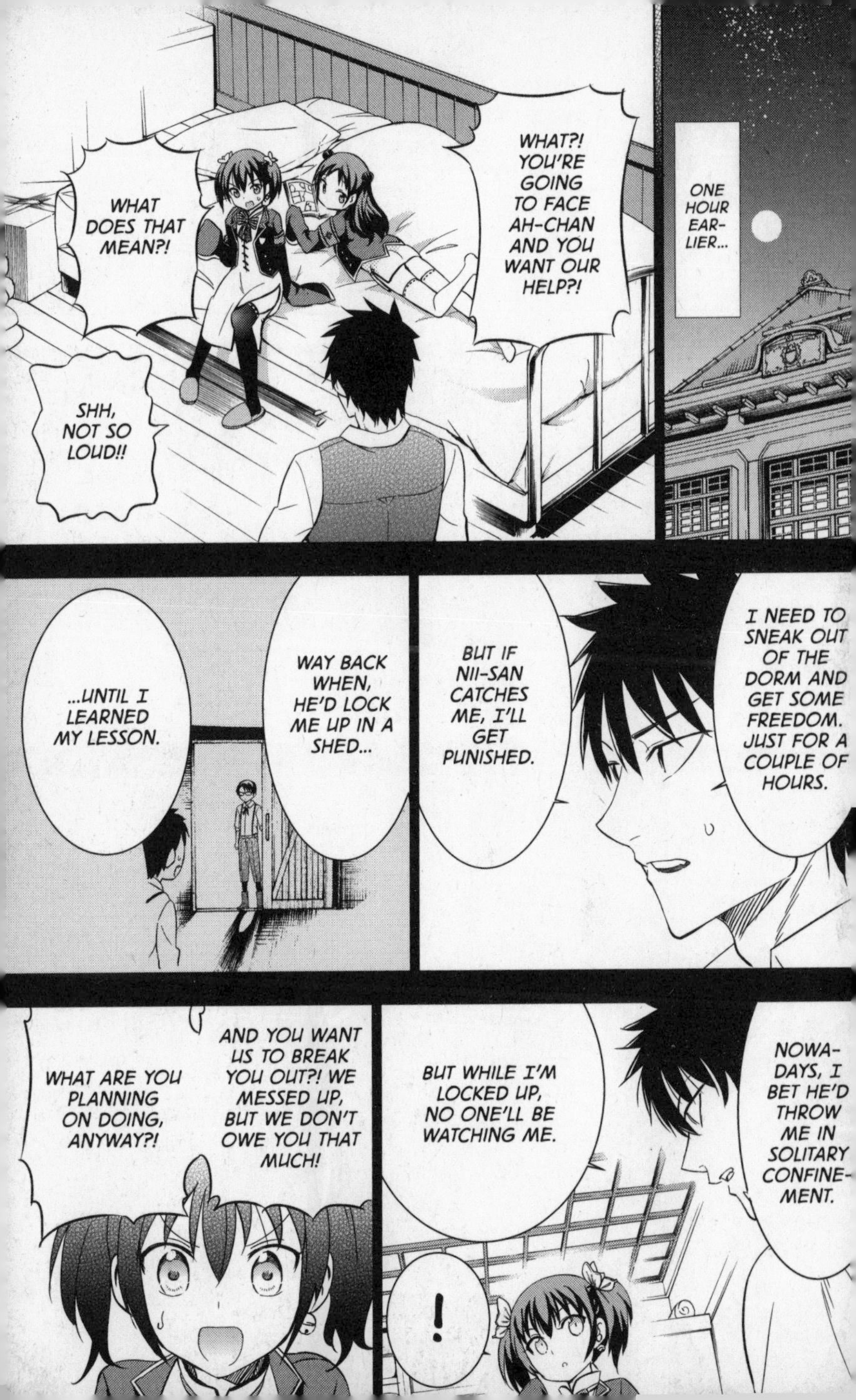
ONE HOUR EAR-LIER...
WHAT?! YOU'RE GOING TO FACE AH-CHAN AND YOU WANT OUR HELP?!
WHAT DOES THAT MEAN?!
SHH, NOT SO LOUD!!
I NEED TO SNEAK OUT OF THE DORM AND GET SOME FREEDOM. JUST FOR A COUPLE OF HOURS.
BUT IF NII-SAN CATCHES ME, I'LL GET PUNISHED.
WAY BACK WHEN, HE'D LOCK ME UP IN A SHED...
...UNTIL I LEARNED MY LESSON.
NOWA-DAYS, I BET HE'D THROW ME IN SOLITARY CONFINE-MENT.
BUT WHILE I'M LOCKED UP, NO ONE'LL BE WATCHING ME.
!
AND YOU WANT US TO BREAK YOU OUT?! WE MESSED UP, BUT WE DON'T OWE YOU THAT MUCH!
WHAT ARE YOU PLANNING ON DOING, ANYWAY?!

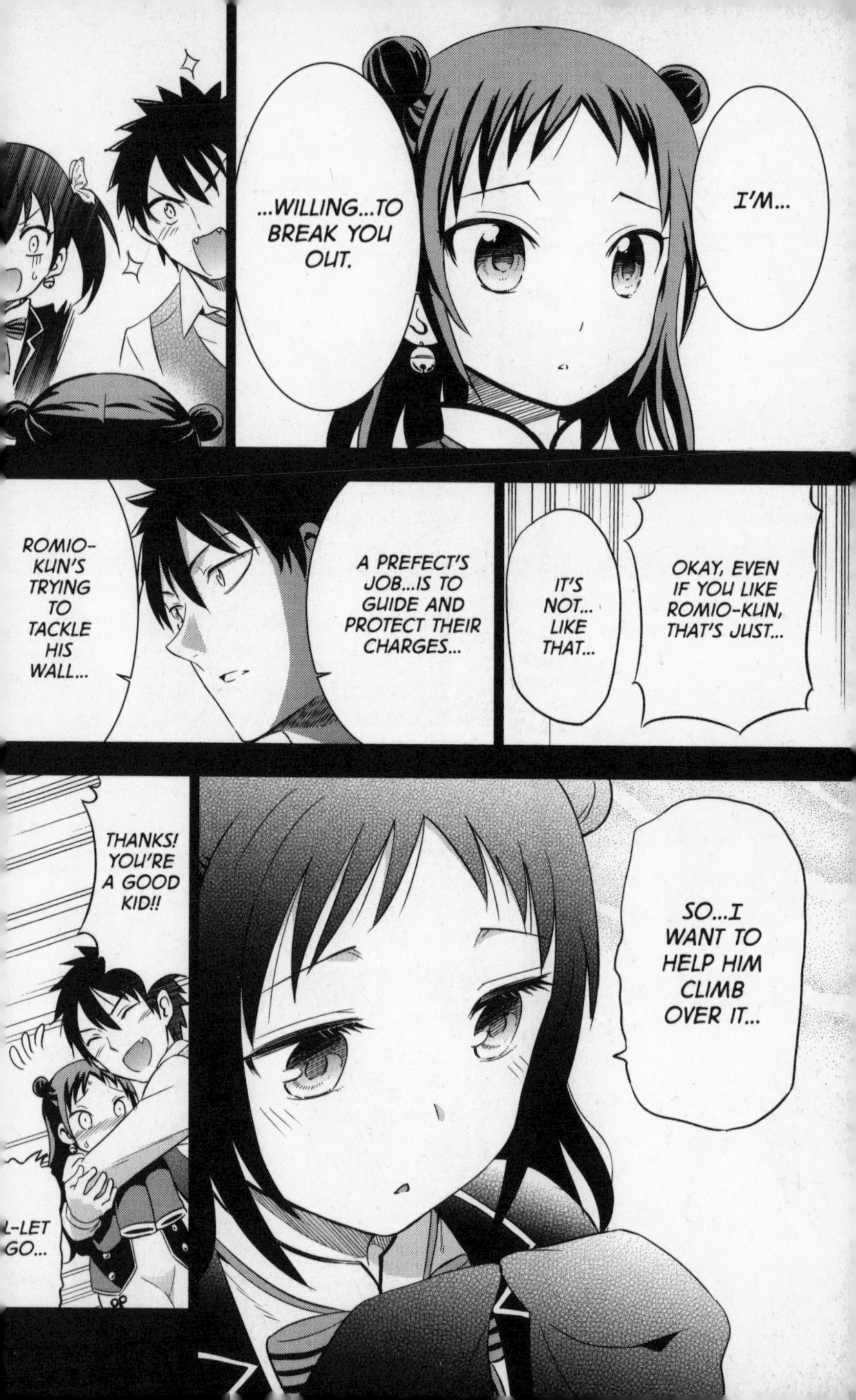
I'M...
...WILLING...TO BREAK YOU OUT.
OKAY, EVEN IF YOU LIKE ROMIO-KUN, THAT'S JUST...
IT'S NOT... LIKE THAT...
A PREFECT'S JOB...IS TO GUIDE AND PROTECT THEIR CHARGES...
ROMIO-KUN'S TRYING TO TACKLE HIS WALL...
SO...I WANT TO HELP HIM CLIMB OVER IT...
THANKS! YOU'RE A GOOD KID!!
L-LET GO...

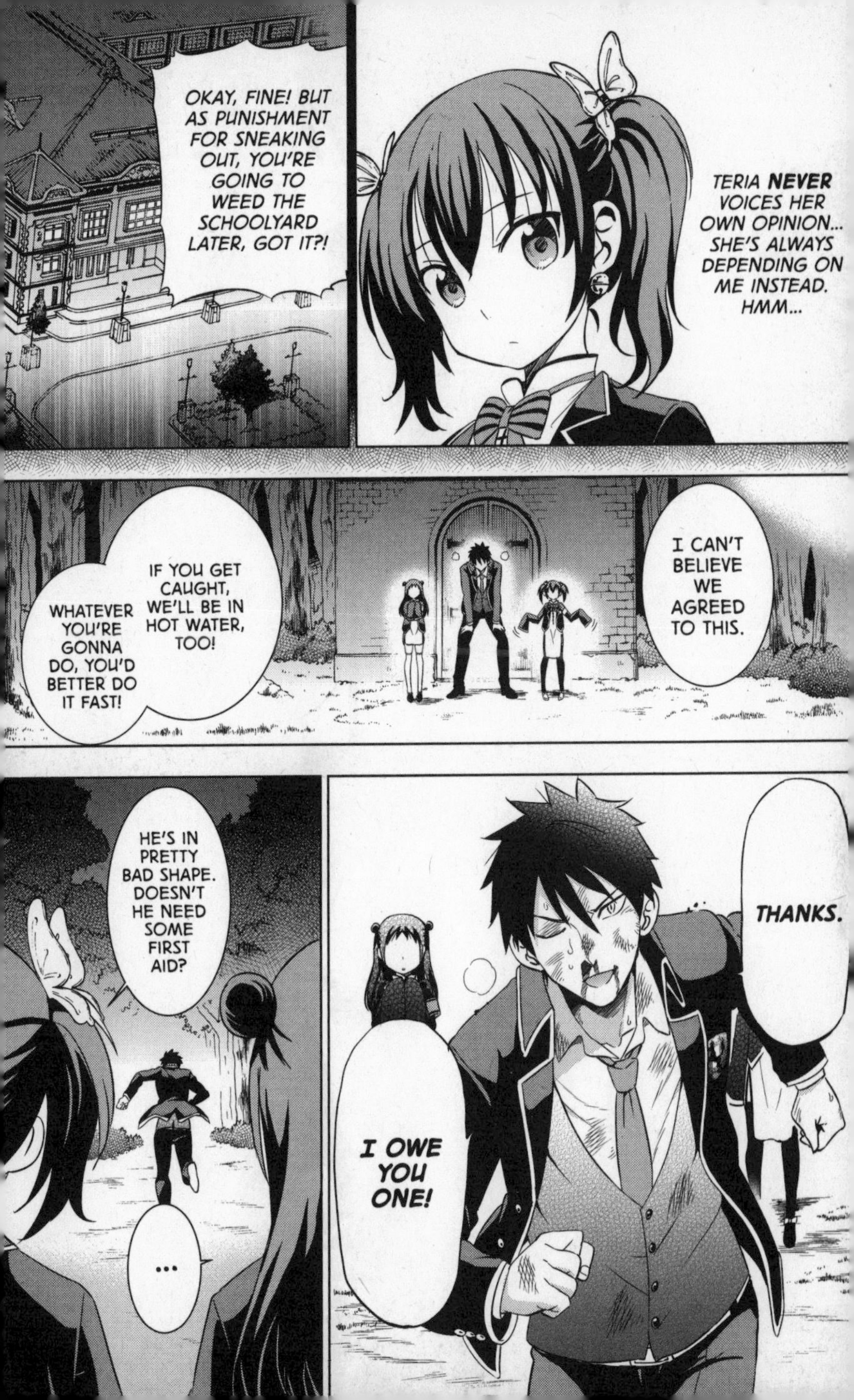
TERIA **NEVER** VOICES HER OWN OPINION... SHE'S ALWAYS DEPENDING ON ME INSTEAD. HMM...
OKAY, FINE! BUT AS PUNISHMENT FOR SNEAKING OUT, YOU'RE GOING TO WEED THE SCHOOLYARD LATER, GOT IT?!
I CAN'T BELIEVE WE AGREED TO THIS.
IF YOU GET CAUGHT, WE'LL BE IN HOT WATER, TOO!
WHATEVER YOU'RE GONNA DO, YOU'D BETTER DO IT FAST!
THANKS.
I OWE YOU ONE!
HE'S IN PRETTY BAD SHAPE. DOESN'T HE NEED SOME FIRST AID?
...

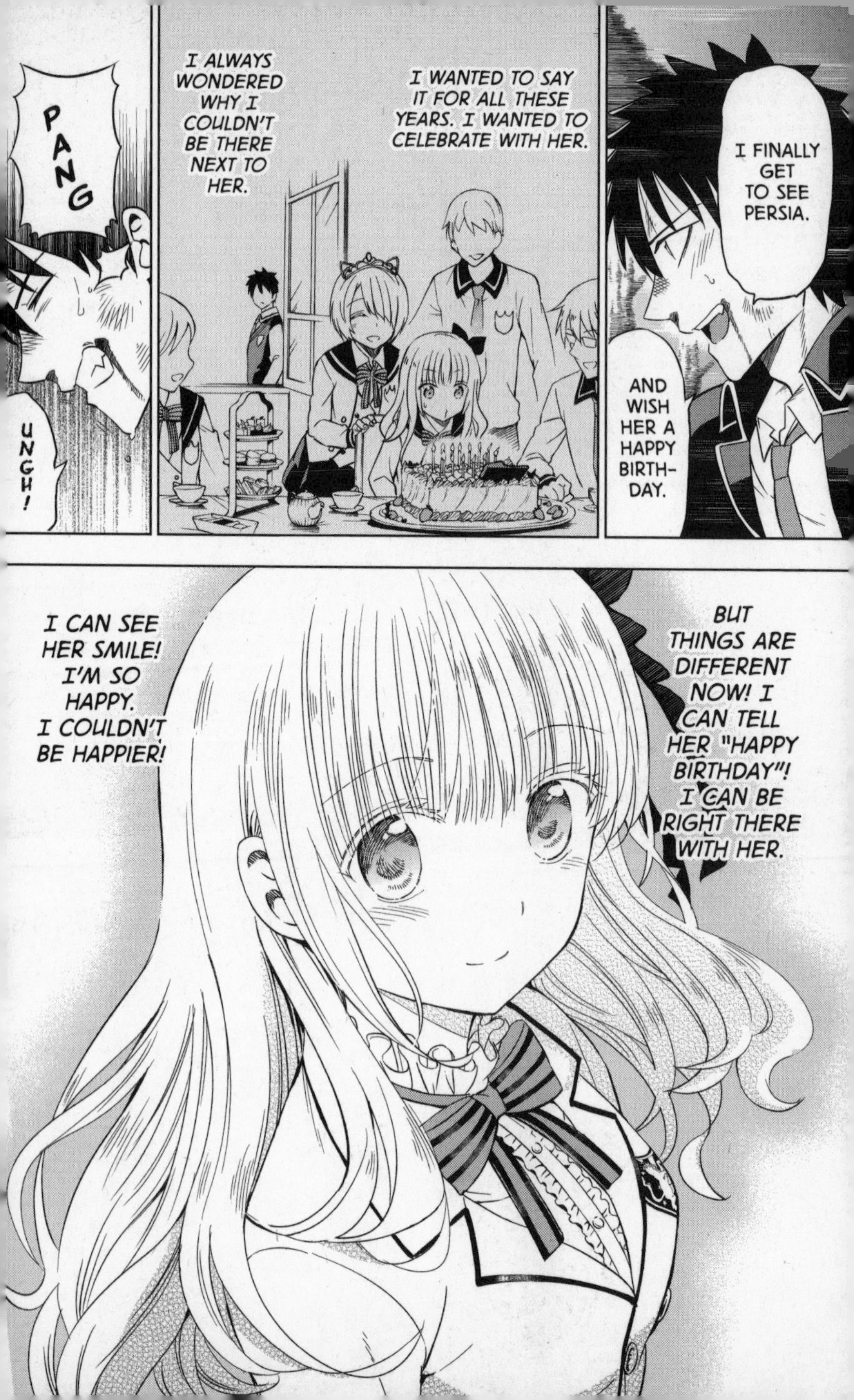
I FINALLY GET TO SEE PERSIA.
AND WISH HER A HAPPY BIRTH-DAY.
I WANTED TO SAY IT FOR ALL THESE YEARS. I WANTED TO CELEBRATE WITH HER.
I ALWAYS WONDERED WHY I COULDN'T BE THERE NEXT TO HER.
PANG
UNGH!
BUT THINGS ARE DIFFERENT NOW! I CAN TELL HER "HAPPY BIRTHDAY"! I CAN BE RIGHT THERE WITH HER.
I CAN SEE HER SMILE! I'M SO HAPPY. I COULDN'T BE HAPPIER!

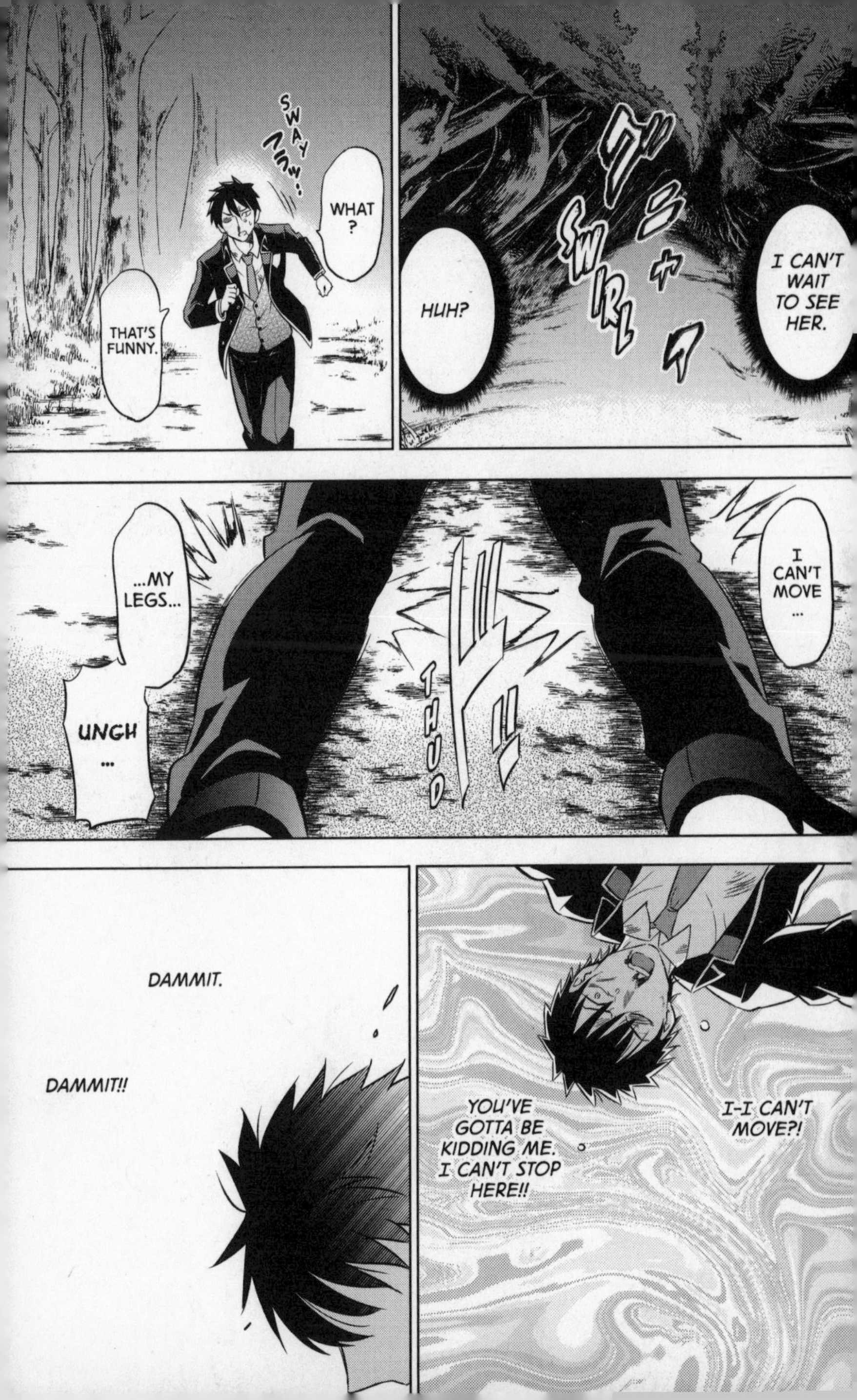
I CAN'T WAIT TO SEE HER.
SWIRL
HUH?
SWAY
WHAT ?
THAT'S FUNNY.
I CAN'T MOVE ...
THUD
!!
...MY LEGS...
UNGH ...
I-I CAN'T MOVE?!
YOU'VE GOTTA BE KIDDING ME. I CAN'T STOP HERE!!
DAMMIT.
DAMMIT!!

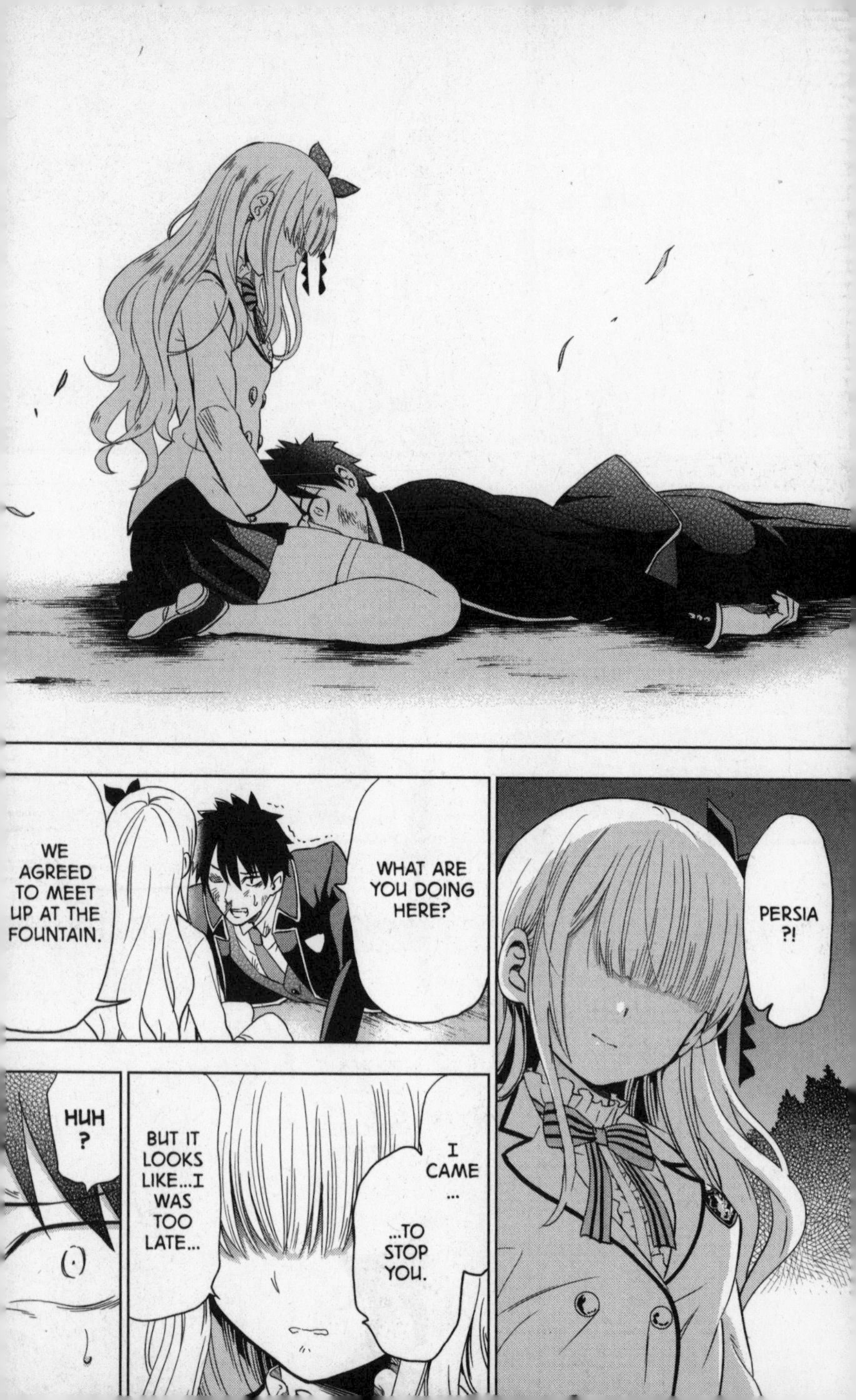
PERSIA ?!
WHAT ARE YOU DOING HERE?
WE AGREED TO MEET UP AT THE FOUNTAIN.
I CAME ...
...TO STOP YOU.
BUT IT LOOKS LIKE...I WAS TOO LATE...
HUH ?

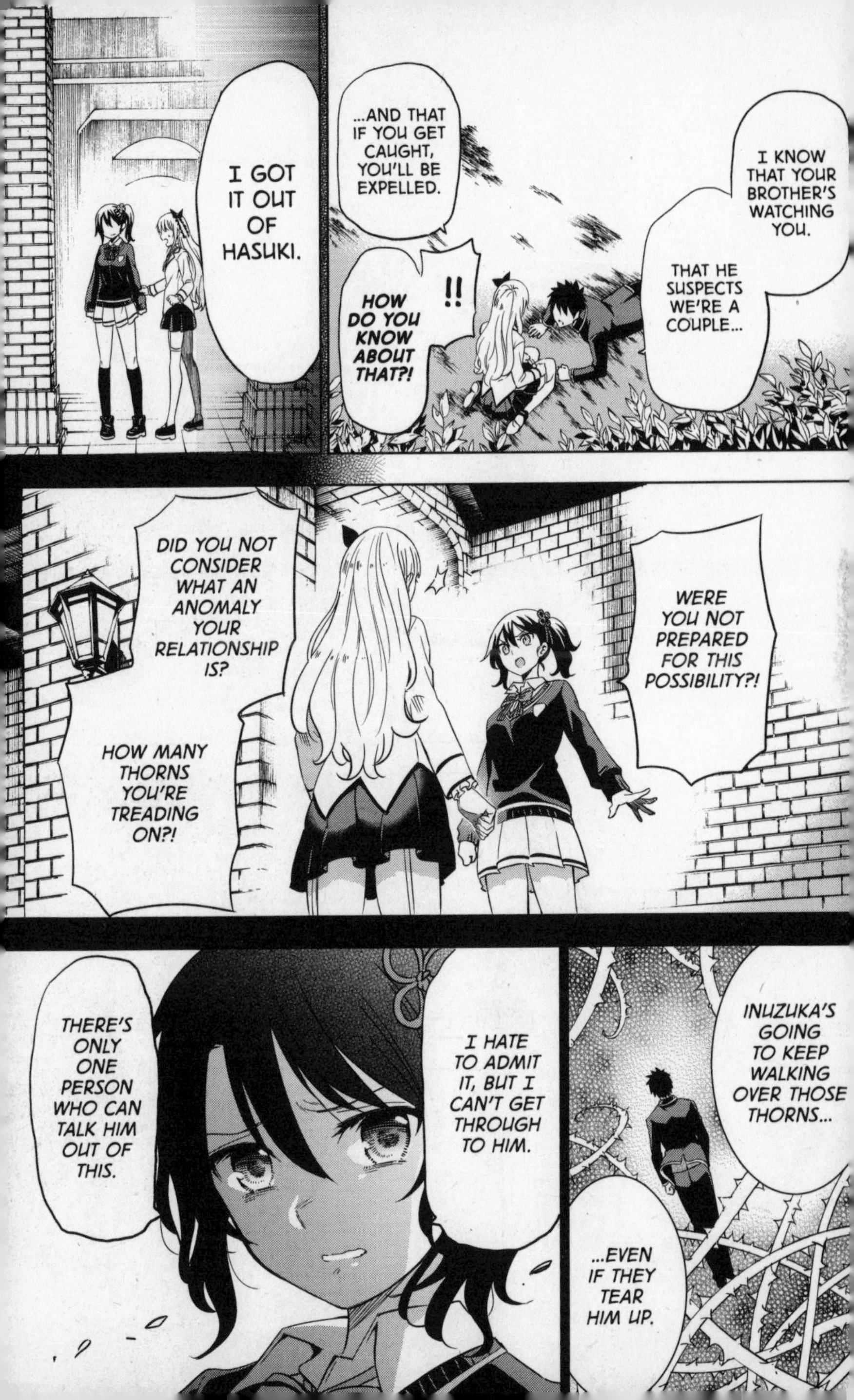
I KNOW THAT YOUR BROTHER'S WATCHING YOU.
THAT HE SUSPECTS WE'RE A COUPLE...
...AND THAT IF YOU GET CAUGHT, YOU'LL BE EXPELLED.
!!
HOW DO YOU KNOW ABOUT THAT?!
I GOT IT OUT OF HASUKI.
WERE YOU NOT PREPARED FOR THIS POSSIBILITY?!
DID YOU NOT CONSIDER WHAT AN ANOMALY YOUR RELATIONSHIP IS?
HOW MANY THORNS YOU'RE TREADING ON?!
INUZUKA'S GOING TO KEEP WALKING OVER THOSE THORNS...
...EVEN IF THEY TEAR HIM UP.
I HATE TO ADMIT IT, BUT I CAN'T GET THROUGH TO HIM.
THERE'S ONLY ONE PERSON WHO CAN TALK HIM OUT OF THIS.

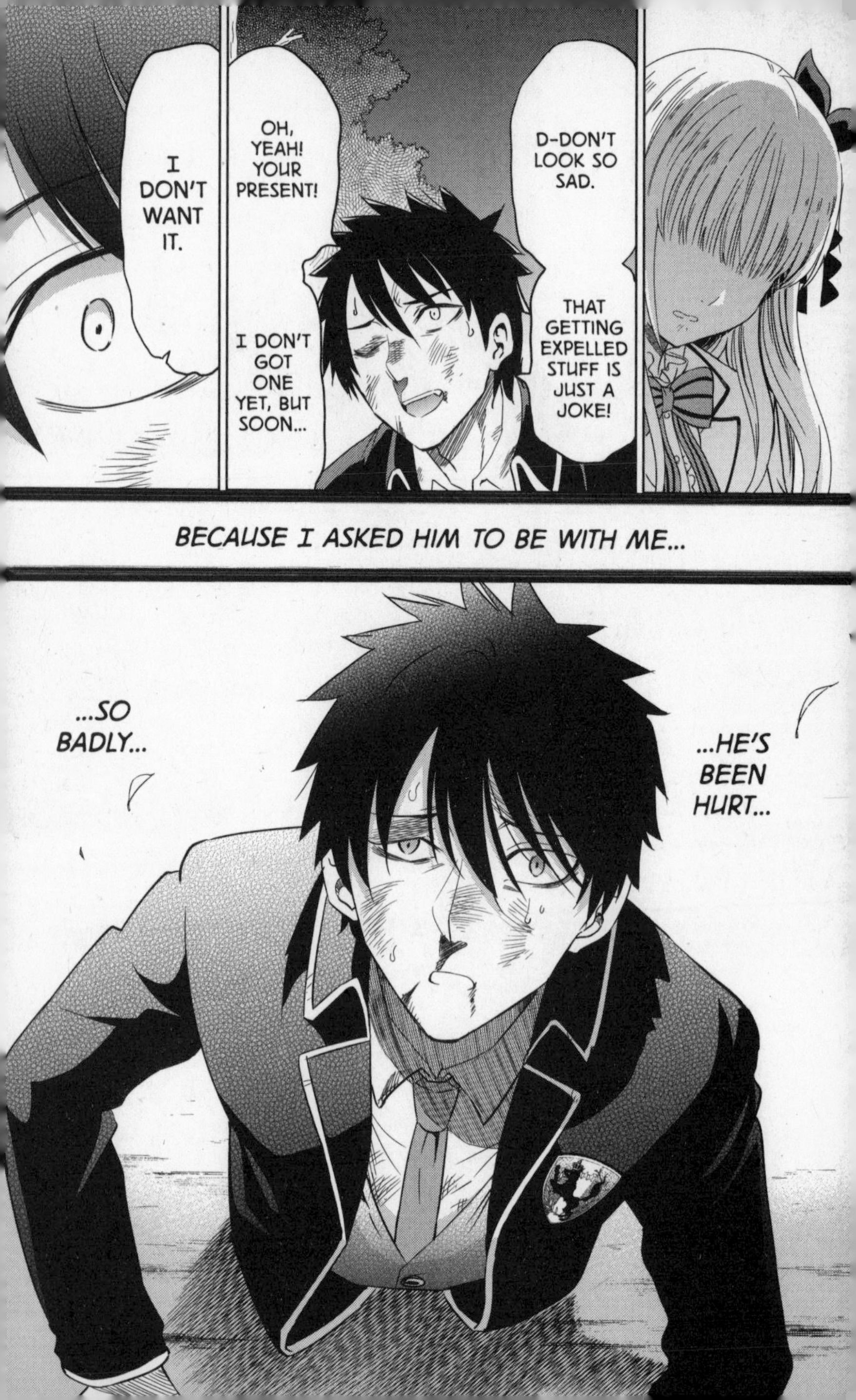
D-DON'T LOOK SO SAD.
THAT GETTING EXPELLED STUFF IS JUST A JOKE!
OH, YEAH! YOUR PRESENT!
I DON'T GOT ONE YET, BUT SOON...
I DON'T WANT IT.
BECAUSE I ASKED HIM TO BE WITH ME...
...HE'S BEEN HURT...
...SO BADLY...

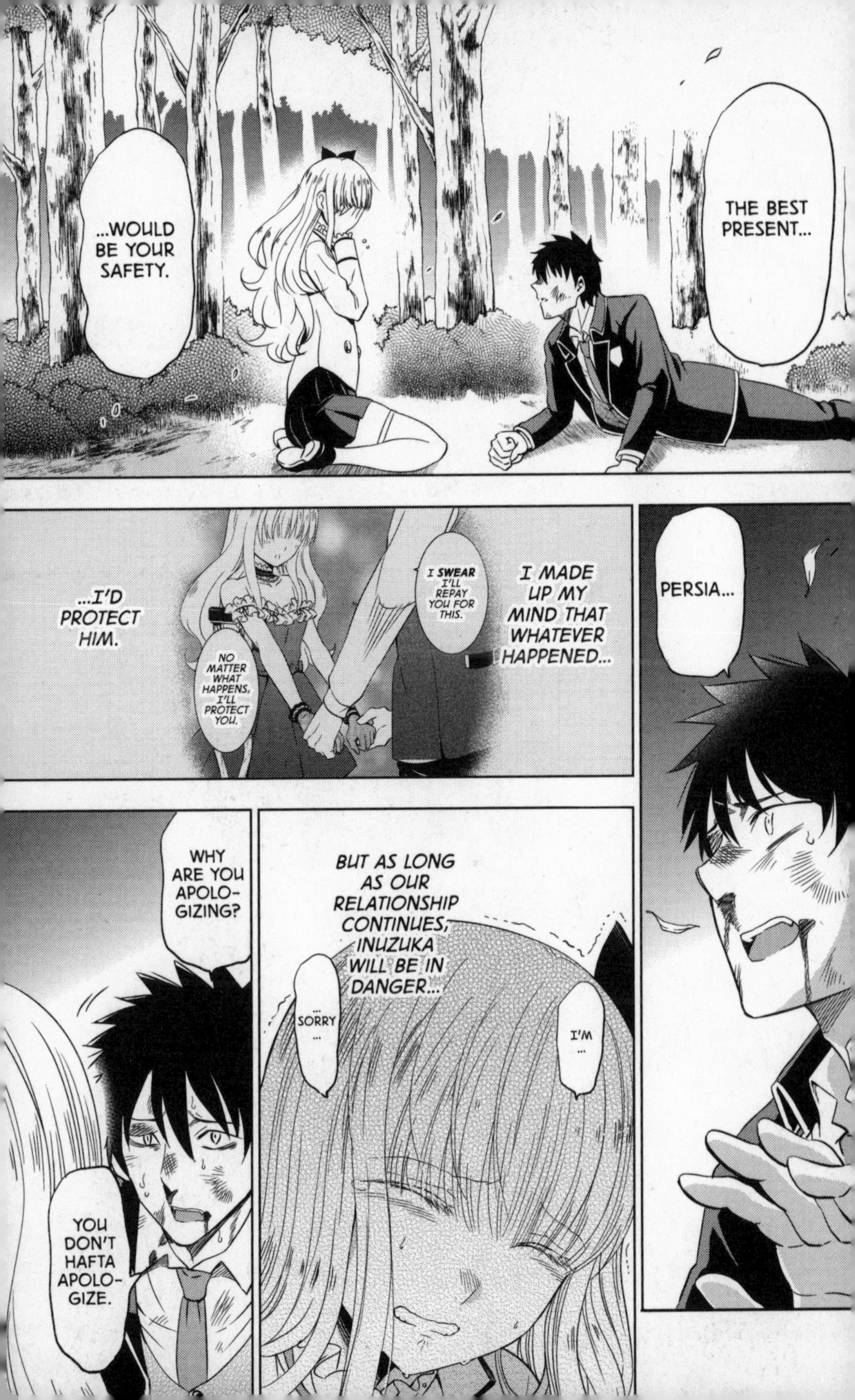
THE BEST PRESENT...
...WOULD BE YOUR SAFETY.
PERSIA...
I MADE UP MY MIND THAT WHATEVER HAPPENED...
I **SWEAR** I'LL REPAY YOU FOR THIS.
NO MATTER WHAT HAPPENS, I'LL PROTECT YOU.
...I'D PROTECT HIM.
BUT AS LONG AS OUR RELATIONSHIP CONTINUES, INUZUKA WILL BE IN DANGER...
I'M ...
... SORRY ...
WHY ARE YOU APOLOGIZING?
YOU DON'T HAFTA APOLOGIZE.

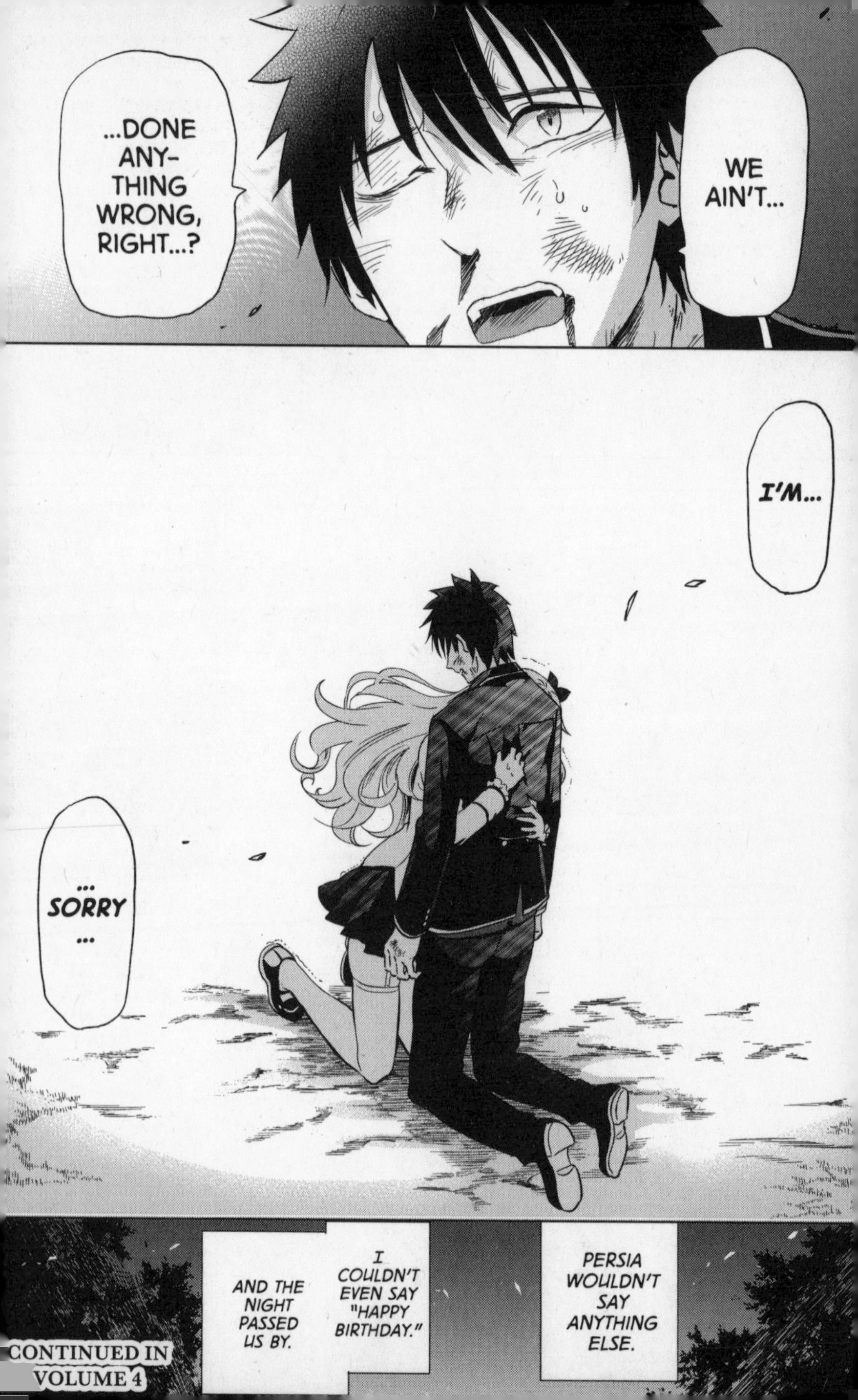
WE AIN'T...
...DONE ANYTHING WRONG, RIGHT...?
I'M...
...SORRY...
PERSIA WOULDN'T SAY ANYTHING ELSE.
I COULDN'T EVEN SAY "HAPPY BIRTHDAY."
AND THE NIGHT PASSED US BY.
CONTINUED IN VOLUME 4

HELLO. IT'S KANEDA, THE MANGA ARTIST WHO GOT STARED AT DISAPPROVINGLY BY A KID WHEN I WENT TO A PARK WITH MY FRIENDS TO TRY FORMING A SPORTS DAY CAVALRY TEAM SO I COULD DRAW THE CAVALRY BATTLE SCENE.

DISAPPROVING LOOK.

AFTE... WOR...

IN THIS VOLUME, I HAD PERSIA SINGING A LULLABY IN ENGLISH.

NORMALLY, THE WHITE CATS SPEAK IN ENGLISH, AND THE BLACK DOGGIES SPEAK IN TOUWANESE—THEIR RESPECTIVE FIRST LANGUAGES.

THEY LEARN EACH OTHER'S LANGUAGES IN SCHOOL, SO THEY UNDERSTAND ONE ANOTHER.

Within the manga, it's all depicted in Japanese in the original edition and English in the English edition.

THE DAH... ACADE... UNIFOR... BASICA... THE SAM... WHATEVE... THE SEASO...

TH... SUMM... CLOTH... ARE J... MADE... LIGH... FABR...

ON ESPECIALLY HOT DAYS, THEY CAN PUT THEIR JACKETS OVER THEIR SHOULDERS.

Ugh, hot...

AS FOR THEIR GYM CLOTHES, THOSE ARE BASED OFF OF THE UNIFORM FOR A REAL-LIFE CRICKET COMPETITION.

A WHITE UNIFORM.

THE GIRLS ARE WEARING GYM SHORTS UNDER THEIR SKIRTS. SUCH A SHAME.

To show the integrity of the games...or so they don't heat up in the sun...or something.

I'M ON TWITTER:

@YOUSUKEKANEDA

I POST ICONS AND OTHER GOODIES. CHECK IT OUT IF YOU'D LIKE.

WELL, MAY WE MEET AGAIN IN THE NEXT VOLUME!

Boarding School *Juliet*

Boarding School Juliet volume 3 is a work of fiction. Names, characters, places, and incidents are the products of the author's imagination or are used fictitiously. Any resemblance to actual events, locales, or persons, living or dead, is entirely coincidental.

A Kodansha Comics Trade Paperback Original.

Boarding School Juliet volume 3 copyright © 2016 Yousuke Kaneda
English translation copyright © 2018 Yousuke Kaneda

All rights reserved.

Published in the United States by Kodansha Comics,
an imprint of Kodansha USA Publishing, LLC, New York.

Publication rights for this English edition arranged through
Kodansha Ltd., Tokyo.

First published in Japan in 2016 by Kodansha Ltd., Tokyo, as
Kishuku Gakkou no Jurietto volume 3.

ISBN 978-1-63236-753-2

Printed in the United States of America.

www.kodanshacomics.com

9 8 7 6 5 4 3 2 1

Translation: Amanda Haley
Lettering: James Dashiell
Editing: Erin Subramanian and Paul Starr
Kodansha Comics edition cover design: Phil Balsman